*Food and Beverage
Management*

Dedication

*This book is dedicated to all the students we have encouraged to learn about
and from the food and beverage industry, all the managers in all the
organizations that have employed, developed and encouraged them,
and all the innovators and people of vision who have inspired us.
In addition thanks should go to all those that have worked hard and put in
long hours to raise the level of professionalism in food and beverage management and by
doing so make the industry the exciting and vibrant one that it is.*

Food and Beverage Management

Fourth Edition

Bernard Davis, BA, MIH
Andrew Lockwood, PhD, BSc, CertEd, FIH
Peter Alcott, DBA, MSc, FIH
Ioannis S. Pantelidis, MSc, HMDip, FHEA, FIH

ELSEVIER

AMSTERDAM • BOSTON • HEIDELBERG • LONDON • NEW YORK • OXFORD
PARIS • SAN DIEGO • SAN FRANCISCO • SYDNEY • TOKYO
Butterworth-Heinemann is an imprint of Elsevier

Linacre House, Jordan Hill, Oxford OX2 8DP, UK
30 Corporate Drive, Suite 400, Burlington, MA 01803, USA

First published 1985
Reprinted 1988, 1989, 1990
Second edition 1991
Reprinted 1992, 1993 (twice), 1994, 1995, 1996
Third edition 1998
Reprinted 1999 (twice), 2001, 2002, 2003 (twice), 2004
Fourth edition 2008

British Library Cataloguing in Publication Data
A catalogue record for this book is available from the British Library

Library of Congress Cataloguing in Publication Data
A catalogue record for this book is available from the Library of Congress

ISBN 13: 978-0-7506-6730-2

For information on all Elsevier Butterworth-Heinemann
publications visit our website at www.bh.com

Printed and bound in Slovenia

08 09 10 11 12   10 9 8 7 6 5 4 3 2 1

Working together to grow
libraries in developing countries

www.elsevier.com | www.bookaid.org | www.sabre.org

ELSEVIER   **BOOK AID** International   Sabre Foundation

Contents

List of figures

List of tables

Preface to the fourth edition

Since the publication of the third edition of *Food and Beverage Management* nearly ten years ago, the Hotel and Catering industry has seen many changes and developments, not the least of which is a change of name to the Hospitality Industry.

Particular changes over this period have been in:

- New technology
- Health and environmental awareness
- Consolidation and the growth of brands
- Customer expectations of our products and services
- The growth in the value of the industry to the economy at the local, regional and global level

This edition also sees some major changes to the presentation of the content of the book without, we hope, affecting the quality and the comprehensiveness of the coverage we have

- Reorganised and condensed the sector chapters to a standard format in the second and third chapters whilst extending the number of sectors covered.
- Added new chapters in developing a food and beverage concept and trends and issues in the industry.
- Added learning activities and mini case examples to every chapter.
- Updated the content to reflect recent changes in this fast moving industry.

This has only been possible by welcoming two new experienced teachers onto the authoring team. Peter Alcott who following a long career in the hospitality industry has found teaching and developing our new young managers of the future a truly rewarding second career and Ioannis Pantelidis who following a successful career in the management of restaurants and hotels discovered his muse in teaching and consulting.

Acknowledgements

The first acknowledgement here must go to Bernard Davis. It was Bernard who wrote the first edition of this text and who led its development over the second and third editions. Although taking a deserved back seat in the detailed development of the fourth edition, he has always been there with detailed comments and criticisms encouraging us to improve the book wherever possible and picking us up when his high standards have not been reached. It is a cliché, but true none the less, that this book would not have been possible without him. He has made such a significant contribution to hospitality education and to the development of food and beverage managers around the world. Heartfelt thanks go to him from all his previous students all over the world for his energy, his determination and his professionalism. Thank you.

Acknowledgements are due to the many colleagues and organizations who kindly contributed to the first, second and third editions, and now especially to those who have given their time and assistance to this fourth edition. In particular, we would like to thank:

Anton Mossiman and Mosimann's Private Dinning
Arthur Potts Dawson and the Acorn House Restaurant
Bank Restaurants
Brian Miller and the Danesfield House Hotel
British Hospitality Association
Burger King UK
CACI Ltd
Christian Bayer and Chris Marsland of DO & CO
Cyrus Todiwala and Café Spice Namaste
Dimitris Tavern
Geac Computers Inc.
Hospitality Assured
Institute of Hospitality

Jane Renton, General Manager of the Jumeirah Lowndes Hotel
Kevan Wallace
Keynote Publications
KFC UK
Lakeside Restaurant and the University of Surrey
Magnolia Restaurant
Menupix
Michael Mack and `s Baggers® restaurant
Michel Roux and Le Gavroche
Micros Ltd
Mintel Research Services Ltd
National readership Survey
National Statistics Office
P&O Cruises
Pizza Hut UK
Radisson Edwardian Hotels
The Compass Group and Scolarest

The London Paper
The Michelin Guide
The Mobil Travel Guide
The Northern Ireland Prison Service
The Zagat Guide
TRI Hospitality
Wagamama Restaurants
Wells and Youngs Ltd

We would also like to thank all at Butterworth-Heinemann for their continued support, encouragement and, above all, patience.

Andrew Lockwood
Peter Alcott
Ioannis S Pantelidis
March 2008

Preface to the third edition

Since the publication of the first edition of *Food and Beverage Management* in 1985 and the second edition in 1991, the Hotel and Catering industry has seen many changes and developments, these being a result of natural progression within the industry, research and development and as a result of outside pressures and government legislation.

Some general trends that were identifiable during the past twelve years, and are continuing, include:

- A continuing increase in food, beverage and energy costs.
- A continuing increase in labour costs and a difficulty in obtaining an adequate number of highly skilled staff.
- An increasingly more knowledgeable customer, demanding more exciting menus, a wide range of 'healthy eating' dishes, a clean smoke-free environment and a high standard of hygiene practices from the industry.
- A continuing concern by the EC and UK Government about all aspects of food hygiene, this being evident with new legislation.
- A much wider acceptance of the use of computers throughout the industry.
- An increasing awareness of the importance of managing quality in all areas of food and beverage operations.

This third edition offers the reader two new chapters, together with a total update of the remaining chapters, with many being enlarged. Over forty new menus are included, together with numerous new tables and figures. This edition is particularly strengthened with the addition of Andrew Lockwood as a co-author of many publications.

Food and Beverage Management continues to be an established source of reading and reference material, not only to students, but to practicing food and beverage managers, controllers and their assistants. The book has been widely accepted by universities and colleges for their degree courses in the UK and overseas, by the HCIMA as a standard textbook for the Professional Certificate, Diploma and Distant Learning, and for the Higher National Diploma. In addition, the book has been found to be a good reference source for advanced GNVQ courses.

Acknowledgements to the many colleagues and organizations who kindly contributed to the first and second editions, and to those who have given their time and assistance to the third edition. In particular, we would like to thank.

Army catering Corps
Automatic Minibar Systems Ltd
Automatic Vending Association of Britain
Avon Data Systems Ltd
British Airways
British Hospitality Association
Brown's Restaurant and Bar
CACI Information Services
Caledonian Hotel, Edinburgh
Catere and Hotelkeeper
Central Statistical Office
Cerco Health Services
Compass Catering
Conran Restaurants
Copthorne London Tara Hotel
Department of Health and Social Security
Dorchester Hotel
Electrolux Ltd
FDS Ltd
Gallup Organization
Girovend Holdings Ltd
Greenalls Group PLC
Guy's and St Thomas' Hopitals
Hicks and Don
House of Commons
Innkeepers Fayre (Bass PLC)
Institute of Directors
Keynote Publications
Landmark Hotel
Langham Hilton
Leith's Events and Parties
Leith's Management
Letheby and Christopher
Marketpower Ltd
Mintel Research Services Ltd
National Health Services

Pizza Express
St Peter's Hospital, Chertsey
Surrey Commercial Services
Surrey County Council
TGI Friday's
Toby Restaurants (Bass PLC)
Virgin Atlantic

We would also like to thank all at Butterworth-Heinemann for their continued support and encouragement.

Bernard Davis,
Andrew Lockwood and
Sally Stone

Preface to the second edition

Since the publication of the first edition of *Food and Beverage Management*, the hotel and catering industry has come to the end of the 1980s and has already begun its progress through the 1990s. In such a relatively short period of time changes have occurred within the industry, both through its own natural progression, research and development and as a result of outside pressures and government legislation.

Some general trends that were identifiable during the past decade and are continuing include:

- A continuing increase in food, beverage and energy costs.
- A continuing increase in labour costs, a decline in the young labour force available for the industry and an increase in the number of part-time employees.
- An increasing interest in healthy eating by the general public with more prominence of vegetarian dishes and menus. Also a requirement by the public for non-smoking areas to be a standard for all types of catering outlets.
- An increasing demand and awareness by the general public for higher hygiene standards for all catering outlets. This demand being as a result of the general awareness through the media of new food legislation and of the out-breaks of food poisoning in the UK. The continuing monitoring of the above will have significant importance to the success of any catering operation in the 1990s.

This second edition offers the reader six new chapters and a total update of all previous chapters with many being enlarged, reflecting the growing importance of their subject areas. The new chapters are *The meal experience*; *The marketing of food and beverages*; *Advertising, public relations, merchandising and sales promotion*; *Financial aspects*; *Food and beverage management in school catering*; and *Food and beverage management in hospital catering*.

Food and Beverage Management continues to be a source of reading material and reference to many practicing catering managers, food and beverage managers, controllers and their assistants both within the UK and overseas. This edition sets out to also cover the new examination requirements for the various degree courses in hotel and catering management, the diploma and certificates of the Business and Technical Education council and for the Hotel and Catering Institutional Management Association.

In addition, the book has been selected by the English Language Book Society since 1988 for inclusion in its hotel catering and tourism list. The English Language Book Society is funded by the Overseas Development Administration of the British Government to make available significant textbooks of British publishers to students in developing countries throughout the world.

Acknowledgements go to the many colleagues and organizations who kindly contributed to the first edition and who have again given their time and assistance to the second. Additionally, we would like to thank the following for their assistance:

AJ's Restaurants
Beefeater Steak Houses
BMRB; Boca Raton Resort and Club
Caterer and Hotelkeeper
Dome Café Bar
Electrolux Leisure Appliances
FAST International Ltd
Franchise Development Services Ltd
Gallup
Girovend Cashless Systems (UK) Ltd
Harvester Restaurants
HCTC
Hillingdon Borough Council
Horwath & Horwath
Hotel Britannia Inter-continental
London; King Edward's Hospital Fund
Liberty Street Restaurants
London Tara Hotel
Market-Power
Media Expenditure Analysis Ltd
Mintel
North West Surrey Health Authority

Pacino's Restaurant
Queen Elizabeth II Hospital
Remanco Systems Inc
Robobar Ltd
South West Thames Regional Health
Authority

St Peter's Hospital, Chertsey
Surrey County Council
West Dorset General Hospital

Bernard Davis and Sally Stone
1991

Preface to the first edition

This book has been written to explain the complexities of managing food and beverage outlets. The purpose is to examine the wide range of subject areas that come within the orbit of operational food and beverage management and to relate these to the applications applied within five broad sections of the catering industry (i.e. fast-food and popular catering, hotels and quality restaurants, function catering, industrial catering and welfare catering).

The book has been planned to cover the examination requirements for the various degree courses in Hotel and Catering Administration and Management; the Hotel and Catering Institutional Management Association; and diplomas and certificates of the Business and Technician Education Council.

In addition, the book has written for practicing catering managers, food and beverage managers, food and beverage controllers and all their assistants who may wish to formalize and update their knowledge, in order to improve the profitability and productivity of their operations and to enhance their customers' satisfaction.

This book is based on our own practical experiences and from first-hand information obtained from practitioners, within both large and small companies and units, in the many segments of the industry, who so generously gave up their time to answer and discuss many of our questions while undertaking research for the book. We are also grateful to the many companies who kindly gave permission for samples of their menus to be reproduced within the book.

In particular the authors would like to express a special debt of gratitude to those people whose assistance to us has been invaluable. To Prof. S. Medlik who gave valuable advice in the structuring of this book and for commenting on the early drafts of some of the chapters, and to Brain Cheeseman (Principal Lecturer, Westminster College) and Barry Ware-Lane (Operations Systems Director, United Biscuits Restaurants), both of whom made invaluable constructive comments to the final draft of the book. Also to David Airy (Lecturer, University of Surrey) for his help and advice with the first two chapters.

Acknowledgements also go to the following organizations for their help and assistance:

The Peninsula Hotel, Hong Kong
The Inter Continental, London
Hilton International, London
Hyatt Carlton Tower, London
British Airways
Sweda International
Berni Restaurants
Pizza Express, New York
New York Restaurant
United Biscuits Restaurants Ltd
The Mandarin Hotel, Hong Kong
The Broadmoor Hotel, Colorado
The Oriental Hotel, Bangkok
The Castle Hotel, Taunton
Grosvenor House, London
Sutcliffe Catering Company: Derbyshire County Council
The Department of Health and social Security
The Home Office
The Automatic Vending Association of Britain
Multimet
Regethermic
The Hotel, Catering and Institutional Management Association

Bernard Davis and Sally Stone
1985

Introducing food and beverage management

The provision of food and beverages away from home forms a substantial part of the activities of the hospitality industry and, indeed, of the economy as a whole. Like the industry of which it is a major part, food and beverage operations are characterized by their diversity. Outlets include private and public sector establishments and range from small independently owned and operated units to large multinational corporations managing global brands and from prison catering to catering in the most luxurious hotels in the world.

It is however very difficult to get hold of consistent statistics about the hospitality industry and about food and beverage operations as there is no one single definition of what the boundaries of the various industry sectors and subsectors are and therefore what should and should not be included.

Activity 1

Before you go any further with this chapter, write down 10 different occasions when you might eat out of the home and attach a different business to each occasion. For example, taking my girl/boyfriend out to celebrate their birthday – The Ivy, popping into town at lunchtime for a sandwich and a coffee – Pret A Manger, and so on.

Chapter objectives

After working through this chapter you should be able to:

- Understand the complexity of the hospitality industry.
- Identify the size and scope of food and beverage operations.
- Distinguish between market and cost orientation.
- Identify the key responsibilities of food and beverage managers and the constraints that may be placed on them.
- Explain the factors affecting the nature of the meal experience and recognize the manager's role in ensuring coherence.

SIZE AND SCOPE OF FOOD AND BEVERAGE OPERATIONS

If the hospitality industry is considered to cover all undertakings concerned with the provision of food, drink and accommodation away from home, this will naturally include all food and beverage outlets. In other words, food and beverage provision is simply one element of a broader hospitality industry. In conceptual terms, this raises few problems except possibly with take-away food establishments where in some cases the food may be taken home for consumption even though it is prepared and provided away from home. In practice, however, there are a number of difficulties in considering the hospitality industry as embracing all food and beverage establishments and outlets. This arises because, following a number of official and commercial attempts at definition, the hospitality industry is often considered to have a much narrower scope. The official definitions have excluded many food and beverage outlets. For example, the Standard Industrial Classification (SIC, 1992) gives hospitality a reasonably broad coverage as shown in the Table 1.1, but even here parts of employee and welfare catering are either omitted or included in other sectors. This book adopts the broadest possible approach, aiming to consider all types of food and beverage operation wherever they may appear.

Table 1.1 provides the latest figures on the size and scope of the UK hospitality industry available from UK government sources. The figures are based on a definition based on the SIC 1992, which will be discussed in more detail later.

The data show a pattern of fairly consistent growth across the industry for the first few years of the 21st century. In terms of numbers of businesses, with the exception of the hotel and motel sector, all other sectors have grown substantially, with the restaurant, cafés and take-away sector in particular growing by around 10% over these 4 years. The hospitality industry as described here has a total of nearly 127,000 separate businesses.

Looking at turnover provides a slightly different picture of the make up of the total of over £70,000 million. For example, hotels and motels show an increase in turnover from 2002 onwards even though the number of businesses has declined. This suggests

Number of businesses	SIC 92 Code	2001	2002	2003	2004
Hotels and motels	55.11 and 55.12	10,890	10,800	10,535	10,416
Camping sites, etc.	55.21 and 55.23	3,928	4,175	4,370	4,702
Restaurants, cafes, take-away food shops	55.30	52,633	54,340	55,475	57,667
Pubs, bars and licensed clubs	55.40	46,320	47,914	47,475	48,146
Canteen operator, catering contractor	55.51 and 55.52	5,217	5,485	5,636	5,765
Total	55.00	118,988	122,714	123,491	126,696

Turnover (£ million)	SIC 92 Code	2001	2002	2003	2004
Hotels and motels	55.11 and 55.12	12,047	11,824	12,172	13,009
Camping sites etc.	55.21 and 55.23	2,220	2,631	3,032	3,616
Restaurants, cafes, take-away food shops	55.30	18,323	18,843	20,145	21,726
Pubs, bars and licensed clubs	55.40	19,163	20,681	21,392	24,481
Canteen operator, catering contractor	55.51 and 55.52	5,985	6,624	6,670	7,382
Total	55.00	57,738	60,603	63,412	70,216

Employment (Thousands)	SIC 92 Code	2001	2002	2003	2004
Hotels, motels and camping sites, etc.	55.1/55.2	370	365	369	379
Restaurants, cafes, take-away food shops	55.30	509	547	575	594
Pubs, bars and licensed clubs	55.40	525	531	540	558
Canteen operator, catering contractor	55.50	256	265	267	267
Total	55	1,660	1,708	1,751	1,798

Source: Annual Abstract of Statistics 2007, Edition No 143, Office for National Statistics © Crown Copyright with permission

Table 1.1
Size and scope of the hospitality industry

either a consolidation of the sector with a smaller number of larger businesses or that each business is showing much better performance. The reality is probably somewhere between the two. The restaurant and pubs, bars and clubs sectors have shown very strong growth in turnover and can be seen to be the dominant sectors of food and beverage operations as a large part of hotel turnover is dependent on room sales. The canteen and contract catering or contract food service sectors have also shown strong growth.

In employment terms, restaurants are easily the largest sector, closely followed by pubs, bars and clubs, with the hotel sector growing more slowly, and the contract food service sector holding steady.

Standard Industrial Classification

The figures given in Table 1.1 come from the UK government and are based on the SIC, 1992. For analytical purposes, economically similar activities may be grouped together into 'industries', for example, into agriculture, motor vehicle manufacture, retail distribution, catering and national government service. A system used to group activities in this way is described as an 'industrial classification'. Such a classification usually starts with a small number of broad groups of activities that are then subdivided into progressively narrower groups so that the classification can be used with varying amounts of detail for different purposes.

The first comprehensive SIC for the United Kingdom was issued in 1948. The classification has been revised on many occasions and in order to comply with EU data standards, the SIC was redrawn in 2007 and the new classification scheme will come into effect at the beginning of 2008. While the old SIC had only four main groups: hotels and other accommodation; restaurants, cafes and takeaways; pubs, bars and clubs; and canteens and contract catering, the new scheme as shown in Table 1.2 is much more comprehensive. There is a lot of information here but it is worth looking in some detail at the various headings to understand the differences between the different classifications.

Section I Accommodation and food service activities

This section includes the provision of short-stay accommodation for visitors and other travellers and the provision of complete meals and drinks fit for immediate consumption. The amount and type of supplementary services provided within this section can vary widely.

This section excludes the provision of long-term accommodation as primary residences, which is classified in real estate activities (section L). Also excluded is the preparation of food or drinks that are either not fit for immediate consumption or that are sold through independent distribution channels, that is through wholesale or retail trade activities. The preparation of these foods is classified in manufacturing (section C).

55 Accommodation

This division includes the provision of short-stay accommodation for visitors and other travellers. Also included is the provision of longer term accommodation for students, workers and similar individuals. Some units may provide only accommodation while others provide a combination of accommodation, meals and/or recreational facilities.

This division excludes activities related to the provision of long-term primary residences in facilities such as apartments typically leased on a monthly or annual basis classified in Real Estate (section L).

55.1 Hotels and similar accommodation
55.10 Hotels and similar accommodation

This class includes the provision of accommodation, typically on a daily or weekly basis, principally for short stays by visitors. This includes the provision of furnished accommodation in guest rooms and suites. Services include daily cleaning and bed-making. A range of additional services may be provided such as food and beverage services, parking, laundry services,

---

Table 1.2
UK Standard Industrial Classification of Economic Activities 2007

swimming pools and exercise rooms, recreational facilities as well as conference and convention facilities.

This class includes accommodation provided by hotels, resort hotels, suite/apartment hotels and motels. This class excludes the provision of homes and furnished or unfurnished flats or apartments for more permanent use, typically on a monthly or annual basis, see division 68.

55.2 Holiday and other short-stay accommodation
55.20 Holiday and other short-stay accommodation
This class includes the provision of accommodation, typically on a daily or weekly basis, principally for short stays by visitors, in self-contained space consisting of complete furnished rooms or areas for living/dining and sleeping, with cooking facilities or fully equipped kitchens. This may take the form of apartments or flats in small free-standing multi-storey buildings or clusters of buildings, or single storey bungalows, chalets, cottages and cabins. Very minimal complementary services, if any, are provided. This class includes accommodation provided by children's and other holiday homes, visitor flats and bungalows, cottages and cabins without housekeeping services, youth hostels and mountain refuges. This class excludes provision of furnished short-stay accommodation with daily cleaning, bed-making, food and beverage services, see 55.10 and the provision of homes and furnished or unfurnished flats or apartments for more permanent use, typically on a monthly or annual basis, see division 68

55.20/1 Holiday centres and villages
This subclass includes the provision of holiday and other collective accommodation in holiday centres and holiday villages.

55.20/2 Youth hostels
This subclass includes mountain refuges but excludes protective shelters or plain bivouac facilities for placing tents and/or sleeping bags, see 55.30.

55.20/9 Other holiday and other short stay accommodation (not including holiday centres and villages or youth hostels)
This subclass includes the provision of holiday and other collective accommodation other than that provided in holiday centres and holiday villages or in youth hostels.

55.3 Camping grounds, recreational vehicle parks and trailer parks
This class includes the provision of accommodation in campgrounds, trailer parks, recreational camps and fishing and hunting camps for short stay visitors, provision of space and facilities for recreational vehicles and accommodation provided by protective shelters or plain bivouac facilities for placing tents and/or sleeping bags but excludes mountain refuges, cabins and hostels, see 55.20.

55.9 Other accommodation
This class includes the provision temporary or longer-term accommodation in single or shared rooms or dormitories for students, migrant (seasonal) workers and other individuals.

This class includes student residences, school dormitories, workers' hostels, rooming and boarding houses and railway sleeping cars.

56 Food and beverage service activities
This division includes food and beverage serving activities providing complete meals or drinks fit for immediate consumption, whether in traditional restaurants, self-service or take-away restaurants, whether as permanent or temporary stands with or without seating. The fact that meals fit for immediate consumption are offered is the decisive factor rather than the kind of facility providing them. This division excludes the production of meals not fit for immediate consumption or not planned to be consumed immediately or of prepared food which is not considered to be a meal (see divisions 10: manufacture of food products and 11: manufacture of beverages). Also excluded is the sale of not self-manufactured food that is not considered to be a meal or of meals that are not fit for immediate consumption (see section G: wholesale and retail trade).

Table 1.2
Continued

56.1 Restaurants and mobile food service activities

56.10/1 Licensed restaurants

This subclass includes the provision of food services to customers, whether they are served while seated or serve themselves from a display of items. The meals provided are generally for consumption on the premises and alcoholic drinks to accompany the meal are available.

This subclass includes restaurants, cafeterias, fast-food restaurants and also includes restaurant and bar activities connected to transportation, when carried out by separate units but excludes concession operation of eating facilities, see 56.29.

56.10/2 Unlicensed restaurants and cafes

This subclass includes the provision of food services to customers, whether they are served while seated or serve themselves from a display of items, The meals provided are generally for consumption on the premises and only non-alcoholic drinks are served. This subclass includes restaurants, cafeterias, fast-food restaurants and also includes restaurant and bar activities connected to transportation, when carried out by separate units but excludes concession operation of eating facilities, see 56.29.

56.10/3 Take away food shops and mobile food stands

This subclass includes the provision of food services to customers to take away or to have delivered. This includes the preparation and serving of meals for immediate consumption from motorised vehicles or nonmotorised carts. The subclass includes take-out eating places, ice cream vans, mobile food carts, food preparation in market stalls but excludes retail sale of food through vending machines, see 47.99 and concession operation of eating facilities, see 56.29.

56.2 Event catering and other food service activities

This group includes catering activities for individual events or for a specified period of time and the operation of food concessions, such as at sports or similar facilities.

56.21 Event catering activities

This class includes the provision of food services based on contractual arrangements with the customer, at the location specified by the customer, for a specific event but excludes manufacture of perishable food items for resale, see 10.89 and retail sale of perishable food items, see division 47.

56.29 Other food service activities

This class includes industrial catering, that is the provision of food services based on contractual arrangements with the customer, for a specific period of time. Also included is the operation of food concessions at sports and similar facilities. The food is usually prepared in a central unit.This class includes activities of food service contractors (e.g. for transportation companies), operation of food concessions at sports and similar facilities, operation of canteens or cafeterias (e.g. for factories, offices, hospitals or schools) on a concession basis. It excludes the manufacture of perishable food items for resale, see 10.89 and retail sale of perishable food items, see division 47.

56.3 Beverage serving activities

This group includes the preparation and serving of beverages for immediate consumption on the premises.

56.30/1 Licensed clubs

This subclass includes the preparation and serving of beverages for immediate consumption on the premises by: nightclubs, social clubs but excludes reselling packaged/prepared beverages, see 47 and retail sale of beverages through vending machines, see 47.99.

56.30/2 Public houses and bars

This subclass includes the preparation and serving of beverages for immediate consumption on the premises by: bars, taverns, cocktail lounges, discotheques licensed to sell alcohol (with beverage serving predominant), and beer parlours but excludes reselling packaged/prepared beverages, see 47, retail sale of beverages through vending machines, see 47.99, operation of discotheques and dance floors without beverage serving, see 93.29.

Source: UK Standard Industrial Classification of Economic Activities 2007 (SIC 2007): Structure and explanatory notes, Office for National Statistics

Table 1.2
Continued

In reading through the new classification, there are a number of interesting issues for note.

- First the very detailed nature of the descriptions and the very precise nature of the language used, including specifying types of activity that are included and also types of activity that are excluded. The activities excluded will appear in the national statistics under a different heading.
- Second, the definition of food and beverage operations as activities providing complete meals or drinks fit for immediate consumption. The emphasis here is on ready to eat food and drink and not on the manufacture or retail of food that needs reheating or reconstitution. This may cause some problems for supermarkets, who sell large amounts of sandwiches – for immediate consumption – but also large amounts of ready meals to take home and prepare for dinner. Where would a rotisserie chicken fit into this description?
- Third, the inclusion for the first time of mobile food stands, specifically mentioned in the classification.
- Fourth, the introduction of the category of event catering, which has seen substantial growth over the last few years, but perhaps strangely the inclusion of industrial or contract food service as part of this category. This 'other food services' category now also includes travel catering, catering at sports grounds, as well as factories, offices, hospitals or schools but only on a contract or concession basis and so still excludes the majority of public sector catering.
- Fifth, what is a beer parlour?

Activity 2

Take your 10 occasions and businesses identified earlier and try to fit them into the categories described above. Why are some easy to categorize and some more difficult? Are there any that you cannot find an appropriate category for?

Classifying food and beverage operations

There are many different ways of classifying food and beverage operations for different purposes. The SIC scheme discussed above is to allow the systematic collection and analysis of national economic statistics, which will now allow comparison across the whole of the EU. Organizations such as Keynote, a well-respected market intelligence company, who prepare very detailed reports on a wide range of industries including hospitality and food and beverage operations, concentrate only on commercial operations in restaurants, fast food, contract food service, hotels, public houses and other (Keynote Publications, 2007). People 1st, the Sector Skills Council for the Hospitality, Leisure, Travel and Tourism industries, whose emphasis is on employees and the development of their skills to match industry needs, split the industry into 14, namely Contract food service providers,

Events, Gambling, Holiday parks, Hospitality services, Hostels, Hotels, Membership clubs, Pubs, Bars and nightclubs, Restaurants, Self catering accommodation, Tourist services, Travel services and Visitor attractions (People 1st, 2007). This is a much broader description of the industry and by including in 'hospitality services' people who are employed 'in house', rather than by a contract caterer, to provide hospitality in travel, retail, education, healthcare, offshore locations, corporate hospitality, government and local authority provision such as care homes and prisons, as well as leisure venues and events, they capture many more people than the 'commercial' only definitions. While these different definitions and classifications are interesting and useful, they do not provide any significant managerial insight.

From this perspective, it is possible to make a number of distinctions between the many different types of food and beverage outlets. First, there is a distinction between those outlets that operate on a strictly commercial basis and those that are subsidized. A second distinction concerns the type of market served. In some cases, the market is confined to restricted groups, as for example, in a hospital or a prison or on a cruise ship, while in other cases the outlet is open to the public at large. A third distinction is between outlets where catering is the main activity of the undertaking, as for example, in a privately owned commercial restaurant, and those where it is a secondary activity, as is the case with travel catering or school meal catering. A final distinction appears between outlets that are in public ownership and those in private ownership. To a certain extent there is a rough compatibility between the distinctions. On the one hand, captive markets tend to be in public ownership and to be a subsidiary activity of the undertaking. On the other hand, the commercial outlets tend to be in the private sector, to serve the general public and to be the main activity of the undertaking. In brief, the subsidized sector is not normally available to the public at large and normally provides catering only as an activity that is both secondary to the main business and available only to restricted groups. These broad divisions, however, do not hold true in all cases. Indeed, the exceptions are numerous and beyond the broad categories, they tend to devalue any generalizations.

Using some of the above distinctions, it is possible to classify food and beverage outlets into a number of broad sectors. Figure 1.1 illustrates one way of breaking down the industry into sectors. The figure shows a distinction between purely commercial operations and those which accrue subsidies in some way. The purely commercial operations may be in public or private ownership and include outlets where catering is the main activity as well as those where it is a secondary activity, as for example, catering in theatres or shops. In the case of the commercial sector, a secondary division is shown between outlets that have a restricted market and those which are open to the general public. The subsidized operations similarly may be in public or private ownership. A distinction is drawn between catering in institutions where public ownership dominates and catering for employees where

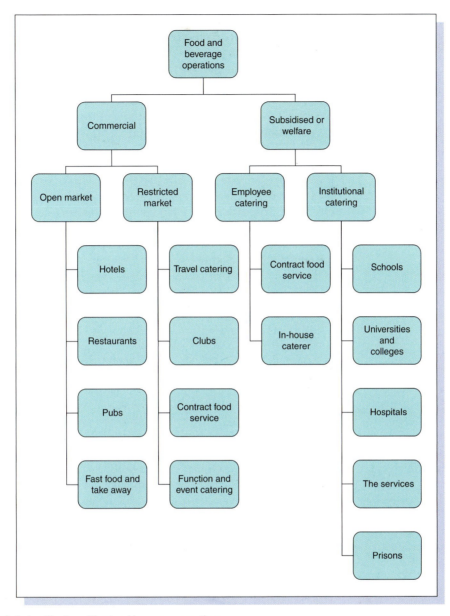

Figure 1.1 A classification of food and beverage operations

private ownership is also of importance. Almost by definition subsidized catering tends to be available only to restricted markets.

As with any classification, there are of course areas of overlap. There are two of particular importance here. The first overlap concerns catering in various private schools, colleges and hospitals, and in some offices and works canteens where the catering is not in any way subsidized but run on strictly on commercial lines. These outlets appear under the heading of the commercial sector as commercial catering for a restricted market, above. The second issue concerns the many subsidized or welfare catering outlets that are operated by catering contractors who are themselves strictly organized on commercial lines. These have not been separated out because although the operators themselves may be commercial companies, this does not affect the fact that the end product is normally subsidized for the market.

There are two reasons for using this classification here. First, it provides a very broad coverage of food and beverage outlets – broader, for example, than many of the official definitions and classifications of the hospitality industry. The second reason for using this classification is that it is based on distinctions that have a significant bearing upon most aspects of the operation of the catering activity. For example, the difference between subsidized catering and commercial catering not only embraces differences of objectives but also covers differences in the markets served, differences in the organizations involved and differences in their marketing and business strategy. These distinctions will be discussed in detail in Chapters 2 and 3.

Activity 3

Take the 10 occasions and businesses you identified earlier and place them on the chart show above. Where do most of your businesses fall?

Cost and market orientation

It is then convenient at this point to discuss the broad distinction between cost and market orientation within the hospitality industry, as these two terms are closely associated with the particular sectors of the industry that have been identified. Examples of cost orientation are identified particularly in the welfare sector such as catering in prisons, for patients in hospitals and often for 'in-house' employee restaurants, while market orientation examples are found in the hotels, restaurants, popular and fast-food sectors. It is arguable that in fact all sectors of the industry need to employ a market oriented approach.

A market oriented business displays the following characteristics:

- A high percentage of fixed costs, for example rent, rates, management salaries, depreciation of buildings and equipment. This high percentage of fixed costs remains fixed regardless of any changes in the volume of sales. A hotel restaurant is an example of an operation with high fixed costs that have to be covered before profit can be made.
- A greater reliance on increases in revenue rather than decreases in costs to contribute to the profit levels of the establishment. The implication here is that in seeking to increase the business's profitability, more emphasis must be given to increasing sales (e.g. by increasing the average spend of the customers or by increasing the number of customers) rather than by reducing costs. For this reason the close monitoring of all sales in a market oriented business becomes of prime importance.

- An unstable market demand for the product, thereby requiring a greater emphasis on all forms of selling and merchandising of the product to eliminate shortfalls in sales and the need to manage the capacity of the business more closely.
- More likely to have a more flexible pricing policy in order to attract customers at off-peak times.

A cost oriented business displays the following characteristics:

- A lower percentage of fixed costs, but a higher percentage of variable costs such as food and beverage costs. The percentage of variable costs in cost oriented establishments varies with changes in the volume of the business's sales. Employee restaurants are often found with a lower percentage of fixed costs. This places less emphasis on achieving high sales volumes.
- A greater reliance on decreases in costs rather than increases in sales to contribute to the budgeted profit levels of the establishment. Thus in seeking to increase the performance level (budgeted revenue and profit) of a cost oriented business more emphasis would be given to reducing the overall costs of the operation in such areas as purchasing, portion sizes and labour levels.
- A relatively stable market demand for the product. In comparison to market oriented businesses, cost oriented operations enjoy a reasonably stable demand for their products. This makes planning and operating more predictable and controllable.
- More likely to have a more traditional fixed-pricing policy.

There are those areas of the hospitality industry that cannot be precisely defined as either cost or market oriented in that they display characteristics of both orientations at different times during their business. In the main, however, most hospitality establishments fall into one of these two categories and this has important implications for the catering and financial policies of the business, which are described later.

Activity 4

Taking the 10 occasions and businesses you identified earlier, categorize them into their cost or marketing orientation. Why are some businesses more difficult to categorize than others?

FOOD AND BEVERAGE MANAGEMENT

What do managers do?

There has been substantial interest in the nature and definition of the work of the manager over many years. Figure 1.2 presents a model, which has been developed to synthesize much of this work for the hospitality industry (Li et al., 2006).

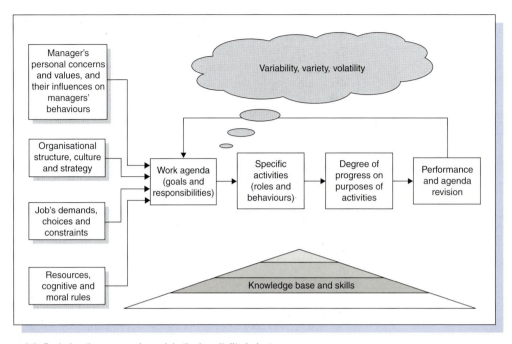

Figure 1.2 Exploring the manager's work in the hospitality industry

Hospitality managers have explicit and implicit goals, or responsibilities, which are concerned with ensuring the organization's continued success and survival, as well as their own personal interests, such as career progression. For hospitality firms, there are three main types of objectives that management must be concerned with, which are to ensure that the guest feels welcome, that facilities work for the guest, and that the operation will continue to provide service while also making a profit (Powers and Barrows, 2003).

The goals that are set are shaped by factors, which include the organizational structure and culture, the economic situation, national culture, available resources, cognitive and moral rules, and their own personal attributes. Managers in the hospitality industry face a more uncertain and complex work environment than in many other industries due to its unique service characteristics. This complexity is then coupled with the cultural differences of different business climates and environments and the managers' personal values.

To reach the goals that have been set, managers in hospitality firms carry out various tasks and activities, covering the standard managerial roles such as planning, organizing, commanding, coordinating and controlling, sometimes called POC[3]. They often act in a seemingly ad hoc way constantly responding to the unexpected resulting from the changing environment. While managers undertake a diversity of managerial activities, what they do and / or what they choose to do are, to some extent, unpredictable and changeable. The way that managers choose to perform the tasks is not always consistent either. Hence, the hospitality manager's work can be characterized by variability, variety and volatility, which represents the informal element of the hospitality manager's work.

However, each managerial activity is often associated with a certain management function. In other words, the purpose of a managerial behaviour can be linked to one of the key functions of management. For example, a restaurant manager may choose to speak to the customers to find out how they view the service offered. S/he will then be able to report on customer satisfaction. The manager may also recognize some weaknesses in service and, consequently, introduce appropriate training activities for staff. Since managers, including those in the hospitality industry, are responsible for the success of their organizations or organizational units, they also need to carry out these functional duties. This constitutes the formal nature of the hospitality manager's work.

While the performance of managers is reflected by the degree of progress in achieving their goals, the effectiveness of the manager's performance is underpinned by their competencies including personal attributes, knowledge and skills. In the case of a food and beverage business, managers must have sufficient knowledge in order to manage daily operations and direct the business strategically. They must be competent in relating to employees and guests, accomplishing operational goals within financial constraints, and responding to customers' requirements immediately so that the quality of real-time service can be delivered. Within an international work environment, hospitality managers must be also competent in appreciating cultural differences and dealing with various situations appropriately.

While this model sets the background to what managers should be doing, research conducted on behalf of the HCIMA (now the Institute of Hospitality) by the University of Surrey (Gamble et al., 1994) was designed to identify the types of management activities that could be seen to be typical of different sectors of the hospitality industry across Europe. Using a critical incident methodology, the research collected situations in which managers felt that their contributions or actions had made a significant difference to the outcome of a situation; somewhere the manager's skills and knowledge were used well, and somewhere the respondents felt their skills and knowledge were lacking. These incidents were then categorized into the four key areas of managing operations, managing the business, managing people and personal skills. Each of these areas was then divided into categories. These 15 categories represent the key areas of skills and knowledge that any manager in the hospitality industry needs in order to be effective. The areas and subcategories are illustrated in Figure 1.3.

Analysing the incidents against the main category areas by level of management provides the data shown in Table 1.3. To allow for the differences in the titles and roles between industry sectors, the following management levels were used:

- *Department head/Junior management*: Managing a section within an operating unit. This would equate to the coffee shop

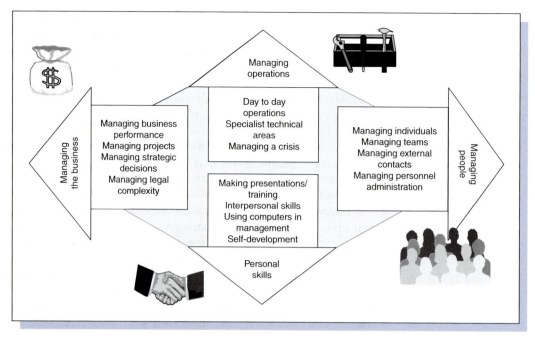

Figure 1.3 Main areas of management activity

Column %	Junior	Unit	General	Area	Director	Owner	Total %
Managing operations	40.3	30.2	20.9	13.4	17.8	29.3	29.0
Managing the business	11.8	23.0	32.6	41.2	41.1	32.0	25.2
Managing people	10.7	16.4	15.9	19.6	12.3	9.5	14.4
Personal skills	37.2	30.4	30.6	25.8	28.8	29.3	31.5
Total %	23.2	36.5	19.6	6.3	4.8	9.6	100.0

Table 1.3
Cross tabulation of main category areas by management level

manager in a hotel operation or the assistant manager of a fast-food operation.

- *Unit manager/Section manager*: Managing a complete unit or a section within a larger unit. This would equate to a unit catering manager working for a contract catering company, an executive chef, or the food and beverage manager of a small hotel.
- *General manager*: Overall control of one large unit composed of a number of sections or a collection of smaller units. This would equate to the food and beverage manager of a large hotel with extensive restaurant, conference and banqueting facilities, or the manager of a small number of catering contracts.
- *Area manager*: Overall responsibility for a number of separate large units or geographic areas.
- *Director*: responsibility for the operation and management of a complete organization.
- Owner/proprietor/partner.

Managing operations recorded the second highest number of incidents across the three subcategories of managing day-to-day operations, specialist/technical areas and managing crises. The analysis by managerial level, shown in Table 1.3 shows a heavy emphasis in this area for the junior managers. This was strongest in day-to-day operations and specialist knowledge but when it came to a crisis the junior managers were more likely to call in their unit or general manager. Owners also get heavily involved in sorting out the crises that may occur within their businesses. Sector comparisons show that hotels and restaurants reported the heaviest emphasis on managing operations while employee catering had the lowest.

The area of managing the business included aspects of managing business performance, managing projects, managing strategic decisions and managing legal complexity. Across the whole sample, this area was in third place behind personal skills and managing operations. More detailed analysis by managerial level reveals some significant differences. Although general managers, regional managers and directors show significantly more incidents in this area, junior managers and unit managers show a low emphasis. This suggests that managers as a whole may be becoming more business oriented but only when they have reached a position of some seniority with an organization. Comparisons across the sectors of the industry reflect this emphasis, with hotels, restaurants and popular catering, sectors with large numbers of junior managers, showing a low emphasis on this area but other sectors, especially contract catering and local authority services, featuring positively.

The managing people area covered managing individuals, managing teams, managing external contacts and managing personnel administration. It was therefore surprising that, given the labour intensity of many sectors of the industry and the natural importance given to this area, there were relatively few reported incidents in this area. One explanation for this anomaly is that the interpersonal skills involved in managing people are not included in this section but are categorized as more generic personal skills. Analysis across managerial level shows unit managers having the highest score in this area with junior managers and owners having low scores.

The area of personal skills includes a range of generic or transferable skills that cover making verbal or written presentations, training, interpersonal skills, using computers in management and self-development. There were more incidents reported in this area than any other and most of these were in the interpersonal skills area, followed by making presentations and training. Using computers in business showed comparatively few incidents and incidents to do with self-development were sadly, for an industry that seemingly values training highly, very sparse. All levels of manager reported large numbers of incidents in the area of interpersonal skills, especially the junior managers who would be new to having to handle these situations. Again there was an even spread across all sectors of the industry but a heavier than expected emphasis in popular catering or fast food. This is perhaps a reflection of the time managers spend dealing with interpersonal issues when the technological issues have been removed from consideration through systematized service delivery systems.

Responsibilities of food and beverage management

The research described above highlights the areas of activity that all managers are involved in but does not look at the specific responsibilities of the food and beverage manager. The significant contribution food and beverage sales can make towards total sales is evident but food and beverage costs can make equally significant inroads into sales. This necessitates the development of an effective system of control for all areas concerned with the food and beverage function. The development of such a total control system begins with the basic policy decisions described previously – the determination of the financial, marketing and catering policies. Working within these three broad policies of the establishment, the food and beverage department is then able to detail its objectives.

Definitions of management are numerous with writers using different words and phrases to describe the same activity, but if allowance is made for this there is some broad agreement about managers' functions.

First, they are involved in the planning process – setting objectives, making decisions about which direction the organization should take, that is, formulating policies. Second, managers decide how these objectives should be achieved and by whom. This involves analysing tasks and assigning them to individuals or groups. Third, managers are involved in staff motivation in such a way as to move the organization through them in the direction formulated at the planning stage, to achieve the stated objectives. Fourth, managers have a controlling function including the comparison of actual performance to that forecast at the initial planning stage and taking any necessary steps to correct any deviation from agreed objectives. The controlling may be done by observation, by analysis of accounting records and reports or by analysis of recorded statistical data.

These four management functions – planning, organizing, motivating and controlling – can be translated into the functions of the food and beverage manager. In a food and beverage department, the planning process involves the setting of several basic policies: a financial policy dealing with envisaged profitability or cost constraints of the establishment; a marketing policy defining the market to be catered for; and a catering policy defining the main objectives of operating the food and beverage facilities and the methods by which such objectives are to be achieved. Such policies would be decided at a senior level of management. The tasks needed to achieve these objectives would then be assigned to individuals who should receive job descriptions detailing the purpose of their tasks, the responsibilities of the individuals, who they are responsible to, etc. Here food and beverage managers work in conjunction with the personnel department in producing job descriptions and appointing on-the-job trainers to help train new staff.

The motivation of the staff of the food and beverage department is an important function of food and beverage managers. This may be undertaken in several ways – for example, by helping individuals who are undertaking common tasks to form into groups so that a 'team spirit' may develop, by encouraging staff–management committee meetings, or at a more basic level to see that full training is given so that job anxieties are reduced for employees from the beginning.

Finally, there is the element of control in the food and beverage department. This involves the checking of actual performance against expectations or forecasts, and in the case of any wide deviations, to locate the problem area and rectify it, and to take whatever steps are possible to prevent the problem occurring again.

The functions of food and beverage managers in coordinating the food and beverage department are therefore numerous, and it is important that they should use all the tools of management available to them. An organization chart should be produced showing the position of the food and beverage department within the context of the total establishment. An organization chart presents graphically the basic groupings and relationships of positions, and a general picture of the formal organization structure.

In larger units, departmentalization becomes more apparent. Figure 1.4 shows the organization of a food and beverage department in a large prestigious hotel.

In this example, the food and beverage manager has six subordinate managers acting as departmental heads and then further levels of assistant managers and the operational teams themselves. The food and beverage department can be seen to represent a major part of the hotel's total organization structure but clearly supported by other departments.

Some units are, of course, too small to adopt anything like this type of organization structure. Indeed, in a small privately owned restaurant, it is often the owner who is 'manager' of all departments. In this instance, the proprietor would also operate as the control department, monitoring all incoming and outgoing revenues and costs, but overall the same main activities still have to be covered.

It is also important to supplement the organization chart with a job description. A job description is an organized list of duties and responsibilities assigned to a specific position. It may be thought of as an extension of the formal organization chart in that it shows activities and job relationships for the positions identified on the formal organization chart. An example of a food and beverage manager's job description may be seen in Table 1.4. Some organizations also produce work schedules; these are outlines of work to be performed by employees with stated procedures and time

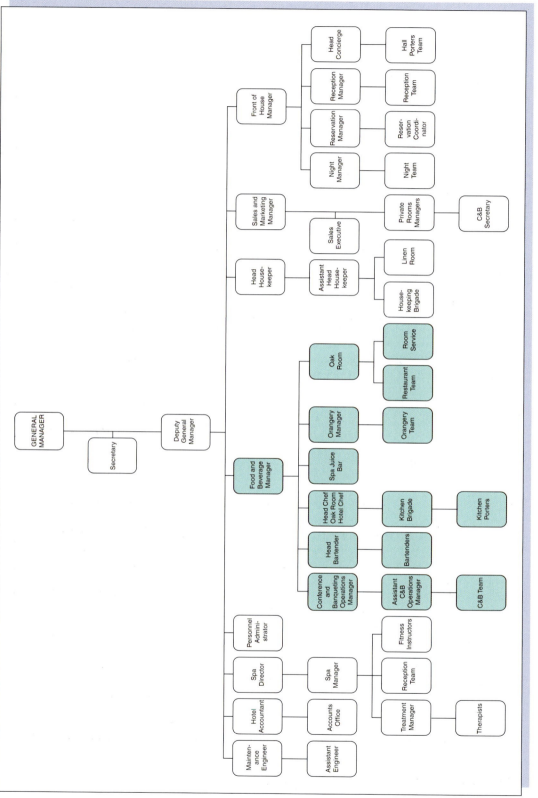

Figure 1.4 Danesfield House Hotel and Spa Organization Chart

DANESFIELD HOUSE HOTEL AND SPA
JOB SPECIFICATION

DANESFIELD HOUSE
HOTEL AND SPA

Food and Beverage Manager
Reporting to the Deputy General Manager

QUALIFICATION REQUIREMENTS:
1. Excellent reading, writing and oral proficiency in the English language.
2. College education, hotel or business administration degree preferred.
3. Five to Ten years in management positions in the hotel and/ or restaurant industry.

PURPOSE:
* To service all guests in a manner which exceeds expectations.
* To provide leadership and management for the Food and Beverage Division and integrate its functions with other hotel departments.
* To plan the continued growth and profitability of the division.
* To accept the responsibility for the health, safety and welfare of the restaurants/ outlets, guests and employees.
* To be accountable for the operations' assets and its personnel's actions.

JOB FUNCTIONS:
1. To prepare quarterly forecasts and business-achieved reports for each Food and Beverage operating department.
2. To coordinate the development, interpretation and implementation of hotel policies, operating procedures and training programs, manuals, directives, menus, work schedules, rules and regulations for the food and beverage staff and personnel.
3. To maintain up-to-date records on food and beverage staff personnel attendance, appearance, standards, work and vacation schedules, labor costs, payroll, absenteeism, turnover and disciplinary action.
4. To approve the employment and termination of food and beverage staff.
5. To be responsible for personal development and training of all F & B Staff.
6. To coordinate the selection, purchasing, storage, inventorying, maintenance and usage of all related food and beverage supplies and equipment.
7. To handle all guest comments in the food and beverage area.
8. To obtain maximum revenue results from the utilization and appearance of the food and beverage areas.
9. To constantly strive to improve the quality levels, performance and standards of F & and B service.
10. To oversee and apply risk assessments of safety, accident prevention, fire drills and first aid.
11. To achieve optimum levels of profitability within all areas of the F and B Operations, by buying and selling produce at optimum prices and maintaining appropriately efficient costs whilst achieving the required service and quality standards.
12. To maintain current prices and approved purveyors listed based on quality, service and cost of all related food and beverage items for requisitioning purposes, store inventories, cost control procedures and forecasts.
13. The ability to aid each Department Head in giving the necessary training to their staff and to assist them in it.
14. The ability to develop new and analyse existing procedures and special promotions that will improve guest patronage under the guidelines of the hotel's overall policies.
15. To develop and maintain effective communications between all operating departments.
16. To respond properly in any hotel emergency or safety situation.
17. To perform other tasks or projects as assigned by hotel management.

Table 1.4
Danesfield House Hotel food and beverage manager job description

requirements for their duties. Tasks are broken down into a careful sequence of operations and timed. They are particularly useful in training new employees and for lower-grade jobs, but have a limited application at the supervisory and management level.

In general, the main responsibilities and objectives of the food and beverage department may be summarized as follows:

1. The provision of food and beverage products and services catering for clearly defined markets to satisfy or exceed these customers' expectations.
2. The purchasing, receiving, storing, issuing and preparation of food and beverages within the establishment for final provision and service to the customer.
3. The formulation of an efficient control system within the food and beverage department with the purpose of:
   - Monitoring food and beverage prices and achieving competitive rates while still ensuring quality standards.
   - Pricing restaurant and special function menus to achieve desired profit margins.
   - Compiling on a daily, weekly and monthly basis, all relevant food and beverage information on costs and sales that may be used by management for forecasting, planning, budgeting, etc.
   - Reconciling actual and forecast costs and sales, and initiating corrective action if discrepancies occur, and finding out and eliminating the causes, for example bad portion control, incorrect pricing, etc.
   - Training, directing, motivating and monitoring of all food and beverage department staff.
   - Cooperating with other departments to become a significant contributor to the organization's short- and long-term profitability.
   - Obtaining in a regular, structured and systematic way, feedback from customers, so that their comments, complaints and compliments may be taken into account to improve the overall standard of service.

Activity 5

Compare the main responsibilities and objectives of the food and beverage department identified above with the job description from Danesfield House Hotel and Spa. Identify where there are any differences between the two? Why might these differences exist?

These are the major responsibilities and objectives of a food and beverage department. Other minor objectives do become important during the day-to-day running of the department, but these often tend to deal with sudden crises or short-term problems and would be too numerous to mention. However, achieving all these objectives is a far from easy task when managers are faced with the inherent complexity and variability of a food and beverage operation.

Constraints on food and beverage management

The management of food and beverage departments has been described as the most technical and complex in the hospitality industry. The specific factors that make food and beverage management relatively more complex are due to particular external and internal pressures.

External factors ● ● ●

The external factors are often seen as the 'major' problems of the food and beverage function. They originate outside the organization and for this reason internal action can rarely solve the problem adequately, although pro-active management may help to reduce their impact. Some of the major external pressures affecting the food and beverage function are listed below.

Government/political ● ● ●

- Government legislation, for example, fire regulations, smoking regulations, health and safety legislation, EU regulations.
- Changes in the fiscal structure of the country, for example, regulations affecting business expense allowances.
- Specific government taxes, for example, VAT.
- Government policy on training and employment, economic development, regional development, etc.

Economic ● ● ●

- Rising costs – foods and beverages, labour, fuel, rates and insurance.
- Sales instability – peaks and troughs of activity occur on a daily, weekly and seasonal basis.
- Changes in expenditure patterns and people's disposable incomes.
- Expansion and retraction of credit facilities.
- Interest rates on borrowed capital.

Social ● ● ●

- Changes in population distribution, for example, population drifting away from certain areas or demographics such as age structure.
- Changes in the socio-economic groupings of an area.
- Change in eating patterns leading to a demand for more varied foods.
- Changes in food fashion, for example, current popularity of take-away foods, home delivery of fast foods, trends in healthy eating.

Technical • • •

- Mechanization, for example, of food production and food service equipment.
- Information technology, for example, data processing in hospitality establishments.
- Product development, for example, organic vegetables, increased shelf life of foods through irradiation, meat and dairy produce alternatives.

Internal factors • • •

Along with external factors, the food and beverage function also has many other day-to-day internal pressures. Internal problems are those originating within the organization and for this reason such problems can usually be solved adequately within the establishment if they can be identified and the root cause removed. The internal problems may be classified as follows.

Food and beverage • • •

- Perishability of food and the need for adequate stock turnover.
- Wastage and portion control.
- Pilferage from kitchens, restaurants, bars and stores, sometimes referred to as 'shrinkage'.

Staff • • •

- General staff shortages or skill shortages within the industry.
- Achieving staffing levels to match peaks and troughs of sales activity.
- Absenteeism, illness, etc.
- Use of part-time or casual staff in some food and beverage departments.
- Poor supervision and training of new staff.
- High staff turnover, particularly in some areas.

Control • • •

- Cash and credit control and collection.
- Maintenance of all costs in line with budget guidelines and current volumes of business, for example, food, beverages, payroll, etc.
- Maintenance of a tight and efficient control of all food and beverage stocks.
- Maintenance of up-to-date costing and pricing of all menu items.
- Maintenance of an efficient food and beverage control system giving analysed statistical data of all business done.

Figure 1.5 shows diagrammatically the potential sources of issues and problems that food and beverage managers need to be aware of if they are to maintain and improve the effectiveness of their operations. Being a food and beverage manager is a challenging and demanding job but with the clear understanding and

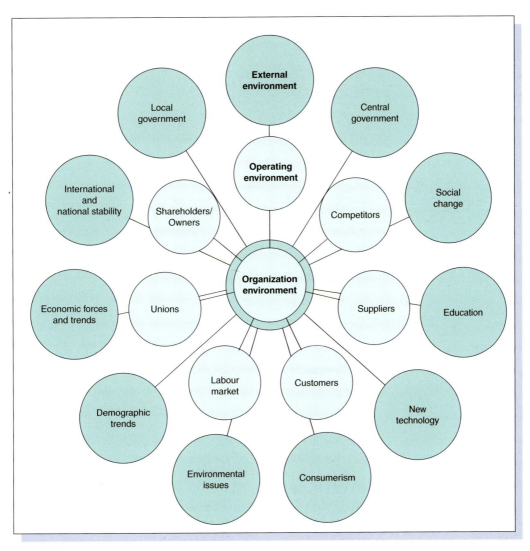

Figure 1.5 A representation of issues in the business environment

systematic approach that the following chapters provide, it can also be a rewarding and satisfying one. One key factor for all food and beverage managers is to understand their customers, the trends in the eating our market and the nature of the meal experience they need to provide.

MANAGING THE MEAL EXPERIENCE

Service industries, such as food and beverage operations, differ from manufacturing in several ways. The customer is present at the time of both production and service. In manufacturing the customer is not present during the production process. In food and beverage operations, the customer is involved in the creation of the service that is consumed at the point of production with little or no time delay between production and service. The customer is not involved in the creation of manufactured products and there may be a considerable time lag between production and service. Services cannot be examined in advance, they are highly perishable and cannot be stored, all adding to difficulties in the quality control of service products; in manufacturing goods can be made in advance of demand and stored allowing more time for control procedures. Finally, services have a larger intangible element in many of their products than manufactured goods do and for this reason have traditionally been more difficult to quantify and evaluate. For all these reasons, the time that the customer spends in the operation and what happens to them during that time is of particular importance.

The 'meal experience' may be defined as a series of events – both tangible and intangible – that a customer experiences when eating out. It is difficult to define exactly where a meal experience actually starts, and indeed ends, although it is usually assumed that the main part of the experience begins when customers enter a restaurant and ends when they leave. However, any feelings customers may have when they arrive at the restaurant, and when they leave, should also be taken into account and included as part of the total meal experience.

The series of events and experiences customers undergo when eating out may be divided into those tangible aspects of the product, that is, the food and drink, and those intangible aspects such as service, atmosphere, mood, etc. See Chapter 11 for a further discussion of tangibles and intangibles in food and beverage operations.

These two components of the meal experience have also been labelled primary and secondary products or core and peripheral elements but although differing in descriptive terms, the underlying concept is the same. It is the appreciation of the different components by the caterer that is important; the tangible and the intangible aspects must be integrated together to present a total product to the customer. If one or two components of the meal experience are out of harmony with the others, the whole product/service mix will be seen by the customer as a number of disjointed parts rather than as a totality.

This experience was first called the 'meal experience' in 1989 (Campbell-Smith) but is now a widely used term throughout the industry and has now been developed even further into the idea of the experience economy.

The experience economy

Food and beverage operations such as TGIFridays, the Hard Rock Café or Planet Hollywood have long understood that there is much more to the total customer experience than the food or the way that it is served. They recognized in putting their concepts together that they needed to provide an additional 'theatrical' element to their operations that would make them memorable and provide added value to their customers. The

Disney Corporation take this theatricality to an extreme by calling their hotel, restaurant and theme park employees 'cast members' and the uniforms they wear 'costumes'.

Pine and Gilmore (1999) argue that in order to differentiate your operation in an era of high competition and the increasing commoditization of service there is a need to provide the customer with a memory of an experience that they can take away with them rather than just a good product or service. They argue that in order to do this the business needs to consider the complete staging of the experience from start to finish and to think of it as an almost theatrical performance expecting employees to act out their roles within a carefully crafted environment. It could be argued that many restaurants have been in this business for a long time, but some operations are taking it even further.

Activity 6

Read the following examples provided from an article in *USA Today*.

Recognizing the need to create memorable experiences, some hotel groups in the United States are no longer selling corporate meeting clients just a room, a sound system, a projector and some bottles of water, but are creating a customized environment that uses sound, food, smell, decor, toys and gadgets to create moods that match the meetings' objectives.

For example, a client wishing to hammer out a financial deal might opt for an environment that eases tension. That could call for low lighting, green tea, worry stones on the tables and a relaxed mix of instrumental music. Those wishing to generate team-building and brainstorm for new projects might consider a joint cooking session, bowls of almonds (reputed to be brain food) and even board games.

Kimpton Hotels began its Signature Meetings initiative last year and now allows clients to customize by selecting from a menu of items and services. Those wishing to break up the tedium with 'elements of wellness' can buy aromatherapy, yoga or massage sessions, 15-minute guided power walks or even stress balls. They can select fruit smoothies, organic coffee and tea or wholegrain cereals for breakfast, and add fun foods including Pop-Tarts, Lucky Charms, macaroni cheese and hot dogs.

Omni Hotels launched a similar campaign – dubbed Sensational Meetings – earlier this year. They change the ambiance of their rooms to complement three different types of meetings:

The Energetic for brainstorming, planning and training provides special lighting, floral arrangements, miniature kumquat trees, and bright-coloured table items along with music by artists including U2, Coldplay and Sheryl Crow. They offer wheat grass shots, juice shots in test tubes, almonds in bright bowls, chocolate with mandarin orange, wild sweet orange vitamin C tea, sparkling pomegranate drink and use brightly coloured table linen and pens with bright inks in an environment scented with lemon.

The Challenging for change management and negotiations with lower lighting, candles, light pastel florals, water features, blue rocks, and bamboo in glass containers to the sounds of classic rhythm and blues, and soul. They offer green tea with jasmine, dark chocolate with lavender, apple cinnamon macaroons and also provide worry stones and blue table linen in an environment scented with lavender, juniper and aloe.

The Recognition for celebrating achievement with many mirrors, floral arrangements, stainless-steel balls, and large mirrored discs with a baby boomer soundtrack featuring artists such as the Beatles, Rolling Stones, Led Zeppelin, the Who and Fleetwood Mac. They offer juice in champagne flutes, chocolate champagne truffles, sparkling cider, Fuse white tea along with metallic table linens, recognition stones in an environment smelling of peppermint and chocolate.

Adapted from an article by Roger Yu, *USA Today* 24/07/2007

Although these seem quite extreme examples, consider ways in which restaurants or coffee bars already attempt to create customized experiences within their operations.

Before customers set out to any operation for a meal, they may already have decided on the type of meal they want or feel would be most suitable for that particular occasion. This pre-meal experience decision may have been taken after the consideration of a number of variables and customers will choose the operation they consider satisfies all or most of their requirements. The general factors affecting a customer's choice of meal experience include the following:

Social • • •

A social occasion is one of the most common reasons for eating out. Such family events as birthdays and anniversaries, special dates (Christmas, the New Year, Valentine's Day and Halloween), a special event (a christening or passing examinations) are all reasons for celebration and eating out. Equally, people decide to go to a restaurant for no other reason than to dine with friends.

For those people who eat out infrequently, may be two or three times a year, the celebration of a special occasion is the most important reason. As the number of meal occasions per year rises, to over four times a year, there is a corresponding increase in the variety of reasons given, for example, to socialize with friends and relatives, as a treat for self or spouse, as a change from eating at home, etc.

Business • • •

Meals may also be taken away from home for business reasons. Generally speaking, the level of restaurant chosen will depend on the level of business being conducted, so that the more important and valued the business, the more expensive and up-market will be the restaurant. Business lunches and dinners are still the most common, although working breakfasts and afternoon teas are also common.

Convenience and time • • •

A food service facility may be convenient because of its location or because of its speed of service. A working couple arriving home may decide to eat out rather than prepare something at home; they do not wish to travel far, nor do they want an elaborate meal, so they choose a local pub, pizzeria or Thai restaurant. A family out shopping at the weekend decide to have lunch in a fast-food operation in the high street. A long-distance commuter has a meal onboard a train knowing that he will arrive home late that evening. Office workers or hospital staff with little time available decide to have lunch in the staff canteen. Housewives out shopping decide to stop for a snack in a shopping centre food court.

All of these are typical examples of convenience eating away from home. They are convenient sometimes in terms of location, sometimes speed, because of the limited amount of time a customer has for a meal, and very often a combination of the two. Most of the facilities used are associated with the mass-market end of the catering industry: fast-food operations; coffee shops; catering facilities in shopping centres; pizzerias; steak houses; cafés in leisure complexes; vending machines in schools; hospitals; offices and other work situations.

Atmosphere and service • • •

The atmosphere and environment of certain types of catering facilities and the social skills of the service staff can be particularly attractive to certain groups of customers. For example, wine and cocktail bars, and champagne and oyster bars in city centres appeal, in particular, to employees who have spent the day working together in offices and wish to meet together after work. The widespread use of 'Happy Hours' in such operations has further encouraged this trend for workers to go straight from their place of work to a catering outlet to socialize. These facilities are also often attractive because of their convenient locations.

Price • • •

The price level of an operation will significantly affect the restaurant choice of customers, particularly 'impulse' buying decisions. For the majority of customers, except perhaps for those few who can afford regularly to patronize high-quality restaurants, there exists a 'trade-off' point between the task and cost of preparing a meal at home, or paying for a meal out. Generally speaking, the higher the disposable income, the higher the trade-off level. For example, a couple may consider it quite acceptable spending up to £40 for an impulse meal experience once a week; another couple may consider this price too high and would only be willing to pay up to that amount once a month. If they thought the meal was likely to cost more then they would trade-off the meal experience at a restaurant for a meal at home, or perhaps a cheaper take-away meal.

The menu • • •

Finally, a restaurant's menu may appear particularly interesting or adventurous, or have been recommended, enabling customers to enjoy a different type of meal from that cooked at home.

Activity 7

Consider each of your 10 operations in turn and decide which of the reasons given above would influence your decision to visit that operation

All of these factors will at some stage affect the buying decision of customers and hence their choice of meal experience, although it is unlikely that any of these variables will operate in isolation – usually two or three factors together will influence customers' choice of operation. Once customers have decided on the type of meal they want, they will start to accumulate different expectations and anticipations. Just as the customers' buying decisions are influenced by a number of variables, so too is the meal experience itself.

Understanding eating out

Understanding the factors affecting customers' buying decisions an analysing who eats out and the frequency that they do is valuable data for all food and beverage managers. The analysis of who the customers actually are is also necessary information, not only for caterers in general, operational management in particular, but also for marketing management. The size and distribution of the eating out market is illustrated in the Table 1.5.

A review of this data shows that fast food as a sector has grown 23% between 2002 and 2007, with more growth in chicken, perhaps fuelled buy health concerns and the introduction of new operations such as Nando's, and less growth in ethnic takeaways and fish and chips. In the restaurant sector, pubs have seen a growth rate of 35% and restaurants including many of the branded chains growing 36%. Much less growth has been seen in ethnic restaurants and in dining in hotels. The biggest growth, however, has been in the 'other' sector which includes cafes, coffee shops and other retail outlets. It would have been difficult over these last 5 years not to have noticed the number of new Costa, Caffè Nero, Starbucks and Pret A Manger operations appearing in towns and cities across the UK.

The analysis of those who eat out can be done in many ways. For example, it can be done by age, by gender, by socio-economic class and by the frequency of eating out – whether once, twice, or three or more times a week. Other examples of the types of analysis that may be done are by marital status, by the number of people in a household, by the number and age of children in the household, and by region within a country or of a specific area, etc.

	2002 £bn	2003 £bn	2004 £bn	2005 £bn	2006 (est) £bn	2007 (fore) £bn	% change 2002–07
Fast food:							
Burgers	1.95	2.08	2.22	2.31	2.41	2.4	23
Ethnic takeaway	1.5	1.55	1.61	1.67	1.75	1.8	20
Pizza and past[a]	1.08	1.14	1.2	1.28	1.32	1.35	25
Fish and chips	0.87	0.91	0.95	0.99	1.02	1	15
Fried chicken	0.76	0.86	0.91	0.97	1.04	1	32
Other fast food[b]	0.13	0.14	0.14	0.15	0.16	0.17	29
Total fast food	6.28	6.67	7.03	7.36	7.7	7.72	23
Restaurants:							
Pub catering	5.35	5.72	6.04	6.38	6.81	7.25	35
Hotel catering[c]	3.94	3.99	4.02	4.12	4.22	4.31	9
Restaurant meals	3.31	3.49	3.76	4.16	4.33	4.5	36
Ethnic restaurants	1.86	1.92	1.97	2.01	2.07	2	7
In-store	1.16	1.21	1.26	1.3	1.38	1.4	21
Roadside	0.47	0.48	0.49	0.51	0.53	0.53	11
Total restaurants	16.09	16.81	17.53	18.48	19.34	19.98	24
Other[d]	1.7	1.77	1.95	2.28	2.56	2.75	62
Total	24.07	25.25	26.51	28.12	29.59	30.45	27

Source: Mintel Eating Out Review, UK, July 2007.
Note: some historical data has been revised
[a] excl. institutional catering and other expenditure on food outside the home
[b] incl. jacket potatoes, sausages, filled croissants etc
[c] incl. drinks revenue
[d] incl. cafés, coffee shops and other retail outlets

Table 1.5
The UK eating out market[a], by segment, 2002–2007

The types of catering establishments that the public choose to eat out at, and the frequency that they do, is also valuable information. An example of an analysis of the types of establishment visited and frequency of visit based on a sample of 2,029 adults aged 15 and over is shown in Table 1.6.

- Major research of this nature is conducted by established market research organizations such as Mintel, Keynote and other consultancy companies, who undertake major studies for the industry in general. Specific and confidential studies to answer particular questions or for particular locations are also undertaken for individual companies. Research is also undertaken by the marketing departments of medium/large hospitality companies. This does not preclude the smaller-size establishment from undertaking systematic research studies, although the sample size is likely to be smaller and the time available to do so is restricted.

	All %	Twice a week or more %	About once a week %	About once a fortnight %	At least once a month %	At least once every 3 months %	Less than once every 3 months %
Pub restaurant/bar	51	67	64	69	52	50	27
Café/coffee shop	32	52	41	46	35	25	13
Chinese restaurant	27	45	39	37	28	17	10
Pizza/pasta restaurant	25	53	35	36	22	16	7
Fish and chip shop/restaurant	24	44	33	27	26	17	9
Indian restaurant	24	46	32	32	27	20	5
British restaurant	24	42	30	26	29	20	9
Burger/fried chicken bar	21	44	27	28	20	14	6
Hotel restaurant	18	36	28	25	17	10	8
In-store restaurant/ cafeteria	16	32	23	24	11	14	6
Other restaurant (e.g. Italian, vegetarian)	16	33	23	19	16	11	4
Other ethnic restaurant (e.g. Thai, Mexican)	11	28	18	15	9	7	2

Source: Mintel Eating Out Review, UK. July 2007

Table 1.6
Frequency of eating out, by venues visited, March 2007

Ideally, basic information should provide:

- sufficient data to aid decision-making;
- accurate and up-to-date consumer profiles, so that an organization is more successfully able to meet the requirements of the consumer;
- competitive analysis, so that an organization can in part measure its own performance.

Research of this nature to understand the needs of the customers should always be ongoing, and not just of an occasional nature.

Food and drink

The type of food and drink that people choose to consume away from home depends on a number of factors which are of particular concern to food and beverage managers. They include:

- The choice of food and drink available: whether the menu is limited or extensive; whether the operation revolves around

	Any venue %	Pub restaurant/ Bar %	Café/ Coffee shop %	Chinese restaurant %	Pizza/ Pasta restaurant %	Fish and chip shop/ Restaurant %	British restaurant %
All	86	51	32	27	25	24	24
Men	85	49	29	29	25	28	25
Women	87	52	35	25	25	20	23
16–19	91	52	30	35	45	40	18
20–24	90	50	26	33	44	28	21
25–34	93	53	34	38	40	30	24
35–44	90	56	41	32	29	28	29
45–54	85	48	36	26	20	18	26
55–64	84	53	31	22	15	20	25
65+	75	44	24	12	4	15	20

Source: Mintel Eating Out Review, UK, July 2007

Table 1.7
Most popular eating out venues visited, by gender and age, March 2007

one particular product, for example, steak houses and pizzerias; or whether there is a varied choice, for example, coffee shops and wine bars.

- Table 1.7 shows an analysis of the most popular types of food and beverage outlets visited by age group and by gender in the last month, from a sample of 2,029 adults aged 15 and over. This shows that 86% of the sample ate out at least once in the last month (an increase from 70% in the last edition in 1996) with pub restaurant and bars being the most popular choice, coffee shops growing strongly in popularity in second place and fish and chip shops and 'British' restaurants as the least popular.
- Looking at the gender differences, it would appear that women eat out more often than men (another change since 1996) and are more likely to visit pub restaurants and coffee shops (the second choice for women in the 1996 survey was fish and chips!). Men on the other hand are more likely to visit Chinese restaurants and fish and chip shops.
- Looking at the age differences, young people are more likely to eat out than older people, but everyone is happy to visit a pub restaurant. British restaurants appear to be more skewed towards an older clientele while pizza and pasta are skewed in the opposite direction.
- The quality of the product offered, for example, locally sourced fresh organics or convenience foods: château or estate bottled or cheaper wine varieties.

- The quantity of product offered, that is, the portion sizes. For example, does the restaurant offer children's meals or smaller portions for children or older people?
- The consistent standard of the product: customers returning to the restaurant for a second or subsequent occasion would expect the product to be of the same standard as they had eaten or drunk before.
- The range of tastes, textures, aromas and colours offered by a food dish, or the taste, colour and aroma offered by a drink.
- That the food and drink are served at the correct temperatures, for example, that the iced coffee is sufficiently chilled, or that hot food is hot when it reaches the customer.
- That the presentation of the food and drink enhances the product offered. This is important at all levels of catering, from cafeteria to fine dining service, where the visual presentation of the meal is very much part of the total experience.
- That the price and perceived value for money are both in line with customers' pre-meal experience anticipations.
- That the quality of the total meal experience matches or even enhances the expectations of the guests.

Variety in menu choice

The type of menu offered by an establishment and the variety of menu choice should also enhance the total meal experience. At the lower level of the market the choice of menu items in a restaurant is usually fairly limited for a number of reasons. First, price. If a customer is paying £10–15 for a three-course meal the range of menu items that can be made available within the cost limits of such an operation is obviously more limited than in operations where the customer's average spending power is higher. Second, the amount of time taken to consume meals at this level of the market may vary between half an hour and one hour, but will rarely exceed this. Proportionately, little of this time is spent studying the menu choice. Third, it may be suggested that customers frequenting this lower level of the market may be uncomfortable if presented with a very large menu selection and may therefore prefer a more limited, but still varied menu choice.

In fine dining restaurants where the average spending power may be well above £50 per head, the menu selection can be much greater. In these establishments which encourage a luxury meal experience, the minimum amount of time customers usually spend on a meal is one and a half hours, and may often be three hours, depending on the size of the group and the occasion. The proportion of the time that may be devoted to reading the menu and selecting from the menu items is correspondingly greater. Customers frequenting these types of establishment would also expect to be offered not only a large menu selection, but also a number of chef's and house specialities and wines.

The menu choice offered by a restaurant is therefore dependent on a number of interrelated factors: the price the customer is willing to pay; the amount of time available for the meal experience; the level of the market in which the restaurant is situated and, consequently, the types of customer likely to frequent that type of operation. Further considerations affecting the choice of menu from the caterer's point of view would be the production and service facilities available, the skills of the staff, the quality and availability of ingredients and the potential profitability of the menu.

Level of service

Broadly speaking the higher the cost of the meal to the customer, the more service the customer expects to receive. In a food court where customers are spending around £5 for a meal, the degree of service received is comparatively little: customers collect and purchase their own food from particular food units, carry it to a table, and may be expected to clear their own dishes from the table at the end of their meal. As the cost of the meal to customers increases so will the amount of service they receive. At the higher end of the eating out market, where customers may be paying over £40 per head for a meal, full service is most likely to be provided. However, the dominance of silver service at this level is increasingly challenged by chefs wishing to take direct control of the presentation of their dishes and so adopting a plated style of service.

The actual service of the food and beverages to the customer may be described as the 'direct' service. Part of the restaurant's total service, however, is also composed of 'indirect' or ancillary services. These might include the provision of cloakroom facilities (somewhere for the customer to leave coats and bags safely); or access to the Internet. It is necessary for a restaurant to identify the level of service it is going to offer in its offer and to extend this standard of service throughout all aspects of the operation. Thus, if a restaurant has a very formal type of food and beverage service, associated with some fine dining operations, the other aspects of the restaurant service should be equally formal – the speed, efficiency and dress of staff; the degree of personalization and courtesy the customers receives, and so on. It is important, therefore, for a restaurant operation to consider not only the service of the food and beverages for which the staff are usually adequately trained, but also to remember the indirect service aspect of the operation, which are all part of the customer's meal experience.

Price and value for money

The concept of value for money will vary from one sector of the market to another and, indeed, from one customer to another. In the majority of cases, however, customers will frequent a restaurant not only because of its food and service, but also because they feel the price they are paying represents good value for money. At the popular end of the market, inclusive 'meal deals' are often offered. For example, in the summer, a steak house operation might offer rump steak and strawberries at an inclusive and competitive price, so that a prospective client is aware in advance what the main cost of the meal will be, and this will help alleviate any concern the customer may have about the total cost. At the top end of the market, menu items are often charged for separately because at this level the total cost of the meal is not such an important factor to the customer as perhaps are the other aspects of the operation, such as the standard and range of food and beverages, the level of service offered and the degree of comfort, décor and atmosphere. However, there has been a growing emphasis recently on set price menus in quality and luxury restaurants, at both lunch and dinner.

Today, some establishments include a percentage service charge in the price of their meals, others will add it separately (commonly 12.5% of the total bill), while some operations do not include a service charge but leave it to the customer's discretion. Prices charged within the UK are inclusive of government taxes, while in some other countries the total amount of tax is shown separately. Some schools of thought consider that by not showing these 'added extras', such as a service charge in the price of the individual menu items, customers may be encouraged to spend more because the prices will appear very reasonable; others consider that customers prefer to know exactly what they are paying for and do not like to see these 'extras' added at the end of the bill.

Interior design

The overall interior design of a restaurant is one of the first physical aspects of a catering operation that a customer will come into contact with. This first impression of the restaurant is very important. Potential customers passing by may like the look of the establishment and decide to come and eat there; customers who have actually planned to eat in the restaurant and like what they see when they enter, will feel pleased with their choice of restaurant.

The interior design of a restaurant is composed of many different aspects: the size and shape of the room; the furniture and fittings; the colour scheme; lighting; air conditioning; etc. As with the previously described aspects of a restaurant, there is a need for a sense of coherence in a restaurant's interior design. The colour scheme of the restaurant should blend and balance and be enhanced by the lighting; tables and chairs should be ergonomically and aesthetically designed so that they not only satisfy their functional purpose, but also look attractive.

The interior design of a restaurant contributes greatly to the creation of its image. A self-service cafeteria in an industrial situation, for example, may consist of a very large dining area, tables and chairs of a standard design and shape, the colour scheme of the restaurant having few variations and lighting arrangements being purely functional. For this type of catering operation a consistently steady seat turnover is required, and this is encouraged by designing the interior of the restaurant so that it does not invite diners to linger over their meal; in addition a separate coffee lounge or area may be provided where customers may go afterwards and in this way vacate their seat for the next diner.

In a luxury restaurant, however, seat turnover is not so critical and, in fact, customers may be encouraged to stay in the restaurant to increase their average spend. In these types of establishment the interior design of the restaurant is made to be very comfortable: the lighting in the restaurant is quite subdued; the colour scheme has warmth and depth; there may be several particular points of interest in the restaurant, such as pictures, murals and large floral displays to hold the customer's interest; tables are farther apart, and may be separated from one another in booths or by partitions; and the chairs are so designed that the customer may sit in them for several hours without feeling uncomfortable.

The interior design of a catering facility needs to be carefully considered at the initial planning stage and if necessary professional advice sought in order to avoid costly corrective measures later. The life cycle of the operation also needs to be taken into account as this will significantly affect the financial investment in this aspect of the catering operation.

Activity 8

Consider each of your 10 operations and list the key elements of their interior design. In what ways is the interior design affected by the purpose of your visit.

Atmosphere and mood

The atmosphere or mood of a restaurant is a difficult aspect of an operation to define, but it is often described as an intangible 'feel' inside a restaurant. Not all restaurants have an obvious type of atmosphere, others try to deliberately create one. For example, some fine dining restaurants have a very formal atmosphere which is created by the dress and attitude of the staff, the decor of the restaurant, the service accompaniments, the type of clientele that frequent these restaurants, etc. Other restaurants, such as pub restaurants or pizza and pasta restaurants, try to create a relaxed informal atmosphere, and one that is very sociable to be a part of and seen in.

The atmosphere of a restaurant is affected by many different aspects of the operation. They include the décor and interior design of the restaurant, the table and seating arrangements, the service accompaniments, the dress and attitude of the staff, the tempo of service, the age, dress and sex of the other customers, the sound levels in the restaurant, whether music is played, the temperature and the overall cleanliness of the environment and the professionalism of the staff. Again, the harmony between the product itself, the service and the overall environment is important. If one of these aspects is out of unison with the others, disharmony may result in the customer gaining a confused image of the restaurant, and the customer will invariably leave feeling unsettled and remembering that one small aspect.

Expectation and identification

A single customer or group of customers arriving at a restaurant for a meal bring with them a series of expectations regarding that restaurant – the type of service they will receive, the price they will pay, the expected atmosphere and mood of the restaurant, etc. The customer's expectations may be varied and numerous, ranging from the restaurant which the customer frequents because they want to be seen there and participate in its social atmosphere, to the small quiet restaurant where the customer may go because of its intimate and personal nature. Upon arrival at the restaurant, if the product presented to customers is in harmony with their expectations, it is very likely that they will be pleased with their choice and have a relaxed and enjoyable meal. Should customers sense disharmony, however, between their expectation of the restaurant and the actual product they find, they may not enter the restaurant but choose another. If disharmony is not realized until customers are seated at the table, it is unlikely that they will leave but will have a less than satisfactory meal.

There is a need for customers to be able to identify and associate themselves with a particular restaurant for a particular meal occasion. They may not always identify with the same restaurant, as their needs and expectations may vary from one meal experience to the next. For example, at a business lunch a customer may require an expensive restaurant with an atmosphere conducive to discussing business; such a restaurant, however, will not be suitable for the same customer to take their family for a special occasion. A customer therefore has different needs and expectations on different meal occasions, and similarly at different times of the day, for example, lunch and dinner. These alternating needs of customers should be identified by a restaurant and catered for differently; for example, the restaurant offering formal business lunches may offer special function catering in the evening when the demand for business meals is minimal. There is a danger in these situations, however, that restaurants may be led into catering for mixed markets, and it is important for a restaurant offering different levels of service at different times of the day, to keep them completely separate, and not attempt to be 'all things to all people'. The first case example in Chapter 11 illustrates some of these problems.

Where different levels of markets are being catered for within the same establishment, it is sometimes possible for separate entrances to be used to service the different facilities, or functions timed so that the guests do not enter the operation all at the same time, and all require the use of the ancillary facilities simultaneously, such as cloakrooms, toilets, telephones, car parking spaces, etc. In a hotel, for example, the speciality restaurant may be situated on the top floor featuring panoramic views, while the night club may be found on the lower ground floor; both facilities operating successfully within the same establishment, but both with separate entrances, ancillary amenities and catering to different types of clientele.

Location and accessibility

The location of a food service facility has been said to be its most important feature. The location of a food and beverage operation must be made after careful identification of the market segments to which it is appealing. For example, a take-away fish and chip shop catering to a market segment identified as couples with children of CD1 socio-economic classification could not be situated further than two or three miles from this market; any distance greater than this and potential customers would consider choosing a fish and chip shop closer to their home.

The restaurant's location in relation to its present markets should not only be considered but also its location to possible future markets. For example, a city restaurant may rely heavily on a number of large local companies for the majority of its lunchtime trade; should several of these companies leave the area the restaurant's demand would be significantly affected. A roadside restaurant's trade would also be affected by the expansion or relocation of a major nearby road and consequently an increase or decrease in the volume of traffic and hence customers. The future expansion on a site with the possibility of catering to larger or more varied markets should also be considered and incorporated into the initial planning stage whenever possible.

The accessibility to a catering operation is another important factor. Customers arriving by car will expect adequate car parking facilities. If customers travel by public transport, the operation should be well served by buses, trains or taxis. If a high street take-away facility expects a large percentage of its business from passing trade there should be a heavy pedestrian flow past its doors.

Food and beverage service employees

Staff employed by a restaurant operation should complement the meal experience of the customers, and they are able to do this in a variety of ways: their social skills; their age and sex; their uniform; the tempo of their service, and so on. The number of staff serving in a restaurant is closely related to the prices charged by the establishment and the level of service that it offers. In self-service operations very few service staff are required; in some establishments the ratio of staff to customers being as low as one member of staff serving twenty to forty customers. However, in the fine dining restaurants offering full service, the ratio may be as high as one member of staff to eight or even less customers. These latter types of operations are, however, charging the customers for this extra-attentive service and must therefore be seen to have an adequate number of staff.

Not only does the number of staff in a restaurant contribute to the meal experience, but also their attitude to customers and the tempo of their service. In a large employee cafeteria where the ratio of service staff to customers may be low and speed of throughput important, the staff are required to work at a fast and efficient speed, and where possible leave the customers to serve themselves. In a luxury restaurant the tempo of the staff is considerably slower and more relaxed because of the higher ratio of service staff to customers. It should be noted that the attitude of the staff is almost totally influenced by the management attitude and the employment climate in which they are working.

The uniforms of the service staff should be appropriate for the level of the catering operation, and again this physical aspect of the restaurant must be seen to be a part of the establishment's total image.

At the end of the meal, staff can do a lot to reassure customers about their choice of meal experience. Because the intangible elements of a service are not visible, they are more difficult to evaluate. Customers, therefore, particularly need reassurance about the product they have purchased. Food service staff may help in several ways: at a basic level by asking if the customers have enjoyed their meal – this verbal confirmation by customers reinforces that their decision was correct in having chosen a particular restaurant; by remembering to offer customers take-home tangible items provided by the restaurant, for example, matches, sample menus, the restaurant's card; by pointing out a special promotion for a future date and enquiring whether the customer would like to make a reservation.

Summary

This chapter has considered:

- The size and scope of food and beverage operations.
- The different methods of classifying the hospitality industry to identify the diversity of food and beverage provision and the implications for food and beverage managers.
- The nature of the job of the food and beverage manager and different ways of identifying what managers do, what they are responsible for and what are the key constraints on their activities.
- The nature of the meal experience and how it can be managed. This starts with an identification of who our customers are and what they want allowing the manager to determine their position in the market and to offer the right product at the right price for the identified market segments.
- The main factors that affect customers perceptions of the total meal experience.

Review questions

1. In what ways might food and beverage operations be classified? What purpose do these different classifications serve?
2. What do the letters POC[3] stand for? How might these functions be distributed in the job of a food and beverage manager in a fast-food operation as opposed to contract food service?
3. In what ways might the expectations of regular customers differ from those of first time users?

Further reading

Campbell-Smith, G. (1989). *Marketing of the Meal Experience: A Fundamental Approach*. Guildford Surrey: University of Surrey Press.

Gamble, P., Lockwood, A. and Messenger, S. (1994). Management Skills in the European Hospitality Industry, 48th Annual CHRIE Conference. Palm Springs, July 27–30.

Keynote Publications (2007). Market Review 2007: Catering Market, Keynote Publications: Hampton Middlesex.

Li, L., Lockwood, A., Buhalis, D. and Gray, D. (2006). Managerial Work Revisited, CHME 15th International Research, *Teaching and Learning Conference*, Nottingham, 10–12 May 2006.

Mintel (2007). *Eating Out Review* – UK – July 2007. London: Mintel.

Office of National Statistics (2007). *Annual Abstract of Statistics*, edition No 143. Basingstoke: Palgrave Macmillan.

Office for National Statistics (2007). UK Standard Industrial Classification of Economic Activities 2007 (SIC 2007): Structure and explanatory notes, ONS: London.

People 1st (2007). www.people1st.co.uk/about-us/our-industries

Pine, B. J. and Gilmore, J. H. (1999). *The Experience Economy: Work is Theatre and Every Business a Stage*. Boston: Harvard Business School Press.

Powers, T. and Barrows, C. W. (2003). *Introduction to Management in the Hospitality Industry 7*. New York: John Wiley and Sons, Inc.

The restaurant sector

Introduction

The enormous variety of food and beverage outlets makes it a challenge when one is trying to differentiate between them. Some are distinctly different (e.g., fast food and hotel restaurants). Others are harder to categorize (e.g., school catering can be categorized as public sector but may be serviced by Contract Caterers). The list of sectors in food and beverage management in this book is not exhaustive and as trends change so will new sectors emerge.

In this chapter the restaurant subsectors are covered with relevant descriptions drawing from the experience of food and beverage managers, educators and research in current sector definitions. For each subsection the basic policies, financial, and catering issues specific to that type of outlet is discussed. Where possible average spent, typical capacity, production capabilities and available technology issues are discussed.

Chapter objectives

After working through this chapter you should be able to demonstrate:

- An understanding of full service restaurants and licensed retail.
- An understanding of hotel and private club restaurant operations.
- An understanding of fast-food restaurant operations.
- An understanding of differences in the areas of finance, marketing, product, service, staffing and technology (FMPSST) between different types of operations.

FULL SERVICE RESTAURANTS AND LICENSED RETAIL

In this section of the chapter full service restaurants are categorized by revenue stream. Operations with food as their main revenue source (fine dining and popular catering) and operations that their main revenue is generated from sales of beverages (bars, nightclubs and pubs) are explored. Examples of mainstream restaurant guides are also explored in this section. As licensing laws differ from country to country the restaurant guides provide a good point of reference when trying to distinguish restaurant types and styles.

Restaurant guides

Consumers will often refer to restaurant guides when they wish to choose which establishment they might wish to visit. Restaurant guides can provide an easy way of classifying food and beverage establishments and for the food and beverage manager listing in a restaurant guide may mean the difference between a successful operation or failure to attract business. An understanding of the most predominant restaurant guides is therefore a necessary asset for any food and beverage manager.

The Michelin guide (http://www.viamichelin.com) is a famous guide awarding restaurants from 1 to 3 stars depending on quality of their cuisine (Figure 2.1). The guide also features the face of the Michelin Man (Bib Gourmand) for restaurants that offer good food at reasonable prices and has a rating for the atmosphere décor and general feeling of the establishment with a scale of five levels ranging from quite comfortable to Luxurious establishment. In 2006, Michelin released a New York city guide. Unfortunately in some cases a Michelin star can be taken by the proprietor as license to charge extravagant prices.

The Mobil travel guide (http://mobiltravelguide.howstuffworks. com) is the USA guide for restaurants and ratings range from 1 star to 5 stars. Ranging from a restaurant that provides a distinctive experience through culinary speciality. To the top of the

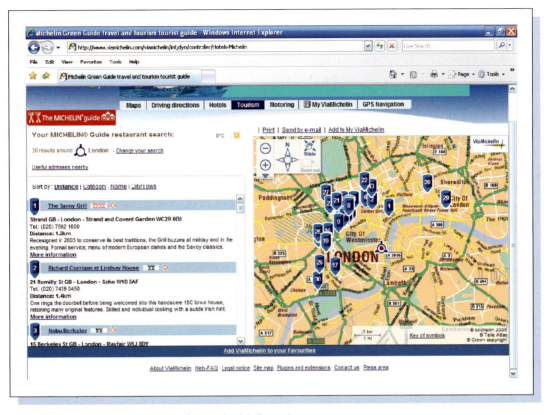

Figure 2.1 The Michelin guide website (*Source*: viamichelin.com)

scale which represents a flawless dining experience in the country (Figure 2.2).

The AAA is another travel guide that rates restaurants on a 1 to 5 Diamond scale. Three, four and five star/diamond ratings are somewhat equivalent to the Michelin one, two, and three star ratings. Specific to the UK the 'Good Food Guide' (http://www.thegoodwebguide.co.uk) is an annual publication using anonymous inspectors to grade restaurants from 1 to 10 were by 1 is a recommended restaurant that makes the top 1% of the countries restaurants whilst a 10/10 would be the equivalent of a 3 star Michelin restaurant. Another guide worth mentioning is the 'AA restaurants and Pub Guide' (http://www.theaa.com/getaway/restaurants/restaurant_home.jsp)

An alternative guide is the Zagat survey (http://www.zagat.com/). The Zagat survey compiles individuals' comments about restaurants but does not pass an official judgment of the establishment (Figure 2.3).

One of the largest web-based restaurant and menu guide is MenuPix.com (http://www.menupix.com). The website features over 16,000 restaurant menus in various US cities. It is a great resource for any food and beverage manager to get ideas on what to do or what not to do when designing their own menus (Figure 2.4).

Figure 2.2 The Mobil travel guide website (US) (*Source*: mobiltravelguide.com)

Figure 2.3 The Zagat guide website (US, UK, FR) (*Source*: zagat.com)

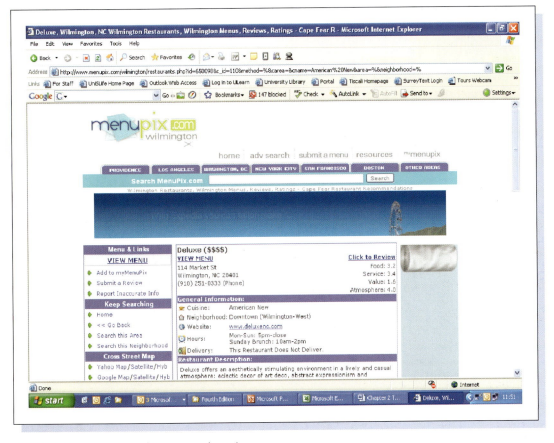

Figure 2.4 Menupix website (*Source*: menupix.com)

Activity 1

Log on to http://www.viamichelin.com and locate your nearest restaurant recommended by the guide with a 3 star rating.

Now see if you can find the same restaurant using the Zagat guide: http://www.zagat.com/. Considering a 3 Michelin star rating is a highly sought after accolade what do customers actually thought of the restaurant? Does the restaurant live up to its 3 star rating? Discuss.

You can try the same activity for a 2 or 1 Michelin star restaurant.

Fine dining

Fine dining restaurants are those establishments that offer very high standards in all aspects of their operation – an extensive à la carte menu, silver service, good quality facilities and décor, service accompaniments, etc. They can be found in four and five star hotels or as free standing restaurants (Figure 2.5).

The percentage of restaurants today that may be described as fine dining restaurants is small; indeed it may be as little as 3–5% of the total number of restaurants in all sectors of the

'For a restaurant of such high standards, like Le Gavroche, maintaining those standards is the highest challenge'
Michel Roux

with permission of Le Gavroche.

Figure 2.5 Le Gavroche (UK, London) (*Source*: Le Gavroche)

catering industry. However, the narrow market for which quality restaurants cater will continue to be present in the future, because there will always be that percentage of the eating-out market that demands the highest standards in all aspects of a restaurant operation, and can afford to pay the high prices charged.

Financial implications • • •

Fine dining restaurants are profit orientated and this is reflected in their financial policies. The higher GP levels of the à la carte and high quality restaurants are mainly due to the lower percentage of variable costs of these operations and the need to cover the higher staff costs.

The high percentage of fixed costs associated with the fine dining restaurants affects the margin of safety of these operations; this is the difference between the operation's break-even point and its maximum potential output. High fixed cost operations have a smaller margin of safety than those with lower fixed costs, so that a drop in the volume of sales would seriously affect the profitability of high fixed cost establishments. In addition, the wide range of price discretion that is available to hotels and quality restaurants further complicates their pricing structure.

The balance between the price level of these establishments and their volume of sales must therefore be carefully calculated, and this again would be contained in their financial policies.

The average spend per customer in the fine dining may range from £50 to £120 or even more per customer.

In the higher average spending power (ASP) operations, the cost of the meal to the customer is not such an important variable in determining the sales of the operation; broadly speaking, the higher the price level of an operation, the less elastic its demand. The demand for those catering facilities offered by quality restaurants and hotels (specifically the à la carte outlets), therefore tends to be relatively inelastic, that is, a large change in price will not have a very substantial effect on the sales of the establishment.

Marketing • • •

Because of the narrowness of the market for which quality restaurants cater, the marketing policies of these operations are able to quite clearly identify their market and target their advertising and merchandising campaigns at this market level.

The high ASP of such establishments must be reflected in their marketing policies; if they cannot compete with other catering operations on the basis of price, they must look to the other aspects of their operation, such as food quality and standard of service as a basis for competition. Often such restaurants will feature a Celebrity chef as their executive chef. Other times the acquisition of a Michelin star due to the quality of the food will send demand levels to such a high that soon the menu prices follow.

Fine dining restaurants are characterized by the need for a high capital outlay and have a correspondingly high percentage of fixed costs; the perishability of their product; and a demand for that product that is unstable. All these factors lead to a high dependence of these operations on the demands of the market, so that hotels and quality restaurants may be said to be highly market orientated. In comparison to the welfare sector cost-orientated operations, fine dining restaurants are more dependent on their market for the survival of their operation, and this has important implications for their basic policy-making decisions.

In fining dining restaurants marketing has to be subtle for example, advertising in quality magazines – obtaining free write-ups of the restaurant in quality newspapers and magazines – joint promotion with credit card companies. These can enhance the type of image the restaurant is trying to create. Often the restaurant will hire a public relations company that has the expertise, resources and networking to do just that.

Product and service styles • • •

The most widely used method of food production in the kitchens of fine dining restaurants is still the conventional method of production, based on the *partie* system. The partie system is a method of kitchen organization in which production is divided into separate areas according to the type of food being produced. In a large hotel kitchen, for example, there may be as many as seven main production parties: roast; vegetables; larder/salads; entree; fish; soup; and pastry, and each of these sections may be further subdivided depending on the quantity of food to be produced by the partie. In fine dining restaurants fresh ingredients define the product and the use of any convenience food stuff is eliminated or reduced to a bare minimum.

Food service styles are not only dependent on the type of catering operation, but also on its price level. Generally speaking, the higher the price level of an operation, the more elaborate and sophisticated the service style becomes. However in fine dining restaurants we have seen a move away from silver service and towards plated service styles. This is mainly because the chef can far better control the appearance of a plate in the kitchen. When a customer is paying £40 for a main course, they would expect excellent quality of food but excellent dish appearance as well. Furthermore the luck of skilled staff in the industry has made styles such as Flambé and silver service redundant. It is worth noting however that a renaissance of the Flambé service in front of the customer might be back on the menu. Although flambé dishes still exist on the menu they are mainly prepared in the kitchen but recent trend would suggest that in fine dining at least Flambé service style might be resurrected.

As the sophistication of food service styles increases with the price level of an operation, so too do beverage service styles. The service of wines, for example, is considerably more elaborate in an à la carte quality restaurant than in an operation featuring a table d'hôte menu. In a quality restaurant an extensive wine list would be available and a wine waiter would serve the wine throughout the duration of the meal. In a lower ASP catering outlet a more limited wine list would be offered and the service of the wine would usually be by the member of staff serving at the customer's table, rather than a separate wine waiter. Adjacent to quality restaurants may be a cocktail bar or some other form of bar where beverages are served to customers at individual tables. In the lower ASP operations, this bar arrangement is not often found; patrons for the table d'hôte restaurant would usually use the main hotel bar.

Staffing • • •

The organization of fine dining restaurants has changed mainly at the top over the past years. An executive chef might often be the owner or the manager of such an establishment as the product is what differentiates the restaurant from its competitors. However the traditional hierarchy will still exist with a sous chef responsible for the operations and the chefs de partie responsible for sections of the kitchen whilst a number of commis chefs will assist the chefs de partie with the more menial tasks.

In the front of house a Restaurant Manager is now often the title used for what in more traditional settings be the Maitre'D a head waiter, a chef de rang responsible for a station with a commis waiter. Also a wine waiter with a commis might be present especially in operations that feature an extended wine list.

Technology • • •

In fine dining restaurants communication between service and production staff is of paramount importance. If the Chef has prepared an exquisite dish only to find it melting away in the hot plate because service staff could not be alerted on time, the restaurant will not uphold its reputations. Electronic point of sale (EPOS) and mobile point of sale systems (MPOS) technology have made huge advancements (Figure 2.6). The waiter can be alerted through the MPOS, the waiter can input specific instructions about a dish without having to physically go to the kitchen. The Chef can instantly alert all waiters with how many portions of a specific dish is left or if he wants to push a particular dish.

Staff performance has become much easier to quantify as a result of technology. POS systems can provide information about an employee, how many customers he/she serves per hour, how much revenue he/she generates, how long it took to

Figure 2.6 Micros POS terminal (*Source*: Micros http://www.micros-fidelio.co.uk)

service a table, how much tips tables leave and the lists goes on. Such information can be used to establish whether a member of staff needs more training, needs to be appraised for brilliant work or needs to be evaluated, as they do not seem to match the required standards. The ease of obtaining such information allows for the information to be shared around with the team and that in its self can help motivate staff as they can share what is going on in the workplace.

Bars, nightclubs and pubs

Although bars strictly speaking are focusing in the sale of beverages only and the provision of entertainment, Nightclubs often feature restaurants within their premises and pubs have taken the food agenda in their premises even further with the relatively new phenomenon known as Gastro pubs. According to Mintel, the UK market shows a positive growth in the future (Table 2.1). The Gastro pub is a traditional pub that has been updated with a full service restaurant that can often be compared in product to a fine dining establishment.

Financial implications • • •

The sale of beverages has always been a favourite with every food and beverage manager. With a gross profit of 65–70% beverages

At current prices	2007 £bn	2008 £bn	2009 £bn	2010 £bn	2011 £bn	2012 £bn	% change 2007–2012
Fast food:							
Burgers	2.4	2.47	2.5	2.49	2.48	2.48	3
Ethnic takeaway	1.8	1.87	1.94	1.98	2.04	2.09	16
Pizza and pasta	1.35	1.42	1.51	1.57	1.64	1.7	26
Fish and chips	1	1.04	1.07	1.09	1.12	1.14	14
Fried chicken	1	1.1	1.19	1.24	1.31	1.37	37
Other fast food	0.17	0.17	0.18	0.19	0.19	0.2	18
Total fast food	7.72	8.07	8.39	8.55	8.77	8.96	16
Restaurants:							
Pub catering	7.25	7.67	8.21	8.5	8.9	9.26	28
Hotel catering	4.31	4.43	4.48	4.54	4.66	4.69	9
Restaurant meals	4.5	4.79	5.15	5.34	5.6	5.85	30
Ethnic restaurants	2	2.02	2.07	2.12	2.2	2.23	11
In-store	1.4	1.5	1.59	1.66	1.75	1.82	30
Roadside	0.53	0.54	0.54	0.54	0.54	0.54	2
Total restaurants	19.98	20.93	22.05	22.7	23.65	24.39	22
Other	2.75	2.99	3.02	3.07	3.21	3.24	18
Total	30.45	31.99	33.46	34.32	35.64	36.6	20

Source: Mintel, 2006

Table 2.1
Restaurant sector forecast – UK

often help to sustain a business through rough times. With night-clubs there may be further income as many charge an entrance fee but this is mainly in order to cover the entertainment expenses such as the fee of a DJ or a band. With new antismoking regulations in place there has been a fear that such establishments would see a significant reduction in their revenues, however in May 2007 it was reported that the antismoking laws have not deterred punters and companies such as Wetherspoons in the UK have announced a 3% higher profits than predicted (Caterer, 2007).

Marketing • • •

Whilst bars and nightclubs tend to attract younger audiences the traditional pub is an establishment seen in the UK that bases its operation mainly in the local community with often a catchment area of no more than 5 mile radius. To counter that pub managers will often have a live music night or put together and advertise event nights such as Bingo nights or Karaoke nights.

Bars and nightclubs will often advertise in local newspapers and magazines as well as local radio and TV stations. Often a nightclub will have young people distributing leaflets when they attempt to advertise a big event. Similarly to a pub they will often have themed nights or a special attraction in an attempt to attract further audiences.

Activity 2

Look at the advertising section of your local newspaper. Choose one restaurant and one bar/nightclub advertisement. What are the common techniques used by restaurateurs to promote their establishments and what are those used by bar and nightclub owners?

Product and service styles • • •

Bars and nightclubs will often feature an extended beverage and cocktail menu. The service in bars and pubs is always counter style service and in some nightclubs one may find table service or in the case of an event a butler style service. This style of service is common when a drink might be included in the entrance price and the customer might give a ticket whilst collecting a drink from staff passing around with a tray full of the specified drink. Pubs will often offer at least ten types of beer and or ale, often products from local breweries might feature in the menu, but today most pubs are owned by large companies that they rent the pubs out to owners who are then obliged to buy the products from the company's brewery.

Staffing • • •

Bars and nightclubs will need to have well-trained bar staff behind the counter as often the volume of business is extremely high and one barperson might have to serve one order per 1–3 minutes. The volume of business in pubs is not as high as in bars and nightclubs and as most punters will require beer the skills needed are not as demanding. Another staff consideration for bars and nightclubs is that of security. As insurance costs can be quite high often an operator will decide to outsource their security to a security company.

Technology • • •

We have already talked about the advantages of EPOS technology but together with advancements in beverage dispensing technology these types of operation that traditionally suffered loses from beverage spillage or theft can now pinpoint exactly what was sold when and by whom. Making it far easier to keep track of stock and reducing opportunities for theft. Wine cooling and dispensing technology has also advanced allowing the establishments to offer more wines by the glass without having to throw the unfinished bottle of wine within a few days. Recent technology in beer dispensing has allowed for extra cool beer to be dispensed and self-cleaning pipes for the beer dispensing system can reduce staff costs.

HOTEL RESTAURANTS AND PRIVATE CLUBS

Hotel food and beverage management may be described as one of the most complex areas of the catering industry because of the variety of catering outlets that may be found in any one hotel. The different types of catering services associated with hotels include the following: luxury haute cuisine restaurants, coffee shops and speciality restaurants, room and lounge service, cocktail bars, banqueting facilities and staff restaurants. (for banqueting and staff catering see Chapter 3). Additionally, some hotels will provide a catering and bar service to areas of the hotel such as swimming pools, and health complexes, discos and other leisure areas as well as often providing some vending facilities.

The type and variety of catering outlets in hotels will depend to a large extent on the size of the hotel. Small hotels of up to 30–40 bedrooms may have a licensed bar, and a restaurant which may offer a limited table d'hôte or à la carte lunch and dinner menu. A medium-sized hotel of up to 100 bedrooms would usually have a licensed bar and two restaurants; these may include a grill room/coffee shop offering a table d'hôte menu and a separate à la carte restaurant. The bar in this size of hotel may also offer a limited selection of snacks. Today, room service in these small- and medium-sized operations is limited; facilities for tea and coffee making within the room are more usually provided as an alternative. In the large hotels with several hundred bedrooms, the largest variety of catering outlets is found – the traditional haute cuisine restaurant alongside the more unusual speciality restaurant; lounge and cocktail bars; several coffee shops, some offering a very limited selection of snacks, others offering more substantial menu items; and varying degrees of room service.

The different types of catering outlets in hotels depend not only on the size of the operation, but also on its nature and the market for which it is catering. A medium-sized resort hotel, for example, where a guest's average length of stay may be 2–3 weeks, may need to offer a variety of food and beverage facilities to cater for the guests' different and changing needs during their stay. A transient hotel, however, such as one situated near an airport where the guest's average length of stay may be one or two nights, may only need to provide comparatively limited catering facilities. As for the future demands for catering services in hotels, this is closely allied to the demand for hotel accommodation itself. The continually growing tourism industry both in the UK and abroad guarantees a future demand for some form of hotel accommodation to be provided for tourists, and with this a demand for food and beverage services.

Private gentlemen's Clubs feature the dining room a type of restaurant that pre-dates the member's only exclusive restaurant concept such as Mosimann's in London. It is worth mentioning as it educates us as to how the member only restaurants have evolved.

Hotel food and beverage outlets

In many hotels, the importance of the food and beverage department in operating an à la carte restaurant and a 24-hour room service, neither of which may be significant net profit contributors, is essential for the hotel to obtain a four or five star grading, with their input of service and facilities enabling the hotel to significantly increase its prices for accommodation. In so doing the hotel is more likely to be able to increase its total revenue and net profit figures. It should be noted that hotels have realized the lost potential of their restaurants the latest figures suggest that the food and beverage area is a substantial source of income for most hotels (Table 2.2) and two main options were followed by many hotel operators (Figure 2.7).

		UK
Hotel revenue source %	2006	2005
Rooms revenue	57.3	56.6
Miscellaneous revenue	7.2	6.8
Food revenue	21.2	21.7
Beverage revenue	9.4	9.7
Other F&B revenue	4.9	5.2
Total F&B revenue	35.5	36.6
	100.0	100.0

Source: TRI Hospitality Consulting Hotel Report 2007

Table 2.2
Food and beverage as a percentage of hotel revenue

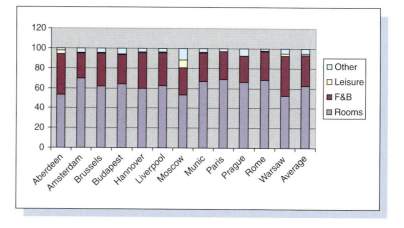

Figure 2.7
Departmental revenue mix by city (*Source*: Adapted from TRI Hospitality Consulting Hotels 2007)

The easiest one is that of outsourcing. With outsourcing the hotel simply rents the space of the restaurant to a management company who in turn create a product that is marketable not only to residents of the hotel but also the public. Catering companies have dedicated branches that specialize in restaurant outsourcing. For example, the Compass Group branch that specializes in outsourcing is Restaurant Associates. The second option for the hotel management is to re-vamp the restaurant themselves. This can be costly at first but the benefits can outweigh the 'rent' received by outsourcing the space. For example, one of the greatest problems hotel restaurants faced is that their restaurants would be located in a middle floor and the customer would have to go through a reception and up an elevator to eventually find a restaurant with often overpriced and outdated menus. Many potential customers would walk by such hotels and not even consider attempting to try out the restaurant. The solution would be to have the restaurant at ground level with an entrance to the high street separate from the entrance the hotel residents might use. Updated menus that can compete with other high street restaurants are crucial as well as highly trained and motivated staff (Figure 2.8).

Financial implications • • •

Generally speaking the average spend of customers in hotel catering outlets, is higher than in similar catering operations found outside a hotel. This is particularly evident with reference to the hotel's high ASP quality restaurants, but also in the less expensive outlets such as coffee shops; here the ASP of the hotel customer may again be higher than in comparable operations found, for example in a town's high street. The higher prices charged by these types of catering facilities result in higher sales per employee, and a higher revenue per trading hour. In fast-food operations with their lower ASP per customer, the long trading hours of these establishments are often necessary in order to achieve high volume sales. In the catering outlets of hotels similar long trading hours are not characteristic of

Figure 2.8 Radisson Edwardian Ascots Restaurant – London UK (*Source*: radissonedwardian.co.uk)

all the facilities; the lower ASP coffee shops may stay open for most of the day, but the higher ASP restaurants in the hotel, like the quality restaurants found outside, will only open for the lunch and dinner periods, approximately 3 hours and 4–5 hours, respectively. In the larger hotels some form of food and beverage service is generally available 24 hours a day and most of the catering facilities are usually open 7 days a week; quality restaurants situated outside the hotel, however, may only open 6 days a week. The catering policy of the hotel or quality restaurant in conjunction with the financial policy of the establishment will, however, determine the opening hours of the operation based on such information as revenue per trading hour, sales per employee per hour, etc.

Payment for food and beverages in hotels may be made in several ways. If customers are residents, the charges may be debited to their hotel account. Alternatively, payment may be made on a cash or credit basis. Generally speaking, the higher the price level of a restaurant, the more likely that credit facilities will be available. Some hotels and quality restaurants include a service charge in the price of their meal, while others leave it to the discretion of the customer. This is the sector of the industry where the practice of tipping is most commonly found and the 'trunc' system of sharing pooled by the employees.

Marketing • • •

The marketing policy of a hotel is very complicated because of its variety of catering outlets and the corresponding variety in the types of customers these facilities will attract; the customer frequenting the hotel's coffee shop, for example, may not be the same customer to use the hotel's à la carte restaurant. The danger of catering for mixed markets within the same establishment must therefore be recognized and planned for accordingly. The marketing policy of a hotel may vary with different times of the year because it can see opportunities for marketing its catering facilities to different markets. A hotel in a coastal resort, for example, may cater largely for families and groups of tourists during the summer months, during which time its catering facilities may be well patronized. In the winter months, however, this market may no longer be available and the hotel may therefore alter its marketing policy and promote its catering facilities as part of banqueting and conference 'packages'. In this way the hotel's catering facilities may be utilized throughout the year without the danger of mixing its markets, and adversely affecting the hotel's total image, whilst also ensuring a consistent revenue and maximum utilization of the hotel's capital equipment.

A hotel's marketing policy will also contain its intentions with regard to its resident and non-resident markets. For example, is the hotel going to concentrate mainly on trade generated from within, that is, residents, or to what extent is it going to attempt to attract outside custom? Some hotels aim almost exclusively at the resident guest and may offer comparatively limited catering facilities, compared with those hotels seeking to also attract the non-resident customer by offering a wider range of catering outlets – restaurants, bars, banqueting facilities, etc.

'Crisscross' advertising is a technique available to hotels where there is more than one type of catering facility in the hotel; for example, the cocktail bar may use tent cards to advertise a special promotion week in the à la carte restaurant. Where the hotel is part of a large organization, inter-hotel advertising may be used which usually features the catering outlets of the group's hotels in the company sales literature which is distributed to all hotel units throughout the country, and sometimes abroad. It is also possible to advertise the food and beverage facilities of the hotel in conjunction with its other services; for example, a number of large hotel chains now offer 'bargain week ends', where for an inclusive price a guest may stay at the hotel for 2 or 3 days on *demi pension* or *en pension* terms. Gourmet and wine weekends may be offered during off-peak winter months. Discounts are given to hotel residents dining in the à la carte restaurant, a free bottle of wine is offered with the meal, or two meals for the price of one during the quieter weekdays. It is important therefore for all possible advertising techniques to be reviewed for the marketing of catering outlets, as they may often not only be marketed in isolation, but also may be advertised in conjunction with the establishment's other facilities such as accommodation.

Product and service styles • • •

Hotel restaurants like fine dining restaurants still use mainly the partie system. Other production styles such as cook-chill and sous-vide are making inroads into this previous bastion of hotel tradition, these inroads are mainly in specific areas, for example, function catering, where they may be used to complement the traditional methods rather than replace them.

The variety of food service styles used in hotels is dependent upon the different types of catering outlets in the establishment. In a small hotel, for example, where one restaurant is used for the service of all meals, and features table d'hôte menus for lunch and dinner, plated meals may be served to the guests by service staff. In a large hotel, however, with four or five different types of outlets, there can be a corresponding variety in the service styles. Breakfast service in the hotel, for example, can be on a self-service basis in the coffee shop, or waiter service in the main restaurant. For lunch and dinner the coffee shop can serve a limited selection of plated snacks and meals directly to customers at their table, and the outlet may also incorporate a self-service buffet or carvery. The hotel grill room or themed restaurant could feature a table d'hôte menu with plated meals, and the à la carte restaurant would offer silver service, both with waiter service. In addition to the main dining areas the hotel bar can offer a limited snack service and the hotel could also offer room service facilities; because room service is, however, a highly labour intensive and time-consuming method of food service, the majority of hotels offering room service today usually provide only a very limited menu selection, except for the large luxury establishments; the room service menus often containing some items from the main restaurant menu. This same variety of service styles is not, however, found in quality restaurants. This level of operation usually only offers a similar service style to that found in the à la carte restaurants of hotels, that is, silver service to the table.

Staffing • • •

Staffing organization in hotels restaurants depends to a large extent on the size of the establishment and the level of service being offered; the larger the operation and the more staff employed, the greater the departmentalization and specialization of the catering personnel. In a small hotel with one restaurant offering a limited menu, there may be as few as five or six production staff and a similar number of service staff; this would constitute the catering department. In a large hotel, however, with a number of catering outlets, the catering department may consist of several hundred personnel. In the smaller hotel little staff hierarchy would be present; in the larger hotel a very clearly defined hierarchy would be identifiable for each catering outlet.

As the staff hierarchy in a catering operation increases, so does the specialization of the staff functions. The *head chef* of a large hotel may therefore have several *sous chefs* who would deputize in his absence, and under the sous chefs would be the *chefs de parties*; these are each responsible for the main sections in the kitchen – roast, vegetables, fish, larder, pastry, soup and sauces, etc. The chefs de parties may have several *commis*, or assistant chefs, reporting to them, depending on the size of the section, and finally there can be a number of general apprentices working in the kitchen in any one of these sections. In the large kitchens organized on this traditional partie system, each section is quite autonomous; in smaller kitchens where less specialization is found, the kitchen staff may be required to perform a variety of tasks that would normally be associated with specific sections in a large production area. The head chef of a large kitchen is usually involved to a far greater extent with the administrative side of the operation, rather than in the physical preparation of meals. In a small establishment, however, the head chef is more involved in the production of restaurant meals, leaving the majority of the administration to the hotel owner or proprietor.

On the food service side of catering operations a similar staff hierarchy is found according to the size of the establishment. In a large operation, for example, the staffing organization for a lunch or dinner service in a quality restaurant serving 80 or more covers, from an à la carte menu, may be as follows: the restaurant manager or his assistant, one head waiter, two chef de rang, one wine waiter, one commis wine waiter, and three commis waiters. In a smaller operation, however, there may only be the restaurant manager or head waiter, and several assistants, with no separate staff hierarchy for beverage service.

Technology • • •

Hotel restaurant service has been changing dramatically as a result of new technology. A challenge that the industry faces is to provide a meal when and where the customer wants it, with guaranteed food safety and nutritional value, offering authentic recipes and customer specific engineered menus.

Guests give their order to a waiter holding a wireless POS the order is transmitted to the Kitchen, speeding service reducing errors, and increasing time spent by server staff with guests. The data from the handheld device, now in the restaurant's computer system, pass through an interface to the inventory and supply ordering software.

Wireless point-of-sale systems are ideal for difficult-to-wire environments such as pool areas, casino floors, leisure centres or common areas, as well as historic buildings and properties with large open spaces, providing point-of-activity revenue opportunities and new service offerings. Wireless pen-based terminals integrated with leading-edge restaurant systems can provide food and beverage facilities with breakthrough solutions that optimize efficiency, diminish lines and eliminate waits in a wide variety of hospitality applications.

Wireless customer pads enable customers to give feedback if they are dissatisfied before they leave the restaurant. Guest pagers that light up or vibrate mean that the hostess does not have to hail customers on a loudspeaker system. Pagers can alert waiting staff when orders are ready in the kitchen. Guest initiated pagers alert servers when a table is ready to have their order taken, saving time and preventing unnecessary trips to the table. Restaurant processes such as order taking, payment processing, inventory control, wait-list management, valet parking, frequent diner program interface and other applications can dramatically increase productivity, reduce costs and improve customer service.

In addition, the introduction of new technologies in Room Service has also allowed greater flexibility. Room service staff can be supplied with internal phones that allow them to be in constant contact with food, beverage and banquet personnel, while roaming throughout the property. The productivity enhancements and responsiveness by re-directing staff to deliver and/or pick up food service orders while being mobile are phenomenal. By installing a wireless transmitter, hotels can provide Internet connectivity to sales people who happen to entertain customers in the hotel restaurant or even to guests who may wish to use their laptops.

New accounting software interface direct with POS systems, enabling credit card authorization and payment, storing customer information for future use and providing up to date reports for managers. Specialized software can analyse profitability, productivity, costing, and realization at multiple levels from company-wide to the individual client or staff member. Tax, Social Security and statistical updates can also be automated and payroll software can maximize payroll processing productivity and enhance profits.

POS and Sales and Catering systems (S&C) have provided new management and accounting tools. Accounting software can print reports that enable the accounting office to spot costs and trends. Managers can visualize better and faster where money is coming from and tactical decisions can be made faster and safer. Computerized systems identify true food and beverage expenses much faster than with systems that do not utilize information technology, and save time in accounting and food and beverage management.

Time and money saved in accounting processes can be invested in training staff or bettering products and services

Dining rooms

Private Gentlemen's Clubs are organizations that resemble hotels but in order for a customer to use their facilities they have to become a member. Often the organization is so exclusive that a 2 year waiting list is a common phenomenon amongst the more exclusive clubs. In such organizations the restaurant often takes the form of a dining room which keeps the traditions of the old fine dining restaurants whilst offering a high quality product at lower prices than their high street counterparts (Figure 2.9).

Financial implications • • •

These restaurants often offer lower prices on their menu as they are subsidized by the membership fee. Often they are there

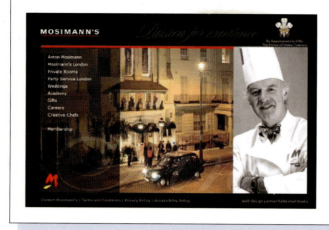

Food was the earliest influence on me as a child. I still remember the wonderful smell of apricots in season. It was fantastic. Coming home from school to find my parents in the kitchen cooking, it all smelt so good. Theirs was basic cooking with seasonal produce. We have lost all that now, products are available all year round and I feel that's a pity, as waiting makes it more worthwhile.

Anton Mosimann

Figure 2.9 Mosimann's private dining – London UK (*Source*: mosimann.com)

simply to offer the service to their members and may not function as a profit making outlet. Considering that these types of restaurants still have labour costs to cover and the fact that they may not offer services to the public they more often make a loss than break even.

Marketing • • •

Private clubs often have their own newsletters or magazines and they will advertise their new menu in those or have notices of a special menu around the premises of the club and in the bedrooms if they offer accommodation. Apart from in house marketing there is not much more they can do to attract the business due to the restrictions imposed in them by the clubs regulations. However, sometimes clubs will allow members of other clubs to use the facilities. Those clubs are known as reciprocal clubs and often are allowed to advertise their services in the reciprocal clubs magazine.

Product and service styles • • •

The product is often of a fine restaurant standard and these are establishments were one would expect to find full silver service and flambé, a Carving Trolley and Cheese or Dessert Trolleys. The menu tends to be restricted however and more often is a Table d'hôte as the low volume of business may not allow for an extended à la carte menu. A well-stocked cellar is often the pride of such establishments and an extended wine list is not uncommon.

Staffing • • •

Customers would expect to find the same hierarchy that is found in a fine dining restaurant. Members Clubs tend to have a smaller team and the environment and pace of business tends to be more relaxed than in a hotel. Unlike a corporate hotel clubs enjoy almost 100% repeat business. As members join they will tend to use the facilities a number of times over a year, staff will often know customers by name. A more relaxed atmosphere and a closer, smaller team reinforces club loyalty which can result in lower staff turnover.

Technology • • •

Often there is limited investment in technology in such dining rooms and although in the kitchen one might find some of the latest equipment in the front of house a basic EPOS will be considered a luxury.

FAST FOOD

Fast food may be defined as that sector of the catering industry primarily concerned with the preparation and service of food and beverages quickly, for immediate sale to the customer. McDonalds, Burger King, KFC and Wendy's are some of the better known fast-food operators.

Although differing from one another in certain aspects, these catering outlets have a number of characteristics which are common to all these types of operations – they offer a limited menu range; the operation tends to focus around one product, namely burger, pizza or chicken. These operations cater mainly for the relatively lower average spend markets with lower prices being charged than those found in other food and beverage establishments; there is a low ratio of service staff to customers with many of these operations being a form of self-service; consumption of the food may be on or off the premises; less rigid meal times are observed by these establishments, with some form of menu usually available throughout the day; and finally, all aspects of the operation are highly standardized, leading to a high volume throughput with resulting economies in food, labour and other operating costs (Figure 2.10 and Figure 2.11).

Sandwich bars

Sandwich bars are fast-food outlets that their main product is sandwiches. They often provide fruit juices and other refreshments and they may venture into the sales of hot beverages. According to Mintel Report (2007) the sandwich showed a 23% increase from 2002 and is now worth over £4 billion. This strong growth

McDonald's brand mission is to 'be our customers' favorite place and way to eat.' Our worldwide operations have been aligned around a global strategy called the Plan to Win centering on the five basics of an exceptional customer experience – People, Products, Place, Price and Promotion. We are committed to improving our operations and enhancing our customers' experience.

Figure 2.10 McDonald's brand mission (*Source*: mcdonalds.co.uk)

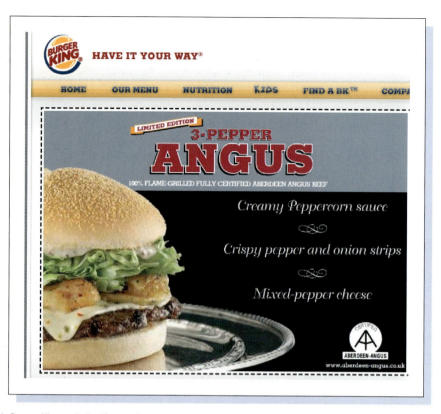

Figure 2.11 Burger King website (*Source*: burgerking.co.uk)

has been driven by the introduction of specialist sandwich bars, as well as a focused innovation and new product development. A possible threat to future growth is the growing competition from other snack style foods and lunch options such as soups, sushi and other convenience foods. On the plus side, the sandwich supply structure continues to expand, thus widening the locations where sandwiches can be purchased. With UK consumers continuing to work long hours and take shorter lunch breaks than their European counterparts the sandwich fits in well with such a lifestyle.

When McDonald's first bought a high share in Prêt A Manger, (http://www.pret.com) a UK-based chain of Sandwich Bars, food and beverage managers around the world realized that sandwich bars have stopped been a mere 'pawn' in the 'Chess board' of food and beverage management. Consumers were looking out for a healthier option and they found it in the marketing promises of sandwich bars.

Retail operations such as supermarkets have ventured into sandwich bars and it is not uncommon to see them in your local Asda, Tesco, BiLo, Wal Mart, etc.

Financial implications • • •

Sandwich bars, rely on high turnovers and the fact that they have very low fixed costs. In some cases extra income may arrive from the sale of hot and cold beverages but the main focus remains the sandwich or baguette.

Depending on the type of operation, goods can be perishable often expiring within a few days of packaging therefore it is important to ensure high sales of the items. The average spend can range from £3 to £5 with food cost at around 20–30% and minimum labour, a sandwich bar can be a very profitable operation that involves relatively low startup costs.

Marketing • • •

Some operations will have a Unique Selling point which might be the freshness of the product or the speed of service or the spirit of hospitality and ethics in the organization. Often organizations will attempt to communicate the essence of their business to stake holders through the use of a mission statement, sometimes the unique selling point of the organization may appear in the mission statement as well. For example, in the Pret A Manger mission statement (Figure 2.12) one can see their unique selling point as the freshness of the ingredients and their passion for food. Sandwich bars will market their product to a huge range of market segments and they are generally placed on a high street or strategic points were there are a high number of people passing by.

Product and service styles • • •

Some operations will place the importance on the quality of ingredients or range of ingredients available. Outlets may have pre-packaged products on sale or prepare products on order. Generally speaking the smaller operations which cannot guarantee a high volume of sales every day will opt for the customized option, whilst larger operations will tend to have a high number of pre-packaged products, although product customization will still be a choice available to their customers.

Although traditionally convenience foods have been used in those type of operations, consumer awareness has generally steered such type of operations to more healthy options. How much convenience food is to be used and when can be the key to a successful operation as often the kitchen space available may only be a counter and the 'Kitchen' is really nothing more than a finishing kitchen. Often big sandwich chains will have centralized Kitchens were they prepare and even assemble the finished product for distribution to the various outlets. Portion control and costing is of paramount importance as the net profit per sandwich sold is minimal so production

PRET: creates hand made natural food, avoiding the obscure chemicals, additives and preservatives common to so much of the 'prepared' and 'fast' food on the market today.

Figure 2.12
Pret mission statement
(*Source*: pret.com)

can be highly standardized. Equipments used are minimal and might involve a toaster or sandwich grill whilst refrigeration space is a must for every sandwich bar.

Service styles tend to be either counter service or self-service. Speed of service is extremely important especially at the peak times which is very likely to be around lunchtime. Some operations will offer seating space with different pricing for eating in or taking away.

Staffing • • •

Staff levels are kept to a minimum. Depending on the size of operation there can be one or two members of staff behind a counter. It is not uncommon for small establishments to only have one member of staff per shift, who may be both producing the end product and serving the customer. It is often the case that one staff member may serve a few hundreds of customers per day. Staff to customer contact time is extremely limited.

Technology • • •

Bar code and scanner technology is not uncommon in established sandwich chains. The technology speeds up service dramatically enabling servers to deal with even more customers per hour. EPOS systems are also used as sandwich bars now analyse their peak times, service levels and even waiting times of customers to ensure faster and better service to their customers. Product popularity can also be tracked and analysed a helpful tool especially when new products are introduced. Stock control software is also extensively used as it can help reduce costs. Really high-tech sandwich bars with seating capacity may offer WIFI connection.

Popular catering (pizza/steak houses/bistro/brasserie, etc.)

These types of outlets have many similarities to fast-food outlets and although they could be categorized as such they often offer full table service and that alone can be considered a reason enough to slightly distinguish them from fast-food type outlets.

Although differing from one another in certain aspects, these catering outlets have a number of characteristics which are common to all these types of operations – their menu is focused around a certain product, for example, pizza (Pizza Hut) or chicken (Nandos, KFC), or offer a limited range of products. The food and beverages sold are of a consistent standard and quality with a high percentage of convenience and pre-cooked foods being used (Figure 2.13).

These operations cater mainly for the relatively lower average spend markets with lower prices being charged than those found in other food and beverage establishments; there is a low ratio of service staff to customers with many of these operations being a form of self-service; consumption of the food may be on or off

Figure 2.13
The KFC Bucket (*Source*:
Courtesy of KFC)

the premises; less rigid meal times are observed by these establishments, with some form of menu usually available throughout the day; and finally, all aspects of the operation are highly standardized, leading to a high volume throughput with resulting economies in food, labour and other operating costs.

Financial implications • • •

Popular catering establishments have a number of characteristics which enable their particular business orientation to be identified. Relatively speaking, they do not require such a high initial capital outlay (relative to other sectors of the industry), nor a high percentage of fixed costs, although they do normally have a higher percentage of variable costs. Although the products offered for sale by these establishments are perishable, they are not as perishable as similar food and beverage products offered by other types of catering establishments; this is mainly due to the high level of convenience foods used by popular catering outlets, and the fact that often most of the foods are 'cooked to order' and do not have to be prepared sometime in advance; also because the products are not so highly perishable, these operations do not suffer from such sales instability as do hotels, for example, and they therefore have a lesser degree of dependence on market demand. All these factors contribute to making the fast food and popular catering operations both cost-orientated (to control costs tightly) and market-orientated (to ensure the volume of business in a very competitive sector of the industry).

In these lower average spend operations, the cost of the meal to the customer is an important variable in determining the sales of the operation; because fast food and popular operations demonstrate a very elastic demand, an increase in an establishment's prices of, for example, 10%, is likely to have a substantial effect on its sales. Variable costs in fast-food operations account for a large part of the product's selling price and the range of price discretion is consequently low. The prices charged by these establishments must therefore be carefully calculated, particularly in relation to competitors' pricing levels. The average spend per customer can be relatively low, ranging from £10 to £20 although these relatively low average spends are compensated by the volume sales achieved.

The financial policies of such operations would include the envisaged profitability of the establishment and the way in which it may be achieved, by controlling costs, balancing selling prices against volume sales, determining the profit margins on the food and beverage items, etc.

Marketing • • •

The marketing policy for the modern popular and fast-food organization is the key to success in this sector of the industry. A study of many of these organizations provides an outline to the marketing policy which may be discussed under the variables of product, promotion, place, price, process, physical evidence and participants. We approach these marketing variables in more detail in Chapter 9 of this book.

Product and service styles • • •

The products sold by popular catering operations are highly standardized and portion controlled, particularly in take-away operations. The larger organizations, such as Pizza Hut, have vertically integrated their supply chains, controlling food production through to product sales, ensuring total product control and specification. Other companies may buy in pre-prepared and packaged products from the food manufacturers and sell them directly to the customer, for example, pre-wrapped pies, biscuits, butter, etc. In this situation the fast-food operation closely resembles a retail trading outlet in which it has bought from the wholesaler and is selling to the customer without altering the product in any way.

This is a particularly useful way for an operation to increase its menu range without increasing the work load on the kitchen staff or requiring additional space or equipment to prepare a menu item with fresh produce.

The menu as a sales tool is important in any food and beverage operation, but is particularly so in these types of operations where staffing levels are reduced to a minimum and the operation's only vehicle for selling its products is via its menu and visual displays. In situations such as takeaways where contact time with the service staff is minimal, the menus are featured very prominently, usually with pictorial representation of the dishes.

In these operations it is not so much a question of whether or not to use convenience foods, but of those available which ones to use and to what extent. The amount of convenience foods used by an establishment will depend on a number of factors: the cost of buying in manufactured foods compared with the cost of producing the same products on the premises; the standard of food that the establishment wishes to offer; the variety of menu items to be offered; whether the additional costs of buying manufactured foods is offset by savings in production and labour costs, etc.

Staffing • • •

Staffing levels are, where possible, kept to a minimum. The ratio of service staff to customers is dependent upon a number of factors which include the type of establishment, the range of menu items, and the prices charged. The labour intensity of an operation is particularly related to its price level; broadly speaking, the higher the price of the meal to customers, the more service they expect to receive. The staff to customer ratio increases as the operation becomes more sophisticated so that in waiter service establishments, for example, one waiter may only serve 12 to 16 customers.

Technology • • •

Apart from the advancements in EPOS and production technologies that is mentioned in previous sections its worth mentioning the use of the Internet that has enabled smaller businesses to use this new and exciting medium for marketing efforts. Restaurants of various sizes around the world have seized the opportunity by creating websites. These can range from simple information 'electronic billboards' sites to more interactive websites where customers can book seats in the restaurant online. Websites are just one piece of the overall marketing strategy that can help operators realize some of their business goals. Innovative and cohesive websites combined with other online tools such as, mail list, newsletters, and auto-responders, can generate a high degree of visibility for a company that is necessary to increase sales or business to business contacts (Figure 2.14).

Takeaway and home deliveries

The take-away, or take-out service as it is more commonly known in the US, is a method of food service that exploits to the full the concept of 'fast foods'. The products offered by these establishments are highly standardized, as are most of the features of the operations – service, sales control, product packaging, etc. The take-away operation offers a limited basic menu to the customer, but within this menu there may be a number of variations on the basic items. These operations aim to achieve volume sales by offering low- to medium-priced foods, and they have become a popular segment of the food and beverage market because they fill a need for a quick snack or meal.

The time between customers placing orders and receiving their meals, aims to be faster than any other method yet discussed; some operations aim for a 30 second service time. The customer may either take the food out of the takeaway to eat, or

Figure 2.14 Bank Restaurant website showing online booking facility

it may be consumed on the premises; a large number of so-called 'take-away' outlets now provide very extensive seating areas, often for more than several hundred.

A number of take-away restaurants would also offer a Home delivery service. The practice, traditionally linked to Pizzas expanded to Indian and Chinese and even sit in restaurants. Home delivery is one of the upcoming markets as it is predicted to have a high growth in the UK in the next few years (Table 2.1).

Financial implications • • •

Traditional restaurants tend to be limited by the number of seats in their facility, a takeaway or home delivery restaurant however, can capitalize on the fact that the faster they produce and deliver food the higher the earnings. Average spend can range from £2 to £8 depending on the type of takeaway and for home deliveries average spend tends to be in the range of £8 to £12.

Marketing • • •

Because take-away outlets aim for a high rate of customer turnover, their situation in relation to their markets is crucial; they are usually found in high streets and main shopping centers where they have a high percentage of passing trade. Although the ASP of customers in takeaways may be considerably lower than for some of the other food service methods discussed, this is compensated by their high rate of customer throughput.

Home delivery operators tends to spend most of their marketing budget in leaflets that they distribute in houses in their catchment area. Apart from the menu itself, other typical information will include operating hours and contact telephone numbers although increasingly operators will accept orders via email or their website. As the majority of consumers will consider such menus junk mail, increasingly the use of the website will be paramount and the operators will revert to using business card style leaflets to draw potential customers to their website portal.

Product and service styles • • •

Today there is a wide selection of products that takeaway can offer for sale; the growth of the traditional fish-and-chip shops has now taken second place to the other types of foods now offered – hamburgers, pizzas, Chinese, Indian and Mexican food, to name a few (see Table 2.1). Menu is normally limited to allow for either pre-cooked goods that can be easily reheated and served to customers or batch cooking which can be an efficient production for a busy high street takeaway. Even fish-and-chip shops will often batch cook a number of portions and keep in a hot plate especially in busy times of the business.

Self-service is therefore a method of food service in which customers collect their own food from some form of service counter, in return for which they pay a lower price for the meal than they would, for example, in operations offering a waiter service. In self-service operations payment for the meal is made either before the meal, for example, in vending operations or after the meal as in some cafeterias.

In the industrial sector of the catering market this method of food service has become firmly established; in the majority of cases people's main meal is in the evening, so that they only require a snack-type short lunch which a self-service operation can adequately provide. In the welfare sector this utilitarian method of food service is also used extensively, leaving the more leisurely dining to that part of the day which is not associated with work.

Staffing • • •

A take-away restaurant focuses its labour expenditure mainly in production staff with just one person serving the customers; often the same person may prepare some easy menu items such as salads. In the case of Home delivery the person in the counter will also take any calls and allocate orders to the delivery staff. The number of delivery staff will vary with the volume of business but a good home delivery restaurant would need at least three delivery staff to be able to deliver orders on time.

Technology • • •

Increasingly home delivery restaurants are utilizing database software, so once a customer has made a call their address and phone number is stored so that the next time they call the call receiver knows correct address customer menu preferences and past purchases. Innovation in credit card and Internet technology has allowed for orders to be made via the Internet enabling the operation to be more efficient.

Coffee houses and Tea rooms

Coffee houses often feature large comfortable sitting areas were customers may purchase hot beverages and cold snacks for consumption primarily in house. Often to take away. In the US from late 1950s onward, coffee houses also served as a venue for entertainment, most commonly folk performers, especially since young audiences are not allowed entry to bars until the age of 21. For example, Bob Dylan began his career performing in coffee houses. A Coffee house is not to be confused with the term Café. In the US the term is used to describe a small restaurant whilst in France a café may sell alcoholic beverages. In the UK the coffee shop market has evolved rapidly since the 1990s and is now a major market with Starbucks leading the way but brands such as Costa and Nero following the example.

Tea rooms are found mostly in Britain and tend to be small businesses that offer a variety of teas as well as scones, pancakes and other cakes. Tea rooms can also be found in countries such as Australia, India and New Zealand and generally countries that have been in some way influenced by the UK. Although the traditional tea room is beyond its maturity stage, tea consumption is on the increase particularly with herbal and aromatic tea varieties, and the concept might find a revival in future years.

Financial implications • • •

Coffee houses in the US according to Mintel (2005) the market experienced 157% growth between 2000 ($3,258 million) and 2005 to reach some $8,372 million. Over the next 5 years sales are expected to grow by a further 125% to reach an impressive $18,839 million by 2010. This is over twice the growth rate seen in the British coffee shops market which is not as established as in the US.

The total number of coffee shops in the US increased by 70% between 2000 and 2005, bringing the total to a staggering 21,400 or one coffee house for every 14,000 Americans. According to Mintel (2005) the number of shops could well continue to rise until there is a coffee shop for every 10,000 Americans.

In the UK, the market is worth over £700 million (see Table 2.3) and forecasts suggest a growth well into 2011 although the market would soon reach maturity stage.

Tea rooms today, are not a significant market in terms of financial implications but they worth a mention from a cultural point of view.

Marketing • • •

The market for coffee shops today is highly segmented. From business people conducting meetings to mothers with toddlers during the day and young people during the weekends it is a

Year	2005 prices £m	Index	At 2006 prices £m	Index2
2001	305	45	355	53
2002	375	56	420	62
2003	450	67	489	72
2004	530	79	561	83
2005	610	90	627	93
2006	675	100	675	100
2007	736	109	716	106
2008	801	119	760	113
2009	874	129	806	119
2010	948	140	848	126
2011	1,023	152	890	132

Source: Mintel

Table 2.3
Market size and forecast of branded coffee shops

product that has attracted such a wide market that it can be hard to distinguish one significant market segment. As coffee shops tend to be opened by a chain, the brand increasingly becomes a prime criteria for consumers when choosing which coffee shop to select.

The tea room market tends to be elderly customers although tea rooms are often seen as a tourist attraction by tourists of all ages.

Product and service styles • • •

The main product is the large variety of types of coffee that the consumer can find in a coffee shop. Apart from the large variety of coffee beans that each shop may feature there can be a variety of products that all are made using the same coffee bean. For example a latte a cappuccino and an espresso can all have the same coffee as the base ingredient. A typical coffee shop menu will feature 10–15 types of coffee and other hot beverages such as tea or hot chocolate. Often the shops may sell their own brand of coffee beans for consumption at home.

Interestingly Starbucks, the global leader of the coffee shop, is diversifying by selling hot food rather than cold snacks. If other brands follow suit the coffee shop concept will be reinventing itself and we may well see a number of coffee shop chains mutating into the café concept often found in France.

Counter service is now a norm in most coffee shops although some privately owned may still offer table service. On the other hand with tea rooms table service is the norm or a combination of counter and table service, where by the customer gives the order over the counter and the product is served at the table.

Staffing ● ● ●

Coffee shops depending on their size will have two or more baristas. A barista is a counter clerk and the word derives from the Italian word for bartender. As the quality of the hot beverage is affected by the skills of the barista it is very important for all staff to be properly trained in the use of the equipment. High street coffee shops tend to have their busiest times during morning hours and the lunch period so the coffee shop manager would have to take that in consideration when creating the rotas.

As most tea houses tend to be family owned businesses the staff tend to be members of the family, in the UK tea houses tend to get busier during the summer months and weekends when tourists would visit the destination but often seating space is so limited that the necessity for extra staff would not normally arise.

Technology ● ● ●

EPOS systems have enabled coffee houses to deal with higher volumes of costumers and better stock control. Even more importantly the advancement of coffee dispensing technology has enabled coffee shop chains to be able to deliver consistent quality of their beverages throughout their branches. The technology however is not yet that far advanced that can deliver a complete finished product and well-trained baristas are still a must.

Summary

In this chapter we explore:

- Food and beverage outlets, focusing in restaurant outlets.
- Activities and type of operations in the food and beverage management.
- Restaurant guides.
- Fine dining and catering in bars, nightclubs and pubs.
- Hotel restaurants and private dining rooms as well as the fast-food sectors were explored highlighting the intricacies of each sector.
- Key differences between types of operations looking at areas of finance, marketing, production and service.
- Differences in the sourcing of staff and the use of technology.

Further study options

Case study: What type of outlet?

Derek always daydreamed about opening his own little restaurant but he had no idea about how to run one let alone where to begin. When he won the lottery he decided that this was the time for him to start his little dream and he decided to go back to the village that his parents lived.

The village has about 5,000 inhabitants and is only 20 minutes by car from a large city. It already has two takeaways and three small restaurants that are doing ok. All three restaurants are mid ranged. A fine dining restaurant opened 3 years ago but it closed after 1 year. There is also a pub in the village that offers a limited menu during lunch period.

Derek is unsure as to what type of property he should open. Money is no object to him now that he won the lottery but he also does not want to invest to an enterprise that is going to loose money for certain.

What would you advise Derek to do next?

If you were Derek what type of operation would most likely attempt to open? Why?

Review questions

1. What are the key differences between a Fast-food operation and a fine dining restaurant?
2. Describe at least two different service and production styles that you would come across in different operations.
3. What is an EPOS and in which type of operations might it be a necessity and in which a luxury.
4. List the key differences in the six operating areas (FMPSST) between a coffee shop and a dining club.

Further reading

Brewin Dolphin http://www.brewindolphin.co.uk/ (accessed 2nd November 2006).

British Hospitality Association http://www.bha.org.uk/ (accessed 20th October 2006).

Caterer, 08 March 2007, JD Wetherspoon's John Hutson welcomes smoking ban http://www.caterersearch.com/Articles/2007/03/08/312049/jd-wetherspoons-john-hutson-welcomes-smoking-ban.html (last accessed 10th March 2008).

Durocher, J. (2001). *Unplugged, Restaurant Business*, 100(1), 79–80.

Feinstein, A. H. and Stefanelli, J. M. (1999). Technology applications in foodservice purchasing: a primer for foodservice marketers. *Journal of Restaurant and Foodservice Marketing*, 3(2), 3–22. The Haworth Press.

Hertneky, P. (2000). The disappearing chefs. *Restaurant Hospitality*, 84(2), 47–50.

Hutchcraft, C. (2001). Scan and deliver. *Restaurants and Institutions*, 111(9), 111–112,114.

Karel, M. (2000). Tasks of food technology in th 21st century. *Food Technology*, 54(6), 56–58,60,62,64.

Menu Pix http://www.menupix.com (accessed 25th October 2006).

Michelin Guide http://www.viamichelin.com (accessed 5th January 2007).

Mintel Reports, Sandwiches – UK – October 2007 http://reports.mintel.com/ (accessed 10th March 2008).

Mobile Guide http://mobiltravelguide.howstuffworks.com (accessed 28th October 2006).

Pret a Manger (2006). http://www.pret.com (accessed 2nd September 2006).

TRI Hospitality Consulting (2007). Hotels 2007 report, UK.

Walton, C, (2007). JD Wetherspoon full-year profits to be below expectations, Caterer and HotelKeeper, http://www.caterersearch.com (accessed 15th August 2007).

Zagat survey http://www.zagat.com/ (accessed 28th March 2007).

CHAPTER 3

Contract, travel and public sector catering

Introduction

In this chapter we examine the contract, travel and public (CTP) sector catering. In many occasions the public sector and travel catering operations, are often serviced by contract caterers. However, there are still occasions where organizations provide their own in-house catering and by dividing the sector into three subdivisions, it allows us to discuss the distinct differences between the various operations. The three subsectors have shown a dramatic increase in the past few years with some sectors such as the cruise ships showing a growth in business looking to continue in the next ten years or more. The chapter aims to give an overview of the sectors to enable the reader to get an understanding of the type of technology often used as well as the marketing and financial implications for each sector.

Chapter objectives

After working through this chapter you should be able to demonstrate:

- An understanding of the *contract* catering sector focusing on:
  - Industrial catering
  - Event management
  - Sport venue catering
  - Leisure venue catering.
- An understanding of the *travel* catering sector focusing on:
  - Airline catering
  - Cruise ship and Ferry boat catering
  - Train catering
  - Roads and Motor side catering
  - Vending machines.
- An understanding of the *public* sector catering focusing on:
  - School catering
  - Universities and college catering
  - Hospital catering
  - Armed forces catering
  - Prison catering.

CONTRACT CATERING

Contract catering has evolved greatly in the past ten years and it is not uncommon to find contract catering companies investing in any of the sectors that are covered in this chapter. Traditionally, contract catering has been associated with non-profit or institutional catering, including workplace canteens, hospitals and schools however, today contract catering firms such as Compass or Sodexho have branched outside the remits of traditional contract catering and today it is not uncommon for contract catering firms to develop brands under which they operate restaurants (Figure 3.1). According to the BHA in 2006 in the UK alone contract catering reached revenues of just under £4 billion, showing a 0.8% drop in turnover from the previous year. Worth noting is the decline of contract catering in Healthcare, MOD, Local authority and private education (see Table 3.1).

For the purposes of this text we shall define contract caterers as: individuals or firms who undertake the responsibility of operating and controlling a company's catering facilities within that company's guidelines for a specified contract arrangement. Contract caterers are usually engaged for a specific period of time, after which the contract may be renewed or dissolved as both parties wish.

Catering contracts can be classified mainly in five types:

1. *Cost plus/management fee*: These are contracts where the client is billed for the cost of the operation plus a management fee.

	2001		2003		2005		% change 2001–2005
	m	**%**	**m**	**%**	**m**	**%**	
Business and industry	588	38	613	36.9	645	41.2	9.7
State education	227	14.7	281	16.9	265	16.9	16.7
Public catering	177	11.4	185	11.1	210	13.4	18.6
Healthcare	238	15.4	232	14	204	13	−14.3
MOD	135	8.7	161	9.7	105	6.7	−22.2
Private education	125	8.1	135	8.1	100	6.4	−20
Local authority	42	2.7	37	2.2	22	1.4	−47.6
Oil rigs, training centres, construction sites	15	1	17	1	16	1	6.7
Total	1,547	100	1,661	100	1,567	100	1.3

Source: BHA/Mintel Reports (December 2006)

Table 3.1
UK contract catering market segments by number of meals served

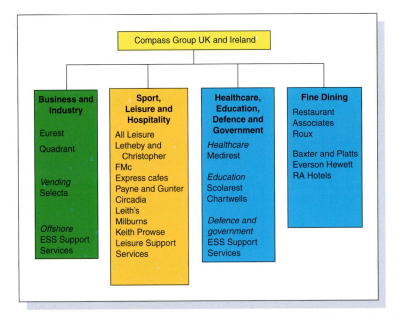

Figure 3.1 Structure of Compass Group the largest catering company in the UK. Compass Group employs 90,000 employees and has 8,500 sites in the UK alone. Worldwide the compass group employees 400,000 employees and annual revenue of approximately £11 billion (*Source*: http://www.compass-group.co.uk)

2. *Fixed price/performance guarantee*: Contracts where the clients agree a total subsidy and the costs may not rise above the agreed figure.
3. *Profit and loss concession*: The client and the caterer agree to share the profits or loss of the operation.
4. *Total risk*: Total investment covered by the caterer who earns all profits.
5. *Purchasing*: A contract for purchasing only.

Contract caterers are involved in all types of industrial catering situations, ranging from the small independent concerns to the large multinational organizations and may become involved for different reasons: for example, the organization's dissatisfaction with the existing services; complaints about the standard of catering have been made at staff meetings and repeated attempts to improve the facilities have failed, or the company does not wish to become involved in operating the catering facilities itself as it may not be its core business or recognizes that it does not have the expertise and so engages the services of contract caterers.

Industrial catering

Industrial catering can be defined as catering taking place in businesses. For example, major retail operators will offer catering to their employees and whilst sometimes they may have an in-house catering division, most often they will hire a contract caterer. Another example of industrial catering is the catering supplied to employees of organizations that provide financial services. Other businesses that may be included would be catering in oil rigs, construction sites, and training or conference centres. Indeed the subsector is so large that it exceeds an annual turnover of £660 million (see Table 3.1). Typical contracts agreed between organizations and caterers tend to be fixed price and profit/loss concession and total risk.

Financial implications • • •

Product pricing is a major issue for industrial catering. The market can be characterized as semi-captive as it would be convenient for employees to use the caterer but they also have the choice to use other food and beverage providers or bring in their own lunch. Of course there are exceptions to this such as catering provided in oil rigs where employees have no alternative but to consume what is provided by the caterer. Supermarkets tend to offer good quality luncheons not only in the form of sandwiches but also in hot and freshly prepared food at very competitive prices. Caterers have to ensure good quality of food is provided with food items that are around the range of £3–£5.

Marketing • • •

Ensuring that the caterer is the prime choice for the employees of the business can be affected by the marketing efforts of the caterer. Day specials and promotional packages (such as food and drink special deals) will often be advertised on a company's intranet or message board. Traditional methods such as flyers may also be used but the speed and cost effectiveness of an email makes it a prime method of communicating with potential clients.

Product and service styles ● ● ●

Counter service and take-away service styles tend to be the preferred service style for such operations, however buffet style and self-service may be used. The main products are snacks and take-away food, so product packaging can be important as some caterers may have limited seating space and employees may also chose to buy the product and consume it later.

Staffing ● ● ●

These operations tend to be staffed by regular members of staff. Caterers will often have other operations in nearby sites so staff mobility between operations can be an option. This flexibility can become important especially when there is need to cover staff leave or sickness periods from one outlet to another.

Technology ● ● ●

Food holding technology is very important. An off-site central kitchen may be used that supplies a number of operations. Ensuring that the quality of food is maintained through the transportation and delivery is paramount. Electronic point of sale (EPOS) technology can help with forecasting of sales thus reducing wastage. Communication technologies such as access to host company electronic boards or intranets and group mailing lists can be a great advantage to the caterer for marketing purposes.

Event management

An increasingly important area in Hospitality Management is that of Event Management. Although event management involves all those aspects that are required to organize a successful event, the provision of food and beverage is often of paramount importance to guarantee the success of the event. Policy decisions relating to function catering are largely determined by a number of characteristics inherent in this type of catering. The first is the season. The second is the concentration of events during these months, which are mainly at weekends, particularly Friday and Saturday events, during which time an operation must seek to maximize its sales potential. Third, a considerable amount of information is available to the caterer in advance of the organized functions; this includes the number of guests to be catered for and for which meal periods, for example lunch or dinner; their time of arrival and departure; the menu they are to be given and the price being paid per guest.

The basic policies relating to function catering are usually quite specific to this form of catering. If function trade is an establishment's only source of business then the policies laid down will only relate to this type of trade. In other establishments, however, such as hotels, the function facilities may be one of a number of catering outlets, although even in these organizations the banqueting department will often have policy decisions relating specifically to this department.

Activity 1

In groups of 3 plan an event. Use a brainstorming session to identify the event concept and key considerations with planning and managing of the event. The event concept can be based on a specific theme, for example an Italian Evening or a Casino Night. You are only limited by your imagination.

Banqueting and functions and large-scale events • • •

Function and event catering may be described as the service of food and beverages at a specific time and place, for a given number of people, to an agreed menu and price. Examples of function catering include social functions, such as weddings and dinner dances; business functions such as conferences, meetings and working lunches; and those functions that are organized for both social and business reasons such as outdoor catering at a sports event, show or exhibition.

Function catering is found in both the commercial and non-commercial sectors of the catering industry. The term 'banqueting' can often be used within hotels to describe the department that deals with function catering. The typical hotel function or banqueting 'season' runs between the months of October and May with the busiest months being December and January. For the rest of the year some of the facilities may be used for providing separate restaurant facilities for tour groups who normally have limited time available for meals and whom the hotel may wish to keep apart from the normal day-to-day restaurant business. The function facilities may also frequently be let on a day or half-day basis for such occasions as antique shows, trade exhibitions, fashion shows, etc. where the requirement of food and beverages may be very limited.

This function season is more noticeable in certain types of establishments, particularly those organizations whose sole purpose is function catering, and those that offer purpose-built facilities such as hotels. In other establishments such as public houses, department store restaurants, industrial cafeterias, etc. the function season is not so evident, as existing dining facilities are usually adapted for function events rather than specific facilities being available; however, even these types of operations are still likely to experience peak periods during the year when the function facilities are in greater demand than at other times. This characteristic fluctuating of demand associated with function catering has implications for such establishments' basic policy decisions, and these are discussed below.

Financial implications • • •

The logistics required for such events can be extremely complicated. Often the event might take place in a location that there is no production capabilities and the food and beverage will have to be produced at another site and then transported and

served on-site. For the company taking on such a project there are the additional costs of transportation to take into account. When negotiating the contract the caterer will have a number of ready-made and costed menus but often in events such as weddings the customer might require a very specific product that the caterer will have to customize. Using the wedding as event example, beverages will often be included in the cost per head or cover. Meaning, cost per customer. Because the margins per head are normally very small the caterer makes the money on the volume of the event.

The pricing structure for an establishment's function catering facilities will be largely determined by its cost structure, with particular reference to its fixed and variable costs. This is most in evidence in the non-commercial sector where functions may not be fully costed, that is not taking into account the fixed costs of the operation. Where the costing of function menus is based mainly on covering food and labour costs, it is important to remember that both of these increase with the size and quality of function offered. However, due to the volume of sales the food and labour costs as a percentage of actual sales will slightly decrease; it is necessary therefore to not only consider the food costs per function but also the potential benefits to be gained from a reduction in labour costs. There are a variety of pricing structures that may be used for costing functions, the adoption of any one being determined by such factors as the type of organization, the standards of food and beverage service to be offered, and the cost structure of the establishment.

Marketing ● ● ●

There is such a varied type of events that a catering company or a hotel banqueting department may use any of the traditional marketing such as Leaflets, radio, TV, magazine and newspaper adverts. According to Brewin Dolphin, a financial research company, the market for weddings is worth £4.2 billion each year with the average wedding to about £16,000 no wonder hotel banqueting departments and contract catering operators are competing for this lucrative segment.

Sample function menus produced by an establishment need to be of a good quality and appearance as the customer will often wish to take them away to study before deciding on the function menu. These sales tools should also be of a standard consistent with the level of operation and the type of image it is trying to project. Function 'folders' containing details of all the different facilities offered by an establishment are often produced by organizations which may be distributed to prospective clients advertising the establishment's function facilities.

A function 'folder' often colour-coded for easy reference by the client, would most likely be composed of the following:

1. An envelope type folder with the company's logo, title and address clearly displayed.

2. A personal letter from the function/banqueting manager to the client.
3. A list of function rooms together with details of the numbers that could be accommodated for different types of functions, for example a formal lunch or dinner, a dinner dance, a buffet type reception, a theatre-style conference/meeting, etc.
4. Plans of the room with basic dimensions, position of power points, telephone points, ceiling heights, etc.
5. Sample menus for lunch, dinner, buffets, meetings, etc.
6. Details of audio-visual equipment available for meetings, for example lecterns, microphones, overhead projectors, screens, etc.
7. Details of accommodation facilities available, often at special rates for guests attending a function/meeting.
8. Coloured postcards of the hotel/function rooms.
9. Relevant simple maps and parking arrangements where necessary.

Product and service styles • • •

The product may vary depending on the type of the event and it may be anything from buffet style service to full table service depending on the customer request. Silver service and family service styles are quite common when table service has been requested. Functions may include a reception stage where canapés and appetisers are served by "satellite waiters". This is often known as the Butler style of service.

Staffing • • •

Caterers as well as banqueting departments will normally have a core of staff and will then use agency staff to cope with larger events. Because of this the quality of service may suffer as the operator cannot guarantee the skill level of the agency staff. Some contract catering companies train their own casual staff and they then have a 'Bank' of casual staff that they may call upon when needed.

Technology • • •

Food holding technology is very important to contract caterers. Because the business is more predictable as the numbers of customers are known hotel kitchens may use their staff to prepare the food for a large function before hand and load it to already plated to specially designed racks that can fit into combination ovens. Food can then be either completely cooked at the time needed and served straight from the racks or pre-cooked/chilled and then re-constituted.

Sport venue catering

Sport venue catering includes catering offered in stadia, football, cricket, rugby, horse racing venues, private health and fitness clubs, golf and other sports. The sector is hard to quantify as each country has a large number of venues and catering operations are largely fragmented. In 2004, Mintel was estimating the sector in the UK to worth £354 million. With the introduction of new venues since 2004 including the Wembley and Arsenal Stadia in London in 2007 and 2006, respectively, the UK sector is estimated to exceed the £400 million mark in revenue today. In the UK there are 365 stadia whilst the USA currently has 1,726. With 9,379 stadia around the world (Table 3.2) the revenues generated through the sale of food and drinks alone must be well over the £10 billion mark today (Figure 3.2). There are three common types of contracts often found between caterers and venue operators. The first is where the venue takes a percentage of the revenue generated by the contract caterer (performance guarantee). The second is where the venue simply leases their facilities therefore enjoying a fixed stream of income (total risk). The third is a relatively newer type of arrangement where both caterer and venue work in partnership setting a joint venture and splitting the profits generated equally (profit and loss concession) (Mintel Reports, September 2004).

Financial implications • • •

With approximately 9% of the world's stadia having a capacity of over 30,000 the logistics required for the catering of such large

	Number of venues
Africa	525
Asia	884
Central America	260
Europe	3,780
Middle East	424
North America	2,125
Oceania	260
South America	1,121
Total	9,379

Source: http://www.worldstadiums.com

Table 3.2
Number of stadia around the world

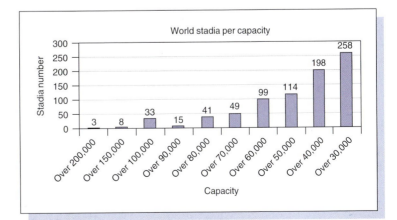

Figure 3.2 Number of world stadia per capacity (*Source*: http://www.worldstadiums.com)

operations can be extremely complex. If we consider the newly finished Wembley stadium in London, UK, the catering logistics required are phenomenal. The stadium has a capacity of 90,000. With 60 bars and 41 food and beverage outlets the stadium hospitality facilities include conference rooms of up to 1,000 capacity and reception rooms for up to 3,000 capacity. With 803 points of sale and a total of 3,000 hospitality employees, Wembley is one of the biggest catering sites in Europe. It includes a 950 cover Atrium restaurant, serving buffet food, the great hall and banquet space for up to 1,500 people, as well as four signature restaurants of 650 covers each, including two à la carte eateries and two brasseries. It also features two Champagne and seafood bars as well as two large free-flow public catering areas, 162 private boxes, two super boxes and a royal suite for up to 400 people Kühn (2007). This example illustrates the fact that stadia incorporate types of food and beverage outlets from every sector described in Chapter 2, making it an extremely complex operation that would require careful planning and organization to ensure success.

Marketing • • •

Many of the venues will try to entice the consumer earlier than the starting time of the event to maximize sales. Often leaflets might be handed at to the public featuring 'early bird' offers as well as the type of food and drinks on offer at the venue. Meal deals often seen in fast-food operations are also a popular promotional tool to increase multiple item purchasing. For example, a consumer may be offered to buy a pint of specific lager and a pie and gets a bag of crisps for free. The major contract caterers such as Delaware North, Compass and Sodexho use the Internet extensively as a marketing and promotional tool.

Product and service styles • • •

Soft and hot drinks and sandwich markets appear to be the most popular items according to Mintel. However, it is not uncommon for exclusive restaurants to be featured in many of the worlds stadia. Therefore the service and product style often seen would incorporate all the production styles and service styles of the sectors illustrated in Chapter 2 of this book. However, it is worth mentioning something specific to stadia in terms of service styles; often catering staff may be seen moving around the stadium selling food and beverages whilst a game is taking place. They can be on foot carrying trays or in some cases in specially converted bicycles that allow the sale of cold bottled beverages or even warm food.

Staffing • • •

Staffing can be a major 'headache' for the human resources management of such an operation. Because of the fluctuation of the events that could range from the corporate entertainment of a handful of people to that of a few thousands the organizations involved tend to have a core of permanent staff whilst they manage an often enormous database of casual staff that can be called upon to cover a certain event. Two major problems emanate from such a setup. The first is that of consistency, so organizations will have to ensure that all staff are trained to ensure standards of production and service are maintained at all times. The second is ensuring that the casual staff in the database get enough work every week to keep them interested in coming back for more work in the future.

Technology • • •

Two key considerations in such environments are paramount: health and safety, and speed of service. Advancements in technology enable operators to have better control of their food production ensuring health and safety standards are maintained throughout the production and service delivery. With large stadia that often have an excess of 500 selling points, EPOS systems and networking technology has to be extremely robust. Technology can also ensure that food production and food holding can be achieved with larger numbers than ever before. The new Wembley stadium in the UK features a beer dispensing system that has the pumping capability of four pints per sixteen seconds with the stadium number of sales points that means at optimum production their 803 points of sale can produce 45,169 pints in fifteen minutes. That is half the total possible capacity of the stadium and in theory it would mean the end of customer queuing for a pint.

Leisure venue catering

Leisure venue catering is catering offered in venues such as museums, theatres, cinemas, historic buildings, zoos, wildlife parks, art galleries. Perhaps, because of the captive nature of the market the key management issues that appear to be prevalent are that of pricing and quality. In the UK, the market has exceeded the £2 billion mark since 2006. However, the growth of the sector compared to that of free-standing restaurants is quite slow suggesting that improvements could be made (Figure 3.3). Although the majority or leisure venues outsource their catering a significant number chooses to keep their catering in house. This is more prevalent in cinema and theatre catering.

Financial implications • • •

Although catering in museums has shown the largest growth in the leisure venue catering in recent years Museums and art galleries in the UK have lost a major competitive advantage. With the introduction of free admission consumers have the option to go to a high street restaurant and re-enter the museum or gallery later. What was once a captive market has now become at best a semi-captive one. This meant that catering in such establishments has to offer a better value for money than it has

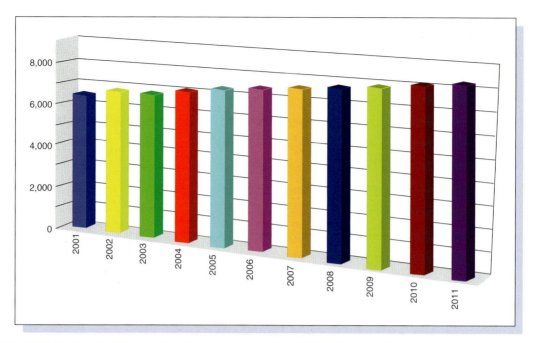

Figure 3.3 Trends in the UK Leisure Venue Catering market, 2001–2011 (in million pounds)
(*Source*: Mintel Reports, March 2007)

done in the past, ensuring that costs remain low whilst quality of product and price remains competitive enough to entice visitors to buy from their outlets. In order to ensure higher profit margins whilst remaining competitive leisure caterers will have to ensure that they maximize their sales per available customer within the venue. That means that vendors must ensure that the long queues that often put off consumers must be minimized.

Marketing ● ● ●

Apart from the common promotional techniques used such as meal deals and discounted offers, catering in leisure venues over the past years had a reputation of bad value for money. Caterers today must not only ensure that customers are enticed to buy their in-house products but also that they develop a brand that communicates quality and efficiency to the consumer. This one of the main reasons leisure venue operators will often chose to outsource their food and beverage provision to well-established contract catering companies. The main operators in the UK are Compass, Sodexho and Elior although there are other operators such as DO & CO, Searcy and Caterleisure (Figure 3.4).

Product and service styles ● ● ●

The majority of visitors purchase snacks or take-away food such as burgers, hot dogs, crisps and chocolate. Therefore the majority of the food provision can take often the form of retail. Counter, buffet and take-away service styles tend to be amongst the more popular for leisure catering (Table 3.3).

Figure 3.4 DO & CO at the British Museum (*Source*: http://www.doco.com)

All events no matter the location share one trait: meticulous attention to detail and as a consequence training by our in-house academies is essential. The British Museum, or any other historic building is one of the most challenging environments a caterer can operate within. One minute it can be empty, then it rains, and within one hour it can be full, which is very difficult to plan for. Alternatively, the museum may provide us with a one-hour window to set up an event for over 1,000 people with hot food and drinks in one of the galleries.

The museum has procedures and protocols for almost everything. Ranging from the serious, such as the evacuation procedures, which results in many customers walking off and leaving their food and bills. To the not so serious, such as the procedure for removing a pigeon perched on the planters in the restaurant, giving the customers cause for concern.

Christian Bayer, Project Manager and Chris Marsland, Food and Beverage Manager of DO & CO at the British Museum explain the challenges of events and running a catering operation at a museum.

Catering by its very nature needs to be flexible and elastic; however the museums are institution governed by their own regulations that can often be inflexible. In order to effectively run a multi-unit catering operation within such a unique space, it is important to understand the limits of what you can change and what you cannot (i.e. playing the system). And, of course, knowing the right people means everything!

	Percentage of a sample of 809 visitors
Cold snacks (e.g. crisps, chocolate, nuts)	47
Hot take-away food (e.g. hotdog, burger, hot pie/pastry	45
Cold take-away food (e.g. sandwiches, ice cream)	45
Hot snacks (e.g. chips, nachos)	30
Hot sit-down meal (e.g. pizza/ pasta, shepherds pie, curry)	27
Cold sit-down meal (e.g. salad, sandwiches)	19
Healthy snacks (e.g. fruit, energy/ cereal bars)	19
Others	1
Did not buy food	15

Source: Mintel Reports (March 2007)

Table 3.3
Types of food bought at leisure venues, 2007

Staffing • • •

In recent years, the minimum wage in the UK has been increased much faster than inflation rates. This has caused an added challenge to operators and for a sector that was traditionally perceived as an expensive one compared to high street vendors transferring the added cost to the consumer farther expanded the gap between consumer expectations and value for money delivered. When catering is kept in house, operators have a separate staff division that focuses on hospitality. Casual staff are also used as there is a fluctuation of visitors depending on day of the week, weather and time of the year. During weekends and school breaks, for example, leisure parks tend to be at their busiest. This in turn does affect the quality of service especially with the larger operators.

Technology • • •

One of the key allies in recovering product and service quality lies in the investment of information technology. The latest EPOS technology can help managers keep track of customer preferences as well as employee productivity, this can be a great tool in allowing the manager to identify a member of staff that may be in need of further training or even award that excellent member of staff that could otherwise go unnoticed.

TRAVEL CATERING

Travel catering (i.e. road, rail, air and sea) has a number of characteristics not commonly associated with other food and beverage outlets. It frequently involves the feeding of a large number of customers arriving together at a catering facility, and who need to be catered for in a specific time, for example, on board a plane. The plane only carries sufficient food and beverage supplies for a specific number of meal periods. If for any reason this food cannot be served to customers, alternative supplies may not be readily available. The service of the food and beverages may be particularly difficult due to the physical conditions within the service area, for example, turbulence on board a plane. The types of restaurants described previously are usually catering for a specific and identifiable socio-economic market. Travel catering often has to cater for 'mixed markets'. Finally, there are the problems of staffing these food and beverage facilities: the extra costs involved in the transportation and service of the food and beverages; space restrictions and the problem of security while the operation is in transit. Four main types of travel catering may be identified: Airline catering, Cruise ship and Ferry boat catering, Train catering and Motorway catering.

Airlines

The major new trend of the past ten years in the Airline industry in Europe has been the introduction and substantial growth of the budget or 'no frills' airline phenomenon. Companies such as Easyjet and Rynair have shown amazing growth. The total airline growth from the year 2000 to 2006 has been an amazing 30% (Figure 3.5) but mainly due to the increase in budget airlines the in-flight catering expenditure had a downward trend in recent years (see Table 3.4).

Airline catering has increased and developed considerably over the past twenty-five years. Originally consisting of sandwiches and flasks of tea, coffee and alcoholic beverages, the progress to today's full and varied service has paralleled that of aircraft development itself. In budget airlines, however, the product has gone back to the basic trolley with sandwiches, snacks chocolate and limited selection of beverages on offer. Airline catering falls into two main areas: terminal catering, and 'in-transit' or 'in-flight' catering.

Financial implications • • •

The cost of a hot meal and beverage to the airline is about £6.50 but the biggest cost to the airline is the waiting to restock the

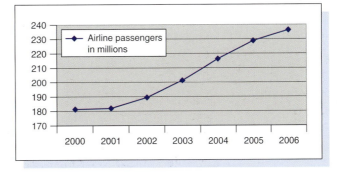

Figure 3.5
UK Airline passengers, 2000–2008 (*Source*: Adapted from CAA)

	2002		2005		2007		% change 2002–2007
	£m	%	£m	%	£m	%	
In-flight	613	72	590	72	577	72	−6.0
Ferry	170	20	155	19	152	19	−10.6
Rail	69	8	75	9	73	9	+4.2
Total	852	100	820	100	802	100	−5.9

Source: Mintel Reports (May 2007)

Table 3.4
UK onboard catering market, by sector

aircraft and time at an airport can mean a big loss of income to the carrier. If, for example, a carrier flies from London, UK to Athens, Greece, it may cost the airline less to stock up for the return trip (Athens–London) as well, limiting the waiting time at the Greek airport. This is especially true for budget airlines as they are well known for their strategy of limiting their turnaround time (see Table 3.5).

Marketing • • •

Airlines have tried to different experiments to alleviate the widely held customer perception that airline food is bland. Some airlines have tried introducing high street brands in their food packaging. Quite often the quality of the food is used in their marketing campaigns as a unique selling point, and airlines will employ a well-known chef to design their menu as part of their marketing efforts (see product and service styles). An interesting resource worth mentioning is http://www.airlinemeals.net/. This website invites members of the public to upload pictures of their in-flight food.

Activity 2

Thinking of the last airline you travelled with, see if you can find some pictures of their in-flight menu on the Internet.
What are your views of the in-flight catering service and food quality in general?
Can you recall any differences between different airline food?

Product and service styles • • •

The in-flight catering service varies considerably with the class of travel, type and duration of flight. For the economy travellers, the food and beverage portions are highly standardized with the meals portioned into plastic trays that are presented to the passengers and from which they eat their meals. Disposable cutlery, napkins, etc. may be used to increase the standard of hygiene and reduce the weight carried and storage space required. Gourmet

Airline	Aircraft km (in thousands)	Number of flights	Flight hours	Number of passengers	Available seat (km in thousands)	Seat (km) used (+%)
Air Atlantique	948	3,305	3,250	21,431	47,918	50.8
Air Southwest	3,209	13,790	12,359	328,084	160,644	61.8
Astraeus	21,629	9,581	29,524	809,968	3,720,734	76.9
Aurigny Air Services	2,688	20,182	10,153	419,552	132,816	67.6
BA Connect	55,483	91,862	130,780	3,302,742	3,480,415	58.9
BMED	20,268	6,271	25,185	376,434	2,813,929	53.6
BMI Group	94,487	125,477	201,039	9,942,528	13,811,843	69.1
British Airways	614,195	266,081	921,161	32,724,392	146,729,551	76.7
British International	396	6,296	2,155	117,256	9,877	74.5
Eastern Airways	13,691	34,370	33,668	500,071	469,063	45.9
EasyJet	228,702	226,185	409,521	27,970,593	33,885,755	81.5
European Air Charter	2,500	1,681	3,944	161,941	324,071	82.1
First Choice Airways	78,515	29,493	113,194	5,517,283	17,737,530	90.7
Flightline	2,762	7,212	7,029	175,525	281,024	48
Flybe	41,228	86,044	79,541	4,536,841	3,987,743	63.3
Flyglobespan	25,135	11,625	37,720	1,489,377	4,205,776	82.5
GB Airways	42,337	21,753	65,653	2,741,717	6,915,735	80.4
Isles of Scilly Skybus	697	6,736	3,128	53,638	10,923	57.9
Jet2.com	32,233	26,808	56,244	2,831,922	5,166,385	77.2
Loganair	6,361	31,399	24,814	496,537	197,148	56.1
Metropix UK	438	169	560	776	6,132	31.1
Monarch Airlines	71,630	32,256	105,672	5,788,234	18,016,794	82
My Travel Airways, UK	54,625	18,573	78,020	3,568,277	13,421,516	91.2
Scot Airways	4,630	8,720	10,468	164,731	143,511	61.4
Thomas Cook Airlines	66,563	23,609	93,525	4,872,999	16,446,072	87.2
Thomsonfly	117,917	54,063	175,953	9,617,416	27,632,857	86.9
Titan Airways	3,481	2,867	4,554	64,677	518,496	70.3
Triair (Bermuda)	293	129	371	659	4,140	29.8
Virgin Atlantic Airways	139,528	18,960	177,897	4,887,541	48,308,314	72.8
Silverjet (October–December)	1,403	446	1,996	90,756	324,403	84.3
XI Airways, UK (September–December)	16,283	5,573	23,373	1,044,726	4,067,039	86

Source: CAA http://www.caa.co.uk/

Table 3.5
UK airline statistics, 2006

food in the airlines is another recent trend. To ensure a "Gourmet Brand" in their menu, Airlines are hiring celebrity chefs such as Guy Martin, of Paris' three star Le Grand Vefour Hotel, working for Air France; Govind Armstrong of Table 3.8 in Miami and Los Angeles, working with Air New Zealand and Christian Petz, of Vienna's Restaurant Palais Coburg, working for Austrian Airlines. Stephan Pyles, of the Dallas restaurant, working with American Airlines whilst Charlie Trotter, the Chicago chef, introduces dishes created for premier United Airlines passengers. The lower than normal air pressure can affect customer perception of taste as well as digestion and executive chefs designing a menu will often taste it mid-air to ensure they have compensated for this. Added to that is the fact food is not cooked on board, it is just warmed. Meals are prepared twelve to sixteen hours in advance chilled and then held at low temperatures.

Service is from a gueridon trolley, where food is portioned in front of the customers and any garnishes, sauces, etc. are added according to their immediate requirements. The crockery used may be bone china and this combines with fine glassware and cutlery to create an atmosphere of high-class dining. Some airlines offer full silver service menu for their first class and business travellers.

A characteristic of airline catering is that this service is often contracted out to a specialist catering firm, which will supply a similar service to many airlines. The meal is usually included in the price of the fare with the exception of budget airlines. The growth in air travel has made competition fierce, and the area of food service is now a particularly competitive aspect of the total service offered by an airline. An interesting concept currently in the USA is that of gourmet meals delivered to the airport by the SkyMeals company (see http://skymeals.com/).

Staffing ● ● ●

Food and beverage outlets at air terminals usually consist of self-service and waiter service restaurants, supplemented by vending machines and licensed bars. The major restaurant brands often seen in high streets can also be seen in airport terminals.

In flight catering service is delivered by the flight attendants, who often see the service of food and drinks as secondary to their responsibility of ensuring the health and safety of passengers, this can be especially true if customers are flying in the economy class. Although health and safety should always remain flight attendants primary responsibility airlines that wish to claim a competitive advantage ought to train and offer incentives to individuals that offer exceptional service.

Technology ● ● ●

The main issues with aircraft are that of space and weight. Ensuring that on-board ovens are lighter, take less space and consume less energy are of primary importance. Advancements in technology may mean that airlines may be able to offer a menu fully cooked on board one day.

Cruise ships/Ferry boats

The cruise ship sector is one of the fastest moving sectors in the hospitality industry. The number of passengers has grown to more than 12 million in 2006 from approximately 500,000 in 1970. Forecasts suggest that by 2012 the global industry will reach 20 million passengers with the USA and UK leading in terms of cruise ship passengers (Table 3.6). Budget or 'no frills' cruise liners are making an appearance with new companies such as Caspi Cruises, Easy Cruise, whilst older budget companies such as Thomson or Louis Cruise Line increase their fleet capacity.

On the other hand, Ferry boat catering has slumped as the numbers of Ferry travellers has dramatically decreased due to the increase of low-cost airlines. In UK, the onboard catering market was valued at £155 million for 2005, a 19% decrease since 2000, and the trend is still going today (Mintel Reports, May 2007).

Financial implications • • •

Whilst cruise ship catering promises growth Ferry boat catering is extremely competitive. Mintel is forecasting a downward trend continuing well into 2010. Traditional cruise liners are looking to be more innovative continuing with all inclusive packages but offering optional extras. Wedding and honeymoon packages are another two products often offered by cruise liners.

Marketing • • •

Cruise liners are expanding their marketing strategies to target non-traditional market segments. Increasing competition in the budget sector forces them to think innovatively in finding ways to sell their product without conflicting the more traditional brands. Special promotions, discounts during low season,

	2001	2002	2003	2004
North America	6,906,000	7,470,000	8,195,000	9,107,000
UK	776,000	824,000	963,000	1,029.00
Continental Europe	1,130,000	1,296,000	1,709,000	1,758,000
Asia (excluding Japan)	600,000	600,000	500,000	450,000
Japan	200,000	220,000	200,000	200,000
Australia	75,000	116,000	154,000	158,000
Latin America	315,000	312,000	320,000	340,000
Others	190,000	360,000	300,000	315,000
Total	10,192,000	11,198,000	12,340,000	13,377,000
% change	1.20%	9.90%	10.20%	8.40%

Source: Mintel Reports (September 2005)

Table 3.6
Ocean cruise passengers worldwide, 2001–2004

special occasions, anniversary gifts to customers are some of the promotional tools used by most liners.

Product and service styles • • •

Sea or marine catering varies from the provision of food and beverages on the short sea route ferries to the large cruise or passenger liners where the catering facilities are an important part of the service offered by the shipping line and are usually included in the price of the fare. On the cruise liners the standard of catering facilities is high because they are an important sales feature in a competitive activity. On the short sea routes, however, price is usually a more important factor and because of the necessity to feed large numbers of people in a short time the catering service provided is usually of the popular and fast-food type. In the cruise liners companies appear to be more innovative than ever with companies such as Princess Cruises serving dinner in customer cabins or suite balconies ensuring extra food and beverage income. The Gourmet 'bug' is also appearing in the cruise sector with celebrity chefs such as Todd English on Queen Mary 2; Nobu Matsuhisa and Wolfgang Puck on Crystal; Marco Pierre White on the new P&O Ventura (Figures 3.6 and 3.7) and Gary Rhodes on two P&O's ships, Oriana and Arcadia. Service styles can range depending on cruise liner from full silver service to self-service and buffet. With Ferry boats the service style often is cafeteria or take away due to the short journeys involved.

Staffing • • •

After casino sales one of the largest revenue generators in cruise liners is beverage sales. Staff are trained extensively in up-selling

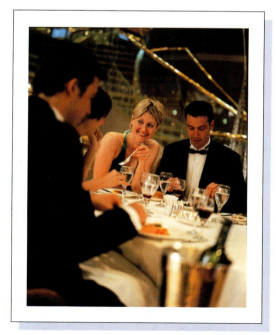

Figure 3.6
Cruise ship dining. Photo courtesy of P&O (*Source*: http://www.pocruises.com)

Figure 3.7 The new Ventura super liner by P&O Launching April 2008, this cruise liner is 115,000 tons with a capacity of 3,600 passengers, 1,200 crew, 1,546 cabins (880 balcony cabins), 11 restaurants, 12 bars, 5 places to shop, 3 places to dance, 5 places for live music, 2-tier theatre, 2 show lounges, a nightclub, 5 pools and 6 Jacuzzis (*Source*: http://www.virtualventura.co.uk)

techniques and with traditional cruise liners the recruitment process ensures that some of the best staff are hired. With the added incentive of tax-free incomes many hospitality professionals consider a few months on a cruise liner. The organization on cruise ships can be extremely hierarchical. Most front line employees tend to stay for only a few trips as the nature of the ship means that there is not much to do but work whilst on a cruise ship.

Technology • • •

Advanced EPOS technology and bar dispensing equipment mean better control of sales, stock control and wastage ensuring better profit margins as well as the facilitation of special discounts. Advancement in waste disposal technology ensures waste is better compacted shredded and incinerated.

Trains

According to Mintel Reports (December 2006), unlike Ferry and in flight catering, rail catering is showing an upward trend in revenues generated. Rail catering may be conveniently divided into two areas: terminal catering and in-transit catering. There are 2,500 rail stations across the UK. The main rival to rail is the low-cost airlines but the introduction of Eurostar in 2003 raised the rail market share in the UK. The improvements of the West Coast Mainline and the introduction of the Pendolinos train by Virgin Trains passenger numbers increased by a 20%. In the US sales reached $79 million in 2005 (Figure 3.8 and Table 3.7).

Financial implications • • •

With a 4.2% increase in rail catering revenue the sector appears a positive one. The main products purchased are hot beverages and snacks so the focus is in the reduction of costs to ensure

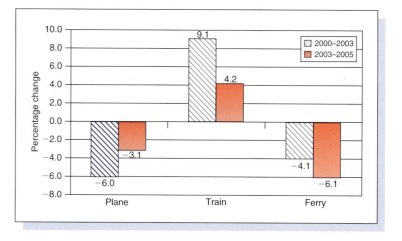

Figure 3.8
UK percentage change in value of the UK onboard catering market, by sector (*Source*: Mintel Reports, May 2007)

F&B sales	$78,929,599
Food	$30,237,417
On train food condemnage	$222,920
Liquor and tobacco	$3,395,625
Total cost of goods sold	$33,855,963
Gross profit	$45,073,636
% Gross profit	57%

Note: F&B – Food and beverage
Source: http://www.narprail.org

Table 3.7
US rail F&B gross profit, 2005

higher profit margins. Spend per passenger increases as the length of journey increases, however some companies offer all inclusive ticket prices which help raise the food and beverage revenue generated.

Marketing • • •

The provision of food and beverage in rails is often used as promotional tool. Ticket inclusive packages are often advertised in an effort to entice customers away from low-cost airlines. The sector is not as aggressive as it could be with its promotional efforts on food and beverage sales. The majority of train companies advertise their services in their in-house magazine whilst some have an e-marketing campaign and also use local and international media advertising.

Product and service styles • • •

Catering at railway terminals usually comprises licensed bars, self-service and waiter service restaurants, fast food and take-away units, supplemented by vending machines dispensing hot and cold foods and beverages. In-transit catering can feature three kinds of service. The first is the traditional restaurant car service where breakfast, lunch and dinner are organized in sittings and passengers go to the restaurant car for service where appropriate seating accommodation is provided, and then return to their seats on the train after their meal. In a Pullman service, these meals are delivered direct to the seat of first-class passengers only. The second type of service is the buffet car, which is a self-service operation in which passengers go to the car and buy light refreshments over the counter. The third is a trolley service where snacks and drinks are delivered to customers at their seats. Innovative approaches to catering on trains are also in evidence such as the operation of 'Cuisine 2000' using cook-chilled foods prepared centrally, buffet cars turned into bistros on the London to Birmingham route, and on the east coast Anglo-Scottish route 'A taste of Scotland' restaurant service.

Staffing • • •

In the UK, the Network rail is undertaking a project that looks to rejuvenate the provision of skills in the rail catering and other rail staff. In partnership with local colleges the programme aims to bring all staff to a National Vocational Qualification standard. For example, in 2004 the country's first Rail Academy – run by York College in partnership with the National Railway Museum the academy was funded with £1.25 million. Other similar initiatives have been introduced all over the UK ensuring that rail employees are well trained.

Technology • • •

There have been a number of advancements in railway kitchen design and technology enabling operators to serve more complicated menus than ever before. Also the same benefits enjoyed by the other sectors with the advancement of EPOS and beverage dispensing technologies are also enjoyed by the rail sector.

Roads/motor side

Road catering has progressed from the inns and taverns of earlier days used by those travelling on foot and horseback to the present-day motorway service areas (MSAs) and other roadside catering outlets. High street fast-food operations are also now appearing both on MSAs and as free-standing drive-through. As an example, in the UK, there are 86 MSAs. Moto is the biggest MSA operator with 42 sites followed by Welcome Break and Roadchef. These three operators control 89% of the market whilst McDonalds are slowly emerging as a significant MSA operator.

Financial implications • • •

The numbers of cars on the road are on the increase. In UK from 1999 to 2004 there was an increase of almost 3 million cars (Figure 3.9). There is a constant decrease of households without cars whilst the percentage of females holding driving licences

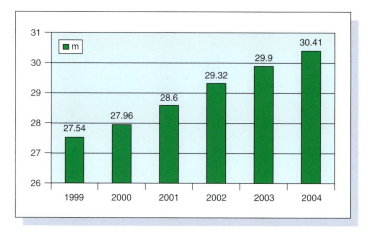

Figure 3.9
UK cars, 1999–2004 (*Source*: Mintel Reports, September 2004)

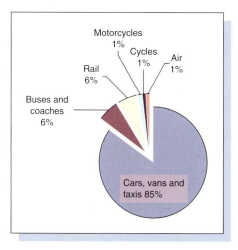

Figure 3.10
UK transport by mode 1999–2003 (*Source*: Mintel, 2004)

has risen from 49% in 1989/1991 to 61% in 2002/2003. This does have implications as demographics change so do trends in consumer expenditure. As seen in Figure 3.10 public transport in the UK only accounts for 12% of traffic, this would suggest a steady growth of motorway catering revenue well into 2010.

Marketing

MSAs main marketing tool are the road signs. The main motive for consumers stopping at such a facility is that of convenience. Advertising is heavily regulated and often operators may not be allowed to use their own brand in motorway signage.

Product and service styles ● ● ●

MSAs provide a valuable catering service to the travelling public and their food and beverage facilities usually include self-service and waiter service restaurants, vending machines, and take-away foods and beverages.

Staffing • • •

These service areas are often open twenty-four hours a day and have a particular problem of staffing as some employees have to be brought to and from work over a distance of 20–30 miles. Also, because of their isolated locations, the hours they are open and the sheer volume of numbers involved at peak periods, these service areas are also particularly prone to vandalism and littering.

Technology • • •

In the USA, public wireless Local Area Network (LAN) is widely available. In the UK, talks for public wireless LAN in MSA's first started in 2003 with the first hotspots installations around 2004. This added service may have an effect on the average food and beverage expenditure of customers in MSAs. The longer a business person spends online whilst at an MSA the more likely they will need to purchase food or drinks.

Vending machines

Vending today has become synonymous with selling from a machine. It is also known as 'automatic retailing' or selling from an 'electronic cafeteria' and involves a machine providing the customer with a product in exchange for some form of payment, coins, credit cards, etc. Although vending was in evidence in the UK prior to the Second World War, mainly in the form of chocolate and cigarette machines, it was not until the 1950s that the vending of drinks and snack items really became established in this country. The markets for vended products have grown steadily over the last forty years. In beverage vending, canned drinks, cartons and bottles have shown the greatest increase in growth whilst snack foods have increased the greatest (Table 3.8).

According to Mintel, the value of the vending market grew by 15% between 1999 and 2004 to reach £2.2 billion. However, the market has actually declined by 3% in real terms, although their forecasts show a steady growth both in revenue and numbers of vending machines showing a 5% steady increase. The number of machines increased by 13% over the same period, indicating that the growth in the market can be attributed mainly to the expansion in the number of machines, rather than a rise in the unit value of products.

Factors to consider when outsourcing vending operations to a contractor:

1. No capital outlay for machine – it is supplied by contractor.
2. Some installation costs paid by client, for example water and electricity.
3. Operating costs such as ingredients, commodities, cups, maintenance, cleaning and servicing done by contractor.
4. Selling prices set between client and contractor. Reimbursement costs, direct and indirect to contractor.

Drinks £m		Confectionery/snacks/meals			Total		
		Index	£m	Index	£m	Index	
2004	815	100	640	100	1,455	100	
2005	877	108	682	107	1,559	107	
2006	917	113	726	113	1,643	113	
2007	974	120	767	120	1,741	120	
2008	1,007	124	798	125	1,805	124	
2009	1,045	128	826	129	1,871	129	

At 2004 prices

Drinks £m		Confectionery/snacks/meals			Total		
		Index	£m	Index	£m	Index	
2004	815	100	640	100	1,655	100	
2005	854	105	664	104	1,727	104	
2006	871	107	689	108	1,775	107	
2007	898	110	707	111	1,826	110	
2008	898	110	711	111	1,830	111	
2009	908	111	718	112	1,849	112	

Source: Adapted from Mintel Reports (December 2006)

Table 3.8
Forecast of expenditure on vended products, by sector

The range of vending machine equipment or hardware is divisible into two major groups:

1. *Beverage venders*: Beverage vending machines have accounted for the largest share of vending sales over the last thirty years and consequently their design has been developed further than the food vending machines. This group is discussed in greater depth later in this chapter.
2. *Food vending machines or merchandisers*: Food vending machines may vend a variety of food products – confectionery, snacks, plated meals, etc. and are usually vended in one of three types of machine:
   (a) *Snack machines*: Confectionery, crisps, biscuits, etc. are usually vended from an ambient temperature machine as these items have a relatively long shelf life and do not have any special temperature requirements. Because of these factors, servicing of the machines except for re-stocking purposes, can be kept to a minimum thereby also reducing operating costs.
   (b) *Refrigerated machines*: Snack items such as sandwiches and rolls have a limited shelf life and need to be date-stamped ('sell-by' or 'use by') and vended through a refrigerated machine. Plated foods such as salads, cold meats, etc. must be vended from refrigerated machines where the holding

temperature is between 2°C and 5°C. At this temperature the food may be kept for 2–4 days, although some operations work on a twenty-four hour cycle only.

(c) *Hot meal machines*: Food for a hot vending service may be vended in a number of ways. The first is the heated food vendor which will hold the temperature of the plated food at about 69°C for up to six hours. The second is the hot can vendor which usually offers a choice of items. The selection of hot canned meals, for example soups, baked beans, pasta dishes, casseroles, etc. are held at a temperature of 68°C in the machine without deterioration in the quality of the food. Money is placed into the appropriate slot and the hot can is vended together with a disposable bowl and suitable cutlery to eat the food with; the can is easily opened by the use of a ring pull top. The third involves the use of a microwave oven adjacent to a refrigerated merchandiser. Cooked food is plated by kitchen staff, rapidly cooled and placed into a refrigerated merchandiser; if limited kitchen facilities are available, ready plated or semi-prepared foods may be bought in from a supplier, plated and put in the vending machine. The food is heated when placed in the microwave, which has an automatic timing device for the different foods which begins when a token or code is put into the microwave. The time taken for a meal to be heated thoroughly depends on whether it is a snack item or a full meal. Snack items being heated from a refrigerated state takes between ten and thirty seconds, and a main meal between forty and sixty seconds, depending on the quantity and depth of the food, and the power supply feeding the microwave. The range of products available for hot meal vending is now quite considerable although snacks and sandwiches still account for the largest percentage.

Within each of these groups the type of vending machine used will depend largely on the type of product being vended. For confectionery and pre-packed goods a simple mechanical unit with a drawer at the base of the column is all that is required; it can be free-standing, wall-mounted or be positioned on a fixed surface and does not require any electricity or water supply. Snack and sandwich vending machines require a power supply only and because their products are easily consumed, the machines can be situated outside wards, in the corridors of hotels, etc. close to the customer market. Machines vending plated meals need to be situated close to the kitchen facilities and adjacent to the dining area; some banks of vending machines are sited such that the kitchen is behind the machines for ease of stocking and the dining area is in front of them. These types of machines may be a rotating drum or revolving shelf design whereby a button is pushed rotating or revolving shelves until the required item is reached and then removed through a flap door.

The basic question of whether to use vending machines or not should be taken after careful consideration of the organization's catering and financial policies and an assessment of what vending has to offer. The main advantages associated with vending include the following:

1. *Flexibility*: Vending can provide a twenty-four hour food and beverage service, either alone or in conjunction with other catering services. Customers can use a vending machine when they want to, rather than only when a cafeteria is open.
2. *Situation*: Vending machines can be sited close to the customer market, for example in office corridors, thus reducing workers' time away from the workplace queuing for a snack or drink; customers are also more likely to take a vended drink back to their workplace and consume it there, rather than spend time away from their work, for example in a cafeteria. Satellite vending machines can also be used to serve areas that would not normally benefit from a catering facility; for example, in a large industrial complex, machines can be sited some distance from the main kitchen and dining area.
3. *Quality control*: In terms of quality, vending machines can sell a consistent product, particularly beverages, pre-packed snacks and bought in meals from a supplier. Meals prepared in the kitchen can also be plated under tighter quality and portion control.
4. *Hygiene control*: Reduced handling of vended foods also reduces the possibilities of food contamination. Many beverage machines now also have built-in, self-clean mechanisms.
5. *Operating control*: Labour savings can be made as once cleaned and stocked vending machines should require the minimum of maintenance, thus reducing labour costs. Wastage, pilferage and cash losses should also be negligible.
6. *Speed*: Vending machines can 'sell' products quickly and efficiently, for example a hot chips machine which can vend portions of freshly prepared chips, always giving a standard product, at a standard price.
7. *Sales promotion*: Products for sale in a vending machine can look attractive and stimulate 'impulse purchases', particularly glass-fronted merchandisers (GFMs) displaying fresh fruits, sweets, etc.

The disadvantages associated with using vending include the following:

1. *Impersonality*: Vending machines lack the 'personal touch' and some customers will always prefer to be served food and beverages in the traditional manner rather than from a machine.
2. *Inflexibility of the product*: Initially the range of products available for vending was quite limited; today, however, vending machines offer a much wider selection, and beverages in particular can be highly customized.

3. *Reliability*: One of the major causes of dissatisfaction with vending machines in the past has been that the coin mechanism could become jammed and the machine would give no service. This in turn left the machines open to abuse and vandalism. Since their introduction the vending machines' coin mechanism has been a mechanical device which could be regularly jammed with foreign coins, washers, etc. Today, however, the electronic coin mechanism can detect even the most accurately produced fake coins, which even when fed into the machine, do not jam it. Electronic mechanisms are constantly being improved and are incorporated into the majority of new machines. These electronic mechanisms are also capable of accepting different valued coins, displaying a running total as they are added and of giving change.

4. *Limiting*: For large-scale food and beverage service, vending machines have limitations. In some situations they are best suited as a backup to the main catering services although a bank of vending alleviates queuing and waiting time. They are also of less use in up-market situations, except in the form of mini-bars, for example in hotels.

Financial implications • • •

The vending market is a retail-based operation and profits rely on high volume turnover, however the sector is highly competitive and pricing wars by different vendors may eat into profits.

According to Mintel Reports (2005) in the UK the vending market grew by 15% between 1999 and 2004, the market has actually declined by 3% in real terms, as the slump in the cigarette segment and inflationary pressures slowed year-on-year growth. The number of machines increased by 13% over the same period, indicating that the growth in the market can be attributed mainly to the expansion in the number of machines, rather than a rise in the unit value of products (Table 3.9). However, in the USA it is expected that sales of the vending industry will fall from $14 billion to $12.5 billion by 2010.

Table 3.9
Forecast of the number of vending machines, 2004–2009

Machines (in thousand units)*		Index
2004	770	100
2005	785	102
2006	805	104
2007	820	106
2008	842	109
2009	866	112

Source: Mintel Reports (March 2005)
*Number of machines in circulation

Marketing • • •

The markets available for vended products are varied and numerous and may be grouped into three main areas:

1. The *general market* vending machines and their products may be situated in areas to which the general public largely has access; for example, shopping courts, MSAs, garage forecourts, airports, seaports, ferries, rail and bus terminals, libraries, swimming and leisure centres, stadiums, exhibition centres, cinemas and theatres.
2. The *industrial market* includes those establishments where vending machines are provided for employers and employees in office blocks and shops, factories and sites, etc. Eighty per cent of companies in the UK having installed vending machines at some or all of their premises.
3. The *institutional market* includes establishments such as hospitals and schools, prisons, sports complexes, universities and colleges and more recently hotels, replacing to some extent floor service.

Product and service styles • • •

Vending operates in a very competitive market and a number of developments and market trends may be identified in the vending sector:

1. *Cashless systems*: The development of card operated vending has probably been the most important technological development in vending. The leading supplier of this type of system is Girovend, the main component being a credit card type of pass or card which can record the user's own data; it can be used for personnel control such as security, identity passes, attendance recording, leisure facilities, etc. For catering purposes, customers can buy any food and beverage items from a vending machine by placing their card into the machine instead of cash; their card is then debited with the amount for the items purchased.
   (a) The card first has to be loaded with credit and this can be done in a number of ways. First, supervised loading whereby a supervisor collects customers' cash amounts and loads the cards via a vending machine; the disadvantage to this method is that the handling of cash is still involved and at least one person has to be employed to do this job. Second, customers self-load their own cards with a cash value before making their purchases. By inserting the card into the loader a customer can check its balance and increase the amount by feeding the appropriate money into the machine; this method's disadvantage is that special loaders are required and cash is still handled. Third, is the direct-debit loader linked to the wages department so that a card holder may direct debit different values from his/her salary; in this way cash handling is eliminated completely.

(b) The advantages to the customer of card vending are that it is a convenient method of payment; loose change does not have to be carried, it is not 'lost' in the machine and, overall, a faster service can be given.

(c) The card holders can be divided into user type groups and these categories may then be separated into different price bands. Vending machines payments can be broken into cashless, free-vend and coin operated systems. This enables different charges to be made for the same product, for example for regular employees, temporary staff, free vend for visitors, etc. Cash refunds can be given to users giving up their cards, or money can be paid back into an employee account; machines can also be programmed to stop accepting stolen cards. Finally, the sales information stored in these machines can be printed out by item, price list or type of user, and a comparison between actual and cash loaded on to the cards can be given; such up-to-date information greatly aids financial control and cost accounting.

2. *Mixed product vending*: Where the design of the machine allows, different products may be vended together and complement each other, for example, pre-packed snacks with carton juices together form a substitute for a main meal at certain times of the day. Smaller units, for example vending confectionery, can also be attached to the side of the larger machines and utilize their coin or card mechanism.

3. *Fresh brew vending*: Machines using fresh brew systems for tea and coffee ensure that a better quality end product is dispensed to the customer. In-cup drink machines where the ingredients are already in the cup also offer better hygiene, operation and servicing, control and range of products. Some beverage machines are now capable of offering 100 different selections for both hot and cold drinks and have capacities of up to 1,000 cups.

4. *Space economization*: The efficient utilization of business space in offices, factories, hospitals, industrial units, etc. is of great importance today. This has led many operations to critically review their catering facilities and the space allocated to them, particularly where a twenty-four hour service is needed. In many situations vending is being used as a space and cost saving alternative to installing traditional catering services. Furthermore, the vending manufacturers themselves are aware of the amount of space vending machines need, and are researching ways of reducing their overall size yet at the same time trying to increase the range and quality of products they can offer.

5. *Compatibility with cook-chill*: The cook-chill method of food preparation serves the vending industry well by allowing plated meals to be prepared in advance and vended for later consumption either in a chilled state, for example salads, cold meats, pâtés, etc. or for use in conjunction with some type of heating system, for example microwaves.

Vending has now established itself as a method of food service that may be considered for many types of operations and situations. In some sectors of the catering industry it is employed as a total feeding system, for example staff cafeterias and restrooms, hospital canteens, etc. in others it is an economic alternative to other types of catering service at different times of the day, for example, night shifts in hospitals, twenty-four hour factories, offices, etc.

Staffing • • •

The reduced labour costs is one of the biggest advantages of the vending machines along with the availability of the product. Operators can stock a large number of machines with a very small number of staff and with very little training. However, often, there are hidden costs such as maintenance costs.

Technology • • •

Without advancements in technology vending machines would not exists and similarly if technology did not evolve the consumer would prefer alternative means of purchasing the goods. Today technological advancements in stock control and maintenance have enabled vending machines to become more reliable. Telemetry and on-site hand-held systems have helped to reduce the number of out-of-stock situations, or quickly identify malfunctioning machines. With advancements in Internet technology vending machines can be easily monitored for conditions and levels of stock. Vending machine technology has improved the storage conditions for perishable goods, and has enabled hot food vending.

PUBLIC SECTOR

The public sector has seen growth in prison catering, college and university, and public catering as well as the services. However, catering in schools, healthcare and local authority has been in decline (Table 3.10).

Schools

The school meals catering service was formerly structured on a dietary basis with a daily or weekly per capita allowance to ensure that the children obtained adequate nutritional levels from their meals. Most of the schools used to operate their dining rooms on a family type service or a self-service basis with the traditional 'meat and two veg' lunch being very much the norm. There has been a shift away from this conventional arrangement to the provision of a snack type lunch as an alternative to or replacement for the main meal. Many schools now provide 'snack meals' such as baked potatoes, pizzas, sandwiches, rolls,

	2001		2003		2005		% change 2001–2005
	Number of outlets	%	Number of outlets	%	Number of outlets	%	
Business and industry	9,002	49.2	8,939	48.6	8,973	51	−0.3
• Business and industry	8,344	45.6	8,473	46.1	8,214	46.6	−1.6
• Government and agency[a]	475	2.6	–	–	–	–	–
• Department store staff	59	0.3	347	1.9	597	3.4	911.9
• Prisons	124	0.7	119	0.6	162	0.9	30.6
State education	4,847	26.5	5,027	27.3	4,506	25.6	−7
• School	4,386	24	4,529	24.6	3,960	22.5	−9.7
• College and university	461	2.5	498	2.7	546	3.1	18.4
Independent schools	813	4.4	919	5	754	4.3	−7.3
Catering for the public[b]	1,420	7.8	1,385	7.5	1,553	8.8	9.4
Healthcare	960	5.2	882	4.8	839	4.8	−12.6
• NHS and trust hospitals	455	2.5	465	2.5	369	2.1	−18.9
• Private hospitals	67	0.4	22	0.1	50	0.3	−25.4
• Private nursing homes	438	2.4	395	2.1	420	2.4	−4.1
Ministry of Defence	401	2.2	522	2.8	490	2.8	22.2
Local authority	543	3	477	2.6	291	1.7	−46.4
• Courts	97	0.5	96	0.5	75	0.4	−22.7
• Police and fire	312	1.7	266	1.4	157	0.9	−49.7
• Town hall	116	0.6	90	0.5	40	0.2	−65.5
• Welfare	18	0.1	25	0.1	19	0.1	5.6
Oil rigs, training centres and construction sites	238	1.3	235	1.3	202	1.1	−15.1
Miscellaneous	65	0.4	–	–	–	–	–
Total	18,289	100	18,386	100	17,608	100	−3.7

Source: BHA/Mintel Reports (December 2006)

[a] Change in reporting categories
[b] Excluding all events

Table 3.10
UK contract catering market segments, by number of outlets

pies, soups, yoghurts, etc. and the children may choose from this selection in a normal cafeteria fashion.

Some areas have drastically cut their school meal service and are simply providing dining-room space for the children to bring in their own lunches from home. Whether this trend will continue in the future is debatable. It does seem likely, however, that now introduced, the snack type meal will remain as an alternative to the traditional school meal. Many local education authorities contract out this service to specialist contract caterers. Celebrity Chef Jamie Oliver started his campaign for school dinners in 2005 and his TV programme was quite influential in government circles that promised increases in the school budget to ensure a better quality of food in schools.

Catering in schools is about much more than simply providing meals for students. We are responsible for ensuring that youngsters are educated about food and are provided with the information that they need to help them make good healthy eating choices. It's vital that students are made aware of the importance of maintaining a healthy and balanced diet early on, so that it becomes ingrained behaviour that they follow for the rest of their lives. We aim to show students that good food and healthy eating is fun and interesting through events such live cookery demonstrations in schools and cookery classes for parents and students which enable them to learn some basic hands-on cookery skills. From September 2007, the new school meals standards introduced by the Government last term will come into force for food served in schools other than lunch, so it's important that we can give them a wide range of healthy and appealing choices throughout the day and not just on our lunchtime menus.

Gill Ward, Scolarest Catering Manager at City of Norwich School, Norfolk.

Universities and colleges

All institutions of further and higher education provide some form of catering facilities for the academic, administrative, technical and secretarial staff as well as for full- and part-time students and visitors. The catering service in this sector of the industry suffers from an under-utilization of its facilities during the three vacation periods and in many instances at the weekends.

Universities are autonomous bodies and are responsible for their own catering services. They are, however, publicly accountable for their expenditure to the Higher Education Funding Council for England (HEFCE) which allocates them funds on behalf of the exchequer. The HEFCE's policy on catering allows for a subsidy on capital costs, that is, buildings and equipment, 'landlord's' expenses and rent and rates where applicable. Apart from a few special exemptions to named universities, they are expected to break-even. University catering units have traditionally been of two basic kinds: residential facilities attached to halls that may serve breakfast and evening meals within an inclusive price per term, and central facilities that are open to all students and staff and usually serve lunches and snacks throughout the day with beverages. These catering facilities have to compete openly with the students' union services and independently staffed senior common rooms (Figure 3.11).

Figure 3.11
University catering. Photo
courtesy of Scolarest

Residential students pay in advance for their board and lodg-
ings. This method has been abandoned by many universities in
recent years who have provided reasonable kitchen facilities in
the residences to enable students to prepare and cook their own
meals if they wish to. Others have introduced a pay-as-you-eat
system for residential students. Unfortunately, this has led to
reduced catering revenue from students.

Non-residential students are provided with an on-site catering
provision that has to compete against all other forms of locally
provided catering, with ease of accessibility and some level of
subsidy being the main attractions. Increasingly, caterers are
turning to ideas from the high street operations to attract and
keep their predominantly young adult clientele.

To offset the losses incurred and to achieve a position of
break-even in catering, universities have seen the advantages of
making their residential and catering facilities available at commercial rates to outside bodies for meetings, conferences and for
holidays during the vacation periods.

Activity 3

Identify all catering outlets and functions in your university/college.
Does an in-house team deliver catering or is it outsourced to a
contract caterer?
Analyse the strengths and weaknesses of catering provision in
your university.

Hospitals

Hospital catering facilities have improved considerably over the
past ten to twenty years with the result that new hospitals in particular are benefiting from well planned and managed catering

services. Hospital catering is a specialized form of catering as the patient is normally unable to move elsewhere and choose alternative facilities and therefore special attention must be given to the food and beverages so that encouragement is given to eat the meal provided.

The hospital catering service is normally structured on a per capita allowance for patients but with staff paying for all of their meals. A decentralized approach was used in many hospitals where the patients' food and beverages were portioned at the point of delivery in the wards. This often resulted however, in patients receiving cold, unappetizing meals because of the time between the food being prepared and the patients actually receiving it. This method of food service is commonly replaced by a centralized approach that involves the preparation of the patients' trays in or close to the main production area. From here they are transported by trucks or mechanical conveyors to the various floors, and from there directly to the patients so that there should be little delay between the food being plated and served to the patient.

Another trend has seen hospital catering open for tender by contract caterers where in many instances a centralized production system for several nearby hospitals may have to be operated to be viable.

In May 2001, the Better Hospital Food initiative was launched. The programme's aims were to:

- produce a comprehensive range of tasty, nutritious and interesting recipes that every NHS hospital could use;
- re-design hospital printed menus to make them more accessible and easier to understand;
- introduce twenty-four hour catering services to ensure food is available night and day;
- ensure hot food is available in hospitals at both mid-day and early evening mealtimes.

Perhaps evidence that caterers are committed on improving the catering of the healthcare sector can be seen at the Hospital Caterers Association, at a recent (26 April 2007) conference programme. The catering experience and food nutrition are prominent subjects as well as cultural and environmental issues in hospital catering (hospitalcaterers.org).

The services

The services include the armed forces: the Royal Navy, Army and Royal Air Force; the police and fire service; and some government departments. The armed forces often have their own specialist catering branches, for example the army catering is provided by the Royal Logistics Corp. Civil service organizations such as the Metropolitan Police force also have their own catering departments. The levels of food and beverage facilities within the services vary from the large self-service cafeterias for

Kevan Wallace MIOH, Assistant Hotel Services Manager Catering, Frimley Park Hospital NHS Foundation Trust gives his insights in catering in hospitals.

The pace of change in hospital catering has been fast. Over the past six years, we have seen the introduction of several initiatives, the best known being Better Hospital Food. This has been largely successful and has achieved much. The spotlight has been firmly on catering in the NHS, whether by contractor or by in-house teams. More attention has been paid to the quality of the food provided to patients. Not only that, but the patient environment is now also a major focus, making meals and mealtime much more a part of the healing process. Protected mealtimes, in-ward and housekeeper facilities can really make a difference to patients on the road to recovery.

It is always a challenge to meet targets set by individual trusts and government, but caterers in the NHS take great pride in what they achieve. The team at Frimley Park Hospital NHS Foundation Trust has recently been awarded Hospitality Assured at their first attempt, and they are only the second in the south-east to have achieved this.

the majority of personnel, to high-class traditional restaurants for more senior members of staff. A considerable number of functions are also held by the services leading to both small- and large-scale banqueting arrangements.

Prisons

There are over 9 million people detained in penal institutions around the world and over 2 million of them are held in US institutions whilst over 1.5 million in China. The population of detainees in all penal institutions in England and Wales is more than 75,000 and continues to grow. Working on a very limited budget, the diet for the inmates is based upon fixed weekly quantities of specific named food commodities with a small weekly cash allowance per head for fresh meat and a further separate weekly cash allowance per head for the local purchase

Figure 3.12
Prison catering. Photo courtesy of Northern Ireland Prison Service (*Source*: http://www.niprisonservice.gov.uk)

of dietary extras of which a proportion must be spent on fresh fruit. The catering within the prisons is the responsibility of the prison governor with delegated responsibility being given to a catering officer, with much of the actual cooking and service being done by the inmates themselves (Figure 3.12).

Summary

In this chapter we explored:

- Contract catering
- Catering in travel
- Catering in the public sector
- Trends in each sector
- An overview of the range of types of catering
- Major differences and similarities between the various operations
- Management challenges in contract catering.

Review questions

1. What are the key differences between travel catering and public sector?
2. What are the production and service styles commonly used in event catering?
3. What are the key subsectors of travel catering?
4. List the key differences between sport venue catering and leisure venue catering.
5. List the key differences between catering in the public sector and industrial catering.

Further study options

Case study: The big day

Juliana and Victor decided on their big day and wanted to have a wedding reception that everyone would remember. They had decided on a Pirates of the Caribbean theme for the reception and wanted their menu to reflect the theme. Money was no object and lobster and caviar would feature as well as oysters and champagne to get the party started. When they approached Franco the Hotel Banqueting Manager he assured them that in their resort they would find everything they needed and his staff would make sure that the day was a success. The couple had identified a small island about

10 miles away from the resort and wanted to hold the main reception there.

Although Franco and his team had never catered outside the resort, Franco decided that he could not let this function slip his hands. With 200 guests and an average expenditure of £40 per cover he decided he would caterer for this function at all costs.

Getting the food and beverage to the island proved to be a difficult task but with the help of his staff Franco and his team were ready for the event, although Franco was slightly worried that he did not have the right equipment to keep all the food at the correct temperatures. Nevertheless the reception proved to be a success and the couple were overjoyed.

However, two days after the event 46 of the guests were ill with food poisoning. The results from the local hospital will be out tomorrow but everyone suspects it was the oysters and the hotel is getting a lot of bad publicity.

Q1: If you were Franco what would you have done prior to the event to ensure no risks were taken?

Q2: Now that the resort is getting bad publicity, what would you advise Franco to do?

Further reading

Bernstein, D. (2005). When the Sous Chef is an Inkjet. *New York Times*, (February 3). http://www.nytimes.com/2005/02/03/technology/circuits/03chef.html/ (last accessed 10th March 2008).

Brewin Dolphin http://www.brewindolphin.co.uk/ (accessed 2nd November 2006).

British Hospitality Association http://www.bha.org.uk/ (accessed 20th October 2006).

Durocher, J. (2001). Unplugged. *Restaurant Business (January 1)*, 100(1), 79–80.

Feinstein, A.H. and Stefanelli, J.M. (1999). Technology applications in foodservice purchasing: A primer for foodservice marketers. *Journal of Restaurant and Foodservice Marketing*, 3(2), 3–22. The Haworth Press.

Hospitalcaterers.org. http://www.hospitalcaterers.org/conference/programme.html (accessed 21st April 2007).

Karel, M. (2000). Tasks of food technology in the 21st century. *Food Technology (June)*, 54(6), 56–58. 60, 62, 64

Kühn, K. (2007). *Delaware to name new Wembley executive chef*, Caterer and Hotelkeeper, http://www.caterersearch.com/Articles/2007/04/12/312855/delaware-to-name-new-wembley-executive-chef.html (accessed 21April 2007).

Mintel Reports, Cars – UK – September 2004: http://reports.mintel.com/ (accessed 21st April 2007).

Mintel Reports, Vending UK – March 2005: http://reports.mintel.com/ (accessed 21st April 2007).

Mintel Reports, Cruises – International – September 2005: http://reports.mintel.com/ (accessed 21st April 2007).

Mintel Reports, World's Leading Outbound Markets – December 2005: http://reports.mintel.com/ (accessed 21st April 2007).

Mintel Reports, Contract Catering – UK – December 2006: http://reports.mintel.com/ (accessed 21st April 2007).

Mintel Reports, Leisure Venue Catering – UK – March 2007: http://reports.mintel.com/ (accessed 21st April 2007).

Mintel Reports, Onboard Catering – UK – May 2007: http://reports.mintel.com/ (accessed 21st April 2007).

Narprail.org.http://www.narprail.org/cms/images/uploads/FB_Econ_Final.pdf (accessed 19th April 2007).

World Stadiums http://www.worldstadiums.com (accessed 10th April 2007).

Developing the concept

Introduction

Starting a new business can be a daunting task for any food and beverage manager/entrepreneur. In London, UK there are around 100–120 closures per year in 2002 to 2003 although these reduced to 60–65 in times of high economic growth such as 2005 and 2006 and although the numbers for new restaurant openings are countering the closures (Akbar, 2007), one can not help but wonder why so many establishments close, often within one or two years of their operation. The answer could very well be that many investors fail to understand their market and often they rush into an investment without ensuring that the potential is there. Often they allow their 'Gut Feeling' to lead their business decisions without taking any steps to minimize the risks involved. It is important that the market is understood and that an initial investment is undertaken to ensure that the much larger investment into the project will be justified. Understanding the first steps that are needed to take in starting a new restaurant will give the reader an insight into the food and beverage business and the key issues that need to be taken into consideration. This chapter aims to give an initial understanding of some of the tools available to prospective food and beverage managers and how current managers approach a new operation (Table 4.1).

Chapter objectives

After working through this chapter you should be able to:

- Have an understanding of a restaurant feasibility study.
- Understand the main parts of a restaurant business plan.
- Have a basic understanding of ways that an operation can be financed.
- Have a basic knowledge of facility design and layout.

Company	Brand name	Number of outlets 2002	Number of outlets 2004	Number of outlets 2006	Change 2002–2006
Bank Restaurant group	Zinc Bar & Grill	4	6	5	1
	Individually named	3	3	3	–
Caprice Holdings Ltd/Richard caring	Individually named	7	6	8	1
Clapham House Group	Gourmet Burger Kitchen	–	–	9	–
	Real Greek	–	–	6	–
	Bombay Bicycle Club (restaurants)	–	–	3	–
Conran Restaurants	Individually named	18	18	19	1
Craftbutton– Paramount plc	Caffé Uno	63	61	53	−10
	Chez Gérard/ Le Petit				
	Chez Gérard/ Brasserie				
	Chez Gérard	13	11	14	1
	Livebait	9	5	4	−5
	Bertorelli/Café Bertorelli	3	3	6	3
	Café Fish	1	1	1	–
Gaucho Grill Restaurants	Gaucho Grill	7	7	7	–
	Destino	–	1	1	–

Table 4.1

Examples of main restaurant operations, by outlet numbers

Company	Brand name	Number of outlets 2002	Number of outlets 2004	Number of outlets 2006	Change 2002–2006
La Tasca Restaurants	La Tasca	17	35	53	36
	La Viña	–	–	3	–
Living Ventures	Est Est Est	22	19	17	−5
	The living room	–	–	13	–
	The bar and grill	–	–	2	–
Loch Fyne Restaurants	Loch Fyne	17	23	25	8
	Le Petit Blanc	–	4	5	–
Ma Potters	MA Potters bar and restaurant	–	–	8	–
	Ma Potters Chargrill	–	–	7	–
Mitchells & Butlers	Browns	13	15	15	2
Noble House Leisure	Yellow River Café	7	8	7	–
	Oriental Restaurant Group	7	6	7	–
	Arbuckles	–	21	11	–
	Jim Thompson's (JT's)	–	14	10	–
Punch Taverns plc (formerly the Spirit Group)	Old Orleans	35	31	33	−2
Rank	Hard Rock Cafe	6	8	7	1
The Restaurant Group	Frankie & Benny's	67	86	105	38
	Garfunkel's	33	30	30	−3
	Chiquito's	26	25	29	3
	Blubeckers	–	–	17	–
	Edwinns Brasseries	–	–	5	–
Town Centre Restaurant Group	Auberge	–	8	9	–
	Azzurro	–	5	4	–
Tragus Holdings	Café Rouge	–	–	82	–
	Abbaye	–	–	3	–
	Oriel	–	–	1	–
	Leadenhall Wine bar	–	–	1	–
Urban Dining Group	Tootsies	–	–	30	–
Whitbread	T.G.I. Friday's	40	41	46	6

Source: Mintel, 2006

Table 4.1
Continued

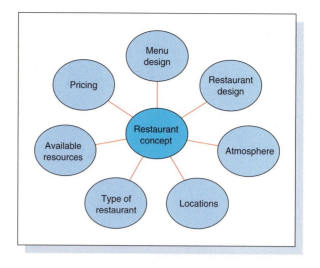

Figure 4.1
Key restaurant concept considerations

THE CONCEPT

Restaurants are businesses that require a creative flair and passion, a good concept is often what separates success from failure. Sometimes the concept will become apparent only after the feasibility study is conducted, but most often the future restaurateur has a good idea as to what she wants to achieve, based on his/her experience and available talent.

The problem arises if the restaurateur is so engrossed in his/her concept that even if the feasibility study clearly shows that the concept is unlikely to work in a particular location they go ahead anyway. There are many examples of concepts that although successful with their first operation they then branched out and found failure when trying to establish a chain of restaurants. For example, the cases of Fish! and Chez Gerard, with extremely successful original concepts they expanded too quick and have had to close a number of their restaurants. A good restaurateur must always keep an eye on the pulse of the market and plan ahead before making key decisions that will affect the business whilst remaining flexible enough to be able to respond to sudden market changes (Figure 4.1).

In choosing a concept there are three primary categories.

1. Restaurants that rely on low margins but high volume of sales (fast food, takeaways, etc).
2. Mid-scale restaurants that offer a full meal but at relatively low prices.
3. Upscale restaurants that rely on high margins (see Michelin star restaurants).

Furthermore, the restaurant may be themed with food from a particular ethnicity such as Chinese, Japanese, Korean, Italian, Greek, Mexican, Caribbean, English, French, German, Indian and Thai to name a few. In the UK, the two most popular Ethnic type of food is Chinese and Indian (Mintel).

The Acorn House Restaurant is a great example of a restaurant concept development focusing on sustainability

Waste management, water usage and energy costs are the three biggest challenges we face today in restaurant management. Governments will charge more and more for commercial waste, it is therefore imperative that we find new and innovative ways to ensure wastage is minimized.

Water is the most underrated resource in our industry. In the future water costs will probably rise to such a degree that it will have a detrimental effect on restaurant profit margins. Restauranteurs should think ahead and manage their water usage effectively, today.

Energy costs will continue to rise and energy efficient restaurants will not be a luxury but a necessity in the near future.

At Acorn House Restaurant (AHR) we carefully consider our suppliers, our use of water and energy, as well as our waste management and the transport of our goods. What we do should not be considered special or different; we are doing what is obvious in conserving the environment whilst still running a successful business.

Arthur Potts Dawson
Co-Director Bliss Restaurant Consultancy
Executive Chef Acorn House Restaurant

Gaps in the market are always a good place to start when considering the concept you wish to develop in the area. If for example, your local area has a good number of Chinese restaurants, you might wish to consider an alternative location or change your theme completely. Restaurant owners tend to consider how formal or informal they want their establishment to be. Then decide on creating the right atmosphere by carefully considering not only the interior design of the restaurant but the menu items featured for the furniture and cutlery crockery used as well as lighting, the acoustics and type of music of the restaurant may feature. Another important consideration is that of selling alcoholic beverages. This decision not only affects the overall feel of the restaurant but also the kind of license the restauranteur will need to possess. The Menu is the next key decision and Chapter 6 covers the Menu in some detail. Pricing is of course of paramount importance as overpriced menu items or menu items that offer no profit may set the business in a difficult financial position. One final decision is whether the restaurant will offer takeaway or delivery service. For some restaurants food deliveries often match revenue generated by sit in customers.

Activity 1

Identify all major Ethnic restaurants in your local area.

Ask a minimum of five of your friends/colleagues about any Ethnic restaurants they have visited in the last year.

Is their answer what you expected given the number of Ethnic restaurants

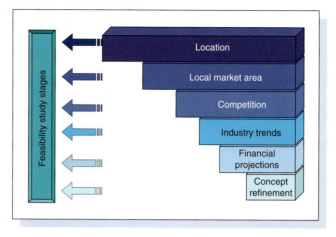

Figure 4.2
The feasibility study

FEASIBILITY STUDY

A key tool to help to reach the decision as to whether a concept is likely to be a success or not is the feasibility study. A feasibility study is a document that is developed after the restaurateur has studied the market and analysed the economy so that he/she has a good knowledge of the environment that the business is proposed to be developed in and the expected return on the investment.

Although there are many guides about conducting feasibility studies the key areas that need to be covered remain largely the same. Here we propose an approach to the feasibility study from the specific to the more generic. Since the most difficult and time consuming task can be the collection of data, starting with the location might save valuable time and resources (Figure 4.2.)

Location

There are two major questions that any future restaurateur wishes to address. What type of restaurant should I open? Where do I open it? The first question is often addressed and redefined by the completion of the feasibility study and the answer to the second question can be the difference between success and failure. Committing resources to a specific site simply because it has a surprisingly low lease without considering the market or the compatibility of the location to concept is a mistake made far too often.

No matter how great the concept of a restaurant is, if it is not accessible it can easily be an empty restaurant. For example, during peak summer times potential customers would prefer to walk in the side of the street that offers shadow if the restaurant is positioned at the wrong side of the road customers would not even consider stopping to look at the menu. A restaurant with limited or no parking that requires a long walk could deter potential customers. Disabled access must also be considered as well as how close the restaurant is to major streets.

A restaurant must also be visible, many restaurants rely on walk in business, if the restaurant cannot be seen or it is hard to find it will be very hard to build a base market for it. Ensuring that signs can be put up to guide potential customers is important. External lighting that both attracts and guides the customer is essential. The building appearance can be a deterrent or an attraction.

How close is the restaurant to potential business sources such as offices, hospitals or hotels as well as how close to potential competitors. It is a good idea to project potential customers by market segment based on distance from the restaurant. The traffic volume can also be a key factor so looking out for traffic and pedestrian patterns as well as identifying peak and off-peak periods is useful.

There are other considerations such as future developments in the area, safety environmental issues and restrictions to name a few. It is important that a complete profile of the location and the immediate area is constructed to ensure that the site is a good match for the type of restaurant intended.

Local market area

Having the location in mind makes it easier to define the geographic size of the market. Overestimating the amount of miles potential customers are willing to travel to get to the business is a common mistake. It is often better to have a pessimistic approach rather than an over optimistic. The next step involves obtaining demographic data about the people that reside or work in the area specified. Demographics such as age, gender, education and income as well as business growth trends, tourist visits, etc. can be obtained through local champers of commerce, business development centres, market reports and local economic development agencies. See Chapter 9 for more on this topic.

Consultancy firms often produce reports that illustrate dining out behaviour and preferences such as menu item preference, dining frequency, preferred restaurants, etc. Such reports can help to understand the economic characteristics of the population and further refine the concept.

Competition

Analysing the competition enables to analyse the demand and opportunities in the market. A common mistake is to only analyse restaurants that fit the particular concept. So a fast-food operator might be tempted to cut corners and only analyse similar operations in the market and avoid investigating other type of restaurants. It is important to remember that each restaurant is competing for customers disposable income and disposable time therefore all food and beverage operators no matter what their concept is will affect the business. By visiting existing restaurants one can gain access to valuable information such as the type of menu offered, quality of food and service, pricing policies and even estimate the turnover of the competitor. How many of your competitors are independently owned and how many are part of a chain that can affect your profitability. Chain restaurants, for example, will have an opportunity to lower prices as economies of scale enable them to buy goods at lower rates. How well can one compete if the same product it offered by a competitor at a far lower price? It is important to also look out for restaurant reviews in the local press or travel guides the reputation the restaurant may have. Existing restaurants are not the only ones one must consider. Recent restaurant closures should be investigated and trying to find the reasons behind the closures will give an insight to the local market. Also any information about future competitors can be extremely important. If for example, you were expecting to be the only seafood restaur-ant in town but you find that such concepts have opened and closed before or that such a restaurant will be opening soon just a few streets away from your location, you may decide to either find a new location, or rethink the concept.

Industry trends

Industry trends can help realize early on potential threats or opportunities that might exist. For example, in times of high economic growth the industry might enjoy higher turnovers as people will tend to eat out more often. It is important to look at how the market demand has been developing over the past three to five years, what types of restaurants seem to be doing well. What trends are there in customer eating and drinking habits? We may see a move away from junk food to healthy eating or an increase in the market segment for vegetarians or vegans. There may be new developments in areas such as food production, customer service, pricing, government regulations to name a few. For example, if you wanted to open an Organic restaurant somewhere in

Jane Renton, General Manager of the Jumeirah Lowndes Hotel, comments on how the smoking ban in the UK influenced the design of their Mimosa Bar and Restaurant.

We recently (November 2006) launched Jumeirah Lowndes Hotel after an £8.5 million renovations project. As the smoking ban of all pubs and private members' clubs in England will affect many hospitality business, it was important for us to retain an al fresco theme for our Mimosa Bar and Restaurant. Our focus is on fresh, seasonal ingredients with vibrant colours and clean flavours. The theme works as Mimosa's most coveted tables are our outdoors tables, where guests can relax and soak up the cosmopolitan atmosphere on Lowndes Square.

Europe you would have to abide with the EU regulations that enable you to use the label 'Organic'.

Financial projections

Once all the data is collected and location, market, competition and industry has been analysed the restaurateur is ready to make some projections to estimate the business turnover and be more specific about expected numbers in areas such as customer average expenditure, number of covers and potential costs.

It is advisable to look at financial projections using weekly, monthly and annual projections as seasonality will affect the business and splitting the year to a number of seasons will make it easier to forecast more accurately. Restaurants are easily affected also by the day of the week, often a restaurant will find that a particular day is the busiest whilst another might be the quiet day. For a new restaurant this might be hard to predict although competitor analysis should have helped. If the restaurant is an existing one historical data makes it easier to do forecasts.

Existing restaurants may wish to do a feasibility study if they consider expanding the business or wish to open a second or third operation.

Refining the concept

The information gained so far will enable the restaurateur to evaluate the business idea and come to conclusions as to whether it is a feasible operation or not. The concept can then be rejected or refined in order to achieve better returns on the investment.

Jones and Merricks (1994) categorize concept development in food service as new concepts, concepts that although not new are entering a market for the first time, modified concepts to provide greater consumer satisfaction, repositioned concepts that target new market segments and extended concepts that aim to appeal to a wider market segment. The key to the concept is customer preference and for most type of concepts this can be relatively easy to predict, however for brand new concepts that have never been tested before it may not be as easy. Often with a new concept the consumer may not know that it would prefer such a product so although asking the consumer may yield negative results, when the product is actually offered it can be found that the consumer actually likes the product.

THE BUSINESS PLAN

The business plan is a document that spells out a company's expected course of action for a specified period, usually including a detailed listing and analysis of risks and uncertainties. For the small business, it examines the proposed products, the market, the industry, the management policies, the marketing policies, production needs and financial needs. It is worth noting that often there is confusion between a restaurant feasibility

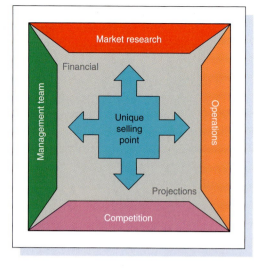

Figure 4.3
Elements of a restaurant
business plan

study and the business plan, this may be so because a number of information that become apparent in the feasibility study will then be used in the development of the business plan. In the business plan the manager addresses significant issues that have been identified in the feasibility study and states how he/she is going to address them.

Who will be reading the business plan can have an effect on how it is written, although the key information remains the same, there is emphasis in different sections of the plan if the operator goes for bank financing (debt finance) as opposed to investors (equity finance). A bank may be looking for a solid plan and assets that will ensure repayments of the loan whilst potential investors may be looking for high returns on investment.

A well-developed business plan makes all the difference when approaching potential investors (Figure 4.3). Investors and lenders will request a copy of the business plan and it is often one of the key tools that helps them make a decision as to whether they will invest or not. The heart of a good business plan is the unique differentiation point. The key innovation that makes the business stand out and ensures potential investors will consider financing the business. The following sections illustrate the main parts of a business plan.

Executive summary

Although this section is the very first of a business plan, it is always a good idea for this to be written last so that it includes all the key points that the operator wishes to put across to potential investors. Most investors will spend no more than five minutes considering a proposal and if the executive summary fails to capture their imagination then it is certain that they will not attempt to read further into the document. The key areas that a good executive summary explores are the company name, the type of restaurant, its unique selling point, the growth of the market and recent trends, the management team and its strengths, financing requirements and projections, how the funds will be used and an outline of the operations and projected return on investment.

Restaurant concept description

The second part of the business plan provides a more detailed overview of the company and the nature of the product/service offering. Typically a sample menu is included. It often includes the history of the concept development the restaurants proposed legal form, for example will it be a limited company, a partnership or single ownership and a mission statement. A time line of key events, for example, how long it will take to have the operation up and running. The description of the concept, and any advantages the concept may have over the competition.

Market analysis

In this section, the information that was gathered in the feasibility study can be utilized. The location can be described, the local market can be defined and analysed, as well as industry trends and actual and potential competition. Any market threats that have been identified should be included here. Potential investors or lenders expect to see an analysis of the weaknesses as well as the strengths, and no weaknesses could mean that the plan is overoptimistic and the researchers may have missed critical information.

PESTLE analysis

Another tool that is often used is the analysis of the external environment to the organization is the PESTLE. The acronym stands for Political, Economic, Social, Technological, Legal and Environmental issues and factors that must be taken into consideration when developing the business plan. This particular tool enables the user to see the bigger picture when deciding how to proceed with their restaurant. Here is a list of some issues under each heading that readers may wish to consider, these are just examples and the lists are far from conclusive but will help the reader further understand the use of the PESTLE tool.

- Political issues (Government policies, Local council and trading policies, Terrorism, War, Political trends).
- Economic (Oversees economy strength, Home economy strength, Local economy strength, Inflation, Distribution trends, Taxation, Unemployment rates).
- Social (Lifestyle changes, Consumer behaviour changes, Population changes, Demographics).
- Technological (New and emerging technologies, Innovative technologies, Communication technologies, Production technologies, Service technologies).
- Legal (Local and country legislation, International or EU legislation, Licensing legislation, Employment law, Environmental legislation).
- Environmental (Sustainability issues, International and local regulations, Consumer attitudes).

	Positive	Negative
Internal	*Strengths* Reputation Strong customer base Unique menu	*Weaknesses* Low profit margins High employee turnover
External	*Opportunities* Open another outlet Future major conference	*Threats* New competitor Change in legislation

Table 4.2

Example of a Restaurant
SWOT analysis

SWOT analysis

Often the strengths, weaknesses, opportunities and threats (SWOT) of the proposed operation will be analysed as part of the market planning process. SWOT involves a systematic analysis of all aspects of the operation, both internally and externally. Strengths and weaknesses are often referred to as internal, opportunities and threats as external.

Taking a fast-food operation as an example, one of its inherent strengths may be a product's quality: customers know that from one purchase to another, they will always receive the same standard quality product. A weakness, however, may be in the limited menu choice available, or the design of the take-away packaging which does not keep the food at the correct temperature for a long enough time. Opportunities may exist for the extension of the menu range by offering additional products, sauces and accompaniments without having the need to purchase additional capital intensive production equipment, or to seek new and more efficient packaging within specific cost standards. Threats may be in the form of competition from other fast-food operators, or from a dramatic increase in the cost of a major raw material item to the operation, which would affect the cost of the product to the customer and the sales mix to the operation.

SWOT's use as a management tool is in its comprehensive analysis of all aspects of an organization. It would, therefore, include a detailed review of all the marketing functions discussed in Chapter 9, and in particular in the formulation of the marketing mix (Table 4.2).

The management team

This is an important section to investors and lenders. How strong the management team is will greatly affect their decision. If for example, Gordon Ramsey would approach a bank for funding of a new venture his profile alone may be an asset strong enough for the bank to finance the operation. It is important that this section illustrates that the management team can effectively run the business and that their collective experience can guarantee a successful project. This is the section where the background of the management team members is illustrated, the experience they have in the field of food and beverage management and what their responsibilities are in this particular project. The organizational structure is illustrated, the type of ownership of the business and who will be in the board of directors, and their experience.

Operations

This part of the plan establishes how the operation will be run and will illustrate the strategies required to implement the business plan. Associated costs will become apparent here as well as service style and standards, production standards and quality control. More specifically the operations plan includes a marketing strategy, a production plan, a service plan, personnel description and customer support.

Business threats

Potential threats that may affect the company are disclosed. By disclosing such possibilities, the restaurateur is letting the reader know up-front that there are risks associated with the business. Potential investors appreciate such honesty and expert businessmen will expect business risks been included in the business plan as a norm. Some of the areas that should be covered are external and internal threats, insurance provisions and contingency plans.

Financial projections

If the business does not make sense financially then there would be no reason as to why one should invest. The financial reports should show a good understanding of the business and its viability. New businesses can also show forecasts but existing companies should also show three to five years of previous actual data. The expected financial statements are normally a profit and loss statement, statement of cash flow and a balance sheet (Figures 4.4 and 4.5). Forecasts are shown in no less than five years. Financial projections are available by month, quarter and annual reports. A break-even analysis is also normally included.

Appendix

In this section, the restaurateur normally includes any supporting information that should be made available to the reader. Examples of such information can be competitor menus, primary data collected such as customer completed questionnaires, examples of menu, promotional materials and advertisements.

FINANCING THE OPERATION

Depending on the size of the business and the experience of the management team there can be a number of avenues available to

(Sterling in millions)	2007	2006	2005
OPERATING ACTIVITIES			
Net Income	£479	£400	£390
Adjustments to reconcile to cash provided by operations:			
Depreciation and amortization	195	162	140
Income taxes	133	87	76
Timeshare activity, net	−195	−102	28
Other	48	19	−22
Working capital changes:			
Accounts receivable	−53	−126	−104
Inventories	−4	−17	15
Other current assets	28	−38	−16
Accounts payable and accruals	219	326	98
Cash provided by operations	850	711	605
INVESTING ACTIVITIES			
Capital expenditures	−1,095	−929	−937
Acquisitions	–	−61	−48
Dispositions	742	436	332
Loan advances	−389	−144	−48
Loan collections and sales	93	54	169
Other	−377	−143	−192
Cash used in investing activities	−1,026	−787	−724
FINANCING ACTIVITIES			
Commercial paper, net	46	355	426
Issuance of long-term debt	338	366	868
Repayment of long-term debt	−26	−63	−473
Redemption of convertible subordinated debt	-	−120	-
Issuance of Class A common stock	58	43	15
Dividends paid	−55	−52	−37
Purchase of treasury stock	−340	−354	−398
Advances (to) from Old Marriott	-	-	−100
Cash provided by financing activities	21	175	301
(DECREASE) INCREASE IN CASH AND EQUIVALENTS	−155	99	182
CASH AND EQUIVALENTS, beginning of year	489	390	208
CASH AND EQUIVALENTS, end of year £	334 £	489 £	390

USAR

Summary Statement of Income
The Tsolias Taverna
For the year ended December 31, 2007

Sales:		
Food	1,045,800	75.85%
Beverage	333,000	24.15%
Total Sales	1,378,800	100.00%
Cost of Sales:		
Food	448,000	32.49%
Beverage	85,200	6.18%
Total Cost of Sales	533,200	38.67%
Other Income	5,100	0.37%
Gross Profit	850,700	61.70%
Operating Expenses:		
Salaries and Wages	332,200	24.09%
Employee Benefits	57,440	4.17%
Direct Operating Expenses	88,440	6.41%
Music and Entertainment	14,200	1.03%
Marketing	30,000	2.18%
Utility Servises	37,560	2.72%
General and Administrative Expenses	56,400	4.09%
Repairs and Maintenance	28,600	2.07%
Occupancy Costs	82,200	5.96%
Depreciation	31,200	2.26%
Total Operating Expenses	758,240	54.99%
Operating Income	92,460	6.71%
Interest	21,600	1.57%
Income Before Income Taxes	70,860	5.14%
Income Taxes	24,801	1.80%
Net Income	46,059	3.34%

Figure 4.4 Example of an income statement and a cash flow statement

End of December, 2007 and December, 2006	2007	2006
(Sterling in millions)		
Assets		
Current assets		
Cash and equivalents £	334 £	489
Accounts and notes receivable	728	740
Inventories, at lower of average cost or market	97	93
Prepaid taxes	197	220
Other	59	58
	1,415	1,600
Property and equipment	3,241	2,845
Intangible assets	1,833	1,820
Investments in affiliates	747	294
Notes and other receivables	661	473
Other	340	292
£	8,237 £	7,324
Liabilities and Shareholders' Equity		
Current liabilities		
Accounts payable £	660 £	628
Accrued payroll and benefits	440	399
Self-insurance	27	36
Other payables and accruals	790	680
	1,917	1,743
Long-term debt	2,016	1,676
Self-insurance	122	142
Other long-term liabilities	915	855
Shareholders' equity		
ESOP preferred stock	-	-
Class A common stock, 255.6 million shares issued	3	3
Additional paid-in capital	3,590	2,738
Retained earnings	851	508
Unearned ESOP shares	−679	-
Treasury stock, at cost	−454	−305
Accumulated other comprehensive income	−44	−36
	3,267	2,908
£	8,237 £	7,324

Figure 4.5
Example of a balance sheet

finance a restaurant. Here we briefly explore some possibilities, although this is not an exhaustive list it aims to give an idea to the reader as to the potential possibilities for financing a restaurant operation.

Commercial bank loans

Getting a bank loan especially if the restauranteur does not have a proven track record can be very difficult. Nevertheless a good business plan most certainly helps. It is may often be the case of managers visiting a number of bank managers before getting a positive response. In cases where this is a loan to fund a second property, having a track record makes thinks easier. If the operator already runs one or two successful restaurants, chances of receiving a bank loan increase. The problem with commercial bank loans is that if the business does not do well you will still have to pay back the loan whilst with investors who purchase equity on the business they share the risk. The advantage of the commercial bank loan is that if the business is a success the restauranteur can still have full control of the business.

Small business grants and loans

There are various opportunities for alternative sources of funding for small businesses for example, the 'Early Growth Fund' a programme that was developed to encourage risk funding for startups and growth firms. It makes available to successful applicants an average of £50,000 another interesting source of funding is the Small Firms Loan Guarantee which considers businesses with viable business plans but was unsuccessful in securing a conventional loan due to lack of assets (Department of Trade and Industry: dti.gov.uk).

As another example, in the US a small business restaurateur has the opportunity to get an Small Business Administration (SBA) loan. To qualify for a such a loan, the restaurateur must first be rejected for a traditional loan. Individual franchisees of large corporations also can be considered as small businesses. The SBA would look for detailed evidence that the operator is able to repay the loan.

Activity 2

Identify at least two potential sources of funding for a 50 cover restaurant in your local area.

What would you need to do to ensure that you stand the best chance of getting funding from your identified sources?

Investors

Attracting investors can be hard but it can be a good way of financing the first operation. Good networking is crucial and often the new restaurateur would seek small investments from a larger number of investors. Investors can offer a loan but more often they will buy equity in the business and a good business structure would ensure that the restaurateur still has control of the business. Investment banks can also be a source of funding but often they will only consider established restauranteurs.

Partnerships

A partnership may be a good way of raising capital but the potential partner should be aware of all the risks involved. There is a number of positive outcomes from having a business partner. For example, the risks and responsibility is shared, other strengths are brought in to the company, often partners will feed of each other in terms of ideas and develop solutions that would otherwise go unnoticed. It is imperative that the terms of the partnership are laid out well in advance because if a partnership turns sour the litigation costs to break up the partnership can be very high. Often friendships may end due to the strain the business may put on them, either because of conflict of interest or because of one partner underperforming.

Personal finances

A personal loan, such as a home-equity loan can provide supplemental funding. Personal savings, Individual retirement (Ira) accounts, Credit cards could be sources of part financing a project. Personal loans may often carry a high interest rate and the added risk of loosing, personal assets.

Venture capital

Well-established restaurateurs may consider the possibility of a venture-capital firm willing to invest. Such firms invest significant funds in companies in which they foresee major expansion. Compared with other investors, venture-capital firms usually require a much greater partnership and will help determine the company's direction. They expect to see a large return of their investment within about five years.

Franchise

A franchise can be a good business set up in ensuring funding. A good franchisor will have a positive impact in the decision-making of banks and investors in lending money to the operation. Companies with successful restaurant concepts (franchisor) may be willing to franchise their concept to the restauranteur (the franchisee). Franchising is an arrangement in which the franchisor (main company) grants to the franchisee (new restauranteur) a license to use particular commercial methods of operation which he has developed. The franchisee contributes the necessary capital to start up an operation, effort and motivation to run the establishment, and agrees to be controlled by the franchisor; the franchisor in return contributes to the training of the franchisee, the procedures of operation and other managerial expertise.

Franchising arrangements are particularly applicable to fast-food outlets because of the way in which these operations lend themselves to standardization and duplication and in this way encourage the development of franchising within the large chain operations.

The advantages to the franchisee are:

1. It offers the opportunity for immediate entry into business.
2. It offers immediate entry into a particular market with a proven successful 'package', that is, a brand product.
3. Assistance is offered in finding and evaluating sites.
4. Assistance is given with initial layouts, shop fitting specifications, and advice with planning applications.
5. Assistance is given with initial training of management and staff.
6. The franchisor provides menus, and sells (or nominates suppliers) all food, beverage, small equipment, etc. to the franchisee.
7. The franchisor provides all operational documents.
8. The franchisor provides regional and national promotional support.
9. The franchisor provides regular advice and assessment.

The advantages to the franchisor are:

1. It enables the franchisor to expand the business with speed using the franchisee's investment capital.
2. It enables the franchisor to achieve market penetration with relative ease and speed using the franchisee's capital, time and energy.
3. It reduces the number (if any) of development staff to find sites and to be involved in lengthy openings of new units.
4. It increases the benefits to the franchisor by providing significantly greater market exposure of the product.
5. It enables the franchisor to be the required supplier of the food, beverages, disposable commodities, equipment and at times fixtures and fittings, to the exclusion of competitors' products in all forms.
6. It enables the franchisor to have the franchisee under a period contract, to pay for entry into the franchise, to pay a commission fee based on turnover, and often to pay a specific percentage of turnover towards regional and national advertising and promotions.

An example of a franchisor would be McDonalds restaurants. The franchisor in this case is McDonalds and the franchisee is any operator that wishes to buy a franchise from Mc Donalds. Often there might be confusion between a franchise and a chain. In a chain all outlets are owned by the main company. In a franchise some outlets are owned by individual operators who then pay fees to the main company. The confusion often happens because companies like McDonalds operate both as a chain and

as a franchise, meaning they own a number of their restaurants but they will also sell franchise to potential investors.

Combination of the above

Any combination of two of the above mentioned methods can be used to finance a project. Realistically a new restaurateur might get a loan as well as re-mortgage a house or get part funding from investors.

FACILITY DESIGN AND LAYOUT

The restaurant design and layout of a restaurant will have a big effect on the meal experience as well as the employees of the restaurant. Depending on the concept and the size of the business there will be different requirements and priorities when designing the restaurant. Here we briefly explore the basic components of a restaurant design and layout.

Activity 3

Figure 4.6 is the layout of the Lakeside Restaurant an 80 cover restaurant in Guildford Surrey, UK.

Considering that this is a training restaurant, can you identify the main differences in terms of layout compared to high-street restaurants?

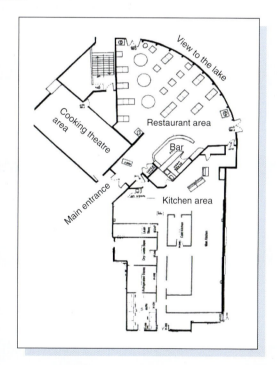

Figure 4.6 The Lakeside Restaurant layout (*Source*: Courtesy of The Lakeside Restaurant)

Customer service area

This area may often be referred to as the 'front of house' by the employees of the business. It is normally what the customer first sees and this area will affect the customer perceptions over the type of operation and the quality of service and even food and beverage the customer might expect. The service area must combine aesthetics as well as practicality so that the meal experience is enhanced by the surroundings and the design of the restaurant. An ethnic restaurant might have a specific theme related to the country of origin of the restaurateur whilst a fast-food type of operation may put more emphasis on functionality rather than comfort. Restaurant space is designated depending on the level of service and generally speaking a fine dining restaurant would be expected to allow far more space per seat than a fast-food operation. Table arrangement will be done so that it allows for maximal use of the space to ensure higher capacity whilst moveable furniture's will enable functions and bigger parties to take place in the restaurant. Other areas may include a hostess station usually found at the entrance of a full service restaurant, a cashier station and in some cases a bar with waiting area for customers that wait for a table to be readied. Public restrooms are also a key area for the restaurant often customers use the level of cleanliness of a toilet as a reflection on the cleanliness of the restaurants kitchen. The layout of the restrooms will require disable cubicles and may require nappy changing facilities and baby feeding area especially if the restaurant is targeting families.

Kitchen area

The kitchen area can be referred to as the 'back of House' or the production area, because this is where the food is produced. Open plan kitchens have been a trend where the process of production becomes part of the meal experience. From a design point-of-view such kitchens can be an added value and can help establish the theme in the restaurant.

Traditionally, the main areas of a kitchen include; the cold preparation section for the assembling of appetizers and salads, and deserts. The cooking station is where main courses are cooked. The hotplate area, where dishes are plated and wait for servers to take to the customers. A dishwashing area is close to the cooking area so that the pots and pans can be easily reached. It is worth noting that most health departments require separate sinks for washing and sanitizing pots, pans and dishes that need to be washed by hand.

A suppliers area or decanting area where goods are received and a food storage area with freezers and coolers, a scale, breakdown table and shelving for your freezer, cooler and dry goods. Linen may also be stored in this area.

Other restaurant areas

Other areas may include an office, employee room and restroom. Often not much thought is given in the design of employee areas but considering that guest satisfaction is often affected

by employee satisfaction restaurant operators must consider designing employee areas that are of as good standard as the restaurant they wish to manage.

Other design issues

The number of people in the UK aged 75 and over is forecast to double over the next 50 years. Elderly and disabled people are significant segments of the market. It is important for managers to take that in consideration when designing not only restaurant interiors but menus and restaurant signage as well. At the best, restauranteurs may design a few of their menu items and restaurant areas to suit the needs of elderly and disabled consumers. However in order to be competitive, managers must consider using an 'Inclusive design' strategy. That is, that every product should be designed with the elderly and disabled in mind.

Summary

In this chapter we explored:

- How restaurant concepts can be developed?
- Feasibility study
- Business plan
- Potential sources of financing a restaurant
- Key issues when considering the design and layout of a restaurant.

Review questions

1. What is a feasibility study and what are its main components?
2. Why is a feasibility study important for a new operation?
3. What is a SWOT analysis?
4. What is a PESTLE?
5. What is the difference between a business plan and a feasibility study?
6. Briefly explain at least five ways of financing a restaurant operation?
7. Why is facility design important to a restaurant operation?

Further study options

Case study: Little Paradise

Mary Smith fell in love with the little bistro in the corner of Worple Avenue and Stiple Street, the first time she laid eyes on the place. It was a small operation no more than 40 covers

at any one time but it had something special about it. Its owner Mr Franco was almost 65 and he would soon retire, so when he put up an advertisement to sell the business Mary was the first to show interest. She was determined to buy that place no matter what, and although she did not have much experience in running a restaurant business, she had years of experience in investment banks as an accountant so she had a good network of friends and she was a quick learner.

The business seemed to just about break even and Mr Franco never lied about the fact that business has been steadily declining over the years. Mary did not think about conducting a feasibility study or checking any historical data of the business. She simply launched in with the enthusiasm of a five-year old seeing her first bicycle.

Within the first months Mary realized that Mr Franco was hiring far too many employees but she was reluctant to let go any of the people as they all seemed to work for years for Mr Franco. Mary's initial funds were running low and the restaurant head chef did not seem to wish to steer away from traditional French Cuisine or try any alternative recipes.

Within the first year Mary's Little Paradise was turning to 'Little Hell', the restaurant did not seem to have a positive cash flow and customer numbers deteriorated whilst a number of equipment needed replacing. In the first year of operations the restaurant made a loss of £35,000. If Mary didn't act soon she would loose both the restaurant and her self-esteem . She needed to turn the restaurant into a success but she had no idea what to do next.

Q1: What were the major mistakes Mary did when deciding to go into the restaurants business?

Q2: What would you advise Mary to do next to help make the business a profitable one?

Case study: Acorn House Restaurant

Developing a unique and innovative restaurant concept such as the Acorn House Restaurant (AHR) may be considered an excellent case study for future hospitality managers. With a philosophy and determination to spread a truly eco friendly message to the restaurant industry, it is an original concept that delivers on its promises.

In November 2006 AHR, opened its doors to the public. The first eco friendly training restaurant in London with a mission statement of not only transforming the way people eat out but also aiming to become an example for the rest of the restaurant industry. The originality of the restaurant does not

lay only in the fact that it is an eco friendly concept but the degree to which it delivers an eco friendly message in every aspect of restaurant design, management and development of its employees, and future hospitality professionals.

History of the idea

In the summer of 2005, restaurant manager Jamie Grainger-Smith and head chef Arthur Potts bumped into one another in a Muswell Hill café. Over coffee and a conversation on the future of the restaurant industry, they began to develop a new concept set to transform the existing restaurant culture (Figure 4.7).

Both Jamie and Arthur, had always recycled, tried to conserve energy in their own homes and use ethical products. The decision to reflect this at their place of work seemed to be a natural one. Together they formed *Bliss Restaurant Consultancy* and in association with *Shoreditch* and *Terence Higgins* Trusts, the AHR idea was born.

The restaurant

AHR is situated on the ground floor of the *Terence Higgins Trust* headquarters at 69 Swinton Street, London, UK. The restaurant is only a five-minute walk from the Kings Cross and St Pancras railway station. The restaurant itself is built from recycled and organic materials. A long modern room can hold 62 covers and the shelves are stocked with fresh produce and various condiments and utensils. The bar next to the main

Figure 4.7
AHR menus and packaging

entrance serves as a station for the take-away menu, the restaurant features and at the other end the kitchen is visible by the customers. The kitchen size was minimized to ensure maximum energy efficiency. The restaurant also features a training room that is utilized to train its staff (see Figure 4.8).

Equipment, furniture and fixtures

The AHR team has gone to great lengths to ensure each decision has a minimum impact on the environment. Organic and recycled materials are used were possible. A great example of the AHR philosophy in practice, is the restaurant's Brazilian cutlery. Since coffee beans have to be imported their research in good coffee directed them towards the procurement of Brazilian fair trade coffee. They import their coffee by boat rather than plane as they have pledged never to use air freight for any of AHR products. To save on excess of transportation they used the same boats that transport their coffee to import their cutlery. The restaurant tables are made from sustainable Norwegian wood and the chair tops are recycled plastic whilst the chair legs are 80% recycled stainless steel. The take-away packaging is from recycled materials and fully biodegradable. The kitchen pass is made from recycled resin plastic, glasses are from recycled glass and even the wall paint is organic to ensure minimum impact on the environment. The menus are printed on re-cycled paper using vegetable ink.

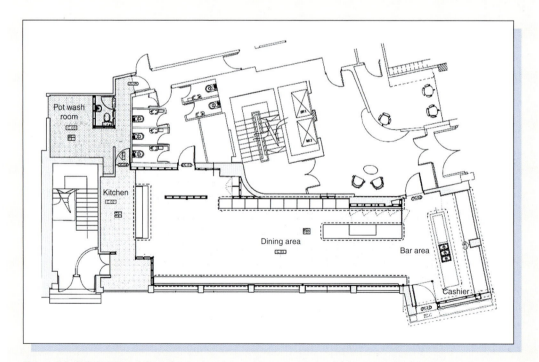

Figure 4.8 AHR Restaurant floor plan

A MENU FOR April

Green & black olives – £3.00
Wilkins Farmhouse cider – £3.60
Rhubarb Bellini – £7.00
Acorn House T-shirts – 10.00

Soups
£6.50 Field mushroom & potato
Beetroot, cardamom & sour cream

Starters
£10.50 Prosciutto di san Danielle, roast aubergine, seeds & sprouts
£9.50 Smoked mackerel with grilled celeriac, salsify & chives
£8.00 Spring beetroot, Jersey Royals, Amalfi olives & chilli
£9.50 Mozzarella di bufala, artichokes & aged balsamic vinegar
£11.50 English asparagus, fresh crab & dandelion

Pastas
£14.00 Tagliatelle, rag of spring lamb, mint & peas
£13.00 Spring herb ravioli & fresh ricotta
£12.50 Artichoke & broad bean risotto

Main courses
£17.00 Duck confit & braised Savoy cabbage
£15.50 Char grilled fish of the day, cardamom & horseradish
£13.50 Aubergine, spinach, goats cheese grilled red chilli sauce
£17.00 Roast pork chop, soy, honey & thyme
£17.00 Pan fried organic salmon fillet & borlotti beans
£18.50 Char grilled leg of lamb, anchovy & rosemary sauce

There will be a discretionary 12.5% service related charge added to your bill!
Acorn House asks you politely to refrain from smoking, for every ones sake!

Figure 4.9
AHR dinner menu

Food

Local produce is in the heart of the menu development at AHR. Items that can not be purchased locally such as peppercorns are imported by boat rather than plane. Seasonality in another characteristic of their menu and although the menu appears fixed for a period of a month the interpretation of each dish is depended on fresh produce available. By supporting the local suppliers AHR is also supporting the Mayor's Food Strategy for London, which aims to create a sustainable food system. A good example of how availability of food might affect menu items is the procurement of fish. Most restauranteurs will go to great lengths of time and money to ensure that particular species of fish is kept in their menu day in and day out. At AHR however the Executive Chef relies on the suppliers to get them the freshest fish available, in their April 2007 dinner menu, for example, char grilled fish *of the day* is featured rather than a particular fish species (Figure 4.9).

The AHR team also wants to put the choice back to the consumer by allowing them certain control on portion quantity and thus reducing wastage as much as possible (Figure 4.10).

Soups
Small – £5.50   Sorrel & pancetta
Large – £6.50   Beetroot, cardamom & sour cream
                  Field mushroom & potato

Cured meats
Selection of three – £8.00   Prosciutto di san Danielle, speck d' aosta, Bresaola,
Selection of five – £10.00   salami Milano, salami Felino, chorizo, Mortadella

Salads
Three salads – £8.00   Purple sprouting broccoli, ginger & vinegar
Four salads – £10.00   Spring greens, juniper & pancetta
                         Borlotti beans, sun dried tomatoes & herb sprouts
                         Grilled salsify, jersey royals & chives

Figure 4.10
Extract from the lunch menu

FIZZ
£25.00   Chapel Down Brut Kent, England NV
£40.00   Nyetimber Classic Cuvee Sussex 1999

Figure 4.11
Extract from the wine list

Beverages

Bottled water at AHR is supplied by *Belu*, a company that makes bottles from biodegradable corn and gives all of its profits to clean-water projects. The take-away menu features juices from England and even the wine list features wines from the UK (Figure 4.11).

Use of suppliers

AHR buys from local small independent suppliers. They focus on seasonal produce and buy fair trade were possible. They have a strict fish purchasing in accordance with the Marine Conservation Society Guidelines which is a UK charity dedicated to the protection of the marine environment and its wildlife. AHR food is organic and all vegetables are purchased from sustainable farmers. The AHR team avoids buying produce associated with industrial farming, as it is causing serious damage to the environment. They pledge never to use air freight and they identify meat suppliers that use positive animal husbandry.

Recycling and composting

The AHR team identifies packaging that can be delivered and sent back to the supplier. Their raw waste is mulched, then processed through an on-site wormery (Figure 4.12) and used to create soil for a vegetable and herb garden on the roof of the restaurants refuge area.

Urban gardening

A great example of the complete circle of the AHR recycling is the vegetable and herb garden at the top of the restaurant's refuge area (Figure 4.13). The garden containers have been built by volunteers from the community and staff of AHR using recycled wood and materials. Lettuce, leeks, onions, zucchini,

Figure 4.12
AHR wormery at work

Figure 4.13
Part of the AHR vegetable and herb garden

basil, coriander and parsley are some of the produce grown in the Kings Cross Urban setting. Grey and rain water is utilized for the needs of the garden. The simple act of planting seeds and witness them grow and later used in the AHR menu instills pride and boosts the morale of the AHR team. The fact that the whole garden is built by recycled materials makes the project even more rewarding.

Energy and water

AHR utilize natural lighting and use renewable green energy. They monitor their energy use in order to curtail usage. Water usage is also minimized and water is purified and bottled on site to decrease transport miles, and usage of plastic and glass. All the cleaning products used at AHR are environmentally friendly. A loop system is in operation for supply and removal of produce to minimize journeys and when transporting in London the AHR van uses bio-diesel.

Educating external and internal customers

Apart from the fact that customers may choose their portion size in order to minimize wastage, they are invited to donate 50p which is used to plant a tree and offset their carbon emissions travelling to AHR. The employees of AHR are trained in the ethical matters related to the protection of the environment, and are encouraged to cycle to work. The philosophy of AHR is clear even in the smallest details, the paintings on the walls depict images that remind the viewer the impacts of deforestation and the destruction of wildlife due to ice melting, but perhaps the strongest message comes from the promotional 'matches' given to every customer at the end of their meal. When other restaurants offer actual matches and unknowingly present a metaphor of destruction AHR 'matches' are herb seed sticks that can be used by customers to grow their own herbs and thus sending them off with a message of regeneration (Figure 4.14).

The people

Arthur Potts Dawson is the co-founder of *Bliss Restaurant Consultancy* and Executive Chef at *Acorn House Restaurant*. He started his career with a three-year apprenticeship with the Roux Brothers, before moving on to *Kensington Place* and *La Tante Claire.* He also worked alongside Rose Gray and Ruth Rogers as Head Chef at the *River Café* where he first began what was to become a lifelong commitment to using organic products and local suppliers. He has been a management consultant at the *Petesham Nurseries Café*, and has also held Executive Chef positions for *Cessonis Restaurant* of the *Soho House Group*, and Executive Chef of another innovative restaurant concept, *Fifteen Restaurant*.

Figure 4.14
AHR mixed herb sticks

Jamie Grainger-Smith is co-founder of *Bliss Restaurant Consultancy* and Restaurant Director at *Acorn House Restaurant*. Amongst his many restaurant projects he re-launched *Monte's* on Sloane Street, with Ben O'Donghue and Jamie Oliver, whom he met at his time working at the world-famous *River Café* in Hammersmith. Jamie has also worked with Alastair Little on Lancaster Road, *Morton's* on Berkeley Square and many others. Jamie was a key player in the development of the *Fifteen Restaurant* project. Working alongside Jamie Oliver he was responsible for the strategic direction and implementation of the restaurant, from finding the location, through interior, ergonomic design, staff recruitment and training. After the *Fifteen Restaurant* project, he was involved in several different projects, one of which being Graze in Maida Vale, another The Hill Restaurant and Bar in Muswell Hill – the latter being a 120 cover restaurant and a 280-capacity nightclub, where his role was to stabilize the business, implement strategies, procedures and gain control of the business.

The Acorn House Trust

Jamie and Arthur launched the Acorn House Trust (AHT) in the spring of 2007. The trust pledges to train 10 new restauranteurs per year that focus in sustainable, environmental friendly restaurant management ethos in Jamie's own words '*respect for all elements involved and awareness of the resources used in the provision of food is central to the AHR training ethos*'. The training programme was created in association with Westminster Kingsway College and the trainees work alongside the AHR full time team for a maximum of thirty-six hours per week. They also spend classroom time in the training room to cover the curriculum which covers sessions in food hygiene and safety, waste reduction, recycling and composting, sustainable farming and socially just and environmentally efficient food distribution, back and front of house, housekeeping, customer relations and developing a business plan.

The partners

The Shoreditch Trust (shoreditchtrust.org.uk), *Terrence Higgins Trust* (tht.org.uk) and *Bliss Restaurant Consultancy* (blissrc.co.uk) are the three organizations responsible for *Acorn House Restaurant*. The *Shoreditch Trust* and Terrence *Higgins Trust* wished to set up a training restaurant for the local community. With the expertise of *Bliss Restaurant Consultancy* this became a reality. Together, the partnership brings together shared values and significant experience in social enterprise and charity projects.

Shoreditch Trust

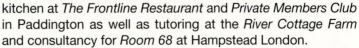

An award-winning charitable regeneration agency committed to developing new models of engagement and change for communities. The Trust has enjoyed significant success in acquiring and developing 16 Hoxton Square, home of the Hoxton apprentice which offers training places to the long-term unemployed in Hackney. The Trust has a social enterprise arm and its stake in Acorn House Restaurant forms part of that activity.

Terrence Higgins Trust

Established in 1982, *Terrence Higgins Trust* is the leading HIV and AIDS charity in the UK and the largest in Europe. It was one of the first charities to be set up in response to the HIV epidemic and has been at the forefront of the fight against HIV and AIDS since. *Acorn House Restaurant* is situated on the ground floor of the Trust's head office.

Bliss Restaurant Consultancy

Formed in 2005, the consultancy's projects include *The Dirt Café* concept the re-development of the menu and kitchen at *The Frontline Restaurant* and *Private Members Club* in Paddington as well as tutoring at the *River Cottage Farm* and consultancy for *Room 68* at Hampstead London.

Acknowledgements

The authors would like to thank the Directors of Bliss Restaurant Consultancy for their time and the information they provided for the benefit of this case study. Special thanks must also go to *Shoreditch Trust* and *Terrence Higgins Trust* for their involvement in this project.

Case study questions

1. Discuss the unique selling point of the Acorn House Restaurant.
2. Perform a cost–benefit analysis for each of the key areas of the AHR.
3. Discuss the implications of portion control management.
4. Conduct a SWOT analysis for AHR.
5. Would the concept work for a large chain of restaurants? What are the arguments for and against?
6. In the case study we see a number of innovative ideas that could be applied to any restaurant, which one you find the most intriguing, why?

Further reading

Akbar, A. (2007). Record number of new restaurants were launched in London last year, The Independent on Sunday, http://www.news.independent.co.uk/uk/this_britain/article2866796.ece (accessed August 27th 2007).

Department of Trade and Industry. http://www.dti.gov.uk/bbf/small-business/info-business-owners/access-to-finance/Small%20Firms%20Loan%20Guarantee/page37607.html (accessed April 23rd 2007).

Huiskamp, R. (2001). *Great Restaurant Concepts: An In-Depth Analysis of Five Noteworthy European Success Stories.* Netherlands: Food and Beverage Publications.

Fuller, S. (2005). *Opening a Restaurant or Other Food Business Starter Kit: How to Prepare a Restaurant Business Plan and Feasibility Study.* Florida: Atlantic Publishing Group.

Guilding, C. (2002). *Financial Management for Hospitality Decision Makers.* London: Elsevier.

Jones, P. and Merricks, J. (1994). *The Management of Foodservice Operations.* UK: Thomson.

Kotler, P. and Keller, K. L. (2006). *Marketing Management*, 12th edn. NJ: Pearson Prentice Hall.

Mintel Reports, Restaurants – UK – April 2006 http://www.reports.mintel.com (accessed 2nd April 2007).

Yee, R. (2005). *Hotel and Restaurant Design.* New York: Visual Reference Publications Inc.

The menu: Food and beverage

Introduction

The menu is the primary selling tool of any establishment that offers food and beverage for sale. For the customer it identifies the items that are available, shows prices and any other charges and together with other external features may characterize the style of food service offered. From the establishments perspective the menu should meet the objectives of the marketing policy, the catering policy and the financial policy.

The marketing policy should guide the catering policy so that the products on offer and the style of operation best meet the needs of the target market. The catering policy is concerned with the size and style of menu to be offered together with an appropriate style of service and this will impact on space requirements, level and type of equipment purchased, and the level of skill and number of staff required. The financial policy aims to achieve revenue and profitability to budget through pricing, cost control and volume.

Chapter objectives

After working through this chapter you should be able to:

- Understand the differences between a Table d'hôte and à la Carte menu.
- Understand the basics of menu planning and menu design.
- Have a knowledge of menu pricing models and applications.
- Understand different types of beverage menus.
- Understand the need for accuracy and honesty in menu descriptions.
- Have a basic understanding of licensing and merchandising.

TYPE OF MENUS

Although there are many types of eating establishments offering many types of meal experiences, there are basically only two types of food menus: the *table d'hôte*; and the *à la carte*. From these two types of menus there are in practice many adaptations of each.

Table d'hôte

Table d'hôte means food from the hosts' table and may be identified by:

1. Being a restricted menu.
2. Offering a small number of courses, usually three or four.
3. A limited choice within each course.
4. A fixed selling price.
5. All the dishes being ready at a set time.

This type of menu usually contains the popular type dishes and is easier to control, the set price being fixed for whatever the customer chooses, or being set depending on the main dish chosen and occasionally may offer and additional item at a supplementary price. It is common practice in many restaurants for a table d'hôte menu to be offered to a customer together with an à la carte menu (Figure 5.1).

Table d'hôte menus can be offered for breakfast, lunch and dinners. Their many adaptations are used for:

1. *Banquets*: A banquet menu is a fixed menu at a set price offering usually no choice whatsoever to the customers, unless the client informs the caterer in advance that certain guests require, say, a vegetarian or kosher type meal, and is available to all guests at a predetermined time.
2. *Buffets*: Buffet type meals vary considerably depending on the occasion, and the price paid, from the simple finger buffet, where all items prepared are proportioned to a small size so

SUNDAY ROAST MENU

STARTERS

Cream of Broccoli and Shropshire blue stilton soup
Served with crusty bread

Chicken liver, brandy and basil terrine
Served with red onion chutney,
salad and toasted crusty bread

Mushrooms
Cooked in a creamy garlic sauce

English Asparagus
Sautéed with butter and crispy cured ham

Scottish smoked salmon
Served with lemon

MAINS

Roasted Sirloin of Scottish Beef
and Yorkshire pudding

Whole Poussin Roasted

Roasted Pork leg
With crackling and fresh apple sauce

Whole Sea Bass
Stuffed with herbs, garlic and lemon

All of the above are served
With seasonal vegetables and potatoes

DESSERTS

Baked Apple with sultana's
and a light caramel sauce

Lemon tart with berries
and a berry Coulis

Chocolate and orange liquor cake
With cream and caramelised orange

Selection of Cheeses
Shropshire blue Stilton, Soignon Goats cheese, Somerset Brie, Mature cheddar

TWO COURSE £13.95   THREE COURSE £16.95

*12.5% discretionary charge will be added to your bill

Figure 5.1
Example of a table d'hôte menu
(*Source*: Courtesy of Magnolia
Restaurant, UK)

that the customer may consume it without the use of any cutlery, to the exotic fork buffets where hot and cold food is available and where many large dishes will be carved and portioned for the individual guest. Buffets are frequently prepared for such occasions as wedding receptions, press receptions, presentations and conferences. Buffets can be classified as a form of table d'hôte menu as they offer a restricted menu, a limited choice of only what is on the buffet; a predetermined set price and all the dishes are available at a set time.

3. *Coffee houses*: A coffee house menu is a more recent form of table d'hôte menu that is commonly used today in hotels and restaurants. This type of menu is characterized by:
   (a) Being a set menu offered often for twelve to eighteen hours of the day.
   (b) Being reasonably priced, with often each dish or section of the menu individually priced.
   (c) Offering a range and choice of items that are suitable for snacks, light meals, lunch or dinner.
   (d) Offering a limited range of foods that are either already cooked, are of the convenience type food category and require little preparation time, or are simple and quick to cook, for example omelet's, hamburgers, etc.
   (e) A simplified form of service being offered, for example plate service, counter service, etc.
       – In some establishments the coffee shop menu may be replaced for two to three hours with a special breakfast menu offering a restricted choice when there is a need to serve a very large number of people in the shortest possible time.
4. *Cyclical menus*: These are a series of table d'hôte menus, for example for three weeks, which are repeated again and again for a set period of, for example, four months. These are often used in hospitals and industrial catering as an aid to establishing a pattern of customer demand for a menu item and as a result assist in purchasing, preparation of items and staffing requirements.

À la carte

À la carte means a free choice from the card or menu and is identified by:

1. Being usually a larger menu than a table d'hôte menu and offering a greater choice.
2. Listing under the course headings all of the dishes that may be prepared by the establishment.
3. All dishes being prepared to order.
4. Each dish being separately priced.
5. Usually being more expensive than a table d'hôte menu.
6. Often containing the exotic and high cost seasonal foods.

Part of an à la carte menu may contain *a plat du jour* or 'speciality of the house' section. This consists usually of one or two main dishes, separately priced, which are already prepared and change daily. À la carte menus are, because of their size and the unknown demand of each item, more difficult to control than the typical table d'hôte menus (Figure 5.2).

A special promotion menu is a form of à la carte menu which is at times offered to the guest in addition to the à la carte menu. This type of menu is concerned with the selling of a particular part of a menu to increase the interest for the customer,

A MENU FOR july

Fresh bread & butter – £1.50
Green & black olives – £2.50
Strawberry Bellini – £6.00

SOUPS

£6.50	Pea, zucchini and their flowers
	Beetroot, cardamom & sour cream

STARTERS

£9.50	Prosciutto di san Danielle with summer artichokes
£9.00	Smoked mackerel, baby leeks, spinach & pickled ginger
£8.50	New potato, French bean, radish & green olive salad
£9.50	Mozzarella di bufala, black figs & purple basil
£8.50	Deep fried vegetables, anchovies & sage, chopped red chilli

Rice & Pastas

£11.00	Tagliolinmi (hand made) of fennel & salami
£12.00	Caramella (little sweets) of sustainable prawns, rocket & chilli
£11.50	Tomato & mozzarella risotto, basil pangratatta

MAIN COURSES

£16.00	Duck confit (from Gascony), tomato & potato 'al forno'
£15.00	Char grilled fish of the day, cardamom & horseradish
£13.00	Aubergine, spinach & goats cheese, grilled red chilli sauce
£15.00	Twice cooked pork belly, soy, ginger & spring onion
£16.00	Pan fried organic salmon fillet, cherry tomatoes & mint

There will be a discretionary 12.5% service related charge added to your bill!
Acorn House asks you politely to retrain from smoking, for every ones sake!

Figure 5.2
Extract of an à la carte restaurant (*Source*: Courtesy of Acorn House Restaurant, UK)

to increase the average spending by the customer and in turn to increase the turnover and profit for the caterer. Promotions may be made by specially printing attractive menus for such items as:

1. Shellfish, when an increased variety of shellfish and special dishes would be made available.
2. Soft fruits, when various types of berry fruits such as strawberries, raspberries, loganberries, etc. would be featured in special dishes.
3. The game season, when pheasant, grouse, etc. would be featured in pâtés, soups and special main course dishes.
4. Dishes cooked or prepared at the table, for example crêpes Suzette, steak Diane, etc.
5. Dishes that utilize seasonal produce many of which are included in the items above.

Activity 1

Design a simple table d'hôte menu suitable for a three star hotel restaurant. The menu should offer three courses and up to three choices per course. As this will be a fixed price menu you need to ensure that all dishes provide the desired contribution margin.

MENU OFFERING

Much has changed in the presentation and service style of the food and beverage offering. Traditionally high-level service consisted of trolley service where food was either cooked or carved at the table and vegetables were silver served or alternatively silver service where each component of the meal was served individually from silver flats or dishes. Table or family service followed this where the main item was plated and vegetables and accompaniments were placed in dishes on the table for guests to help themselves. At the lower end of restaurant service was plated service where the whole meal was pre-plated and finally self-service where the customer selected and collected their meal from a service counter. Menu development followed these service styles so that the more expensive trolley or silver service styles reflected in more expensive menu items, printing and general restaurant ambience. Changes in food presentation style initiated by nouvelle cuisine and continued through the development of celebrity chefs now finds plated service regarded as the normal choice in many of the worlds top luxury restaurants. The chef literally creates the dish on the plate complete with vegetables, sauces and accompaniments creating a presentation or picture of the dish. Menus need to reflect this change in presentation style and the change in status of plated meals. In particular menu descriptions need to be both informative and accurate because all items are already on the plate and customers may dislike one component or have intolerance for some food items. Descriptions have also developed a wider range of and greater use of adjectives similar in many ways to that used to describe works of art, and for the chef restaurateur this is the image that they want to portray as part of the establishment's and their own identity.

Content of food menus

The content of food menus varies with the type of menu, the segment of the market it is aimed at, the occasion, the food cost available, the country or region, etc. Table d'hôte menus are often of three to four courses only. A hotel room service breakfast menu will offer three or four courses from both a traditional breakfast and a continental style breakfast together with a number of ancillary items such as newspapers, magazines or early morning beverages and will also offer a range of breakfast delivery times depending on the establishment.

À la carte menus often differ for lunch and/or dinner periods, although it is not uncommon for the same à la carte menu to be offered throughout the day. In the UK, for example, traditionally the heavier type items, for example thick vegetable-based soups, farinaceous dishes, meat puddings, meat stews, steamed fruit and sponge puddings, would normally be found on a lunch menu; whereas the lighter and often more delicately flavoured dishes would be found on a dinner menu, for example speciality consommés, poached fish with delicate flavours and often complicated garnishes, hot and cold sweet and savoury soufflés, etc. However, many of these traditional dishes now feature on menus at any part of the day as part of a marketing campaign in what marketers would refer to as retro dishes or dishes that where popular in the past, went out of fashion only to re-emerge once again on our menus. This applies particularly to dishes that nutritionalists suggest are bad for us, for example steamed suet puddings for which, nostalgia is a strong buying force. For a traditional full à la carte menu, the courses or sections of the menu would be divided up into a possible 14 sections. It is from this full outline of the sequence of sections that a table d'hôte menu or a special luncheon or dinner menu could be constructed. The combination of the various sections of the menu depends very much on the occasion, the prices to be charged and the wishes of the customer. There is an established order of sequence of sections of the menu, which by tradition are followed. This accepted sequence enables the caterer to compile the separate courses on table d'hôte and à la carte menus and to suggest to clients suitable special and/or function menus of varying lengths. It is very seldom the practice for all of the possible courses of a menu to be served, but as a general rule it is possible to state that when a large number of courses are served that the portion sizes are relatively small. The classical European menu structure identified by M. J. Leto and W. K. H. Bode consists of 16 courses excluding coffee. They are in order of service cold starter, soups, hot starters, egg and farinaceous, fish, small hot meat dishes, large meat joint, small cold meat course, sorbet, roast with salad, vegetable course, potato course, warm sweet course, cold sweet course, cheese course and fresh fruit.

Menu planning

As stated earlier the menu is the key marketing and selling tool available to the restaurateur and as such meticulous attention to detail is the key to making this work successfully and is a positive step towards a profitable food and beverage enterprise. The menu communicates a wide range of information to the customer both in terms of the words used to describe dishes, referred to as 'copy' and more subliminally through colour, layout, quality of material used, and style and needs to be reflected conceptually throughout the whole restaurant (Figures 5.3 and 5.4).

The menu, together with other physical attributes of a property contributes to creating a level of expectation from the customer. Meeting this customer expectation or in fact exceeding this expectation should be the primary objective of the restaurateur in the quest for a successful and profitable business. Because the menu plays such a pivotal role in operational style, pricing structure and overall concept design it is important at the planning stage that the location is right for the planned menu type, that the market exists within this catchments area and that it works with regard to the local competition. In an affluent residential area a small restaurant may be successful with high priced, high quality

In his new restaurant at the Compleat Angler hotel in Marlow, Dean Timpson explains that he can focus much more on the food offering. After more than seven years as executive chef at Marlow's Compleat Angler hotel, Dean Timpson was offered the opportunity of opening a restaurant with his name above the door at the 64-bedroom property.

Almost £1m was spent on creating fine-dining restaurant Dean Timpson at the Compleat Angler and the hotel's other eaterie, the brasserie-style Bowaters, by dividing the former Riverside restaurant in two.

Timpson explains that cooking for a far smaller number of covers than before and being able to focus exclusively on the restaurant – which is open for lunch Wednesday to Sunday and for dinner Tuesday to Saturday – is allowing him to significantly raise the level of cooking. He has also sourced new suppliers for the restaurant, so is working with the very best ingredients. At lunch, as well as the à la carte, Timpson offers a three-course market menu for £24.50, with three options per course. Crayfish and smoked salmon tortellini with red chard is among the current starters on this menu, with fillet of turbot with pea and truffle risotto among the mains, and passion fruit mousse with mango jelly and coconut ice-cream a dessert option.

In the evening, alongside the à la carte, a six-course tasting menu is offered and is selling strongly, with about 25% of diners choosing it. Meanwhile, the à la carte features five dishes at each course, with dishes selling evenly across the menu, says Timpson.

Duck eggs from a local farm are put to good use in a starter of poached duck egg with asparagus and morel foam (£10), while sautéd scallops with English pea purée and a confit of pork belly (£15) is a similarly seasonal alternative to start.

At main course Timpson is particularly proud of the loin of rabbit and langoustine with prune purée and cabbage (£24). 'It's a dish I've been working on for six years, and I've now got it exactly as I want it,' he says. 'It's a lovely balance between earthy, savoury and sweet flavours'.

Figure 5.3
New menu concepts can rejuvenate a restaurant

What's on the menu

- Duo of foie gras with pineapple purée and caramelized pineapple, £14
- Quail ballotine wrapped in Parma ham with rhubarb purée and pickled walnuts, £13
- Cornish red mullet with saffron mayonnaise and a tomato dressing, £12.50
- Roast suckling pig with pak choi and Granny Smith apple sauce, £26
- Cornish monkfish wrapped in Parma ham with marinated tomatoes and asparagus, £23
- Fillet of sea bass with orange dressing, baby spinach, clam and razor clam lasagne, £27.50
- Dark chocolate soufflé with mint ice cream, £7.50
- Strawberry parfait wrapped in chocolate with honeycomb caramel, £8
- Chilled apricot soup and apricot mousse served with champagne, £7.50

Figure 5.4
The Compleat Angler, Marlow, Buckinghamshire website: www.deantimpson.co.uk (*Source*: Caterer & Hotelkeeper, June 2007)

items and a low volume of customers whereas in a less affluent area, perhaps with a high student population on restricted budgets a small restaurant may have more success with a take-away menu. These two examples are rather polarized and often boundaries are not quite so clearly defined but it serves to demonstrate the need to consider these aspects before embarking on a restaurant style or menu plan (Figures 5.5 and 5.6).

Themes • • •

The design of a menu concerns more than the typography, colour, graphics, and shape or production material, important as these areas might be. Today's consumers are well aware of a modern computers ability to produce high quality print and graphics. With

Figure 5.5 Special event menu for exhibition at the British Museum (*Source*: Courtesy of DO & CO)

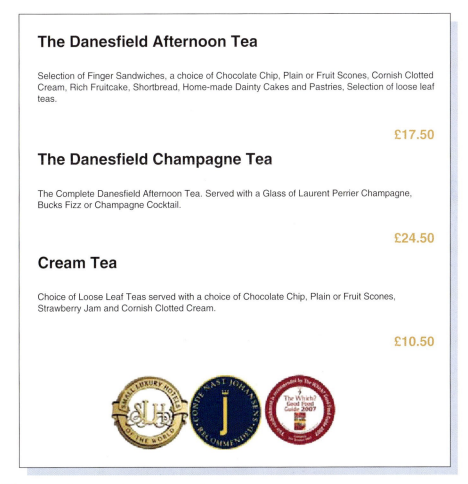

Figure 5.6 Afternoon tea menu at Danesfield House Hotel

a little sophisticated software and a good quality colour printer production of high quality colourfully designed menus with large amounts of graphics is relatively simple and inexpensive. A catering business, therefore, relies more heavily for its overall design appeal on what and how it describes the menu items. The use of language often causes difficulty particularly mixing different languages, for example English and French. By adding French the restaurateur may seek to add classical named dishes but by mixing the language the dish is described in pseudo-English or French and often becomes an unrecognizable hybrid. If part of the restaurants theme is to represent another country then the menu may be written in the corresponding language but it is essential that an accurate description of each dish be given properly translated into English. In this way special themes or events can be reflected in the menu design and content (see Figure 5 2).

Menu presentation

Comparatively lower production costs and modern materials should ensure that menus are always kept clean and presentable. Damaged, soiled menus or those that have prices overprinted or in some cases where new prices have been stuck over existing prices are not acceptable and customers will regard the establishment as being of a low standard.

Menus should be easy to read, clear and precise and enable a customer to calculate approximately how much they are likely to spend and show clearly if any additional charges are to be made, for example service charge. Menu items should have accurate descriptions where required, reflect the expectations of customers in terms of the style of restaurant the menu portrays and the service style they should expect. The menu should reflect the restaurant offering in line with current market trends and customer expectation. 'Menus should be designed to market the restaurant, entice diners to eat. The average customer spends only two minutes reading the menu. The term "reading" may be an overtly optimistic expression of what is no more than a quick scan. In only two minutes your menu must communicate the full range of food and beverages offered and sell the guest on what to purchase to both satisfy them and your financial objectives', Bates (2004, p. 30).

Activity 2

Design a leaflet that can be handed out to customers as they leave the restaurant informing them of a special event of your choice. Use the typography, colour, graphics, and shape or production material to support the text and reflect the type of event you are offering. Once complete pass to a friend or colleague and see if they have all the information they need to make a decision about attending from the information and style of your leaflet.

Layout of the menu

The larger the menu the more time consuming it is for customers to make their selection of food or wine. However, if it is too short customers may not be entirely satisfied by what is offered. Caterers need to adjust the length of their menu to the particular needs of their customers; bearing in mind that the longer a menu becomes the more management control will be necessary. What often is particularly confusing and embarrassing – unless the customer is very knowledgeable – is the length of wine lists offered in many restaurants. Unless wine lists of this type are extremely well laid out and contain additional help to customers to aid their selection, they will do very little to help the potential sales of a restaurant. The layout of a menu should take into consideration how a customer normally reads a menu. This is illustrated in Figure 5.7. This skilled use of the important areas on a menu must be utilized to enable an establishment to achieve its budgetary targets.

Size and form

The size and shape of a menu can add to and complement the uniqueness of the facility. A food or beverage menu must be easy for the customer to handle and in no way confusing to read. The various forms that the menu can take are unlimited, from a menu chalked up on a blackboard, to a large illuminated display board with photographs, conventional menu cards, tent cards, placemats, menus printed in the shape of a fan or even hand printed onto silk handkerchiefs as mementoes for the guests at a banquet. There are cost implications, particularly where the services of a professional printing company are involved and therefore consideration for the length of time that a menu might be used or the level of soiling that might be expected should be included as part of the decision-making process.

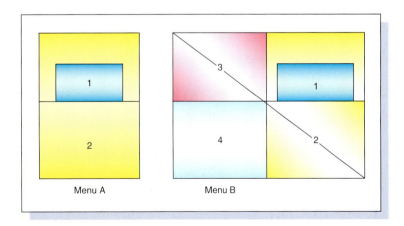

Menu A   Menu B

Figure 5.7
Menu layouts and how guests
read a menu

MENU PRICING

Menu pricing needs to fulfil two needs, for the caterer the need to make adequate profits and for the customer the need to satisfy getting value for money. In both cases the requirement for accuracy is paramount. Customers today are more sophisticated in their dining habits, more people eat out, many are well travelled and nearly all have gained perceptions of quality and value for money from watching celebrity chefs and other food programmes on television. Some aspects of profitability are discussed in Chapter 7 but essentially profitability as far as the menu is concerned has three elements: margin per item, sales mix and volume. A restaurateur's policy on pricing should take a holistic view of the business and include expected return on investment, market demand, competition, where price should be measured against quality, industry standards for style of operation, location, particularly where this may impact on business overheads including staff costs, rents and council charges.

The research shown in Figure 5.7 is taken from work done at the Culinary Institute of America in California. Because much of the time spent on analysis of profitability and pricing, often referred to as menu engineering, it is easy for restaurant owners to lose sight of the fact that they are actually talking about pounds, dollars, euros, etc. and that percentages do not always reveal the true story as shown in Figures 5.8 and 5.9.

Pricing models

There are a number of well-established pricing models commonly used some of which are better suited to commercial undertakings whilst others are more frequently used in 'not for profit organizations'. In this respect benchmarking against others in the sector may provide a good 'feel' for a suitable pricing model.

Cost plus pricing • • •

Cost plus pricing takes the ingredient or food cost element of a menu item and simply adds a predetermined multiplier or markup. Most commonly used where a simple pricing model will provide the desired return and there are few additional costs. Typically, this could be something like a house wine where little further expense will be incurred and the restaurateur simply multiplies the buying price by say three, so cost price is £4 selling price becomes £12 plus or including any sales tax. This simple pricing approach may aid decision making when for example on the telephone to a supplier or perhaps in a market. By simply applying a set multiplier they can get a good estimate of selling price (see Figures 5.8 and 5.9).

Alternatively by adding a fixed markup of say 150% the wine becomes £10. This simplistic pricing method also allows the chef or buyer to make quick purchase.

MANAGER ONE

For illustration, let's take a look at a series of simplified menu abstracts from three different managers pricing the same menu. In the first example, you'll see that this manager budgeted for a 33% food cost and took the safe route to achieve that goal by setting the pricing on each of the individual menu items to meet that same percentage. Safe, because no matter what the customers order, theoretically his food cost should come in on budget and everyone should be happy. Right? Well, before we answer that, let's look a little further.

Item	Selling price	Sold	Total sales	Cost per unit	Margin	Total cost	Profit	FC%
Roast chicken	$9	9	$81	$3	$6	$27	$54	33%
Grilled veal chop	$36	1	$36	$12	$24	$12	$33	33%
Sautéed Salmon	$13.50	4	$54	$4.50	$9	$18	$36	33%
Total		14	$171			$57	$114	33%

MANAGER TWO

Our second manager used a different approach to menu pricing. Using the same menu items, but raising the price on the chicken by $3 and lowering the price on the veal by $12 the natural reaction of her customers was for them to buy less chicken and more veal. And what about the food cost percentage? It went up of course, to a whopping 40%, but the profit went up as well – in fact, by quite a bit. She deposited more money in the bank even though her food cost comes in at five points higher than that of manager number one. Manager number two focuses on real dollars, not just percentages.

Item	Selling price	Sold	Total sales	Cost per unit	Margin	Total cost	Profit	FC%
Roast chicken	$12	5	$60	$3	$9	$15	$45	25%
Grilled veal chop	$24	5	$120	$12	$12	$60	$60	50%
Sautéed Salmon	$13.50	4	$54	$4.50	$9	$18	$36	33%
Total		14	$234			$93	$141	40%

Figure 5.8 Sales mix matrix

Competition pricing • • •

Competition pricing as the name suggests copies the prices of competitors. As a short-term strategy this may achieve increased business but it can easily spiral out of control into a price war. What are unknown are the competitors cost structure and margins maybe severely compromised.

Rate of return pricing • • •

The basis for this method is an attempt to establish a break-even matrix based on predicted costs and sales. So, for example, if a

MANAGER THREE

Okay, so maybe our second manager is a bit more aggressive than you're comfortable with. Manager number three takes a more conservative approach. Some of his customers consider that $9 chicken dish as an entitlement so he decides to leave that dish and its price alone. However, our manager has simply decided to reduce the price on the veal enough to increase its appeal, moving some customers (two in this example) who would have ordered the chicken to get the veal. The food cost again goes up, this time to 37% but even still, this manager's profit continues to be better than that of the first manager.

Item	Selling price	Sold	Total sales	Cost per unit	Margin	Total cost	Profit	FC%
Roast chicken	$9	7	$63	$3	$6	$21	$42	33%
Grilled veal chop	$28	3	$84	$12	$16	$48	$48	43%
Sautéed Salmon	$13.50	4	$54	$4.50	$9	$18	$36	33%
Total		14	$201			$75	$126	37%

Menu pricing should be more dynamic than setting a percentage based on the budgeted food cost percentage and using that same pricing factor across all items. A lower food cost percentage does not mean higher profitability. And finally, the next time you hear someone brag about their low food cost percentage, you cannot be so sure that their profitability is high.

Figure 5.9 Sales mix matrix 2 (*Source*: Adapted from Marriott Streamlines Menuing. Lodging Hospitality, 2007)

restaurant investment is £300,000 and the required return on this is 20% then the restaurant seeks profits of £60,000 per year. By modelling the costs, sales price and volume the emerging data will indicate what levels this needs to be in order to achieve the desired return. It would then be necessary to take it a stage further and carry out a feasibility study to see if the model fits the operational style of the restaurant. This model is unlikely to give definitive menu prices although they may be indicative and therefore help in the initial restaurant setup decision.

Elasticity pricing • • •

This pricing method considers the market and its sensitivity to price change. If the restaurant operates in a market where price is a determinant of demand a lower price may increase volume sufficiently to give better profitability. The market may also allow supply to be a determinant of price thereby allowing price increase without undue effect on volume. Fast-food operations, particularly branded burger restaurants in urban areas have been demand led and very price sensitive, particularly when market share becomes an important aspect, however when these same restaurants are located on motorway service stations they become supply led and prices can increase.

Backward pricing ● ● ●

Backward pricing considers what the customer or market will bear in terms of price. Often used in manufacturing, for example confectionary or canned drinks less common in restaurants but useful when trying to establish or develop a new product. Requires fairly accurate ingredient and processing costs to be established and relies heavily on volume forecasts.

Prime cost ● ● ●

Prime cost and its variant actual cost endeavour to provide more accurate cost models. Prime cost attempts to calculate labour cost in addition to food cost and actual cost attempts to include overheads. Both of these may be modelled via data from electronic point of sale (EPOS) systems over time and may also be benchmarked against industry standards for the sector. For example, it maybe established that Pizzeria's have an average food cost of 20%, an average labour cost of 30%, average overhead costs of 30% and require a return on investment of 20%. In this model if pizza ingredients cost £1 the operator has £1.50 towards labour, £1.50 towards overheads and £2 towards return on his investment that equates to a selling price of £5 plus sales tax where applicable. Whilst this model is more sophisticated and has the propensity to be more accurate modelling against industry standards or using data from the operations EPOS system can be misleading. In the first cost matching across all categories may not be possible and in the second EPOS data by its nature is historic and previous sales may not be attainable in the subsequent trading period, a drop in volume will load each remaining sale with additional levels of cost.

Departmental profit margins ● ● ●

The approach to menu pricing must follow from the outline of the basic policies and from the determined departmental profit targets. Each department will have a significant role in the total organization and its individual profit targets will normally be unrelated. For example, in a hotel the profit required from the à la carte restaurant may well be far lower than that of its coffee shop. The existence of the à la carte restaurant may be mainly of an image status for the hotel as against being a major profit contributor. What is necessary is for the total sum of the individual departments' contributions to equal (at least) the desired contribution to the revenue for the whole establishment.

Differential profit margins ● ● ●

It is unusual to apply a uniform rate of gross profit to all of the items found on a food menu or beverage list, although this simplistic method of costing can at times still be found in the non-commercial sector of the industry. In the non-commercial sector of the industry one of the advantages is that where a uniform rate of gross profit is applied (e.g. 60%), reference to the takings can quickly show the costs at 40% gross profit irrespective of the sales mix and an immediate comparison can be made to the actual usage of materials. The reasons for not applying a uniform rate of gross profit in the commercial sector are those stated in Chapter 7, that is, it ignores such things as capital investment; it emphasizes the cost too much; it ignores competition; etc. Further, it could distort the range of prices and values of items on a menu in that a low food/beverage cost item would end up being priced at a very low price, while a high food/beverage cost item would be exorbitantly priced. In addition, it does not allow any flexible approach to the selling of items. Differential profit margins take into account the sales mix of items from a food menu or beverage list and hopefully provide the competitive balance of prices so that in total it is attractive to the customer and achieves the desired gross profit and revenue for the department.

Special pricing considerations

Sales tax • • •

Depending on the government in power, it is likely that some form of sales tax may be enforced during its period of office. It is important to the customer to know whether prices displayed or quoted are inclusive of this sales tax or not. Additionally, the caterer needs to realize that any money collected on behalf of the government has at some time to be paid to that government and that it should not be included when calculating revenue or average spend figures, etc.

Service charge • • •

This is an additional charge, made to customers, at a fixed percentage of the total cost of the food and beverage served. The fixed percentage is determined by management, printed on the menu/beverage list, with the objective of removing from the customer the problem of determining what size of tip to give when in a particular establishment. As this charge is to be distributed to the staff at a later date, usually on a points system, it should be treated similarly to a sales tax and not included in the calculation of revenue for food and beverages or in the calculations of average spend figures.

Cover charge • • •

This is an additional charge to a meal in restaurants to cover such costs as the bread roll and butter and items included but not priced on a menu. Care should be exercised as to whether to implement this or not as it is most likely to cause aggravation to some clients when it is applied.

Minimum charge • • •

Restaurants to discourage some potential clients from using the premises and to discourage clients from taking up a seat and only purchasing a very low priced item often enforce this.

Menu pricing applications

The exact method of pricing used by an establishment will depend on such matters as which sector of the industry the establishment is in; the level of profit/subsidy required; its basic policies; etc. It is important though to remember that the price in itself can be a valuable selling tool and a great aid in achieving the desired volume of sales. Whilst menu pricing is not quite a science there are a number of ways that the restaurateur can remove some of the guesswork by adopting one or more of the pricing models previously discussed.

Table d'hôte menus • • •

This type of menu is characterized by being a restricted menu, offering a small range of courses with a limited choice within each course and at a fixed selling price. The price may be just one price for any three courses chosen, or may vary in price depending on the main course chosen.

The method of pricing chosen should take into account the departmental profit required and the differential profit margins of the menu. Based on the forecasted sales take-up by guests, the *average* should be taken to fix the price. The average may well be the true figure, rounded off, when the objective is to attract as many customers as possible to choose from the menu; or alternatively, it may be an *average plus* figure when it is being offered with an à la carte menu and it is not desired to encourage too many guests away from the à la carte menu by making the price differentiation too attractive.

À la carte menus • • •

This type of menu is characterized by being a larger menu than a table d'hôte menu offering a greater choice of courses and dishes within each course, and each item being individually priced.

The method of pricing here is again to take into account the departmental profit required and the differential profit margins for each course and then to price each item separately using standard recipes. In addition, note should be taken of the potential sales mix within each course so as to achieve the desired profit margin.

Banqueting menus • • •

This is a specific type of table d'hôte menu offering normally no choice to the customers. The specific difference in pricing this menu is that apart from the food and often the liquor, all the additional items are normally priced and charged separately. Examples of such items are flowers for each table, a band, meals and refreshments for the band, services of a toast master, hire of a microphone, printing of a special menu for the function. Many companies are now trying to customize this restricted choice, for example Marriott have created a package for business functions that combine menu choices with technology requirements banqueting style operations as shown in Figure 5.10.

Figure 5.10
Designing menu options for customer needs. (*Source*: Brand Report, Lodging Hospitality 2006)

Marriott International recently introduced new menus for its meetings and events at all Marriott and Renaissance properties. The company states that the new menuing process will make it easier for meeting planners to choose and customize items for their events and to communicate their selections.
The company surveyed meeting planners and Marriott personnel to help design the menus. As a result, planners can now select from an a la carte menu of meeting choices – breakfast, lunch, dinner, beverages, breaks, receptions and technology – in one user-friendly and colourful document.

The pricing of a banquet menu for a client is commonly found to have a flexible element to it, in that it is not uncommon for a banqueting manager to offer additions to a menu at no additional cost to the client in order to obtain the business during a slack trading period or for a particular gap in a week. For example, the banqueting manager may offer as a free addition to the standard printed menu such things as a soup course, a sorbet, *petits fours*, etc. Further, the charge for the hire of the function room may be reduced or removed altogether (see also Chapter 19).

Pricing of beverages

The method used to price beverages is similar to that for pricing foods. As in the case of foods, first, the departmental profit target and gross profit percentage should be set, followed by differential profit margins based on the sales mix achievable. The sales mix breakdown depends on the type of operation and how detailed the breakdown of sales is required. The gross profit percentage of house brand beverages (i.e. the particular brand of beverage that is offered to the customer, when a specific brand is not requested) is usually higher than on other brand beverages as it is normally made available by the supplier at a special discounted rate (see Table 8.8 for an example of differential profit margins applied to a bar).

Pricing may be more accurately calculated for beverages as little, if any, processing of the drinks takes place; drinks being purchased by the bottle (e.g. beer, wine) or by a specific stated measure (e.g. 6-out) from a bottle of known standard size (e.g. wine, 75 cl). The mixing of drinks is, like food, usually prepared using a standard recipe particular to an establishment.

Subsidized operations

There are many operations within the non-commercial sector of the industry that are subsidized in some form or other. Subsidies may take the form of completely free premises, capital equipment, services, and labour or the catering department may be required to pay a percentage of these costs with the balance being the subsidy. Pricing in this situation may, for example, require the sales revenue to cover the food costs only; or food costs plus specific named expenses (e.g. all labour); or food costs plus a named percentage (e.g. 20%) as a contribution to all overheads. Pricing in this situation is frequently done on a cost plus basis, depending on the level of subsidy. When more than the food/beverage cost has to be recovered, it is important that prices are competitive enough to encourage a high enough volume of sales.

Recipe costing and menu testing software, for example StarChef. NET (www.chef365.com/) or fourthhospitality (fourthhospitality. com/fourth/RandM.html) are readily available allowing the restaurateur to compare performance of various menu items using different recipes for price comparison.

Menu engineering examined by authors Kasavana and Smith (1982), and Keiser et al. (2008) consider the menu in terms of cost, margins and volume analysed to identify menu items under four performance types, namely, plowhorses, stars, dogs and puzzles (see Figure 5.9). Plowhorses are highly popular menu items with average to low contribution margins, stars are highly popular menu items with high contribution margins, dogs have low popularity and low contribution margins and puzzles have low popularity but high contribution margins. As we can see this analysis focuses on the contribution margin, that is the difference between the cost of ingredients and the selling price for each menu item. This is a relatively straightforward approach with information readily at hand but it ignores both overhead and labour costs that are more difficult to attach to individual menu items. Attaching a level of work output or productivity is time consuming, may vary over time or by staff member. Overhead may be averaged across each menu item but this may be grossly inaccurate. Ignoring either of these has the potential to be very misleading as the following example suggests. Let us examine the 'Stars' a high volume and high contribution menu item like Pizza. The ingredient costs for a cheese and tomato pizza are very low in comparison to selling price yielding on average a gross margin in excess of 85%. However, making pizza is a time-consuming process and cooking pizza is energy intense because a high oven temperature needs to be maintained throughout the service period. In many cases pizza is also finished as the order is received into the kitchen so in addition to the preparation time it is labour intensive at the time of sale requiring the restaurateur to plan labour levels accordingly.

Pricing remains a relatively flexible task, depending on the ease and cost of menu printing and should be considered with a view to appealing to the target market and restaurant sector in which it is situated. Pricing to low may make to item attractive but will not generate the desired return, pricing to high may put customers off.

Adding value

In pricing a menu it is necessary to consider the relationship between menu items so that the pricing structure appears balanced and acceptable in today's marketplace. A general observation suggests that starters and desserts are priced at similar levels and main dishes on an upward sliding scale starting just higher than the most expensive starter or dessert. For the caterer it is necessary to give some consideration to ingredient costs but these generally only represent between 20% and 30% of the menu price averaged across the whole menu and a more detailed explanation of this is given in Chapter 6. From the customers perspective however, the ingredient value often has everything to do with the perception of value of the price being charged. It is this dilemma that makes pricing a difficult and complex process because much of modern pricing is based on perceptions of added value, supply and demand, trends and fashion, perceptions of quality and market forces and it is the caterers responsibility, skill, training and value adding techniques that allows high profits to be made on low ingredient costs. As an example, let us consider one food item that has been around for at least the last fifty years, the fish cake. Fish cakes were one of the staple food items used in welfare catering, cheap and easy to produce, ideal for using up fish and potato leftovers and easy to buy in ready-made. Using fresh ingredients it typically costs less than one-pound per portion to produce and using leftovers the cost is literally pence. In a staff restaurant they may sell for three to four pounds per portion, in a typical high street restaurant, with the addition of a few salad leaves, a little flavoured mayonnaise and an imaginative menu description they will sell for ten or eleven pounds per portion and in both restaurant examples, through appropriate marketing it allows the caterer to capitalize the value added and the customer to consider the item value for money. In this way items on the menu with relatively low food costs and therefore high contribution margins are beneficial to profitability. Reputation also allows the restaurateur to add value to the dining experience so for example, a restaurant that can claim to have three Michelin stars may offer an exclusive menu that commands a substantial price (see Figure 5.11).

MENU KNOWLEDGE

When we consider that a menu is the primary sales tool for any restaurant operation it follows that product/menu item knowledge is important. Aside from issues concerning allergies, special diets or preferred tastes discerning customers will expect waiting or sales staff to have a thorough understanding of all dishes both in terms of ingredients and preparation and cooking. Good menu knowledge is an essential aid in the sales process, it provides an opportunity to discuss and where appropriate to up-sell more expensive or more profitable dishes. It also gives the customer assurance that the establishment is managed professionally.

Sales mix

Although generally food costs only account for 20–30% of menu item cost averaged across the menu there are often considerable variations. It may be seen from the example above that different

MENU SAMPLE FOR TASTING MENU
ONE HUNDRED AND FIFTEEN POUNDS

NITRO-GREEN TEA AND LIME MOUSSE (2001)
OYSTER AND PASSION FRUIT JELLY, LAVENDER
POMMERY GRAIN MUSTARD ICE CREAM, RED CABBAGE GASPACHO
QUAIL JELLY, CREAM OF LANGOUSTINE, PARFAIT OF FOIE GRAS
OAK MOSS AND TRUFFLE TOAST
(Homage to Alain Chapel)

SNAIL PORRIDGE
Joselito ham

ROAST FOIE GRAS
Almond fluid gel, cherry, chamomile

'SOUND OF THE SEA'

SALMON POACHED WITH LIQUORICE
Artichokes, vanilla mayonnaise and 'Manni' olive oil

BALLOTINE OF ANJOU PIGEON
Black pudding 'to order', Pickling brine and spiced juices

HOT AND ICED TEA (2005)

MRS MARSHALL'S MARGARET CORNET

PINE SHERBET FOUNTAIN (PRE-HIT)

MANGO AND DOUGLAS FIR PUREE
Bavarois of lychee and mango, blackcurrant sorbet,
Blackcurrant and green peppercorn jelly

PARSNIP CEREAL

NITRO-SCRAMBLED EGG AND BACON ICE CREAM
Pain perdu, tea jelly (2006)

Selection of wines by the glass to accompany this menu,
Available per person at £90, £145 or £295 (min. two)
This menu is designed to be enjoyed by the whole table

An optional 12.5 per cent service charge will be added to your bill

Figure 5.11 A tasting menu from the Fat Duck at Bray (*Source*: www.fatduck.co.uk/menu_degustation.html)

food or beverage items may carry significantly different levels of profit contribution. Other examples include the cost of making a soup as compared with an offering of smoked salmon or the cost of producing a steak and Guinness pie as opposed to an offering of grilled steak and although these dishes in themselves invite pricing differentiation overall the menu needs to have a complimentary pricing structure so that the differentiation appears well

structured and meets all the other pricing criteria for customer acceptability. Sophisticated sales data analysis through the use of EPOS systems allows the caterer to examine changes in profitability as changes to the mix of sales go through the system. Analysis of the sales report will identify sales trends and the effects that these have on profit margins, service requirements and kitchen production. By making adjustments to menu content the caterer is able to manipulate sales mix that can influence revenue, service and production demands. The manipulation of menus or menu engineering, mentioned earlier in this chapter is examined in more detail in Chapter 7 but essentially as one approach to sales analysis it provides the caterer with intelligence on how the menu is performing and suggests areas for further analysis. The level of sophistication for menu planning that EPOS systems provide and the reports they generate are examined in more detail in Chapters 6 and 7.

Nutrition

The 21st century has seen much public concern over the nutritional content of food. The provision of food and beverage in certain categories of establishment has required caterers to pay particular attention to nutrition and traditionally these have included schools, hospitals, prisons, the armed forces and any establishment regarded as having a 'captive market'. More recently public awareness has made nutrition or rather the lack of the correct nutrition a greater concern across the whole strata of society. Obesity at all ages, poor eating habits within the school meal service leading to poor eating habits later in life, levels of nutrition in hospitals and care homes as changes in demographics lead to a more elderly population the part that food plays in behavioural studies both for school children and prisoners. Whilst food remains fashionable and trendy in other sectors of society, lifestyle, image and high-level publicity for more healthy food means that caterers in all sectors need to take account of nutrition as part of their regular review of menu planning and design.

Group activity

One of the popular recommendations for a healthy lifestyle is eating five fruit and vegetables per day. Below you will see a list of five vegetables and fruit. Divide the group in half, one group to defend this selection the other to argue against.

Bananas, baked beans, canned tomatoes, potatoes and seedless grapes, each of these has both good and less good attributes, discuss.

Menus and the law

There are a number of legal issues connected with the preparation of both food and beverage menus. As stated earlier in this chapter, menus need to be accurate but they also need to be

honest in their descriptions of what is on offer. The law requires that all descriptions applied to meals or their accompaniments must be accurate, whether given in writing or by illustration, on menus, blackboards, windows or any other means, including verbal descriptions by staff. Food labelling law states clearly that failure to inform customers honestly or to give misleading information is an alleged criminal offence. The legal framework and enforcement of compliance in these areas is part of the responsibility of the local council Trading Standards department. The local council also has responsibility for issues concerning public health via the environmental health department and liquor licensing.

Food description problems

Using the term 'chicken fillet' or 'chicken breast' on a menu implies that you are providing a whole unprocessed product. If you then use a product where packaging is labelled 'reformed' or 'chopped and shaped' then it is not an unprocessed product and therefore the menu description should reflect this. An example of an item that commonly causes problems in this respect is the dish Chicken Kiev described as a chicken breast stuffed with garlic butter coated with egg and breadcrumbs and deep fried, it is a product that is commonly 'bought in' rather than made on the premises and a close examination of the label will reveal that it is often a reformed reshaped product. Furthermore to use the term 'home-made' when the product has in fact been bought in or 'home cooked' when the product is merely an assembly of convenience products put together and cooked is also an offence so, for example, opening a can of stewed steak and kidney into a dish then adding a frozen pastry lid and baking it in the oven would not constitute a home cooked steak and kidney pie. Some products are required to contain minimum quantities of ingredient before they can be sold, for example burgers have to contain a minimum or 80% meat before being sold as a burger. Descriptions of cooking methods also come under scrutiny; roasted joints of meat that have been steamed and flash roasted should not be described as roasted meat. The roasting process is a clearly defined process (please see Chapter 6) and is not the same as the process available in highly technical ovens that use very low temperature steam over a long cooking process. This process considerably reduces weight loss because the product does not lose much moisture and is subsequently coloured via a short period of high temperature. Whilst this process has obvious advantages for the caterer the end product bears little resemblance to a properly roasted joint. Other common terms used in error are cheese when it is a cheese substitute, smoked when really the product is smoke flavoured and butter when margarine is used. There are a further range of descriptions about which the caterer needs to be completely certain, which are factually correct before using them, for example stating that food is fresh or low calorie, that it is suitable for vegetarians, vegans or coeliacs, that it is a proprietary

brand product for example Hellmann's mayonnaise when it is for example a decanted Tesco own brand product, that a product has come from a certain region for example Scotch beef when it is not from that region or where to your knowledge ingredients used have undergone an irradiation process and this is not declared. In making statements concerning the weight of a menu item, for example steak, it is important to state that the weight quoted is when raw, a 160 g fillet steak will weigh up to 40% less if cooked to well done. Chapter 6 gives an example of a food specification and these can be written for most menu items which will enable more accurate menu descriptions to be followed.

BEVERAGE MENUS/LISTS

The criteria used to prepare a wine menu, or drinks list, are the same as those used when preparing a food menu as outlined earlier in this chapter. Wine menus and drinks lists fall under the requirements of licensing regulations some of which are described above and these can change from time to time and those operating licensed premises need to be aware of these changes. The use of the wine menu, or drinks list, as a selling tool cannot be emphasized enough. Customers eating in a restaurant do not have to, and will not feel embarrassed if they do not purchase a drink. It is the caterer's ability to interest and gain the confidence of customers that is likely to lead them to purchase a drink. Most beverages require fewer staff to process them and the profits from them is therefore higher than those from food and so it goes without saying that this is an area that requires time and attention from the caterer to obtain the full benefit. Beverage lists should be specifically prepared for the particular unit in which they are being sold, because the requirements vary greatly. A restaurant themed to a country or region might offer both food and beverages from that area's wines and beers. To use a general-purpose wine menu may not be suitable but such is the power of 'brands' it might be prudent to include a few as these are likely to aid sales. What is also important with beverages is that there should be a follow-through with the correct serving temperature being adhered to and the correct traditional glassware used, particularly when available to make the brand. The sales of wines and cocktails in hotels and restaurants are generally lower than they should be for such reasons as poor selling, overpricing and the snobbery that goes with wines and cocktails which tend to put customers ill at ease.

Types of beverage menus/lists

The various types of beverage menus are numerous, but for simplicity they may be grouped as being of six kinds: full wine menus, restricted wine menus, banquet/function menus, bar menus, room service beverage menus and special promotion beverage menus.

Within this general heading wine menus may be subdivided as follows:

1. *Full wine menu or lists*: This kind of menu would be used in an up-market hotel or restaurant where the customers' average spend would be high and where the time available to consume their meal would be likely to be in excess of one and a half hours. Like all menus, a full wine menu is difficult to design. Certain wines must be on the menu if a restaurant is of a particular standing; it is the question of the selection of wines within the various types based on the manager's experience and the analysis of customer sales that make it difficult to keep a correct balance and restrict the choice to reasonable limits. A full wine list may resemble a small book, often being of 15–40 pages in length. Because of the size and cost it is often the practice to have the menu contained within a quality cover and to be of a loose-leaf form so that the individual pages may be updated when required and replaced (Figures 5.12). It is also the practice for many restaurants to give a brief description of the major types of wine as well as provide a map to show the origin of the wine. The price range for this type of menu is high because of the quality of the products. The layout would usually be in the following order:
   (a) House wines
   (b) Champagnes and other sparkling wines
   (c) Red wines
   (d) White wines
   (e) Port, sherry, liqueurs

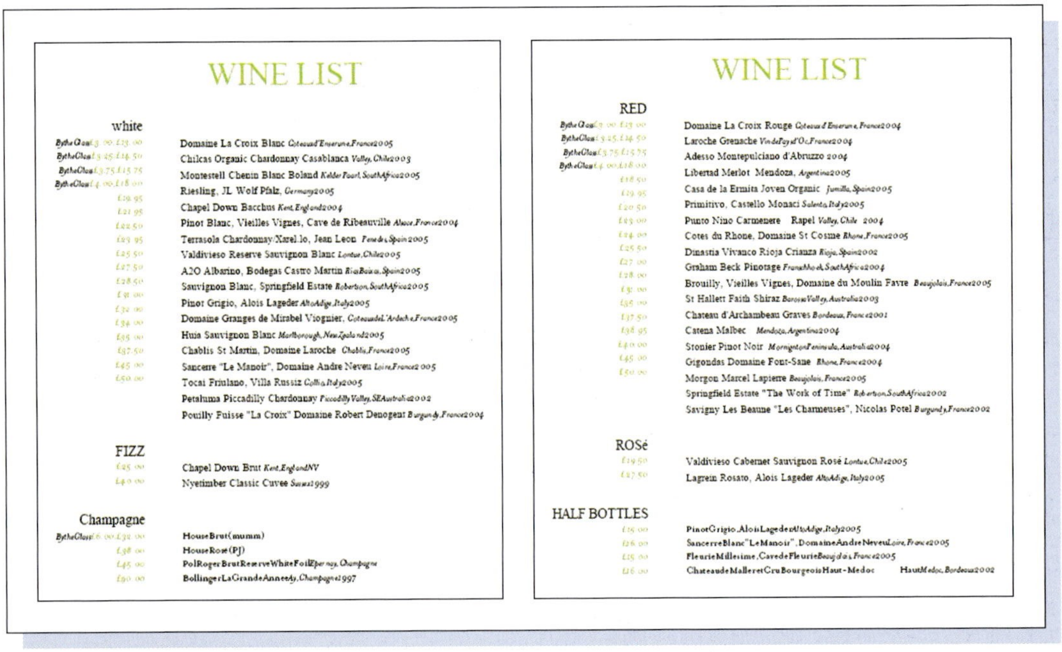

WINE LIST

white

By the Glass £3.00 £13.00 Domaine La Croix Blanc Coteaux d'Enserune, France 2005
By the Glass £3.25 £14.50 Chilcas Organic Chardonnay Casablanca Valley, Chile 2003
By the Glass £3.75 £15.75 Montestell Chenin Blanc Boland Kelder Paarl, South Africa 2005
By the Glass £4.00 £18.00 Riesling, JL Wolf Pfalz, Germany 2005
£19.95 Chapel Down Bacchus Kent, England 2004
£21.95 Pinot Blanc, Vieilles Vignes, Cave de Ribeauville Alsace, France 2004
£22.50 Terrasola Chardonnay/Xarel.lo, Jean Leon Penedes, Spain 2005
£23.95 Valdivieso Reserve Sauvignon Blanc Lontue, Chile 2005
£25.50 A2O Albarino, Bodegas Castro Martin Rias Baixas, Spain 2005
£27.50 Sauvignon Blanc, Springfield Estate Robertson, South Africa 2005
£28.50 Pinot Grigio, Alois Lageder Alto Adige, Italy 2005
£31.00 Domaine Granges de Mirabel Viognier, Coteaux de L'Ardeche, France 2005
£32.00 Huia Sauvignon Blanc Marlborough, New Zealand 2005
£34.00 Chablis St Martin, Domaine Laroche Chablis, France 2005
£35.00 Sancerre "Le Manoir", Domaine Andre Neveu Loire, France 2005
£37.50 Tocai Friulano, Villa Russiz Collio, Italy 2005
£45.00 Petaluma Piccadilly Chardonnay Piccadilly Valley, SE Australia 2002
£50.00 Pouilly Fuisse "La Croix" Domaine Robert Denogent Burgundy, France 2004

FIZZ

£25.00 Chapel Down Brut Kent, England NV
£40.00 Nyetimber Classic Cuvee Sussex 1999

Champagne

By the Glass £6.00 £32.00 House Brut (mumm)
£38.00 House Rose (PJ)
£45.00 PolRogerBrutReserveWhiteFoil Epernay, Champagne
£90.00 BollingerLaGrandeAnnee Ay, Champagne 1997

WINE LIST

RED

By the Glass £3.00 £13.00 Domaine La Croix Rouge Coteaux d'Enserune, France 2004
By the Glass £3.25 £14.50 Laroche Grenache Vin de Pays d'Oc, France 2004
By the Glass £3.75 £15.75 Adesso Montepulciano d'Abruzzo 2004
By the Glass £4.00 £18.00 Libertad Merlot Mendoza, Argentina 2005
£18.50 Casa de la Ermita Joven Organic Jumilla, Spain 2005
£19.95 Primitivo, Castello Monaci Salento, Italy 2005
£20.50 Punto Nino Carmenere Rapel Valley, Chile 2004
£23.00 Cotes du Rhone, Domaine St Cosme Rhone, France 2005
£24.00 Dinastia Vivanco Rioja Crianza Rioja, Spain 2002
£25.50 Graham Beck Pinotage Franschhoek, South Africa 2004
£27.00 Brouilly, Vieilles Vignes, Domaine du Moulin Favre Beaujolais, France 2005
£28.00 St Hallett Faith Shiraz Barossa Valley, Australia 2003
£31.00 Chateau d'Archambeau Graves Bordeaux, France 2001
£35.00 Catena Malbec Mendoza, Argentina 2004
£37.50 Stonier Pinot Noir Mornington Peninsula, Australia 2004
£38.95 Gigondas Domaine Font-Sane Rhone, France 2004
£40.00 Morgon Marcel Lapierre Beaujolais, France 2005
£45.00 Springfield Estate "The Work of Time" Robertson, South Africa 2002
£50.00 Savigny Les Beaune "Les Charmeuses", Nicolas Potel Burgundy, France 2002

ROSé

£19.50 Valdivieso Cabernet Sauvignon Rosé Lontue, Chile 2005
£27.50 Lagrein Rosato, Alois Lageder Alto Adige, Italy 2005

HALF BOTTLES

£15.00 PinotGrigio, AloisLageder Alto Adige, Italy 2005
£26.00 SancerreBlanc "LeManoir", DomaineAndreNeveu Loire, France 2005
£15.00 FleurieMillesime, CavedeFleurie Beaujolais, France 2005
£16.00 ChateaudeMalleretCruBourgeoisHaut-Medoc HautMedoc, Bordeaux 2002

Figure 5.12 Wine list extracts (*Source*: Courtesy of Acorn House Restaurant)

(f) Cognac, armagnac, gin, vodka, vermouth, whisky

(g) Beers, lagers

(h) Mineral waters, fruit juices.

2. *Restricted wine menus or lists*: This kind of menu would be used in a middle type market operation where the demand for a full wine menu is very limited. It is also likely to be used when a highly skilled wine waiter is not required and where the waiting staff serves all food and beverages. The planning of a restricted wine menu is difficult and can best be done by an analysis of previous wine sales. It is usual that this type of menu would feature a few well-known branded wines with which the majority of customers can identify. The price range for this type of menu would be lower than that of a full wine menu and would need to bear some relationship to the food menu prices. Another feature on a restricted menu is likely to be the sale of wine by the carafe and by the glass.

3. *Banquet/function menus*: This type of menu is of the restricted type in that it will offer fewer wines than a full menu. The contents of the menu will depend very much on the type of banqueting being done, but in general it is usual to offer a selection of wines with a varying price range so that it will suit a wide range of customers and their tastes. Again, banqueting wine menus will usually list some well-known branded wines. A point which must not be forgotten with branded wines is that customers frequently will know the prices charged for them in the local supermarket or wine store and therefore the caterer must be very careful as to the markup on these wines so as not to create customer annoyance.

4. *Bar menus and lists*: This type of menu is basically of two types – the large display of beverages and their prices which is often located at the back of or to the side of a bar and is often a legal requirement in many countries; or small printed menu/lists which are available on the bar and on the tables in the bar area. The large display of menus and prices would be in a general type of bar where the everyday types of drinks are served; the small printed menus/lists being found in lounge and cocktail bars. The cocktail bar menu/list usually contains cocktails (Martinis, Manhattans, etc.); mixed drinks (spirits with minerals); sherries and ports; liqueurs and brandies; wine (often by the glass); and minerals and cordials. The layout for a cocktail bar menu/list need not follow any set order, the emphasis for the layout being on merchandising specific items.

5. *Room service beverage menu*: The size and type of a room service menu will depend on the room service offered. For a luxury type unit the menu will be quite extensive, being a combination of items from the full wine list and from the bar list. In a middle type market unit the menu is likely to be quite small, being a combination of items mainly from the bar list plus a few wines only from the restricted unit wine menu/list. Because of the high labour costs for room service staff, a practice today in many hotels is to provide a small refrigerator in each bedroom stocked with a limited quantity of basic drinks.

Figure 5.13 Extract of a beverage menu (*Source*: Courtesy of Wagamama Restaurants)

The market for champagne and sparkling wine has shown accelerating growth since 2003, now worth an estimated £1.22 billion. A number of factors including changing habits in leisure and in eating and drinking have contributed to that growth, as has also the greater exposure to and familiarity with all types of sparkling wines. Among the many factors that have buoyed demand, price discounting has also played its part, becoming a prevalent feature of the market. There is also the presence of competitively priced own-label champagne and sparkling wine.

Figure 5.14 Growth in demand for champagne (*Source*: Mintel intelligence report Champagne and sparkling wine, UK, 2006)

There are many types of beverage units available specifically for use in bedrooms, some of which include a computer-based control system, which automatically records the removal of any item from the unit and records it as a charge to the customer (Figure 5.13).

6. *Special promotion beverage menus*: This type of menu may take many forms from a free pre-function reception to promote a particular beverage, to the promotion of after-lunch and after-dinner liqueurs by the use of attractive tent cards, or to the promotion of the cocktails of the month. Fortunately the suppliers willingly give assistance with beverage promotional menus by providing free advertising and promotional material and by offering the particular beverage free or at a special purchase price (Figure 5.14).

Activity 3

Design a cocktail of your choice with a list of all ingredients in accurate measurement together with the method for making it.

Now design a simple tent card including price, name of drink, an accurate legal description that also makes it sound exciting and interesting.

Licensing

The new Licensing Act 2003 came into force on 24th November 2005, the key aims of which are to allow more flexible opening hours, provide a single premises licence to supply alcohol, regulated entertainment and refreshment late at night and provide a new system of personal licences relating to the supply of alcohol. A full explanation of the 2003 act can be found on the UK government website. The local authority rather than the magistrates' court issues premises licences and personal licences. For most restaurateurs applying for a licence will be done through a solicitor or specialist agency and will require the applicant to have as a minimum qualification the National Certificate for Licensees or the National Certificate in Licensed Retailing.

Description on beverage menus • • •

Much of the regulation that covers food menus also applies to beverage menus or wine lists but there are additional regulations concerning portion sizes. Beer and cider can only be sold in 1/3 pint or 1/2 pint or multiples of 1/2 pints unless sold in cans or bottles. Any glass used to sell draught products must be crown stamped unless dispense is by pump measure. Spirits must be sold in measures of 25 ml or multiples thereof. A notice must be displayed in the bar area informing customers of the measures served. Wine sold by the glass can only be dispensed in measures of 125 ml, 175 ml or multiples thereof and any glass used to sell wine by the glass must be crown stamped. Unstamped glasses may be used where wine is sold either by the carafe or the bottle. It is interesting to note the mix of both imperial and metric measure that is enshrined in licensing regulations. As with branded food items one branded spirit, beer or soft drink cannot be substituted by decanting into another branded container so Sainsbury's Cola cannot be sold as Pepsi Cola and Sainsbury's vodka cannot be sold as Stolichnaya. It is an offence to adulterate beer or spirits with water or other substances to make it go further.

The general rules for the serving of wines

The practice of serving a different kind of wine with each food course is seldom observed today other than for the very formal occasion or for a special gastronomic event.

The choice of wine by a customer is highly individual and the once traditional rules of what wines should only be served with a particular food are not always observed today. Some aspects of the practice that have stood the test of time and are accepted and commonly practiced today are:

1. The progression of wines in a menu would be that light and delicate wines are served before fuller bodied wines, that simple wines are served before the higher quality wines and that young wines are served before the older wines.
2. When several wines are to be served with a menu the order of serving is normally accepted as being first a dry white wine followed by a red wine and finishing with a sweet white wine.
3. Wines from several countries may be served with a meal providing that there is an affinity between the different wines and that they are accepted partners with the food.
4. Champagne may be served throughout a meal with dry champagne being served with all courses other than with the sweet course when semi-sweet champagne would be better suited.
5. Rosé wines may also be served throughout a menu although it would be unusual for a formal or special gastronomic occasion.
6. Dry white wines are normally served with fish, shellfish and white meats such as poultry, pork and veal.
7. Red wines are normally served with red meats, for example beef, and with game, for example all game birds, venison and hare.
8. Sweet white wines are normally served with the sweet course.
9. Port is accepted as being ideal for serving with cheese and dessert.

MENU MERCHANDISING

The efficiency by which menus are merchandised to customers can affect the demand for the use of the food and beverage facilities as well as influence the selection of items and thereby the sales mix of an outlet. The menu is without doubt one of the most important sales tools that caterers have but which unfortunately they often fail to use to the best or fullest advantage. As mentioned earlier in this chapter, it is necessary for all menus to be correct against the checklist of general presentation, cleanliness, legibility, size and form, layout and content. We are concerned here with the way in which caterers can most efficiently utilize the menu to optimize their sales. The merchandising of catering operations involves the point of sale promotion of their facilities using non-personal media. Unlike advertising it is not a paid for form of communication, but like sales promotion is more concerned with influencing customer behaviour in the short term.

Once customers are inside a restaurant they have already made their decision as to the type of establishment they wish to eat in; their subsequent decisions are concerned with what particular aspects of the product they will now choose. Customers may decide to eat at a restaurant because they have seen it advertised, and will therefore bring to the restaurant pre-conceived ideas as to the standard of food, level of service, etc. that they will receive. It is important at this stage that the point of sale merchandising of the restaurant should support its advertising campaign in order to achieve a sense of consistency and totality. For example, if the restaurant has been advertising speciality dishes for a particular week, these must be available when the customer arrives at the restaurant.

The major types of merchandising that may be employed by a catering operation include the following.

Floor stands

Floor stands or bulletin boards are particularly effective if used in waiting and reception areas to advertise special events, forthcoming attractions, etc. In these areas in hotels, restaurants and clubs, people may be waiting in a queue or for the arrival of other guests, and therefore have the time to read the notices on these stands. In the workplace they can be placed in areas with a high throughput of pedestrian traffic, for example in corridors, and in general locations where people congregate such as beside vending machines. The announcements on these stands must be kept attractive and up to date or the messages grow old and ineffective. Some self-service operations use floor stands at the head of the waiting line to show the menu in advance and selected specialities of the day.

Posters

Posters have a wider circulation than the previously described floor stands. They may be displayed in reception areas, elevators, cloakrooms, in the restaurant dining area itself, in fact they may be placed in any strategic positions where people have the time available to read their messages. Consideration must not only be given to the area in which these advertisements should be placed, but also their positions within these areas. In elevators, for example, they are often placed at the back when the majority of people face forwards or look upwards as soon as they enter a lift and therefore only give a poster at the back a momentary glance. Similar thought should be given to the position of posters in reception areas; for example, their height should be at eye level and they need to be placed away from the entrance and exit doors which people tend to pass through quickly.

Wall displays

Illuminated wall displays are used extensively by fast-food operations showing enlarged colour photographs of the food and beverages available. They are also used by wine bars, cocktail bars and lounges and look particularly attractive at night. Blackboards are often found in pubs, bars, school cafeterias and theme restaurants where the dish of the day and other specials can be changed regularly along with their prices.

Tent cards

Tent cards are often placed on restaurant dining tables to promote special events, attractions, etc. Regarded as a valuable merchandising tool because guests will almost inevitably pick the card up and read it at some point during the meal, and they may even take it away with them. They may be used to advertise special dishes or wines, or announce forthcoming events such as a Christmas Day menu or New Year party. Again, these cards should be changed regularly to hold interest and must always be up to date and clean. In hotels or other operations which have a variety of catering outlets, these tent cards are very useful in advertising the other facilities within the same establishment. In a cocktail bar, for example, tent cards may be used to advertise the à la carte restaurant, and in the restaurant the customers' attention may be drawn to special function arrangements the operation offers. This type of merchandising can help to make customers aware of the operation's alternative facilities and hence boost sales in these areas.

Clip-ons

Menu clip-ons are most commonly used in restaurants to advertise speciality items, plats du jour, special table d'hôte lunches offered in an à la carte restaurant and so on; they may also be used on wine lists to promote a particular wine or region. Both tent cards and clip-ons are useful tools for the hotel or restaurant to feature the higher profit earning food and beverage items.

Summary

- Menus, whether for food or beverages have significant impact on attracting diners to an eatery.
- The colour, design and content descriptions all play their part in persuading diners to enter the premises.
- The menu becomes the key selling tool together with service staff that promote profitable dishes and drinks.
- The menu aids the creation of a theme or style and promotes creativity and expression for both kitchen and service staff.
- The menu produces the revenue and with careful management can deliver high profitability.
- Provided that other aspects of the meal experience meet customer expectations the menu can become a talking point long after the customer has gone.
- It is of the utmost importance that the menu reflects accurately and honestly the food and beverage product being sold so that customer expectation and restaurant delivery match.

Further study options

From reading this chapter you will realize that creating a menu verges on being both an art and a science. Whilst all menus should have a good nutritional content, customers are generally more informed and are more interested in what they eat, and those used in school meals, the prison service and hospitals have a particular need for nutritional content to be at the fore-front of design. It therefore makes nutrition an interesting topic for further study. Most hospitality courses include something on nutrition but for those with a particular interest there are a number of texts available. The Manual of Nutrition is a UK government publication produced by the Ministry of Agriculture Fisheries and Food (MAFF) and provides a basic text from which to start. Menus are also the main tools restaurateurs use to generate revenue and profit so it makes sense to examine further the various pricing models mentioned in this chapter and in Chapter 9. In addition there are a number of basic management accounting and menu engineering texts available, *Management and Cost Accounting* by Drury and *Menu Engineering a Practical Guide to Menu Analysis* by Kasavana together with *Analysing and Controlling Foodservice Costs* by Keiser, which covers both subjects are all good examples. For those interested in the design side of menu presentation, whether for special events, seasons or promotions the ability to print menus in-house, especially for one-off events or promotions, or to produce eye-catching website designs are useful skills to acquire. There are a number of further study options. Attending a short course at your local further education college will teach you, even with modest computer software, how to produce good graphics and layouts. There are also useful texts and software on graphic design, the use of colour and website design, SerifSoftware (www.freeserifsoftware.com/) and *The Non-Designer's Design Book*, 2nd edition by Robin Williams are good examples.

Case exercise

You are the food and beverage manager of a three star city centre hotel. Following refurbishment and recent changes to licensing law you have been asked to produce a new bar tariff and wine list.

Using various sections of this chapter design the process you would adopt to complete this task and the rationale for your choice.

Review questions

1. The menu is described as a primary selling tool, what guidelines are used to ensure this is the case?
2. What are the two main types of menu from which others are derived?
3. Consider three key factors in designing a menu layout.

4. What is meant by 'sales mix' and why is it so important?
5. There are a number of different menu pricing models, what is different about the 'prime cost' method?
6. Menu engineering is a useful sales' analysis tool, what are the four descriptors used and what do they represent?
7. In what situation would you expect the 'nutritional content' of a menu to be particularly important?
8. Statements made on a menu are contractual, what implication does this place on the caterer?
9. What type of menu is most likely to have both imperial and metric units of measure?
10. How would you describe menu merchandising?

Further reading

Bates, D. (2004). Pleasure reading: Menus should be designed to market the restaurant, entice diners to eat. *Nation's Restaurant News*, 38(23), 30–80. 7 June 2004, p. 2

Caterer and Hotelkeeper 21st June 2007 'Menuwatch: The Compleat Angler', Marlow, Buckinghamshire www.deantimpson.co.uk

Green, E. F. et al. (1987). *Profitable Food and Beverage Management: Operations*. Jenks, Oklahoma: Williams Books.

Kasavana, M. (1990). *Menu Engineering: A Practical Guide to Menu Analysis*. Lansing, MI, USA: Hospitality Publications.

Kasavana, M. and Smith, D. I. (1982). *Menu Engineering: A practical Guide to Menu Pricing*. Lansing, MI, USA: Hospitality Publications.

Keiser, J., DeMicco, F. J., Cobanoglu, C. and Grimes, R. N. (2008). *Analysing and Controlling Foodservice Costs: A Managerial and Technological Approach*. NJ, USA: Pearson Education Inc.

Leto, M. J. and Bode, W. K. H. (2006). *The Larder Chef: Food Preparation and Presentation*, 4th edn. London: Butterworth-Heinemann.

Lodging Hospitality (2006). *Brand Report: Renaissance Thinks Outside the Box*, 62(15), 8–10. Penton Publishing.

Marriott Streamlines Menuing. Lodging Hospitality, 1/8p, 20-Minute University, The Culinary Institute of America, *Restaurant Business*, 62(14), 15 September 2006, p. 10; 10 September 2007, p. 47.

Morrison, P. (1996). Menu engineering in upscale restaurants. *International Journal of Contemporary Hospitality Management*, 8(4), pp. 17–24.

The 3 Michelin star Fat Duck Restaurant at Bray August 2007 www.fatduck.co.uk/menu_degustation.html

http://www.culture.gov.uk/about_us/tourismleisure/licensing_act.htm

http://www.danesfieldhouse.co.uk/dining/dining.html

CHAPTER 6

Food and beverage operations: Purchasing and storage

Introduction

Food and beverage operations largely follow a basic input, process, output model. The inputs are the food and beverage ingredients and materials, the process includes storing, preparation, cooking, etc. and the outputs are meals and beverages to be sold via the service concept. Conceptually, food and beverage operations start with an idea for a theme or a desired style of restaurant. This will inform the first practical influence on the operation, the menu. Other influences will include the available space, the layout of the premises, the service style and if part of a group the number and the geographical locations. If the restaurant is located in a multi-operational site, for example a hotel, a food court, a hospital or a shopping mall, then other influences may affect the operational style and indeed the concept.

Whilst the operational process necessarily runs from input to output the design of such a process usually starts in reverse. An output objective is formulated via the catering policy, the marketing policy and the financial policy. Therefore the operational aspects of the restaurant are designed in such a way so as to support the menu style, the service style, the financial objectives, staffing and quality issues. The final part of operations concerns controls, how these are implemented and measured. Food and beverage control may be defined as the guidance and regulation of the costs and revenue of operating the catering activity in hotels, restaurants, hospitals, schools, employee restaurants and other establishments. Controls are necessary for a number of reasons from the more obvious with respect to maintaining profitability, quality and reliability to those less obvious, staff morale, disciplinary problems and recruitment costs. Food and beverage control processes are considered in more detail in Chapter 7.

The 1995 Food Safety Act clearly outlines the legal requirements associated with the purchase, delivery, storage, handling, processing and sale of food and beverages and is detailed in the section headed health and safety.

Chapter objectives

After working through this chapter you should be able to:

1. Write a purchasing and storage schedule for any food and beverage item.
2. Write a detailed specification for a food item.
3. Recognize the value of a purchasing schedule to management.
4. Understand the contribution to profitability such a schedule can make.
5. Work out stock turnover.

PURCHASING

Purchasing can be defined as 'a function concerned with the search, selection, purchase, receipt, storage and final use of a commodity in accordance with the catering policy of the establishment'. This suggests that the person employed to purchase foods and beverages for an establishment will be responsible for not only purchasing, but also for the receiving, storage and issuing of all commodities as well as being involved with the purpose for which items are purchased and the final use of them. In many organizations this job role may come under the heading of procurement and be a function of the finance department.

The purchasing function as illustrated in Figure 6.1 is vitally important in the control cycle. Should it be managed inefficiently it creates problems that often result in an unsatisfactory level of both costs and profit for the establishment and dissatisfied customers. With no specifications for commodities there would be neither quality standards nor quantity standards resulting in over-ordering or under-ordering, as yields for items would be

Policies set by management	Determines market segment aimed at, target price to be paid, the quality required and the price to be charged to customers. Sets Standard Operating Procedures (SOPs) to regulate purchasing function
Menu	Determines the choice of items available to customers
Volume forecasting (see also purchasing and storing)	Determines the quantity to be purchased
Requisition (paper or electronic)	Indicates the particular requirements of each sales outlet
Purchasing	Selects suppliers, contracts, minimum and maximum quantities and quantity discounts available. Ensures adequate temperature controlled storage is available. Specifications for individual items and to ensure continuity of supply
Receiving	Inspects for quantity and quality reports to control any discrepancies, checks conformity with required temperature statutes and maintains records for HACCP. Checks delivery vehicle temperatures as laid down in SOPs
Storing	Correct storage for each item, ensures that all temperature sensitive items are stored quickly and correctly and ensures freezers and refrigeration are not overloaded
Production	Preparation of items purchased
Selling	Provision of satisfactory products at the correct selling price/cost and quality
Control	The measurement of performance of all outlets involved, adherence to company policy and SOPs and provide feedback to management

Figure 6.1 The purchasing function

indeterminable. The receiving department would only be able to check on quantity and not on quality. The work in the stores and preparation departments would be difficult with the quality of produce varying greatly. Finally, it would be difficult to measure satisfactorily the performance of departments if they were continually being provided with non-standardized commodity items.

Responsibilities of the purchasing function

Many of the responsibilities of the purchasing manager have been subsumed into other job roles particularly in smaller organizations. Typically, the senior chef or the chef's clerk will place orders with suppliers or in the case of liquor stocks the restaurant manager or cellar manager will place orders. In the vast majority of cases, other than perhaps the small owner-operator establishments, orders would be placed with approved suppliers with terms and conditions pre-approved by management and usually controlled by the finance function. In larger organizations a purchasing clerk or procurement officer within the finance office may cover the purchasing role.

1. Maintain and adequate supply – since customer service is really the only thing sold, running out of a key item frustrates an operator's customer service goals, so adequate stock that prevents running out is crucial to good management.
2. Minimize investment – this objective seems to conflict from the first, however buyers must find some kind of trade-off between the investment level and the risk of running out, a compromise between the investment level and ensuring a continual flow of products.
3. Maintain quality – maintaining quality is not the same as establishing a quality level. Some buyers have little control over the quality they must purchase but do have a major responsibility to maintain the level of quality once set by management. The ability to maintain quality will vary amongst products, branded goods are relatively straightforward, fresh produce may vary drastically. The buyers responsibility is to ensure adequate strategies are in place to overcome any difficulties.
4. Obtain the lowest possible price – which may not necessarily be the lowest price quoted. Buyers need to be aware that the price comparison should reflect the yield of the product.
5. Maintain the company's competitive position – may be viewed as attempting to gain better prices than the competition. In reality better prices are often the prerogative of companies with higher buying power either though their size or perhaps through belonging to a consortia.

Figure 6.2

Purchasing objectives (*Source*: Adapted from Purchasing: Selection and Procurement for the Hospitality Industry, 6th edn. 2005)

The duties of the purchasing function will vary between establishments but however this role is covered and it will usually include aspects of the following:

1. Responsibility for the management of purchasing/procurement and keeping purchasing records, recording the receiving and correct storage of goods.
2. The purchasing of all commodities within their responsibility.
3. Ensuring continuity of supply of those items to user or departments.
4. Finding cheaper (for same quality) and more efficient sources of supply where this forms part of the job role.
5. Keeping up to date with all the markets being dealt with and evaluating new products.
6. Research into products, markets, price trends, etc.
7. Co-ordinating with production departments to standardize commodities and therefore reduce stock levels.
8. Liaising with production, control, accounts and marketing departments.
9. Reporting to senior management usually through establish communication channels.

In large establishments the purchasing function may be responsible for a wide range of non-food items including small equipment, cleaning materials, linen etc. According to Feinstein and Stefanelli (2005, pp. 108–109) there are five essential goals or objectives that the purchasing function should achieve (Figure 6.2).

THE PURCHASING PROCEDURE

Think of purchasing as a cycle, not a one time activity. Purchasing is not just a matter of phoning or emailing another order. You don't want to run out, nor do you want to overstock', (Brown, 2005; p. 395).

The procedure can be broken down into eight steps:

1. Each section of the organization will have established stock levels and a procedure for stock replacement. This may be a requisition form from an authorized member of staff, for example, head chef, restaurant manager or from the storekeeper. With more sophisticated electronic point of sale (EPOS) systems currently in use many stock out or low stock alerts are raised automatically by the system. In larger organizations these systems may even generate an order and send it electronically to the approved supplier.
2. The selection of the source of supply is usually agreed in advance by the department manager or by head office so that contracts can be agreed, for example the price to be paid, delivery performance with particular reference to the time, date and the place of delivery.
3. The ordering process is electronic, telephone or written order.
4. The acceptance of goods ordered and the adjustment of any discrepancies in quality or quantity of goods delivered, checking delivery notes/invoices.
5. Checking the temperature of the goods on delivery and recording this in writing.
6. Checking the condition of packaging or containers and rejecting those that are not in good condition.
7. Periodically checking the temperature of the delivery vehicle and recording this in writing.
8. The transfer of commodities to the ordering department or to the stores or cellar.

The procedure should meet the requirements of the Food Safety Act 1995 and the established Hazard Analysis and Critical Control Point (HACCP) for an establishment which should reflect the type of establishment and the market it is in, for example, a hospital or first-class restaurant so that any hazard may be viewed within this context; the location of the establishment in relation to that of its suppliers; the size of storage facilities available; the forecast of future requirements; the shelf life of the food or beverage item. Whatever the establishment a sound purchasing policy and control system should be implemented if satisfactory standards are to be achieved.

'Purchasing is not a separate activity. What how and when you buy must always reflect the overall goals of your establishment. Trends change – so must you, the purchaser.

Use a simple five-prong purchasing strategy, you want to buy:

1. The right product
2. The right quality
3. At the right price
4. At the right time
5. From the right source.

Write your plan down on paper save it any place where other members of staff will read it, you never know when someone will have to deputise', (Brown, 2005; p. 396).

The selection of a supplier

With global markets and competitive pricing selecting a supplier should be given careful consideration. Seeking a new supplier requires caution and detailed enquiries need to be made in at least the following areas. Initially larger organizations will carry out routine credit reference checks to ensure that companies are bona fide.

1. Full details of the firm and the range of items they are selling.
2. A copy of recent prices lists.
3. Details of trading terms.
4. Details of other customers.
5. Samples of products.

In all cases of food purchasing a visit should be made to any potential supplier to see the size of the company, the full range of products, the size of processing and storage facilities, the size of their transport fleet and to meet members of the management team. It is an essential process that should be recorded as part of the organizations HACCP policy and forms part of the due diligence criteria.

Selected suppliers will be added to an approved suppliers list and will be periodically evaluated for their performance using performance criteria established for each range of goods. Typically this would include price, quality and delivery.

PRICE AND QUALITY PERFORMANCE

Whilst the price paid for goods is important it is value for money and fitness for purpose that guides most buying decisions. Essential to any business is continuity of supply and the building of a sustainable relationship with a supplier that are often greater importance than saving a few pence per item.

The cheapest item is not necessarily the best buy; often a cheap item is of a low quality and may not perform well against purchase specifications, for example not obtained from an ethical source, genetically modified, not organically produced.

Delivery performance

This is the ability of the supplier to meet agreed delivery times and dates with the buyer. Prompt deliveries mean that the goods will be delivered when required and when staff is available to check them efficiently for quantity and quality. The delivery of food is regulated under the Food Safety Act 1995 temperature controls and falls under the establishment's record of HACCP.

Aids to purchasing

The preceding pages have attempted to reduce the complexity of the total purchasing activity to a simplified outline. There are, however, two main problems that continually confront buyers. They are:

1. Keeping up to date with what is available in all the markets in which they are dealing.
2. Keeping up to date with the current prices for all commodities. This is very important, as it enables buyers to negotiate with suppliers more efficiently and to compare the prices that they are being charged.

In order to reduce these difficulties, buyers need to be aware of what general information services are available that will help them. These aids may be grouped under some six headings:

1. *The supply trade press*: Trade journals are published weekly and cover most of the commodities to be purchased. They give valuable current general information and indications of future trends.
2. *The commodity trade organizations*: These organizations will readily provide information to caterers about a particular commodity, such as the types available, how they should be stored and names of local and national suppliers.
3. *The catering trade press*: These papers and journals contain items of commodity news and information of present and future prices.
4. *The national press*: Leading newspapers publish commodity market news with details of the range of prices being paid in certain markets.
5. *Government publications*: These are available from agricultural departments giving a variety of information such as a national food survey response, availability of specific commodities and current food legislation.
6. *Published price indexes*: These are produced by government departments, consumer associations and by trade journals. These indexes start from a particular date in time listing large groups of commodities and monitor the change in prices from that initial period, also recording changes on a yearly and monthly basis. This is of great significance to the caterer as it provides information of general and specific price trends and a comparison against the prices that he has paid for commodities recently.

THE PURCHASING OF FOODS

When purchasing food it is necessary to consider what the true cost of the item will be in relation to what the printed price list from the supplier states it to be. The true cost calculation has to take into account the invoice price less any discounts claimable; storage cost of the item (this is particularly relevant when purchasing large quantities at a special price and includes the problem of a further security risk); and the production costs. The calculation of a true cost may well indicate that it is cheaper to buy in five-case lots as against a fifty-case lot at a lower price, or that the production costs involved with an item make it too expensive to buy it in that state, and that it may be cheaper in the long run to buy the item already processed by a manufacturer.

There are seven main buying methods that may be used for purchasing foods. The particular method chosen often depends on the location of the establishment, the type and size of the business, its purchasing power and the type of food being purchased.

It is important for buyers to have accurate figures available of the consumption/usage of major items so that they may decide which method of purchasing to use and also as essential data for the negotiation of the purchasing price.

Purchasing by contract or tender

Purchasing by contract relates specifically to large scale catering operations, for example Wimbledon fortnight, where specific foods are needed in large quantities (e.g. strawberries). There are two common types of contract used: the organization will advertise the tender in the trade press, for example offers are invited to supply fresh fruit and vegetables for the period of one year or for a specific event.

1. *The specific period contract* which aims at determining the source of supply and the price of goods for a stated period often of three or six months. This reduces the time and labour of negotiating and ordering to a minimum, plus it has the added advantage of assisting with budgeting and pricing, when the prices of items are fixed for a period of time. Items with a fairly stable price, such as milk, cream, bread, etc. can be contracted in this way.
2. *The quantity contract* that aims at ensuring continuity of supply of a given quantity of an essential item at an agreed price over a particular trading period. The purchase of frozen fruit and vegetables for use in a banqueting or a summer season are typical examples when the supply could be affected by the weather conditions with subsequent price fluctuations and where a quantity contract is advisable used.

Note that a contract is a legal document and that the conditions of the contract should be prepared by the firm's solicitors to safeguard against possible areas of dispute or, alternatively, prepared using the guidelines available from one of the professional bodies.

Purchasing by 'cash and carry'

This method is of particular interest to the medium and small establishments whose orders are often not large enough to be able to get regular deliveries from wholesalers and food manufacturers. 'Cash and carry' food warehouses are situated in all towns and resemble in layout and operation that of very large food supermarkets. Whilst the 'cash and carry' food warehouse is only available to traders there are often equally good prices available in retail supermarkets/superstores particularly for small quantities or highly perishable items like bread and milk. Many supermarkets are now open for twenty-four hours.

The particular advantages of buying by 'cash and carry or retail superstores' are:

1. The warehouses are situated near to most catering establishments and their hours of business are usually longer than those of most food wholesalers.
2. Small or large quantities may be purchased at competitive prices.
3. Customers are able to see what they are buying, as against buying just from a price list or catalogue. They may also see special displays of a particular food company's products and be able to taste them.
4. Customers may use the warehouse as often as they like and in doing so they keep the level of stocks held low. Also, when there is a sudden increase in their business it is easy for caterers to replace their stock.

There are two disadvantages of buying by 'cash and carry':

1. Caterers have to provide their own staff and transport to collect the items from the warehouse.
2. Caterers have to pay cash for the items they purchase.

Purchasing by paid reserve

This method is used when it is necessary to ensure the continuity of supply of an item for the menu, which is of particular importance to a restaurant. Large catering companies may purchase the entire output from one supplier or group of suppliers particularly where these products are a feature. Examples of products that are purchased by this method are organically grown fruit, vegetables, hand reared or specially bred meat or the entire haul of local fishermen. For this to be successful the trading has to be equally fair to both parties and therefore requires a certain level of trust in the relationship.

Total supply

It is a method offered only by a few major suppliers who are able to offer a full supply service of all commodities to caterers. This has the advantages of only having to negotiate with one supplier; a reduced volume of paperwork; and far fewer deliveries. The main disadvantage is that of being tied to one major supplier, whose prices may not be as competitive as when using several suppliers and whose range of certain commodities may be limited. It is not commonly used by commercial enterprises but is used, for example by the British Army for logistical reasons including delivery overseas sometimes in hostile areas.

Purchase specifications for food

A purchase specification is a concise description of the quality, size and weight (or count) required for a particular item. Each specification would be particular to an establishment and would have been determined by members of the management team (Figure 6.3) (e.g. the purchasing manager, head chef and the food and beverage manager) by reference to the catering policy, the menu requirements and its price range. The relevant members of the management should keep copies of the specifications, the goods received clerk and the food control clerks and sent to all suppliers on the 'approved suppliers list'.

The reasons for preparing specifications are:

1. It establishes a buying standard of a commodity for an establishment so that a standard product is available for the kitchen and restaurant to prepare for the customer.
2. It informs the supplier in writing (and often aided by a line drawing or photograph) precisely what is required, and it assists the supplier in being competitive with pricing.

	Product specification strip–ion–special trim i.e. contre–filet
Definition	1 Taken from hind quarter of Aberdeen Angus beef
	2 Taken from a sirloin XX
Weight range	1 Between 10.5 – 12.5 k
	2 Average weight per delivery between 11.25 – 11.75 k
Surface fat	1 An even covering of fat not exceeding a thickness of 19 mm
Suet deposits	1 To be completely removed
Length of 'tops' (flank)	1 Not to exceed 25 mm
Depth of 'eye' muscle	1 The main 'eye' muscle to be not less than 75 mm
Gristle content	1 All small 'caps' of gristle on the underside of the 'eye' muscle to be removed
	2 'Back strap' gristle, which is situated on top of the striploin together with its covering of surface fat to be completely removed
Side chain	
Boning	1 To be completely removed
	All boning to be done cleanly so that:
	1 No bone fragments remain
	2 All rib and vertebrae bones are removed
	3 No rib fingers remain
	4 No knife cuts deeper than 12 mm

Figure 6.3 An example of a classical product specification for a catering cut of beef (*Source*: Adapted from Bernard Davis, Food Commodities, 2nd edn. Butterworth-Heinemann, 1991)

3. It provides detailed information to the goods received clerk and the storeman as to the standard of the foods to accept.
4. It makes staff aware of the differences that can occur in produce, for example, size, weight, quality, quantity, etc.

Whilst a detail product specification can be written it still may not achieve the level of quality assurance desired, and sometimes this cannot be checked by the organization, for example, if a product has been subjected to irradiation or has been genetically modified. The regulation of food in the UK is controlled by the Food Standards Agency and although they do not prescribe specifications to a level desired by the caterer they do provide safeguards and standards in line with European Community and UK Regulations. Grading of fruits and vegetables produced in the EC, and the classification of carcass meat, and regulation in the use of genetically modified or irradiated produce is well established.

'A product specification, sometimes referred to as 'product identification', is a description of all the characteristics in a product required to fill certain production and/or service need. It typically includes product information that can be verified upon delivery and that can be communicated easily from buyers to suppliers. Unlike the product specification, which includes only information about the product, the 'purchase specification' implies a much broader concept. The purchase specification includes all product information, but, in addition, it includes information regarding the pertinent supplier services buyers require from suppliers who sell them products. They usually seek long-term relationships with several primary sources and intermediaries and, before entering into these relationships, want to iron out every detail concerning product characteristics and desired supplier services', Feinstein and Stefanelli (2005, pp. 149–150).

Part of a purchase specification may include details of ethical sourcing, food air-miles, fair trade products and sustainability. Many customers are interested in these areas and if details can be included either on menus or other promotional material it can create additional marketing advantage.

Branding has assisted caterers to be more prescriptive when writing specifications as brands come with their own 'branded' quality assurance and tight specification. Brand protection usually means that suppliers will offer money back guarantees for products or produce that fails to meet customer expectations. This together with regulation on packaging and labelling assists caterers to purchase goods with confidence.

Whilst many establishments still use this type of purchase specification it requires both considerable knowledge to understand the specifications and considerable time and effort to write the initial specification. Even when this is done an item such as striploin although it may often be roasted whole it takes considerable skill to turn a striploin into portion-controlled steaks. With the move towards more convenience products many organizations prefer to order pre-cut steaks and joints at a price and quality determined by the supplier.

Group activity 1

Consider an item of meat, fish or cheese that you buy on a regular basis. Without using any brand names write a purchase specification for that item. Once completed pass to another member of your class and ask them if they feel confident of buying the right item.

THE PURCHASING OF BEVERAGES

The purchasing of alcoholic and non-alcoholic beverages, like that of foodstuffs, has the aim to purchase the very best quality of items, at the most competitive price, for a specific purpose. As beverages will frequently contribute more to profits than foods, and as they require considerably fewer staff to process them into a finished product for the customer, it is essential that adequate attention be given to this area. What is important to bear in mind always when purchasing beverages is that branded products are more likely to be attractive to the customer.

With beverage purchasing the following points are generally noticeable:

1. There are fewer and often restricted sources of supply.
2. The high value of beverage purchases so consideration of stock holding size, value/cost and security are important issues. Wines particularly need proper storage particularly if you intend to keep them for any time.
3. That free advice and assistance with purchasing are given by the wine and spirit trade, this particularly helpful with regard to setting and maintaining a good wine list.
4. That quality factors are difficult to evaluate and require special training to identify them. Also customers expect product knowledge from staff particularly when serving wines so this requires setting up or attending tasting sessions several times a year; your wine supplier usually facilitates these.
5. There are far fewer standard purchasing units than for food which makes pricing and stock control more straightforward.
6. There is an established standard of product. Many items like minerals, spirits, etc. will have a standard that will not vary over the years and items such as a well-known wine from an established shipper will be of a standard for a specific year, whereas with food items there may be several grades and a wide range of un-graded items available. In addition, food items may be purchased in different forms such as fresh, chilled, frozen, canned, etc.
7. The prices of alcoholic beverages do not fluctuate to the extent that food prices do.

A beverage selected for a wine list should match the operational style of the restaurant or wine bar and meet with customer expectations. It should complement the food menu and

be available for purchasing over a long enough period and at a price that is competitive. The continuity of supply of any wine selected as the house wine and this should be established before it is added to a wine list. Unusual or bin end wines may offer variety and interest to the wine list and should not be discounted just because they are in short supply.

Wine shippers

These are firms that purchase wine in the country of origin and ship it to whatever country it is to be sold in. Usually shippers are concerned with the wine from a particular region only. This means that the range of products that they are to sell is limited. Further to this problem, shippers are unlikely to want to deal with customers other than prestigious establishments or the very large companies. The products of wine shippers are usually bought from a wine and spirit wholesaler.

Wholesalers

These are usually the subsidiary wine companies of the large breweries or independent wine companies. The brewery companies sell their own label products as a first preference to other proprietary products. Wholesalers offer a very wide range of all beverages as well as a regular delivery service to the caterer. In addition they can assist the caterer with promotional literature for both bar and restaurant sales. As the beverage supply industry is highly competitive wholesalers will offer a range of marketing and merchandising support to selected clients.

Cash and carry

This method was discussed earlier in the chapter in relation to food. Cash and carry businesses or supermarkets offer a very limited range of spirits, wines, beers, etc. at very keen prices, but no other service. They are useful in emergencies or when special offers are being made.

Auctions

This is a method of purchasing that has limitations in that it usually is only for the sale of wines. It can be a useful way of buying 'end of bin' wines in small quantities from a private home or from another hotel or catering establishment. Provided that the wine buyer has a good knowledge of wines this can be an interesting and useful source for wines for a special occasion. It would be unlikely that the quantity offered would justify this method of purchasing of wines for inclusion in a standard wine list.

Purchase specifications for beverages

Generally beverages are sold and purchased by the brand name label of the product, each having a consistent quality and quantity standard of content for each selling unit. Specification for

wines also includes the details of vintage and shipper country of origin, alcoholic content and with the exception of France the grape variety.

It should be particularly noted that as the quality, consistency and quantity are virtually guaranteed the price to be paid for the product is very important, as it is the one factor that is not constant. It is for this reason that close attention is given by the purchaser to offers by suppliers of quantity discounts and promotions.

RECEIVING OF FOOD

In many catering establishments the receiving department is not considered to be a very important one, and people with little or no specialized knowledge often staff it. Unless this department operates efficiently, it becomes the weak link in the food control cycle and nullifies all effort in the rest of the control cycle. It may also pose problems in meeting the requirement of the organizations HACCP policy.

It is important to realize that all goods being received into an establishment have a monetary value and that it is essential to ensure that exactly this value in goods is properly accounted for and received. It is also important to remember that often these goods will have a selling value several times their original purchase in price in a matter of hours and most certainly come within the requirements of food temperature control regulations.

The main objectives are to ensure that for all establishments are:

1. The quantity of goods delivered matches the quantity that has been ordered. This means that goods may have to be weighed or counted.
2. The quality of goods delivered is in accordance with the specification stated.
3. The prices where stated are correct.
4. When the quantity or quality (or both) of the food delivered is not in accordance with the purchase order or an item is omitted from the order a credit note is provided by the driver. When this happens it is important to inform the end user as soon as possible.
5. An accurate record is made on the delivery note, recording details of the delivery including temperature and condition of packaging.
6. Goods should be decanted into clean storage containers where appropriate, for example, meat should be un-wrapped and stored in covered clean containers before being placed in refrigeration.

For larger organizations a purpose built delivery bay may be required. It is essential that staff employed in this department are trustworthy and fully trained in the clerical procedures and in quality inspection and also that the staff are provided with

the adequate facilities to do the job properly, such as a large and well-lit area, large scales with tare weights, copies of all purchase specifications and an office with a telephone. Further, whenever possible the purchasing officer should seek co-operation from the suppliers requesting them to arrive at set periods during the day, to spread the pressure of work at the receiving bay. Spot checks on this area are made by a member of the food and beverage management team periodically to help prevent fraud or pilferage, irregularities can go unnoticed for many weeks and be discovered only by accident or as a result of an enquiry into the reasons for the high cost of food purchased in relation to the sales.

High cost processed foods

In the majority of catering establishments such items of food as meat, especially processed meats such as hams, and fish such as smoked salmon, constitute the most expensive of the purchased foods. Because of this high cost it is not uncommon for units operating a detailed control system to set up a form of special control of these items:

Bar code tagging expensive food serves many purposes:

1. It aids the control of expensive foods.
2. It allows the receiving clerk to record each item, and to check against the delivery note/invoice.
3. It assists in obtaining a more accurate daily food cost percentage figure.
4. It assists in controlling the stock levels of these items.

The operation of bar code tagging of any items is as follows:

1. On receiving the items they are read by a bar code reader attached to a commuter system.
2. This matches the item to the order/stock item/purchase requisition.
3. Receipt of the goods is logged onto the EPOS control system where it may be identified in a number of different formats depending on the company, for example per kilo or per portion.
4. The system is accessed as required by sector manager accounts office, chef or bar manager.
5. As sales go through the till the EPOS system reduces the stock holding proportionately.
6. In a sophisticated system EPOS may generate a new order requisition or order directly from the supplier.

STORING AND ISSUING FOOD

The main objective of a food store is to ensure that an adequate supply of foods for the immediate needs of the establishment are available at all times. Food storage comes under food safety

regulations and forms part of the organizations HACCP policy. 'The basic goal of storage management is to prevent loss of merchandise due to: (1) theft, (2) pilferage and (3) spoilage', Feinstein and Stefanelli (2005, p. 328).

Foods when accepted at the receiving department are categorized as perishable and non-perishable items. The perishable items go straight to the kitchens, where they would be stored in either refrigerators or cold rooms depending on the item. Perishable foods going direct to the kitchen are often referred to as being on direct charge in that they will usually be used within one to three days of delivery by the kitchen. It is a requirement that different foods, meat, fish, dairy produce, fruit and vegetables, and deep frozen foods should be stored separately from each other. In practice some smaller establishments may mix certain categories but need to ensure there is no possibility for cross-contamination and that storage temperatures are not compromised. The non-perishable items (e.g. canned foods) go to a food store where they are unpacked, checked for any damage and placed on racking. The layout for the stores will vary between organizations but should facilitate ease of use and may include electronic stocktaking.

Issuing of food

Depending on the organization this may take place at set times during the day and may require a requisition note signed by an authorized person, for example head chef or restaurant manager. The pricing of issues is usually at the 'as purchased price', ignoring any small discounts. This is made easy in the case of non-perishable foods by marking the current price on all items when they first come into the store. The control office often does the pricing of perishable items after they have been issued as they have access to the suppliers' invoices. Issuing may be done electronically by attaching product codes or reading codes from a chart as goods are issued.

STOCKTAKING OF FOOD

The main objectives of taking stock are:

1. To determine the value of goods held in stock. This will indicate if too much or too little food is held in stock and if the total value of stock held is in accordance with the financial policy of the establishment. The total value of food held in stock is also required for the profit and loss accounts and the balance sheet, by the organization's accounts department.
2. To compare the value of goods actually in the stores at a particular time with the book value of the stock which will have been calculated with the simple formulae of:

$$\begin{array}{c} \text{Value of opening stock} + \text{purchases} \\ \text{during the period} - \text{requisitions} \\ \text{made in the same period} \end{array} = \begin{array}{c} \text{value of} \\ \text{closing} \\ \text{stock} \end{array}$$

This will highlight any differences and indicate the efficiency of the stock control system in operation.

3. To list slow moving items. This will bring to the attention of the purchasing officer, the head chef, etc. those items that are in stock and for which there has been no demand, since the last stocktaking. Usually these items will then be put on to a menu to sell them before they deteriorate, or returned to the wholesaler and credit obtained.

4. To compare the usage of food with food sales, to calculate the food percentage and gross profit.

5. As a deterrent against loss and pilferage.

6. To determine the rate of stock turnover for different groups of foods. This is calculated by the formula:

$$\frac{\text{cost of food consumed}}{\text{average value of stock at cost price}} = \begin{array}{c}\text{rate of stock turnover}\\ \text{in a given period}\end{array}$$

For example, in a twenty-eight-day trading period the cost of food consumed was £3,000. The opening stock on day 1 was £800 and the closing stock on day 28 was £700.

$$\text{rate of stock turnover} = \frac{3000}{\frac{800 + 700}{2}} = \frac{3000}{750} = 4.0$$

This means that in the twenty-eight-day trading period the total value of stock turned over four times and that an average of one week's stock was held during the period.

The rate of stock turnover will vary depending on the frequency of delivery, the commodity, the size of storage space available and the amount of money the establishment is prepared to tie up in food stocks.

Typical stock turnover figures for a month are at least twenty for perishable items (i.e. deliveries most days) and four for non-perishable items (i.e. deliveries once a week).

Stocktaking lists should be printed in a standard format and in some way related to the layout of the storeroom. This is so that stocktaking can be done methodically moving around the storeroom so that nothing is missed out; also, so that it aids the checking of figure-work by facilitating the comparing of like pages with like pages from previous stocktakes to ensure that there is normally a near standard stock of items between periods. In larger organizations stocktaking may be done electronically either by typing in codes or via a bar code system. Electronic systems have the advantage of speed and ease of use and therefore can reduce labour costs; can simultaneously calculate value both per stock item and total stock holding.

Stocktaking will typically be done every trading period (e.g. each month, every four weeks), or more frequently if a problem has arisen. Ideally, the stocktaking should take place at the end of a trading period and before the operational start of the next trading period. This usually means that the stocktaking will take place late in the evening or early in the morning. The end-of-year stocktake is usually done in greater detail and with some more thoroughness than for a trading period and will involve more staff, usually including the head of the control department to oversee and manage it. Professional stocktakers will often be used particularly for the end-of-year stocktake.

Activity 1

Given the stock turnover period shown in the example above make an argument for which of the following offers the caterer the best purchasing method; using wholesalers who provide thirty days credit or using a cash and carry where prices are 7% cheaper. You may use any of the information in this chapter on which to make your case.

RECEIVING OF BEVERAGES

The objectives for beverage receiving are similar in many ways to those of food receiving. However, as the value of beverage purchases is high and the potential for losses is also high, it is important that due attention is given to the receiving of beverages.

The main objectives are as for receiving food deliveries plus:

1. Crates and cases should be opened to check for such things as empty, missing or broken bottles.
2. An accurate record is kept of all chargeable empties delivered and returned.
3. Deliveries of beverages are timetabled with the suppliers so that those responsible for liquor storage are available.

STORING AND ISSUING OF BEVERAGES

Once beverages are received and checked they must be secured appropriately. Ideally and in larger organizations the storage of beverages is separated into five areas as follows:

1. The main storage area for spirits and red wine held at a dry and draught-free temperature of 55°F–60°F (13°C–16°C). This area is also used for the general collection and preparation of orders for the various bars and the storage of keg beers when there is a reasonable turnover.
2. A refrigerated area of 50°F (10°C) for the storage of white and sparkling wines.

3. A further refrigerated area of 43°–47°F (6°C–8°C). This is really necessary only when the turnover of kegs is slow as otherwise they may be stored at 55°F–60°F (13°C–16°C).
4. An area held at a temperature of 55°F (13°C) for the storage of bottle beers and soft drinks.
5. A totally separate area, from those above, for the storage of empty bottles, kegs and crates. This area needs to be as tightly controlled as the beverage storage area, not only because of the returnable value of the crates and bottles, etc. but to prevent free access by bar staff when an 'empty for full' bottle method of issuing is in operation.

The merchandise is unpacked in the cellar and stored correctly (table wines with an alcohol content of less than 16% by volume are stored on their sides, bottles of fortified wine, spirits and vintage ports are stored upright) on shelves or racks in the same order as on the standard bottle code/bin list. The objective for preparing a standard bottle code/bin list is to eliminate the confusion of bottle sizes, spelling of names and different brands, and to establish an appropriate starting point for the control of beverages.

As the majority of food and beverage operations currently use EPOS systems the establishment of a bin system is relatively straightforward. Each product is coded into the sales system-identifying unit of measure/s available and the price/s charged. This can be linked to a stock control system that informs management of current stock level at any given time. This can then be physically checked as required.

Cellar records: If the value of cellar stocks is high it will almost certainly be controlled via an electronic record system, where this is not the case it is usual for the following cellar records to be kept.

A cellar inwards book: This provides accurate reference to all beverages coming into the cellar, and posting data for the cellar man's bin cards. Whenever necessary it is a useful check against the perpetual beverage inventory ledger held in the food and beverage control or accounts office.

Bin cards: These are provided for each individual type of beverage held in stock and record all deliveries and issues made, the cards being fixed on the shelves or racks against each beverage, the bin card numbers referring to the same bin numbers as the wine list and originating from the standard bottle code list.

Cellar control book: This provides a record of all daily deliveries to the cellar and the daily issues of each beverage from the cellar to the various bars and should cross-check with the entries on the bin cards and the various EPOS sales and inventory control system.

Ullages and breakages: It is necessary for any ullages and breakages to be recorded, together with an explanation, and countersigned by a member of the food and beverage management department. The frequency of the recording of any ullages and breakages would determine the necessity for management to take corrective action.

The term 'ullage' is used to cover all substandard beverages such as bottles of weeping wines, bottles of wine with faulty corks, unfit barrels of beer, etc. which, whenever possible, would be returned to the supplier for replacement. Breakages of bottled beverages usually occur by mishandling by cellar and bar staff.

Empties: Many of the containers of beverages such as crates, kegs, beer bottles, soda siphons, etc. are charged for by the supplier against a delivery. It is therefore necessary that control be maintained on these charged items to ensure that they are returned to the supplier and the correct credit obtained.

Hospitality book: This is necessary to record the issue of drinks to the kitchen and other grades of staff as laid down by the company policy.

Issuing of beverages

Issuing of beverages generally takes place at set times during the day and may require a requisition note signed by an authorized person. When stock is transferred from storage to sales point it may be entered onto the sales database depending on the system in use. The importance of recording the transfer of liquor stock only becomes necessary when either the person responsible for the stock changes or additional people have access to stock (i.e. bar staff). In these cases a duplicate copy of the transfer may be used, one for each party concerned.

The pricing of issues for beverages is different from that for food in that two prices are usually recorded, the cost price and the selling price. The cost price is recorded to credit the cellar account and for trading account and balance sheet purposes. The selling price is recorded for control purposes to measure the sales potential of a selling outlet using the basic formula:

$$\frac{\text{opening stock} + \text{purchases} - \text{closing stock}} = \text{total beverage consumed}$$

$$\text{total beverage consumed} = \text{beverage revenue}$$

It should be noted that the above formula might be calculated for the value of stock and purchases either:

1. At cost price in order to compare the usage with the actual sales and to ascertain the profit margin and beverage gross profit.
2. At sales price in order to compare potential sales with the actual recorded sales.

It is usual for the beverage revenue to be different from the sales potential figure because of such factors as a high percentage of mixed drinks being sold or full bottle sales being made over the counter of a bar.

Stocktaking of beverages

The main objectives of stocktaking are as those set out for food however it may be done more frequently:

1. To combat its higher susceptibility to pilferage.
2. To allow for more frequent orders and therefore less stock holding of expensive items.
3. To control the quality and condition of some highly perishable, short-life items for example real ales.

The rate of stock turnover is calculated the same way as food stock turnover:

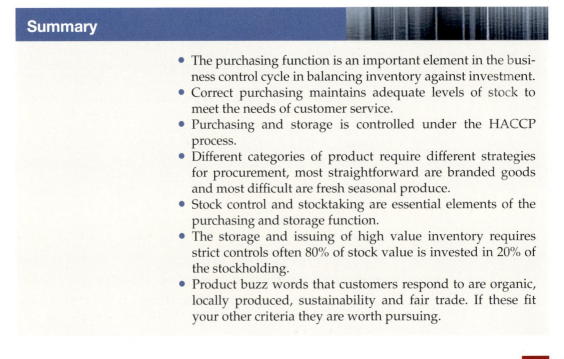

$$\frac{\text{cost of beverage consumed}}{\text{average value of stock at cost price}} = \text{rate of stock turnover}$$

The rate of stock turnover for beverages will vary from unit to unit depending on such things as the size and type of the unit and its storage facilities, its location and whether it 'puts down' wine as an investment. Typically it will follow a similar pattern to stock turnover of food. Instituting 'par stocks' or stock levels based on usage, estimated demand, case sizes and delivery times may control the rate of stock turnover. Many organizations take advantage of weekly stock deliveries, which reduces the need to carry large values of stock or tie up large areas for storage.

Summary

- The purchasing function is an important element in the business control cycle in balancing inventory against investment.
- Correct purchasing maintains adequate levels of stock to meet the needs of customer service.
- Purchasing and storage is controlled under the HACCP process.
- Different categories of product require different strategies for procurement, most straightforward are branded goods and most difficult are fresh seasonal produce.
- Stock control and stocktaking are essential elements of the purchasing and storage function.
- The storage and issuing of high value inventory requires strict controls often 80% of stock value is invested in 20% of the stockholding.
- Product buzz words that customers respond to are organic, locally produced, sustainability and fair trade. If these fit your other criteria they are worth pursuing.

Further study options

Further reading on a wide range of articles on the business of purchasing, supply chain management and inventory control can be gained from:

1. International Journal of Information and Operations Management
2. International Journal of Purchasing and Materials Management
3. European Journal of Purchasing and Supply Management
4. Journal of Purchasing and Supply Management
5. Inventory Management Report.

For those who are perhaps interested in developing a career in this field:

1. The Chartered Institute of Purchasing and Supply (CIPS). Incorporated by Royal Charter in 1992, lead body in purchasing and supply chain management with courses, training, seminars and conferences available internationally.
2. European Institute of Purchasing and Management (EIPM). Founded in 1990, EIPM is the European centre for education and research into purchasing and supply management.

Study exercise

The Duck and Drake is a successful, privately owned 'free house' pub with an annual turnover of £400,000; 60% of the turnover is wet sales (beverage), 30% is food (using rather ad hoc menus) and the remaining 10% is from gaming (pool and slot machines). As owner-operators they view the turnover at the end of their second year as successful and have lived well off the business including most of their own food and beverage requirements. They are unaware of exactly how the sales revenue is made up by each component and what margins they make. They have also not seen the need to introduce any systems for controlling stock or purchases, relying instead on their own experience, an annual chat with their accountant where they look at the purchases against revenues and a family environment of honesty.

A brief look at the accounts identifies the following:

Beverage sales	£240,000	cost of sales	£115,000
Food sales	£120,000	cost of sales (including for own use)	£54,000
Gaming income	£40,000	50–50 share scheme	

Although successful in the eyes of the owners this business is not performing as well as it could. A new member of the restaurant staff has given the following feedback to the owners for the past couple of weeks gained from talking to the customers whilst serving them.

1. We don't come here as often as we would like because it is hard to know what's still going to be available on the menu, when we arrive, and it's embarrassing when one has guests!
2. I like to have a steak when I am out but I don't have them here anymore, they are so unreliable.
3. I hope the wine I have ordered is not that supermarket wine I had last time, it had their brand on the label and was four times the price!
4. Well I haven't been here since Christmas; I wasn't very well after that turkey dinner.

Advise the owners on what procedures they should adopt in terms of purchasing and storage that would mitigate these customer comments and generally improve the performance of the business.

Review questions

1. Define the main requirements of the purchasing function.
2. Define the main purchasing objectives.
3. How can you control quality as part of the buying process?
4. What is the advantage of buying through a 'cash and carry' outlet?
5. What are you seeking to achieve from a purchase specification?
6. How is a purchase specification different from a product specification?
7. Why is a beverage purchasing specification generally less difficult to write than a food specification?
8. What legislative policies cover the purchase and storage of food in the UK?
9. How can stock control improve profitability?
10. Why would a food and beverage manager be interested in the rate of stock turnover?

Further reading

Briggs, R. (2000). *Food Purchasing and Preparation (paperback)*. London: Continuum Publishing.

Brown, D. R. (2005). *The Food Managers Guide to Creative Cost Cutting*. Ocala, Florida: Atlantic Publishing.

Davis, B. and Lockwood, A. (1994). *Food and Beverage Management – A Selection of Readings*. Oxford: Butterworth-Heinemann.

Feinstein, A. H. and Stefanelli, J. M. (2005). *Purchasing: Selection and Procurement for the Hospitality Industry*, 6th edn., Hoboken, NJ: John Wiley Inc.

Mintel, (2006). *Intelligence Report Champagne and Sparkling Wine March 2006* Mintel International Group Limited.

Stevens, J. (1987). *Measuring Purchasing Performance*. London: Business Books.

Food and beverage operations: Production and service

Introduction

Food production may be defined as that phase of the food flow (i.e. from the purchasing of the foods to service to the customer) mainly concerned with the processing of raw, semi-prepared or prepared food-stuffs. The resulting product may be in a ready-to-serve state, for example in the conventional method (cook-serve); or it may undergo some form of preservation, for example cook-chill or cook-freeze, before being served to the customer.

Beverage production may be defined as the processing of the raw, semi-prepared or prepared beverage product, so that it is in a ready-to-serve state before being served to the customer. For example, a raw beverage product such as tea would need to be fully processed before being served, a semi-prepared product such as a cordial would require only partial preparation, and a bottled fruit juice or bottle of wine may be termed a fully prepared beverage product. The fine dividing line between food and beverage production and food and beverage service is not always distinguishable. The point at which production ends, and service begins, is often difficult to define.

It is often necessary, therefore, to include certain aspects of, for example, food service when describing food production methods, in order that the production method may be seen in the context of the whole catering operation, and not in isolation.

The decision as to which food and beverage production method to use in a particular catering operation is taken at the initial planning stage – at this point the market to be catered for, and hence the type of catering facility to be offered, has been decided upon. The initial planning of a food service facility is critical to the long-term success of the operation, and one which must be afforded time, finance and commitment in order to avoid costly mistakes later. As a minimum it is essential that the food production and service model chosen is suitable for the type of operation the organization requires whilst at the same time meeting all the requirements of the food hygiene regulations and in particular the holding temperatures for hot or chilled food. On a practical note it is often very helpful to invite the local Environmental Health Officer (EHO) to the premises in advance of setting out the kitchen or installing equipment. Getting them 'on side' at this early stage can form the basis of a good working relationship in the future and minimize any risk of not complying with regulation or good practice.

Chapter objectives

After working through this chapter you should be able to:

- Understand the wide variety of processes available for food and beverage production.
- Understand the principles, practices and complexity of modern food safety legislation.
- Understand the contribution to profitability of using the correct food and beverage production method for a particular type of outlet.
- Match food and beverage service to an appropriate food and beverage production method.

Hazard analysis and critical control point

Hazard Analysis and Critical Control Point (HACCP) is a systematic approach to identifying and controlling hazards, whether they are microbiological, chemical or physical in nature. Although in many food and beverage operations a number of the hazards are likely to be the same, each establishment is required to undertake an analysis that can identify any potential hazard for that particular organization. The local EHO will be able to offer advice on how best to approach this together with some ideas on what records you would need to keep for the particular service in question.

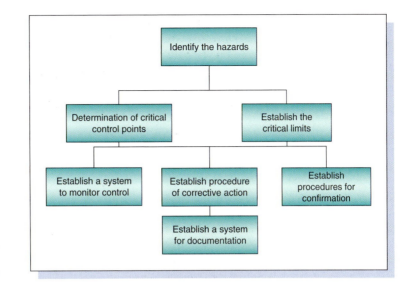

Figure 7.1
Based on an HACCP procedure
developed by the Lakeside
Restaurant University of Surrey

There are seven key stages for HACCP on which a food safety management system can be designed and implemented (see Figure 7.1). The process is systematic and will need to be applied to each group of products.

The planning of food service facilities

The planning of food service facilities is more complex than many other types of planning projects. This is due to some of its unique characteristics, including the following:

1. The wide variety, choice and grades of raw materials available.
2. The high perishability of some raw materials.
3. The wide variety of semi-prepared and prepared products available.
4. The perishability of the end product.
5. The fast turnover of some foods, for example items delivered fresh in the morning may be prepared and served to the customer at lunchtime, and the revenue banked by the afternoon.
6. The product is rarely taken to the customer, the customer has to go to the product to purchase it, and consume it, usually on the premises.
7. The product cannot be stored for any length of time.
8. A wide variety of customers may be catered for within the same establishment.
9. There may be a variety of production and service methods in operation in any one outlet.
10. The process has to comply with the HACCP policy.

An inherent problem in food production planning is that customer demand for the food service facilities is not constant; the restaurant, cafeteria or fast-food outlet is only in demand at certain times during the day, mainly breakfast, lunch and dinner, and this results in peak periods of activity at certain times during the day, and troughs of comparative inactivity in between. This problem is further compounded by the catering facility having to offer different menu items or 'products' for each meal period, and sometimes even a different type of food service for the different meal periods. For example, a hotel restaurant may offer a continental style buffet service for breakfast, a table d'hôte menu at lunchtime with a plated service and an à la carte menu in the evening with silver service.

It is necessary to emphasize the importance of efficient food service planning. It involves a number of interrelated processes, each dependent on the other, which together form a totally integrated system. Cost limits are always present for each stage of the planning process, and funds are allocated specifically for the actual building, the interior furnishings, equipment, etc.; such funds must be used wisely, as short-term savings often result in long-term costs.

Badly planned facilities suffer daily because of initial poor planning, their poor labour utilization, loss in food quality standards, high running costs and general lack of acceptance by customers. Adequate food holding temperature controls at the point of service for both hot and cold food are essential requirements in planning a food service area (see Figure 7.2). The likely outcome of a poorly designed food service area are increases in the number of 'short cuts' staff are willing to make in order to make their work processes more efficient or easier.

Objectives

The first step in the planning of a catering facility is a written statement of the operation's objectives. The primary objective of a food service operation must be the provision of a catering outlet aimed at satisfying a particular market segment of the population. Allied to this main objective are the catering facility's other objectives, some taking precedence over others in different

Section		Service hotplate refrigeration				
Date	Time	Storage unit	Unit temperature	Product temperature	Action required	Recorded by
01/03/07	11.00 AM	Grilled meats fridge	+ 1°C	+ 2°C	None	J. Holland
01/03/07	11.10 AM	Cooked meat counter fridge	+ 3°C	+ 4°C	None	J. Holland

Figure 7.2 Extract from refrigeration temperature record book *Lakeside Restaurant*

catering situations; for example, a commercial restaurant's main objective may be to maximize returns on capital in the shortest possible period, whereas an industrial cafeteria's main objective may be the provision of a subsidized catering facility in which case the net profit is no longer the most important objective.

General planning objectives can, however, be identified for all types of catering facilities and these may be listed as follows:

1. *Customer appeal*: The main objective of a catering facility is to provide a catering service for a clearly defined sector of the market. Once the sector of the market to be catered for has been identified the planning of the facility can begin. When customers enter a restaurant, cafeteria or any other type of food service operation, they bring with them certain expectations about the type of operation it is, the standard of food and the level of service they will receive; the image created by the catering facility must be in congruence with their image of the restaurant if the facility is to have appeal to customers. For many hotels food and beverage has not generated the same levels of revenue as that of rooms division but certainly during the last decade hotel restaurants have sort to turn this around not only as a revenue centre but also as part of their wider marketing effort (see Figure 7.3). It is important that this harmonization between the customer and catering operation is extended throughout the facility. For example, in a high-class restaurant the customer would expect an extensive à la carte menu, silver service, only linen on the tables, the service staff to be correctly attired in uniforms, etc. All these individual aspects of the operation combine to portray a total picture to the customer. It is important, therefore, that at the planning stage the catering operation is planned as a whole so that all the different aspects of the production and service combine to produce a facility that is aimed at a particular market segment.

2. *Cost control*: Whatever the type of catering facility, costs must be controlled; in a catering operation these include the initial

Figure 7.3
Hotels' look to increase revenue from food and beverage (*Source*: Perlik, 2006)

'Hotel operators need to think like restaurateurs today' says Al Ferrone, senior corporate director of fired and beverage for Beverly Hills, Calif.-based Hilton Hotels Corp. 'Our food service operations can no longer simply meet basic dining needs. They have to offer the same quality dining experience as a top-notch free-standing restaurant'.

'There's been a shift in focus toward food service on the part of hoteliers', says Phil Davies, senior director of food and beverage development at Marriott International in Bethesda, MD. 'It's highly competitive, not just among hotels but between hotels and local restaurants'.

Food service also has become more profitable. While food revenue at full-service hotels rose a modest 4.4% last year, direct operating expense of food departments grew only 1.9%, resulting in an 18% improvement in department profitability.

Notes: Hospitality Research.

planning and building costs, and the daily running costs, such as food, labour and fuel. Some operations are built specifically with a profit target to achieve such as commercial restaurants and cafeterias, and even those operations such as subsidized catering facilities should be aiming to keep costs to a minimum so that any 'profits' made, may be put back into the operation, and hence reduce the overall running costs of the operation.

3. *Facilitate production and service*: This involves ergonomically designing the layout of production and service areas and equipment, both in the kitchen and the restaurant and bars. Workplace design is particularly important: which equipment should be mounted; and which should be free-standing; storage facilities; the height and width of the working benches; the height, size and shape of tables; the lighting, heating and noise limitation requirements; etc. All of these attributes of a food service facility, if carefully planned, result in a safely designed working area and a smooth flow of employees and materials.

4. *Materials handling*: The movement of materials in a catering operation should be planned so that minimal handling is involved. Where possible the materials flow should be as direct as possible, for example from the storage area to the workbench for preparation. Cross-flows of traffic and backtracking should be avoided as they are not only time consuming, but they are also potential accident hazards. Many aids are available to the planner when designing materials handling for a catering operation: flow process charts, string diagrams, travel charts, etc., are all aids to designing a materials-handling system that minimizes actual handling. The time spent by employees handling materials may be translated into labour costs – while the employee is transporting or moving the materials, he is not preparing them ready for sale. Mechanical aids should be used where they will alleviate the human handling of materials, for example conveyor belts, trolleys, carts, etc. These can all be incorporated into the original plans. Any mechanical aids or labour-saving equipment should be purchased only if it is seen to be cost effective.

5. *Labour utilization*: The planning of efficient labour utilization is very dependent on the use of management tools such as work-study, motion economy, etc. The tasks that are to be performed in the production and service areas of the catering operation must be identified and the most efficient method of performing those tasks analysed, so that detailed job descriptions and work schedules may be produced. The ever-increasing labour costs in catering operations today necessitate the planning of efficient food production and service areas that result in greater employee productivity.

6. *Supervision and management*: At the planning stage consideration must also be given to the task of supervising and managing the catering operation, particularly the production and service employees. This involves allocating adequate time and facilities for meetings between the management and staff,

training and demonstrations, etc. so that this becomes an ongoing process by management rather than something that is available to all employees at their commencement of employment, but is never refreshed. Management of the catering facility in other areas should also be given consideration; for example, supervising the day-to-day food, labour and fuel costs. Efficient feedback information systems need to be incorporated that are able to supply management with the type of information necessary for them to make decisions concerning the efficient running of the catering operation.

7. *Hygiene and safety standards*: Hygiene and safety standards are both factors that must be built into a catering operation at the planning stage; this is essential for the well-being of both the customer and the employees. In the UK at present EHOs have powers to inspect and, if necessary, close premises whose hygiene standards are not high enough. The acts governing the hygiene control of premises and the current fire regulations also have to be taken into account and strictly observed by all catering establishments. In any new layout or design within licensed premises the fire officer will need to be informed. It is also beneficial to invite comment from the environment health department at the local council so that further alterations are not required following a subsequent inspection.

8. *Cleaning and maintenance*: Closely related to the safety and sanitary conditions of the food service facility is the consideration at the planning stage for easy cleaning and maintenance of the premises. Here a number of factors need to be taken into account: the construction and finishes of floors, walls and ceilings; the design of the equipment, such as mobile units that can be pulled clear of the wall and cleaned behind; sufficient space under the equipment so that the floor can be washed; etc. The regular maintenance of equipment is also particularly important if costly breakdowns and possible accidents are to be avoided.

9. *Flexibility*: Flexibility at the initial planning stage can save on an operation's long-term costs. Most catering facilities undergo some form of change during their life cycle, and advance planning for this can help the transition or changeover period considerably. Most changes in a food service operation occur in the materials being used and/or in the production techniques; for example, the introduction of a high percentage of convenience foods to an operation would reduce its labour and equipment requirements and more kitchen space would become available. Possible changes such as these should be considered at the initial planning stage, so that they may be efficiently managed by the operation when and if they become necessary. It is not uncommon that all of the finance to plan and operate a production facility is not available initially and that the planning has to be implemented in stages when the finance is available, often over a two- to three-year period. For example, a catering operation may not be able to purchase some specific items of

equipment until the second year of operation; it is important at the planning stage that this has been taken into account and that the basic services of gas, electricity, water, drainage, lighting, ventilation, etc. are fully accessible and have allowed for an increase in capacity.

If the optimum use is to be made of available money, materials and manpower, the major requirements listed above should be used as the basis for planning a food service facility. Without adequate planning at the initial stage, the operation will lack direction and may result in trying to be 'everything to everyone'. The operation may then be faced with the situation of attempting to cater for mixed markets, for which it has not been designed, and therefore does not have the necessary facilities.

FOOD PRODUCTION METHODS

In examining food production methods currently in operation, reference must be made to the traditions of catering which have had a profound effect on the production methods in operation today.

Food production methods in the catering industry evolved over a period of time when there was an abundance of labour. The design of the traditional kitchen, first introduced into the UK in the latter half of the 19th century, grew up around the division of tasks into *parties* (similar tasks with numerous foods were carried out by a particular group of people). This was the development of the *partie* system. The rigid demarcation between the sections meant that the staffing ratio was high in comparison with the number of meals served.

During the first half of the 20th century there was little or no technical change in the kitchens of hotels and restaurants. Most managers and chefs had been trained in the old traditional methods that gave reasonably satisfactory results, and to them there seemed little reason to change. It is only during the last thirty years that changes in the old traditional methods have evolved. These changes were slow to appear and started in the manufacturing industry rather than in the kitchens of hotels and restaurants.

The major firms of food suppliers did technical research and their products slowly became accepted by the catering industry, as skilled catering staff began to be in short supply. This was further encouraged by the rising costs of space that was necessary for a traditional kitchen. Traditional kitchen tasks were beginning to disappear at increasing speed. In 1966 the first cook-freeze operation in the UK began, and from this derivatives have evolved from both cook-freeze and cook-chill methods. The following represents a study of the main food and beverage production methods currently in operation. It is important to note that all food processing comes under the Food Safety Control of Temperatures Act 1990.

Conventional methods

Traditional partie method • • •

In the conventional partie method, the majority of food is purchased raw, very little falling into what we now call the 'convenience foods' category. Facilities are provided for the receipt and storage of goods, the preparation, cooking, holding and service of food, and for dishwashing facilities (see Figure 7.4).

During each day the use of labour is intermittent, rising to a peak just before the service of each meal. The same situation exists with the cooking equipment, good utilization for short periods, but overall poor utilization of capital plant. This in turn leads to poor use of electricity and gas appliances which are often turned on in the morning and left on during the day, although only efficiently utilized for a few hours. Altogether it is an expensive way of running a kitchen; expensive because of the manpower needed to operate it, and its space, equipment and energy requirements.

Conventional production with convenience foods • • •

Convenience foods may be introduced into a traditional production kitchen. Conventional production using convenience foods may range from a partial to a virtually complete reliance on the use of the wide variety of convenience foods now available. However, the best use of such convenience foods can only be by means of a planned catering system.

It is basic to the systems approach that the operation be considered as a whole, taking into account the effects that a change in one part of the system might have on another part. Therefore, if convenience foods are to be introduced into a traditional kitchen previously using all fresh produce, the effects upon labour, equipment, space, and more important, the customer, should all be considered.

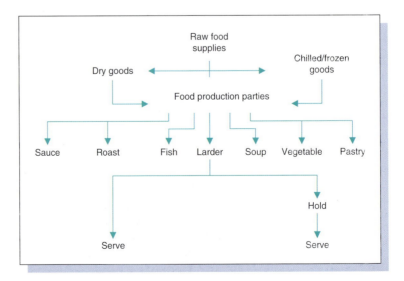

Figure 7.4
The main division of activities in the conventional *Partie* food production method

Centralized production methods • • •

Centralized production methods involve the separation of the production and service components of the food flow system either by place or time or both. Food that is centrally produced is either then distributed to the point of service in batches or is pre-portioned; it may be transported in a ready-to-serve state, for example hot, or it may need some form of regeneration in a satellite or end-kitchen, for example chilled or frozen food. This form of food production became popular in the 1970s and 1980s mainly due to the demand in the welfare sector for this type of centralized production and its associated savings. However, because of the changing nature of the hospital catering service in particular, central production units (CPUs) are no longer in such demand mainly due to their high operating costs. Modern hospital catering offers high quality food and beverages cooked and served to a high standard and offers a wide choice (see Figures 7.5 and 7.6).

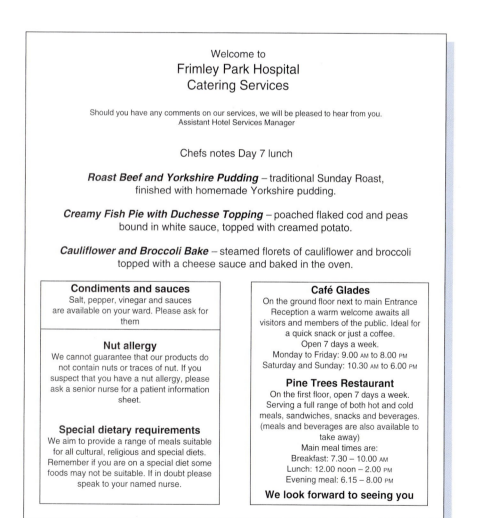

Welcome to
Frimley Park Hospital
Catering Services

Should you have any comments on our services, we will be pleased to hear from you.
Assistant Hotel Services Manager

Chefs notes Day 7 lunch

Roast Beef and Yorkshire Pudding – traditional Sunday Roast,
finished with homemade Yorkshire pudding.

Creamy Fish Pie with Duchesse Topping – poached flaked cod and peas
bound in white sauce, topped with creamed potato.

Cauliflower and Broccoli Bake – steamed florets of cauliflower and broccoli
topped with a cheese sauce and baked in the oven.

Condiments and sauces
Salt, pepper, vinegar and sauces
are available on your ward. Please ask for
them

Nut allergy
We cannot guarantee that our products do
not contain nuts or traces of nut. If you
suspect that you have a nut allergy, please
ask a senior nurse for a patient information
sheet.

Special dietary requirements
We aim to provide a range of meals suitable
for all cultural, religious and special diets.
Remember if you are on a special diet some
foods may not be suitable. If in doubt please
speak to your named nurse.

Café Glades
On the ground floor next to main Entrance
Reception a warm welcome awaits all
visitors and members of the public. Ideal for
a quick snack or just a coffee.
Open 7 days a week.
Monday to Friday: 9.00 AM to 8.00 PM
Saturday and Sunday: 10.30 AM to 6.00 PM

Pine Trees Restaurant
On the first floor, open 7 days a week.
Serving a full range of both hot and cold
meals, sandwiches, snacks and beverages.
(meals and beverages are also available to
take away)
Main meal times are:
Breakfast: 7.30 – 10.00 AM
Lunch: 12.00 noon – 2.00 PM
Evening meal: 6.15 – 8.00 PM

We look forward to seeing you

Figure 7.5 An example of Sunday lunch menu using cook-chill production system (*Source*: Frimley Park Hospital 2007)

Smaller version CPUs are gaining popularity in the commercial sector, particularly amongst restaurant chains as a means of providing standardization of product across outlets.

The advantages of centralized production include:

1. The separation of the production and service activities allows the unit to work at a consistent level of efficiency rather than 'peaks' and 'troughs' often found in a traditional kitchen.
2. By concentrating the skilled production staff at the CPU, a higher standard of preparation and presentation should be possible, as satellite kitchens do not require such skilled staff.
3. Bulk purchasing reduces the raw material costs and helps to reduce the overall cost per meal.
4. The introduction of a 'storage stage' between production and service allows the production unit to work to maximum efficiency and with a better utilization of staff and equipment.

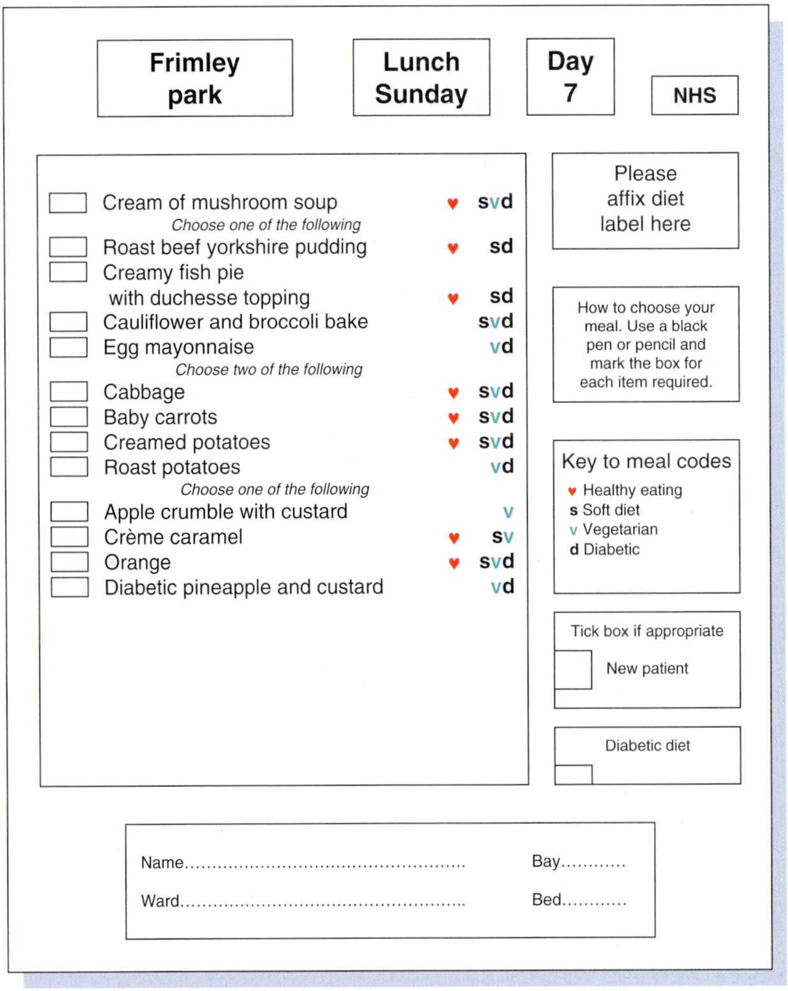

Frimley park | **Lunch Sunday** | **Day 7** | **NHS**

Cream of mushroom soup — ♥ s v d
Choose one of the following
Roast beef yorkshire pudding — ♥ s d
Creamy fish pie
 with duchesse topping — ♥ s d
Cauliflower and broccoli bake — s v d
Egg mayonnaise — v d
Choose two of the following
Cabbage — ♥ s v d
Baby carrots — ♥ s v d
Creamed potatoes — ♥ s v d
Roast potatoes — v d
Choose one of the following
Apple crumble with custard — v
Crème caramel — ♥ s v
Orange — ♥ s v d
Diabetic pineapple and custard — v d

Please affix diet label here

How to choose your meal. Use a black pen or pencil and mark the box for each item required.

Key to meal codes
♥ Healthy eating
s Soft diet
v Vegetarian
d Diabetic

Tick box if appropriate
New patient

Diabetic diet

Name.. Bay............
Ward.. Bed............

Figure 7.6 Reverse side of menu (Figure 7.5) where patient enters meal information

5. Better working conditions and more social hours are generally available for the production teams.
6. Energy consumption can be reduced by careful scheduling and by a continuous run of single products.

The disadvantages of centralized production include:

1. The high capital investment of planning and constructing a CPU.
2. Unless fully utilized the cost per meal can rise dramatically.
3. Production failures or stoppages due to power failure, hygiene problems or food contamination outbreaks can quickly escalate and have much greater repercussions than a problem in an individual kitchen.

Basic principles of cook-freeze and cook-chill systems ● ● ●

1. That all raw foods used should be of a good microbiological quality.
2. That the initial cooking of the foods will ensure the destruction of the vegetative stages of any pathogenic microorganism present.
3. As some microorganisms produce spores which are not killed by normal cooking procedures, it is vital that the temperature range from +7°C to 63°C at which these organisms can quickly multiply, must be covered as quickly as possible to restrict growth during cooking. The same attention needs to be applied when regenerating the foods.
4. Cross-contamination must be avoided throughout the process, particularly between that of raw and cooked foods. Physical separation of pre-preparation and cooking areas is essential to aid this.
5. The storage and distribution conditions for cooked and chilled foods must be strictly controlled to ensure their quality and safety.
6. The reheating and service procedures for the food must be strictly adhered to, to ensure the food's safety with the temperature of all food being strictly monitored.
7. The entire process is subject to HACCP.

Cook-freeze production ● ● ●

The term 'cook-freeze' refers to a catering system based on the full cooking of food followed by fast freezing, with storage at a controlled low temperature of −18°C or below, followed by subsequent complete reheating close to the consumer, prior to prompt consumption. Cook-freeze is a complete food production process from the initial raw food through to the final service of the product and is largely done by food manufacturing companies rather than by caterers (Figure 7.7).

1. *Quality of food*: Raw food should be purchased against a tight specification to ensure quality and consistency. For large

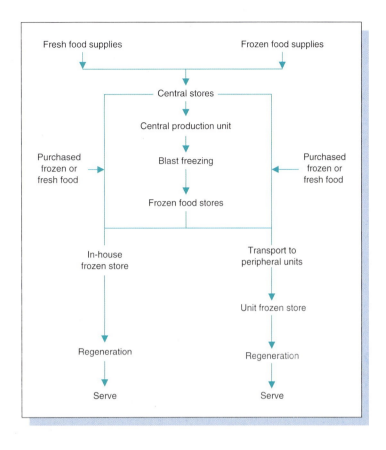

Figure 7.7 The main division of activities in the cook-freeze food production method

operations laboratory testing of all incoming foods should be a standard procedure. Inspection of suppliers' premises with regular checks on their quality and control procedures is also a standard practice.

2. *Food storage*: All foods should be kept under strict temperature control, in hygienic conditions until required for preparation. Care should be taken to avoid cross-contamination and to ensure strict rotation of all stock.

3. *Pre-preparation*: This includes all preparation of foods prior to any cooking. It is standard practice to keep this stage in the process physically separate from any further stage for hygiene and safety reasons with all staff handling raw foods to be restricted to this area.

4. *Cooking*: Ideally, cooking should be done in batches. The cooking must be sufficient to ensure that heat penetrates to the centre of any food and results in the destruction of non-sporing pathogens. This is achieved when the centre of the food reaches a temperature of at least 70°C and is held there for at least two minutes. This should always be carefully checked using a probe thermometer. At times it may be necessary to adjust the recipes to account for large-scale batch production and to account for chemical changes in the food as a result of storage for up to eight weeks at very low temperatures. Modern technology in oven design has improved the efficiency of this process, for

example combination ovens or combi ovens as they are known can produce both dry and wet heat and any combination of these across a wide temperature range. The ovens have built in temperature probes and the oven can be set to cook until the programmed core temperature is reached. In addition the oven contains a microprocessor that allows the whole cooking cycle to be downloaded onto a computer so that the process can be closely monitored and also provides for a permanent record of the batch processed. This could be important if at sometime in the future the cooking process was called into question as it could provide evidence of due diligence in the case of a food poisoning incident. The microprocessor also allows complex cooking processes to be undertaken so where for example a moist mid-range temperature was required to reheat the product followed by a period of dry high temperature to 'brown off' the product this could be programmed into the oven. Pre-programming is useful in maintaining consistent quality and safe food processing with the minimum of operator skill so, for example, a food handler as opposed to a fully trained chef could load up the oven with chicken and simply press the 'roasted chicken' programme. Microwave combi ovens also have microprocessors which allow for 'programmed' cooking but instead of dry or moist heat they combine microwave energy with infrared. This allows a frozen product to go through a thawing stage, a reheating stage and a browning stage. More sophisticated microwave ovens also have bar code readers so that manufactured food regeneration can be programmed via a manufacturers bar code for the product thus considerably reducing the likelihood of the product either being incorrectly cooked/heated or failing to meet quality standards.

5. *Portioning*: Within a time limit of thirty minutes all hot food should be portioned into single or multi-portions prior to freezing. Whatever type of container is used the depth of the food should be restricted to a maximum of 50 mm. Rapidly cooling food prior to storage is governed by the Food Safety Act and should form part of the HACCP assessment.

6. *Blast freezing*: In order to preserve food quality and prevent any growth of bacteria all cooked food should be placed in a blast freezer within thirty minutes of final cooking and being portioned. Food should be frozen to at least $-5°C$ within ninety minutes of entering the freezer and subsequently brought down to a storage temperatures of at least $-18°C$.

7. *Cold storage*: The shelf life of pre-cooked frozen food varies according to type but, in general, may be stored up to eight weeks without any significant loss of nutrients or palatability. A simple but clearly understood system of marking every container is essential, showing the product name, batch number production and expiry date to aid stock rotation and for quality control.

8. *Distribution*: All distribution should take place using chilled insulated containers for any short journeys or refrigerated vehicles for longer journeys.

9. *Regeneration*: Frozen food can be thawed to +3°C prior to being regenerated, or regenerated directly from its frozen state. Food should be heated to a minimum of 70°C for at least two minutes. The service of the food should follow the regeneration as soon as possible or within a maximum time of ninety minutes with the temperature strictly controlled and not allowed to fall below 63°C. Food such as cold desserts will only require to be thawed prior to serving, but must be held in chiller cabinets until served.

10. Any foods regenerated and not consumed must be destroyed and not reheated or returned to a refrigerator.

Cook-chill production • • •

The term 'cook-chill' refers to a catering system based on the full cooking of food followed by fast chilling, with storage in controlled low storage temperature conditions just above freezing point and between 0°C and +3°C, followed by subsequent complete reheating close to the consumer prior to prompt consumption. It has a short shelf life compared to cook-freeze of up to five days including the day of production, distribution time and regeneration (Figure 7.8).

The cook-chill process involves:

1. *Raw foods – storage and pre-preparation*: The purchasing, control, storage and pre-preparation of raw materials to be used in the

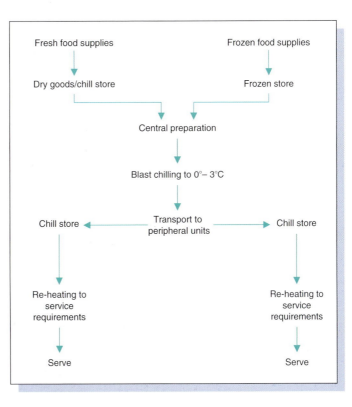

Figure 7.8
The main division of activities in the cook-chill food production method

cook-chill process have the same stringent requirements as the previously described cook-freeze process.

2. *Cooking*: The cooking must be sufficient to ensure that heat penetrates to the centre of any food and results in the destruction of non-sporing pathogens. Recipe formulation is seldom necessary, but the use of a combi oven is a beneficial as previously described for a cook-freeze process.

3. *Portioning*: The hot food should be portioned into single- or multi-portioned containers to a maximum depth of 50 mm prior to blast chilling, within thirty minutes of the cooking being completed. This is in order to preserve the appearance, flavour, nutritional quality and safety of the food.

4. *Blast chilling*: All food should be chilled to between 0°C and +3°C within ninety minutes of being placed in the blast chiller. The reasons are to preserve the food quality and to prevent the growth of bacteria.

5. *Chill storage*: The shelf life of pre-cooked cook-chilled foods has a maximum of five days including the day of preparation, distribution time and regeneration. The food should be stored between 0°C and +3°C in a chilled store containing only cook-chill products. This is because of the importance of maintaining this tight temperature range and to prevent any cross-contamination. A very clearly understood system of marking each container is essential, showing the product name, batch number, and production date and expiry date, to aid stock rotation and for quality control reference.

6. *Distribution*: Distribution should take place only in chilled insulated containers for short journeys or refrigerated vehicles for longer journeys. The distribution stage of this system is difficult to control effectively as an increase of temperature to +5°C is the maximum permitted for short journeys after which the temperature must quickly be brought down to between 0°C and +3°C. Should the temperature reach between +5°C and +10°C before regeneration the food must be consumed within twelve hours or destroyed. If the temperature exceeds +10°C before reheating the food must be destroyed. These regulations apply equally to the storage stage as well as to the distribution stage.

7. *Regeneration*: Chilled food must be regenerated within thirty minutes after removal from its chill store. Food must be heated to a minimum control temperature of at least 70°C and held there for at least two minutes for reasons of palatability and safety.

Sous vide • • •

The sous-vide food processing technique (meaning under vacuum) was developed by the French in the late 1970s as a way to reduce shrinkage in foods while maintaining the flavour and lends itself readily to adaptation as a cook-chill variant. The system involves the preparation of quality raw foods, pre-cooking (e.g. browning) when necessary, putting the raw foods into special plastic bags or pouches, vacuumizing and sealing the pouches and then steam cooking to pasteurization temperatures. The food product can be served direct to the customer at this stage or rapidly chilled to +1°C to +3°C and stored at between 0°C and +3°C for a maximum of twenty-one days (Figure 7.9).

'In the United States, fine-dining operations mostly viewed the process of cooking bags of vacuum-sealed food in temperature-controlled water baths as the domain of high-volume industrial feeders, but that mindset is changing. As top-tier chefs explore techniques that coax different tastes and textures from ingredients, sous vide is gaining prominence in some leading kitchens', Perlik (2006).

The sous-vide method increases the potential shelf life of normal cook-chill in three ways:

1. By vacuumizing the plastic bags or pouches the growth of most bacteria is restricted.
2. The food is cooked at pasteurization temperatures aiding the destruction of most microorganisms.
3. The food being sealed within the bags or pouches is protected during storage and regeneration from any cross-contamination.

The potential advantages of 'sous vide' to the caterer in addition to those offered by a cook-chill system are:

1. The flavour, palatability and nutrients are all improved, relative to normal processing, because all the contents are held within the sealed pouch.
2. The pouches provide a convenient package for safe handling and distribution, and prevent cross-contamination.

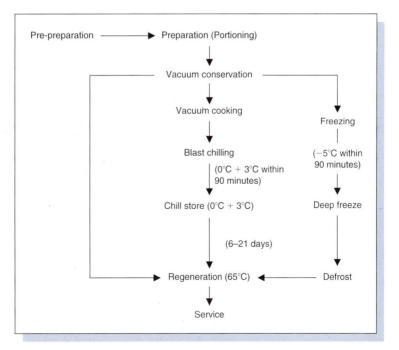

Figure 7.9
Summary of the possibilities of the sous-vide process

At the Mandarin Oriental, Parlo's team uses temperature-controlled bain-maries to prepare pork belly. The pork is packaged with whole garlic cloves and cure seasoning, slow-poached for fifteen hours and cooled using ice baths or a blast chiller. For service, individual portions are sautéed crispy and paired with seared scallops.

Executive Chef Joshua Skenes attaches a $1,300 immersion circulator to a 30-litre basin for sous-vide recipes at Stonehill Tavern at the St Regis Monarch Beach Resort and Spa in Dana Point, California. He relies on the technique to tenderize tougher meats such as short ribs and to evenly cook delicate proteins, including duck breast.

'Sous vide slowly breaks down connective tissue like a braise, but braising is an extraction method while sous vide is a concentration method,' says Skenes, who cooks vacuum-sealed short ribs for twenty hours at 170F.

Figure 7.10
Innovated use of sous-vide cooking process (*Source*: Perlik, 2006)

3. Shrinkage of the cooked product is reduced, increasing the yield by up to 20% compared to normal cooking losses.
4. It can offer a flexible production method to catering units of all sizes with particular applications to à la carte and function menus.
5. It has a longer shelf life than cook-chill, of up to twenty-one days.

The disadvantages of the sous-vide production method are:

1. Sous vide involves higher set-up capital and operating costs than cook-chill.
2. Its higher production costs limit its application and are prohibitive to certain sectors of the industry, particularly schools and hospitals.
3. Exceptionally high standards of hygiene are fundamental.
4. Complete meals cannot be produced, as certain foods need to be processed differently, for example meat and vegetables.

More recently sous vide has seen something of a revival particularly in the United States, and where it was once seen as a method of mass producing food for the welfare sector it is now gaining prominence in more upscale eateries (Figure 7.10).

BEVERAGE PRODUCTION METHODS

The term 'beverages' in this context is used to describe both alcoholic and non-alcoholic drinks. The degree of preparation necessary before these different beverages can be served to the customer varies, but in the majority of cases it is the non-alcoholic beverages that fall into the categories of raw and semi-prepared products, and the alcoholic beverages that are in the main already fully prepared.

1. *Raw beverages*: These are beverage products that require a higher degree of preparation, in comparison to the other categories, before being served to the customer. Examples of such beverages are tea, coffee, cocoa, which may require up to fifteen minutes before reaching a ready-to-serve state. The

preparation of these raw beverage products may be away from the service area and customer, for example a stillroom in the kitchen of a large hotel, although in some speciality restaurants or coffee shops the tea or coffee making facilities may be an integral part of the total food service being offered by the catering operation.

2. *Semi-prepared beverages*: These are beverage products that do not need to be prepared from the raw product state, but neither are they ready to serve. Examples of semi-prepared beverages are fruit cordials that only require the addition of water; iced coffee and cocktails may also be included in this category. The preparation of these semi-prepared beverages may also form part of the service, for example the showmanship of mixing cocktails in a cocktail bar.

3. *Fully prepared beverages*: These are beverage products requiring virtually no preparation before being served to the customer, for example bottled fruit juices, spirits, wines, etc. In the majority of cases fully prepared beverages are dispensed in front of the customer, whether, for example, spirits at a bar or wines at a table.

The style of beverage production in a catering operation should be complementary to the food production method; therefore in a high-class restaurant a full range of alcoholic and non-alcoholic beverages would be available. In a cafeteria operation, however, a limited range of beverages would be offered, and such non-alcoholic beverages as tea, coffee or orange squash, may actually be 'prepared' by customers themselves, for example, by the use of a vending machine or a tea, coffee or soft drinks machine.

The beverage production method in a catering operation should be afforded the same importance and consideration as the choice of the food production method. Tea or coffee, for example, is often the last part of a customer's meal and reputations can be made or marred on the taste of these beverages. Beverages production should also not be left to unskilled staff – this applies to the employees in the stillroom making the tea and coffee or the barmen mixing drinks and cocktails. The necessary requirements for good beverage production include the following: good quality raw materials – for example, a good blend of tea or coffee; the right equipment necessary for performing the job correctly – properly cleaned stills or machines, the provision of cocktail shakers, strainers, etc. if cocktails are being offered; and finally, the employees must be trained for the tasks they are to perform. The standard of beverage production in a catering establishment and the standards of hygiene and cleanliness in beverage equipment should be regularly checked. The method of beverage production must be such that it will operate within the financial limits, and meet the profit targets of the establishment, as laid down in the financial policy. Mismanagement in beverage production can have a substantial effect on the establishment's gross profit, in the same way as shortcomings in food production can, and for this reason must be afforded sufficient time, consideration and finance so that a suitable method of beverage production is chosen for the particular catering operation. The 21st century has seen a substantial growth in coffee shops where of course the beverage 'coffee' is the theme of the establishment and its' central selling product. The market comparator for coffee shops concerns both the quality of the coffee and other beverages served together with the general ambience.

FOOD AND BEVERAGE SERVICE METHODS

Introduction

Food service may be defined as that phase of the food flow (i.e. from the purchasing of the foods to service to the customer) mainly concerned with the delivery and presentation of the food to the customer, after the completion of food production. In some situations food service may include an element of transportation due to the separation of the food service facilities from the food production, for example of a centralized cook-freeze operation serving peripheral units.

Beverage service may be defined as that phase of the beverage flow wholly concerned with presentation of the beverage to the customer after the completion of beverage production. In beverage service there may be little or no element of transportation as the beverage production and any real distance rarely separates service facilities.

As with food and beverage production, there are a number of food and beverage service methods. It should be remembered, however, that unlike food and beverage production, food and beverage service is that part of the catering operation seen by the customer, and it is often, therefore, this aspect of a restaurant that can make or mar an establishment's reputation. The critical point, at which customers' tempers fray in food service operations, is at the service counter or table. The customer service cycle follows a clearly defined path that is used in many industries; customers report problems to staff, staff relates the problem to management, management investigate the problem and plan a solution, solution is implemented hopefully to the satisfaction of the customer, who then might relate this to the staff, etc. If the food and beverage service method is to be successful there must, therefore, be a clear understanding of the problems that occur at the food service point and hence the basic requirements that should be met by any food service method are:

1. Ensure there is a robust customer/staff feedback process in place.
2. The system chosen must be in keeping with the total concept of the catering facility and be perceived as value for money by the customer.
3. An ability to display food and beverages attractively and provide facilities to preserve the temperature, appearance and

the nutritional quality of the food and beverage products, for example, buffets and carveries.

4. Offer good quality control. This is particularly important in self-service display cabinets where numerous portions of similar food and beverage products may be offered for sale.

5. Provide an efficient service. If dining in a high-class restaurant, the customer usually has more time available to consume his meal than if he is dining, for example in a self-service cafeteria, but even in this market of more leisurely dining the service should not be too slow.

6. Provide an atmosphere of hospitality and attractiveness; organization and cleanliness should be emphasized throughout.

7. Ensure good standards of hygiene and safety are maintained. Chances of contamination of food and equipment are increased in proportion to the number of food handlers, and the length of time the food is held. Every possible precaution should be taken to ensure correct temperatures are maintained to inhibit the growth of bacteria, ensure hand contact with food and food handling equipment is kept to a minimum and all food service staff practise good personal hygiene. Also, when staff have to use equipment it must be safe for them to do so and they should have received full instructions on the operating and use of the equipment.

8. Operate within the cost and profit targets of the establishment, as detailed in the catering and financial policies.

These basic requirements should be met by any food service operation, regardless of the simplicity or elaborateness of the service method. Other more specific requirements related to particular food and beverage service methods are discussed under the various service method headings further in this chapter.

Food service methods

In order to deliver the food produced in a kitchen to the customer some form of food service is required. This may vary from full silver service in a luxury restaurant or hotel, where the food is brought to the customer's table, to a self-service cafeteria where customers collect his or her own food from a service counter.

Traditionally, full waiter service was the predominant method of food service. However, a greater degree of informality when eating away from home, and the need for increased productivity due to rising costs, has led to other food service methods and styles being developed. These include the traditional cafeteria and its many derivatives, counter service, take-away foods, vending and the numerous tray service systems, used particularly in the welfare sector.

The mode of food service employed by an establishment will depend on a number of interrelated factors: the type of establishment, for example whether it is an industrial cafeteria providing low-priced meals, or a high-class restaurant offering more complex and expensive dishes; the type of associated food production method, for example whether using traditional or conventional production, or a comparatively more recent method such as sous-vide; the type of customer to be catered for and the type of menu to be offered; the availability of staff and their skills; the space available and finally, the cost and profit targets of the establishment, as determined by financial considerations.

In some operations more than one type of food service may be offered in the same establishment; for example in a large office block there may be a cafeteria for use by the majority of staff, a waiter service restaurant offering a plated meal service for use by middle management and a silver service for top-level management. Where there is more than one level of food service offered, these different operations may be supplied from only one kitchen, although in large office blocks catering for a cross-section of customers on different levels of the building, several kitchens may have to be used.

Whatever the food service method, however, the business of eating out should be a pleasurable one. The main objective of an operation should be to present the customer with food of good quality at the correct temperature and served attractively, to ensure acceptability (Figure 7.11). The service method used must also be economically compatible with the policies and objectives of the organization. This demands efficiently designed food service facilities from the outset, taking into account all aspects of the food service operation, and particularly the market to be catered for and therefore the customer requirements.

Classification of food service methods

For the purpose of this book, the following classification of food service methods is used: self-service, waiter service and special service arrangements, as the majority of identifiable food service methods may be easily classified into these categories.

Self-service • • •

The simplest food service method currently in operation is the self-service method. Self-service methods may be described as those operations in which the service staff do not come to the table and serve customers their meals; customers in fact select their own food, cutlery, etc. and carry them to a dining area themselves. Such a method may be completely self-service such as in a vending operation, or it may be aided self-service, for example those cafeteria operations where counter staff are available to help the customer in portioning and serving the food on to a plate.

Speed and economy are the two major reasons for choosing a cafeteria-type service – such facilities are able to serve large groups of people quickly with limited personnel. Essentially, cafeterias consist of a service counter arrangement, so that customers are able to see the food in advance of making a choice and a dining area. The counter or counters are made up of various heated and refrigerated units displaying food and beverages.

Warsaw Hotel Finds Innovative Way To Use Induction Technology

The Courtyard by Marriott Warsaw International Airport Hotel's Brasserie Restaurant is making strides in cooking technology with a new induction heating system used to keep buffet dishes warmer – and fresher – for the benefit of staff and hotel guests alike. The Brasserie's induction cooking method works by keeping dishes warm with an electrical current frequenting from 1 to 3 kHz, Which circulates within ceramic plates. Placing ferromagnetic cookery in these plates closes the electrical circuit and generates heat in the pans without heating the plates themselves."The cookware, not the surface heats up; it keeps the whole area cooler, and it's literally impossible to start a fire," says Randy Villareal, senior vice president of New York based Tishman Hotel Corp., which manages the nearly year old property. "Plus it is much more flexible in terms of temperature control. Meals are warmed without the threat of scorching or over cooking."

The system was custom-built into the buffet by French manufacturer Bonnet, creating "a clean and sleek look," Villareal says. The cost was approximately US$22,000 for the entire line. However, the real expense is the investment in the chaffing dishes, which have special metal bottoms that induce the current. Still, Villareal says, ROI comes by way of 60% savings in energy costs. "It's well worth the expense, especially in the buffet where there is typically so much energy wasted," he says. Villareal adds that while induction cooking has been getting greater attention in the US market lately, many hotel restaurants have yet to make the switch. Villareal calls induction "the kitchen of the future", and adds this is one of the first hotels in Warsaw to use induction- and one of the first of its kind to use it in a buffet line. The hotel also uses more traditional induction cooking at the buffet's omelet-making station. The management company is starting to incorporate induction cooking throughout its global hotel system

Figure 7.11 Using induction cooking technology in food service (*Source*: Strauss, 2004)

The traditional cafeteria

The traditional cafeteria arrangement consists of a straight line of counters where customers enter at one end of the line, pick up a tray and pass along the full length of the counter selecting menu items on the way. A tray rail runs the full length of the service counter on which customers rest their tray while passing along the line. The service counter and dining area are separated either by a rail or partition, and payment for the menu items selected is usually made at the end of the line where the cashier is seated.

The rate of flow through the cafeteria line varies according to a number of factors including the variety of choices offered, and hence the length of the line, the customers' familiarity with the cafeteria layout, the speed of the cashier, etc. In practical situations between four to six customers per minute can pass along a commercial single-line cafeteria, while in a cafeteria with limited choice, for example a school cafeteria, eight to ten may be the norm.

The rate of flow through a traditional cafeteria arrangement may be increased by installing more than one straight line, for example counter lines in parallel with the service facilities in between; although customer throughput may be increased still further by dispensing with the traditional straight lines and replacing them with food 'stations' or 'banks' which may be arranged in different layouts within the cafeteria. Such layouts are all encompassed within the term 'free-flow' cafeteria.

The free-flow cafeteria • • •

This type of cafeteria design is also known as the 'hollow-square'. Separated counters for hot or cold foods are usually placed along three sides of a room, with the fourth side open for traffic entering or leaving, so that a U-shape arrangement of food stations is formed. In a free-flow cafeteria, food stations may be positioned at right angles to the counter, or be staggered at an angle, forming an 'echelon' or 'saw-tooth' arrangement. On cruise ships counters are normally placed centrally with freestyle seating to both sides and forward (see Figure 7.12). The ability to configure flows to fit physical areas of different shapes and sizes are one of the attractions of this style of service. Customers entering the square can go directly to the hot or cold sections without having to wait in line for their food, although during peak periods short lines may form at the most popular stations.

The beverage sections may either be placed in the centre of the square, or in the dining area itself so as to be readily accessible for the diners. Thought should, however, be given to the ease of supplying stations when the traffic area is crowded, particularly supplying centrally located stations.

The free-flow cafeteria is also able to accommodate a call-order bar where grilled and fried items are cooked to order; this is unlike the traditional cafeteria where it is essential that the line keeps moving steadily, and no allowances can be made for call-order facilities, unless they are separated out completely from the traditional line or adequate by-pass facilities are allowed.

The free-flow service method is a scatter approach to food service that is particularly useful for serving large numbers of

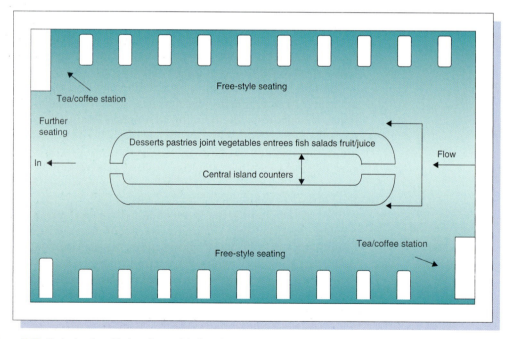

Figure 7.12 Typical cruise ship free-flow cafeteria

people that arrive together. As many as 15–20 customers per minute may be served in this type of cafeteria arrangement; this number may be increased once the customers have become familiar with the layout (Figure 7.13).

Payment for the meal is made as the customer leaves the free-flow area although on cruise ships payment for all meals is pre-paid as part of the fare. In standard cafeterias there are usually a number of cash points available, enabling several customers to pay at the same time.

In both the traditional and free-flow cafeteria systems, the positioning of the cutlery, condiments and drinking water is beyond the cash point, so as to reduce holds-ups as much as possible. It is also important to consider the method of clearing as it is desirable that customers always see clearly what tables are free for them to sit at. Clearing can either be done by employing staff to do this or by requiring customers to clear their own tables.

The carousel • • •

The carousel or 'roundabout server' consists of a number of rotating shelves (usually three) at different heights, all of which are approximately 6 ft in diameter, and rotate at one revolution per minute. Food is passed from the kitchen to a plating table still on the servery side of the carousel, from which the carousel is fed with hot and cold plated foods.

A typical carousel layout may be as follows: the bottom shelf accommodates cold foods – salads, sweets, etc. This shelf is usually pre-cooled by a refrigerator element and a crushed ice bed may be used to ensure a low temperature during the food service period. If the hot food shelf is placed above the cold shelf on the carousel, it is extended out over the lower cold shelf to ensure that the warmth from the overhead heat does not affect the cold shelf below. On the top revolving shelf bread rolls, butter, etc. may be displayed. Trays, cutlery, napkins and beverages are usually separated out from the carousel on dispensers, although some of these items may be on one of the revolving shelves.

Today's passenger has more options. Now the major cruise lines – Norwegian, Carnival, Princess, Royal Caribbean, Cunard, Seabourn and others – have restaurants on board offering an array of cuisine including contemporary, Japanese, Thai, steak house, French bistro and more. 'We know our demographics and build our menus accordingly. The average cruise length is seven days', Tobler reports.

And with regard to menu changes, additional items are added continually to meet current trends, from sushi items to gourmet bites. 'Since food and service are now available at any time of the day or night, staffing requirements have been increased to meet our needs and certain middle management implemented to assure the service runs smoothly', says Poirier.

Freestyle cruising: 'We are now giving people different dining options in a resort style environment', Tobler adds. Norwegian Cruise Lines launched its own 'Freestyle Cruising' programme in May of 2000. Under the programme guests dine when they want, wherever they want, and with whom they want. The Freestyle Cruising ships offer several 'main' restaurants as well as a variety of alternative venues where passengers can enjoy dinner any time between 5:30 PM and 12 midnight, says Tobler.

Figure 7.13
Changes in dining patterns on cruise ships (*Source*: Fiss, 2003)

The carousel unit consists of a number of servery areas where the customer remains stationary, taking his choice of meal from the revolving carousel, and placing it on his tray. Payment is made to a cashier or cashiers on the restaurant side of the carousel.

The carousel may serve between 500 and 720 people an hour, between 8 and 12 a minute. The customers' rate of flow depends on a number of factors – familiarity with the carousel arrangement, the range of dishes offered, the rate at which shelves are refilled by operators on the servery side, etc.

The carousel is not used to any great extent as a method of food service in the catering industry, although where it is used it would appear to be working effectively. It is a form of food service that is really only suitable for catering operations which have repeat custom, for example a staff cafeteria, rather than those operations where there are always new customers arriving who are not so familiar with the method, for example department stores. The carousel has a limited application as a method of food service, although it may be particularly suitable for some catering operations that have specific requirements or restrictions.

Activity 1

You are the food and beverage manager at a large entertainment venue. In addition to both the 'before show' and the 'after show' food and beverage operations you are required to offer snacks and drinks during the twenty-minute interval. What do you consider to be the biggest challenges to the success of this service and what would be the key measures that you would need to put in place to ensure you provided an adequate service.

Vending ● ● ●

Vending today has become synonymous with selling from a machine. It is also known as 'automatic retailing' or selling from an 'electronic cafeteria' and involves a machine providing the customer with a product in exchange for some form of payment, coins, credit cards, etc. Although vending was in evidence in the UK prior to the Second World War, mainly in the form of chocolate and cigarette machines, it was not until the 1950s that the vending of drinks and snack items really became established in this country. The markets for vended products have grown steadily over the last fifty years. In beverage vending, canned drinks, cartons and bottles have shown the greatest increase in growth over the three decades to 1996 and in the last decade snack foods have increased sales the greatest (Figure 7.14).

The markets available for vended products are varied and numerous and may be grouped into three main areas:

1. The *general market* vending machines and their products may be situated in areas to which the general public largely has access; for example, shopping courts, motorway service areas,

Key Points

1. Vending remains reliant on coin-operated systems because alternative technology is expensive and the low average transaction values make it difficult to justify.
2. Drinks are the most popular products sold through vending machines and, of the three major sectors (drinks, cigarettes, confectionery/snacks/meals), are showing the strongest growth.
3. Drinks growth has been driven by trading up to fresh-brew, organic and ethical products in hot drinks and by a move towards bottles and away from cans in cold drinks.
4. In the confectionery/snacks/meals sector, growth has been driven by higher sales of confectionery, particularly in the education sector, although this will shortly stop due to the introduction of minimum nutritional standards.
5. Cigarette vending has been hit by a combination of the wider 24-hour availability of cigarettes in alternative outlets, a combination of rising prices forcing venues to change their machines and the introduction of a smoking ban throughout the UK.

Figure 7.14
Vending performance key indicators (*Source*: Mintel Report, June 2007a, b, c)

garage forecourts, airports, seaports, ferries, rail and bus terminals, libraries, swimming and leisure centres, stadiums, exhibition centres, cinemas and theatres.
2. The *industrial market* includes those establishments where vending machines are provided for employers and employees in office blocks and shops, factories and sites, etc. Eighty per cent of companies in the UK having installed vending machines at some or all of their premises.
3. The *institutional market* includes establishments such as hospitals and schools, prisons, sports complexes, universities and colleges and more recently hotels, replacing to some extent floor service.

The range of vending machine equipment or hardware is divisible into two major groups:

1. *Beverage vendors*: Beverage vending machines have accounted for the largest share of vending sales over the last thirty years and consequently their design has been developed further than the food vending machines. This group is discussed in greater depth later in this chapter.
2. *Food vending machines or merchandisers*: Food vending machines may vend a variety of food products – confectionery, snacks, plated meals, etc. and are usually vended in one of three types of machine:
   (a) Snack machines: Confectionery, crisps, biscuits, etc. are usually vended from an ambient temperature machine as these items have a relatively long shelf life and do not have any special temperature requirements. Because of these factors, servicing of the machines except for re-stocking purposes can be kept to a minimum thereby also reducing operating costs.
   (b) Refrigerated machines: Snack items such as sandwiches and rolls have a limited shelf life and need to be date-stamped ('sell-by' or 'use by') and vended through a

refrigerated machine. Plated foods such as salads, cold meats, etc. must be vended from refrigerated machines where the holding temperature is between 2°C and 5°C. At this temperature the food may be kept for two to four days, although some operations work on a twenty-four-hour cycle only.

(c) Hot meal machines; Food for a hot vending service may be vended in a number of ways. The first is the heated food vendor that will hold the temperature of the plated food at about 69°C for up to six hours. The second is the hot can vendor that usually offers a choice of items. The selection of hot canned meals, for example soups, baked beans, pasta dishes, casseroles, etc. are held at a temperature of 68°C in the machine without deterioration in the quality of the food. Money is placed into the appropriate slot and the hot can is vended together with a disposable bowl and suitable cutlery to eat the food with; the can is easily opened by the use of a ring pull top. The third involves the use of a microwave oven adjacent to a refrigerated merchandiser. Cooked food is plated by kitchen staff, rapidly cooled and placed into a refrigerated merchandiser; if limited kitchen facilities are available, ready plated or semi-prepared foods may be bought in from a supplier, plated and put in the vending machine. The food is heated when placed in the microwave, which has an automatic timing device for the different foods which begins when a token or code is put into the microwave. The time taken for a meal to be heated thoroughly depends on whether it is a snack item or a full meal. Snack items being heated from a refrigerated state take between ten and thirty seconds, and a main meal between forty and sixty seconds, depending on the quantity and depth of the food, and the power supply feeding the microwave. The range of products available for hot meal vending is now quite considerable although snacks and sandwiches still account for the largest percentage.

Within each of these groups the type of vending machine used will depend largely on the type of product being vended (Figure 7.15). For confectionery and pre-packed goods a simple mechanical unit with a drawer at the base of the column is all that is required; it can be free-standing, wall-mounted or be positioned on a fixed surface and does not require any electricity or water supply. Snack and sandwich vending machines require a power supply only and because their products are easily consumed, the machines can be situated outside wards, in the corridors of hotels, etc. close to the customer market. Machines vending plated meals need to be situated close to the kitchen facil-ities and adjacent to the dining area; some banks of vending machines are sited such that the kitchen is behind the machines for ease of stocking and the dining area is in front of them. These types of machines may be a rotating drum or revolving shelf

	2002		2004		2006*		% point change
	Thousand units	%	Thousand units	%	Thousand units	%	2002–2006
Confectionery/snacks	78.9	79	85.8	80	96.0	81	21.6
Other food/meals	21.4	21	21.6	20	21.9	19	2.3
Total	100.3	100	107.5	100	117.9	100	17.5

Figure 7.15 Number of UK confectionery, snacks and meals vending machines, by type of food dispensed, 2002–2006 (*Source*: Mintel estimate, based on AVA census data trends for 2002–2005)

design whereby a button is pushed rotating or revolving shelves until the required item is reached and then removed through a flap door.

The number of vending machines to be installed in a particular establishment will depend on the numbers to be catered for, frequency of use of the machines, the travel distance by staff to use of the machines, etc. As a general rule of thumb one drinks machine is capable of serving between 150 and 250 customers. Should a full vending service be offered, that is, beverages and food items, the provision of two machines would be capable of serving between fifty and one-hundred customers. It is also worth noting that in many establishments vending is not used to cater for all the operation's needs, but often to simply supplement them; thus in a number of catering operations there may be a combination of a cafeteria arrangement and a bank of vending machines, the latter providing snack and beverage products, for example, which could be separated out from the main cafeteria line.

The basic question of whether to use vending machines or not should be taken after careful consideration of the organization's catering and financial policies and an assessment of what vending has to offer (see Figure 7.16). The main advantages associated with vending include the following:

1. *Flexibility*: Vending can provide a twenty-four hour food and beverage service, either alone or in conjunction with other catering services. Customers can use a vending machine when they want to, rather than only when a cafeteria is open.
2. *Situation*: Vending machines can be sited close to the customer market, for example in office corridors, thus reducing workers' time away from the workplace queuing for a snack or

- Despite the fact that it is now possible to procure a wide range of hot snacks and hot meals from a vending machine, consumers remain relatively unenthusiastic about buying, with the result that the number of machines selling refrigerated and/or frozen and other products has remained little changed during the past 5 years.
- This is a reflection of the way consumers view the role of vended products, which is usually as a supplement to their regular meals and drinks or a treat, rather than a substitute for it.
- However, there are several sectors – for example, healthcare – where employers have a legal obligation to provide food 24 hours a day for their employees and vending is an ideal low-overhead way of doing this.
- Technical developments in this area may result in a greater uptake in the future, with advances such as *Selecta's* Steamplicity, *Bon Appetit's* The Little Tasty Food Outlet and Feed Rapide (a joint venture between the Vending Corporation and 3663) likely to result in improved perceptions of the quality of vended hot food.

Figure 7.16
Hot foods vending still not much in demand (*Source*: AVA Mintel Report, June 2007a, b, c)

drink; customers are also more likely to take a vended drink back to their workplace and consume it there, rather than spend time away from their work, for example in a cafeteria. Satellite vending machines can also be used to serve areas that would not normally benefit from a catering facility; for example, in a large industrial complex, machines can be sited some distance from the main kitchen and dining area.

3. *Quality control*: In terms of quality, vending machines can sell a consistent product, particularly beverages, pre-packed snacks and bought in meals from a supplier. Meals prepared in the kitchen can also be plated under tighter quality and portion control.
4. *Hygiene control*: Reduced handling of vended foods also reduces the possibilities of food contamination. Many beverage machines now also have built-in, self-clean mechanisms.
5. *Operating control*: Labour savings can be made, as once cleaned and stocked vending machines should require the minimum of maintenance, thus reducing labour costs. Wastage, pilferage and cash losses should also be negligible.
6. *Speed*: Vending machines can 'sell' products quickly and efficiently, for example a hot chips machine that can vend portions of freshly prepared chips, always giving a standard product, at a standard price.
7. *Sales promotion*: Products for sale in a vending machine can look attractive and stimulate 'impulse purchases', particularly glass-fronted merchandisers (GFMs) displaying fresh fruits, sweets, etc.

Disadvantages associated with using vending include the following:

1. *Impersonality*: Vending machines lack the 'personal touch' and some customers will always prefer to be served food and beverages in the traditional manner rather than from a machine.
2. *Inflexibility of the product*: Initially the range of products available for vending was quite limited; today, however, vending machines offer a much wider selection, and beverages in particular can be highly customized.

3. *Reliability*: One of the major causes of dissatisfaction with vending machines in the past has been that the coin mechanism could become jammed and the machine would give no service. This in turn left the machines open to abuse and vandalism. Since their introduction of the vending machines' coin mechanism has been a mechanical device which could be regularly jammed with foreign coins, washers, etc. Today, however, the electronic coin mechanism can detect even the most accurately produced fake coins, which even when fed into the machine, do not jam it. Electronic mechanisms are constantly being improved and are incorporated into the majority of new machines. These electronic mechanisms are also capable of accepting different valued coins, displaying a running total as they are added and of giving change.

4. *Limiting*: For large-scale food and beverage service, vending machines have limitations. In some situations they are best suited as a backup to the main catering services although a bank of vending alleviates queuing and waiting time. They are also of less use in up-market situations, except in the form of mini-bars, for example in hotels.

If an organization decides to use vending as a catering facility, the next question to be answered is whether to remain 'in house', or to employ a contractor. The main cost structures for each of these groups may be itemized as follows:

Client or in-house operated service • • •

1. Capital outlay for machine, outright purchase, lease, rented or instalment, plus depreciation of machines and loss of interest on capital. Choice of machine made by client.
2. Installation costs such as for electricity and water supplies.
3. Operating costs such as ingredients, commodities, cups, daily sales and cost records, maintenance, cleaning and servicing.
4. Selling prices set by client, all cash takings to the client.

Contract operated service • • •

1. No capital outlay for machine – contractor supplies it.
2. Some installation costs paid by client, for example water and electricity.
3. Operating costs such as ingredients, commodities, cups, maintenance, cleaning and servicing done by contractor.
4. Selling prices set between client and contractor. Reimbursement costs, direct and indirect to contractor.

In the USA, 95 contractors operate per cent of vending installations. In the UK, this figure is approximately 50%, although it appears to be increasing (AVAB). Any operation considering using vending as a total or part catering service needs to give careful thought to choosing a supplier; the above factors need to be taken into account, other operations using the contractor should be visited and discussions entered into with both management and staff committees as to the best way of introducing a vending system into the organization.

Vending operates in a very competitive market and a number of developments and market trends may be identified in the vending sector:

1. *Cashless systems*: The development of card operated vending has probably been the most important technological development in vending. The leading supplier of this type of system is Girovend, the main component being a credit card type of pass or card which can record the user's own data; it can be used for personnel control such as security, identity passes, attendance recording, leisure facilities, etc. For catering purposes, customers can buy any food and beverage items from a vending machine by placing their card into the machine instead of cash; their card is then debited with the amount for the items purchased. The card first has to be loaded with credit and this can be done in a number of ways. First, supervised loading whereby a supervisor collects customers' cash amounts and loads the cards via a vending machine; the disadvantage to this method is that the handling of cash is still involved and at least one person has to be employed to do this job. Second, customers self-load their own cards with a cash amount before making their purchases. By inserting the card into the loader a customer can check its balance and increase the amount by feeding the appropriate money into the machine; this method's disadvantage is that special loaders are required and cash is still handled. Third, is the direct-debit loader linked to the wages department so that a cardholder may direct debit different values from his/her salary; in this way cash handling is eliminated completely. The advantages to the customer of card vending are that it is a convenient method of payment; loose change does not have to be carried, it is not 'lost' in the machine; and, overall, a faster service can be given. The cardholders can be divided into user type groups and these categories may then be separated into different price bands. This enables different charges to be made for the same product, for example for regular employees, temporary staff, free vend for visitors, etc. Cash refunds can be given to users giving up their cards, or money can be paid back into an employee account; machines can also be programmed to stop accepting stolen cards. Finally, the sales information stored in these machines can be printed out by item, price list or type of user, and a comparison between actual and cash loaded on to the cards can be given; such up-to-date information greatly aids financial control and cost accounting.
2. *Mixed product vending*: Where the design of the machine allows, different products may be vended together and complement each other, for example, pre-packed snacks with carton juices together form a substitute for a main meal at certain times of

Within the hot drinks market generally, there has been a sizeable increase in demand for ethical products, with the result that vendors have allied themselves to a dizzying variety of accreditation schemes, the most popular of which are fair trade and *Rainforest Alliance*.

Although the fair trade scheme is well established and enjoys high levels of awareness among consumers, the *Rainforest Alliance* scheme is an alternative which has been growing in popularity among producers, while in the tea sector there is also the Ethical Tea Partnership.

Unilever – whose tea brands include PG Tips and Lipton – announced in May 2007 that it would be seeking *Rainforest Alliance* accreditation for all its tea plantations. Other companies to sign up with the organization include *Lavazza*, with its Tierra brand of coffee.

In addition, major tea suppliers such as *Unilever*, *Tetley* and *Twinings* are also members of the Ethical Tea Partnership, which exists to ensure that the tea used by its members is ethically sourced and that workers on tea estates are fairly treated and enjoy decent living and working conditions.

Figure 7.17
Ethical products play growing role (*Source*: AVA Mintel Report, June 2007a, b, c).

the day. Smaller units, for example vending confectionery, can also be attached to the side of the larger machines and utilize their coin or card mechanism.

3. *Fresh brew vending*: Machines using fresh brew systems for tea and coffee ensure that a better quality end product is dispensed to the customer. In-cup drink machines where the ingredients are already in the cup also offer better hygiene, operation and servicing, control and range of products. Some beverage machines are now capable of offering 100 different selections for both hot and cold drinks and have capacities of up to 1,000 cups (Figure 7.17).

4. *In-room beverage vending*; Mini-bars in hotel rooms offer a wide range of alcoholic and non-alcoholic beverages, snacks and confectionary. The use of these is monitored electronically so that when a guest opens the mini-bar door it sends a microwave signal (wireless connection) to a computer database located in the hotels billing office. Once the signal reaches the database it alerts the room attendant that the mini-bar is being used. At a set time each day (or before the guest checks out, whichever is first) the room attendant checks and replaces the stock in the mini-bar and logs this onto a hand held wireless processor that simultaneously adds the items used directly to the guests bill. The system is efficient because the room attendant only has to check the rooms where the mini-bar door has been opened and last minute sales can be quickly added to the guests bill at checkout.

5. *Space economization*: The efficient utilization of business space in offices, factories, hospitals, industrial units, etc. is of great importance today. This has led many operations to critically review their catering facilities and the space allocated to them, particularly where a twenty-four hour service is needed. In many situations vending is being used as a space and cost saving alternative to installing traditional catering services. Furthermore, the vending manufacturers themselves are aware of the amount of space vending machines need, and are

| | 2002 | | 2004 | | 2006* | | % change |
	Thousand units	%	Thousand units	%	Thousand units	%	2002–2006
Traditional	210.6	52	225.3	55	234.0	57	11.1
In-cup	91.0	23	90.4	22	82.0	20	−9.9
Cans/cartons/bottles	99.7	25	95.5	23	96.0	23	−3.7
Total	**401.3**	**100**	**411.2**	**100**	**412.0**	**100**	**2.7**

Figure 7.18 Number of UK drinks vending machines, by dispensing method, 2002–2006 (*Source*: Mintel estimate, based on AVA census data trends for 2002–2005)

researching ways of reducing their overall size yet at the same time trying to increase the range and quality of products they can offer.

6. *Compatibility with cook-chill*: The cook-chill method of food preparation serves the vending industry well by allowing plated meals to be prepared in advance and vended for later consumption either in a chilled state, for example salads, cold meats, pâtés, etc. or for use in conjunction with some type of heating system, for example microwaves.

Vending has now established itself as a method of food service that may be considered for many types of operations and situations. In some sectors of the catering industry it is employed as a total feeding system, for example staff cafeterias and restrooms, hospital canteens, etc. in others it is an economic alternative to other types of catering service at different times of the day, for example, night shifts in hospitals, twenty-four hour factories, offices, etc. (Figure 7.18).

Group activity

For many years, your organization has used the services of a tea lady who three times a day has wheeled a trolley with tea, coffee, cakes and snacks and at lunchtime home-made sandwiches throughout the building and is very popular. She is about to retire and you are considering replacing her with a vending operation. Write a brief plan considering both the process that you would use and what issues you would consider.

The carvery • • •

Carvery type operations are not a new phenomenon. They were in evidence in some hotels during the middle part of the 20th century where they gradually took over from the gueridon or carving trolley. Over the past ten to fifteen years they have experienced a certain revival and several large pub chains are now featuring them together with a number of hotels throughout the world.

Carvery restaurants essentially offer a three-course meal (exclusive of drink) at a set inclusive price. The first course is served by the waiter and usually offers a selection of five or six items. The main course is selected from the carvery counter and served by customers themselves, although usually aided by a control conscious chef. A waiter also serves the sweet course, like the first course.

The carvery counter may be a straight line, circular or more usually U-shaped. On this counter is placed a selection of hot meats, vegetables and potatoes, sauces and gravies. The counter itself consists of a series of hot plates and containers with the addition of overhead heat lamps to also help keep the food hot. A separate cold table may also be featured in some operations offering a selection of cold meats and salads.

Carvery style service is a speciality food service method and for this reason it has limited application. It is found mainly in hotels, private restaurants, steak houses and pubs, and may be used for special function catering. It is something of a 'fashionable' food service method in that it experiences periods of popularity and then fades into the background; at present the carvery method of food service may be said to be 'in fashion' particularly in the public house sector of the industry.

The buffet • • •

The buffet is a method of food service that is a modification of true self-service. It is a food service arrangement in which foods are displayed attractively on one, or a series of tables and presentation is an all-important factor.

Customers collect a plate from one end of the table and move along it helping themselves to the foods of their choice. Buffets may be a combination of hot and cold foods, all hot or all cold. In a fork buffet cutlery is provided for the customer with which to eat the food; in a finger buffet most of the food is kept to fairly small mouth-size pieces, and little or no cutlery is provided.

Buffets may be used in conjunction with a restaurant operation or for private functions. In a restaurant style operation customers pay a fixed price for the buffet and for this price are able to return as many times to the buffet table, as they would like. At private functions it is more usual to have service personnel continually circulating among the guests serving the food and the beverages and clearing tables.

Buffets are used very successfully by some hotels and restaurants for featuring special weeks, for example a Spanish week, a Scandinavian evening, etc. and for special sales promotion of, for example, foreign foods or wines. It is also an adaptable method of food service in that some operations may use buffet service for particular meal periods, for example breakfast, lunch or dinner, and revert to another type of food service for the other meals (see Figure 7.11).

Activity 2

You are the food and beverage manager of a 250-bedroom hotel where most of the revenue comes from business guests and you operate a buffet breakfast, which is efficient, effective and makes good profits. Following changes in the hotels marketing weekends are now very busy with families and leisure guests and you note that your food costs for breakfast have risen dramatically and are no longer profitable. Make a case for changing the breakfast service at weekends from buffet to menu and plated. What other aspect should be considered?

Buffet service also enables a facility to feed large numbers of people in a given time with less staff requirements. Compared with other types of food service, however, the buffet method can have a higher food cost; this is because good displays of food must be given which often involve presenting fairly large quantities of the items, and because it is time consuming to prepare and garnish all the buffet food in order to achieve a good display. The higher food and labour cost in the kitchen may, however, be offset by a lower restaurant labour cost as fewer service personnel are required.

Take-away or take-out service ● ● ●

The take-away, or take-out service as it is more commonly known in the USA, is a method of food service that exploits to the full the concept of 'fast foods'. The products offered by these establishments are highly standardized, as are most of the features of the operations – service, sales control, product packaging, etc.

The take-away operation offers a limited basic menu to the customer, but within this menu there may be a number of variations on the basic items. These operations aim to achieve volume sales by offering low- to medium-priced foods, and they have become a popular segment of the catering market because they fill a need for a quick snack or meal. Since 2002, there has been a steady growth in the home delivery sector of the market and this growth seems set to continue (see Figure 7.19).

The time between customers placing orders and receiving their meals, aims to be faster than any other method yet discussed; some operations aim for a thirty-second service time. The customer may either take the food out of the takeaway to eat, or it may be consumed on the premises; a large number of so-called 'take-away' outlets now provide very extensive seating areas, often for more than several hundred.

Because take-away outlets aim for a high rate of customer turnover, their situation in relation to their markets is crucial; they are

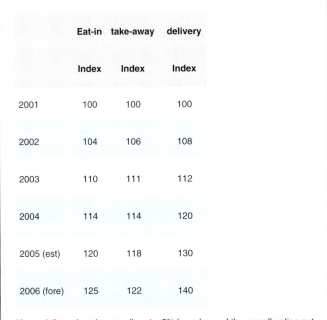

	Eat-in	take-away	delivery
	Index	Index	Index
2001	100	100	100
2002	104	106	108
2003	110	111	112
2004	114	114	120
2005 (est)	120	118	130
2006 (fore)	125	122	140

Home delivery is only a small part – 5% by value – of the overall eating out market in the UK. However, it is the fastest-growing sector and is also growing at a mush faster rate than either the eat-in or take-away sectors.

Figure 7.19
Comparison of performance of different sectors in the eating out market, 2001–2006 (*Source*: Mintel Report, October 2006a, b).

usually found in high streets, shopping malls and motorway service stations where they have a high percentage of passing trade. Although the average spending power of customers in takeaways may be considerably lower than for some of the other food service methods discussed, this is compensated by their high rate of customer throughput. Some fast-food operations are designed solely for take-away food and little or no provision is made for customers to eat in, which considerably reduces the space required and therefore the operational cost. Typically, these have been fish-and-chip shops and sandwich bars but there are many other examples. Some fast-food outlets can be described as restaurants as they have small seating areas in relation to their cooking capacity. Many also offer a delivery service and the most notable of these are pizzerias where deliveries can represent over 70% of sales.

Today there is a wide selection of products that takeaways can offer for sale; the growth of the traditional fish-and-chip shops has now taken second place to the other types of foods now offered – hamburgers, pizzas, Chinese, Indian and Mexican food, sandwich bars, etc.

Self-service is therefore a method of food service in which customers collect their own food from some form of service counter, in return for which they pay a lower price for the meal than they would, for example, in operations offering a waiter service. In self-service operations payment for the meal is made either before the meal, for example in vending operations, or after the meal as in some cafeterias.

In the industrial sector of the catering market this method of food service has become firmly established; in the majority of cases people's main meal is in the evening, so that they only require a snack-type short lunch that a self-service operation can adequately provide. In the welfare sector this utilitarian method of food service is also used extensively, leaving the more leisurely dining to that part of the day, which is not associated with work.

Waiter service • • •

Waiter service involves the transportation and service of food to the customer – whether at a table, counter or bar – rather than customers collecting their own food. This method of food service has also been termed 'aided' or 'personalized' service.

In terms of customer throughput the traditional waiter service to a customer seated at a table is a much slower method of food service than the self-service methods. However, with waiter service speed and price are no longer necessarily the most important factors governing the selection of the food service method. Other factors now become more important both to the caterer and the customer – the provision of a more elaborate service, more leisurely dining facilities, a wider variety in menu choice, etc.

Counter or bar service • • •

This method of food service is an appropriate example to illustrate the transition between self-service and waiter service, as it offers the informality of the self-service methods, and yet also combines that degree of extra service given to the customer commensurate with waiter service.

In bar service customers sit on stools or chairs at a counter, the shape of which may be a straight line, or as is more usual, U-shaped. The latter shape allows the waiter to serve a considerable volume of trade single-handed. The average sized U-shape counter accommodates between 10 and 14 customers, served by one member of staff; two staff may man larger counters catering for between 20 and 28 customers. This type of food service is not designed for large groups of people arriving at once, but for a steady stream of people arriving alone, in couples, or even in parties of between 4 and 6. With these numbers being the average size of the party, the seat turnover using a counter arrangement may be considerable.

The covers are laid up and cleared in front of the customer by the waiter behind the counter. Orders are taken by the waiter and dispatched to the kitchen; here the food is plated, which is then brought to the counter and placed before the customer. The distance between the food production area and the counter is usually minimal which facilitates easy handling of the food and hence speed of service to the customer. An example of this type of service can be seen at many international airports where 30 or 40 customers, sit on stools around a U-shaped servery offering sushi and other cold fish delicacies from a central island on which they are displayed. This enables the waiters to serve the customers very rapidly, offers a good display of foods which may encourage impulse buys and leaves the kitchen staff to prepare replenishments as required in a kitchen situated in a non-sales area. This last factor has a particular advantage if the kitchen is servicing not only the counter arrangements, but also other restaurant facilities or can be located in a less expensive location.

Table service ● ● ●

Table service is a method of food service in which the waiter brings customers' food to the table and places it in front of them, either pre-plated, or if it is silver service, served with a salver on to a plate and then placed in front of customers. Table service is the most leisurely of the service methods so far discussed; customers may still take as little as half to three-quarters of an hour to eat their meal, but are more likely to take between one-and-a-half and two hours, and may even take three to four hours, often depending on the size of the party.

There are basically two types of menus available in table service from which customers may select their meal. The first is the à la carte menu in which all the items on the menu are individually priced and customers select and combine dishes according to their choice. The other is the table d'hôte menu, which consists of a number of items combined together to produce a set meal, at a set price. A set table d'hôte menu may, for example, include a choice of two appetizers, three or four entrées including vegetables and a choice of two or three sweets; a beverage, for example coffee, may also be included in the price. The use of the term 'table d'hôte' is today frequently replaced by the term 'fixed price menu'.

There are a number of different styles of table service, these include the following:

1. American service in which the guest's meal is portioned and plated in the kitchen, brought into the restaurant by the waiter and placed in front of the customer.
2. French service, which is the most elaborate of the table service methods, involves preparing the guest's food in the kitchen, arranging it on silver salvers that are then brought into the dining room and placed on a small cart called a *gueridon*. On this gueridon is a small heater called a *réchaud*, used for heating or flaming the guest's food, which is then served from the silver salvers on to the guest's plate and placed in front of the guest.
3. The Russian style of service illustrates the food service method commonly referred to as silver service; the food is prepared and portioned in the kitchen and placed on to silver salvers, which are then taken into the restaurant. A dinner plate is placed in front of the guest and the food is served on to the guest's plate.
4. English service, which is the least common of all the table service methods described and is usually only used for private functions. The food is prepared in the kitchen, but not portioned, instead the complete joint of meat, for example a

whole turkey, is presented to the guests before carving. The host or one of the service personnel then carves and portions the meat and places it on to a plate with the vegetables, and the plate is then placed in front of the guest.

These are the four main traditional methods of table service, although variations do of course occur within the different styles. Service carts, for example, are not used exclusively in the French style of service; they may be used in a number of the other service styles, although not perhaps to the same extent. Some of the following food service methods are also, in the strict sense of the word, table service, but they have been included here by the titles under which they are more commonly known, as within these following methods different types of table service may be used.

Banquet service • • •

Banquet service is usually associated with large hotels, although today many food service operations are employing this type of food service as a profitable sideline, for example hospitals, colleges and universities, and small restaurants.

The variety of table arrangements used in banqueting service are numerous, using either round, square, rectangular and other interlocking-shaped tables; if there is a 'top' table on which sit the host and the most important guests this table is usually served first. The number of people that may be catered for in banqueting service can be as small as six to eight for a private dinner party, to a large convention of several thousand people. The food served to the customer may either be pre-plated in the kitchen (American service) or portioned on to the plates in front of the customers (Russian service). A further method is to use one of these types of service for the meat/fish main course and to allow customers to help themselves to the vegetables and accompaniments placed on the table in service dishes with the necessary serving equipment.

The advantages of this food service method are that the number to be catered for is known well in advance; the specific time of dining is also known; and a set menu for a set price is established. This enables the service of large numbers of people to be undertaken by a comparatively small number of service personnel, usually one waiter serving between 10 and 12 customers.

Room and lounge service • • •

Room service is a method of food service, which, like banqueting, is most commonly associated with the larger hotels, although some motels and smaller hotels do also offer a degree of room service. Today, however, even in the larger hotels, it is not a method of service that is as common as it was in former years.

From the customers' point of view, hotel guests do not usually choose to eat their meals in their rooms, they prefer either to use the hotel's restaurant facilities, or to dine outside the hotel. From the management's point of view it is a method of food service that is very expensive to provide – a great deal of time and cost is involved in serving customers in their rooms, particularly if a full meal service is offered; for this reason most hotels offering room service today only offer a very limited menu selection or snack items only. The high cost of providing a floor service includes the basic problem of a fluctuating demand with the need to have staff always available to provide the service, the lifts to transport the food from the kitchen, as well as the need for trolleys, tables, trays, heating plates, etc. Furthermore, the special requirement of service pantries on most floors necessitates valuable revenue space being used for food production, which could be more efficiently contained and organized elsewhere, thus releasing service area pantries for other uses.

Today, the provision of lounge service is almost exclusively confined to up-market hotels and to resort type establishments. With many of the larger middle market hotels offering daylong coffee shop service, the need for hotels to offer food and beverage refreshments in the lounge areas has been reduced. Like room service, the provision of lounge service is highly labour intensive, distance from the production area may be considerable and demand uptake by the customer can fluctuate greatly.

Car or drive-in service • • •

Car service commonly consists of two types of service: the first where customers remain in their vehicles in the drive-in area to consume their meal; and the second where customers buy their food and beverages and then leave the drive-in to consume them elsewhere. The former type of car service operations have not increased in popularity in the last ten to fifteen years, although there are still many operations in the USA where they are almost exclusively still found.

Waiters (usually called carhops) take the customers' orders and return with the food placed on trays – these fit on to the car door or steering wheel. The customers eat their food in their cars, the carhops removing finished trays. Payment for the meal is made directly to the carhops.

This method of food service has declined in popularity for almost the same reasons as room service; mainly because it is a very labour intensive service method with often a long distance between the production area and the customer, also because people generally prefer to eat their meal, if only a snack, at a counter or table in a dining area, rather than in a car. Today, many drive-in operations are now providing a restaurant or dining space for their customers, so that they do have an alternative to eating in their car.

The second type of car service is an extension of the fast-food system of takeaway and involves customers ordering their requirements from a menu board which are transmitted usually via a microphone at the entrance to the drive-in. Customers then drive to the exit where they collect their purchases and pay at the same time. These fully computerized systems allow a rapid throughput of customers and parking areas do not have to be provided, unless the drive-in is also offering dining facilities. This method of drive-in takeaways is growing in popularity faster than the original concept as it does at least allow customers a choice of where to consume their meals.

Waiter service is therefore a method of food service in which customers receive some form of personalized service from the catering facility, in return for which they pay a higher price for the meal than would be paid, for example, in a self-service operation. On a simplified scale, the higher the cost of the meal to the customer, the more service the customer expects.

There are a limited number of establishments today which offer the elaborate, traditional service styles described, particularly the true French service; rising costs, especially labour costs, have to a great extent limited this type of service out of the market, although there will always be a small section of the total market that is able to pay the high prices charged. The majority of restaurants offering a waiter service today use either the American or Russian styles of service, depending upon the price the customer is willing to pay.

Special service arrangements • • •

In some catering situations it is a necessity for the prepared food to be transported and served directly to the customer – it may, for example, be a patient in a hospital ward, a passenger on board a plane or an elderly person living at home. In such cases as these, 'special' service arrangements may be used. There are a number of special service arrangements available and in the majority of cases are based on similar concepts and have very similar characteristics; it is convenient, therefore, to take a particular sector of the catering industry, the welfare sector, and to discuss the special service arrangements found in hospitals, as it is in these types of catering situations that most special service arrangements are found.

Centralized tray service • • •

Today, there are a number of centralized tray meal systems available for use in hospital catering. Although differing from each other in certain aspects, the basic menu selection procedure for patients is very similar. Menu cards are distributed to patients on the previous day; patients can then make their own selection of food for the following day from the choice on the menu card. Also included on the card are the desired portion sizes of the meal and any particular dietary requirements customers may have.

The menu cards are collected from the wards and returned to the catering officer who then prepares a production schedule for the following day based on the number to be catered for, the quantity of food to be produced, etc. Individual diet cards are then prepared for every patient in the hospital; these are later placed on the tray before it moves along the conveyor belt, so that the operatives can read exactly what is to be given to each patient.

When the food has been prepared for a particular meal period, the food is loaded into heated or refrigerated 'bains-marie', which are wheeled up to the conveyor belt and plugged into a mains socket to keep the food at the correct temperature throughout the service period. Cutlery for the meal is wrapped in a napkin (or pre-wrapped cutlery may be used) and placed on to a tray with the patient's menu card. The trays automatically move along the conveyor belt and the next item to be placed on the tray is some form of heated plate receiver, on top of which is then placed the conventionally styled plate. As the tray moves along the conveyor belt the operatives place the requested menu item and portion size on to the plate. By the time the tray reaches the end of the conveyor belt a complete meal has been assembled; one or two supervisors then check the tray's items against the menu cards before putting lids over the plates and placing the completed tray into the mobile holding cabinets, or tray trolleys, which are then sent to the wards. Using this special service arrangement several hundred complete meals can be prepared in a very short time and with constant supervision. Depending on menu selection, dietary requirements, garnishes, etc. 500 tray meals can be completed in one to one-and-a-half hours. If a cook-chill conveyor belt is being used, the ambient temperature of the kitchen should be 5°C or below.

There are, of course, other special service arrangements, found particularly in hospitals in the USA. Differential heating containers (DHC), for example, use metallized shielding over prepared trays to control the input of microwave on the various components of a meal. Other arrangements also include those that are almost totally computerized – from the analysis of the patients' meal choice to the assembly of the patients' trays. At present, however, the sophistication and cost of such special service arrangements are limiting factors to their more widespread use.

Special service arrangements are generally recognized as being a most effective way of serving 'captive audience' customers. One of their main aims is to provide meals that are both standardized and nutritionally balanced; using such systems as have been described these objectives can be achieved. Centralizing tray service preparation saves duplication of space and equipment, rationalizes labour requirements and individual meals can be ordered to suit customer requirements. As well as the above savings there may also be savings on food costs due to centralized portion control, and elimination of waste from excessive ordering.

It should be remembered, however, that where special service arrangements are used, such as in hospitals, customer satisfaction is of particular importance. The presentation of the tray, food arrangement, colour combination, garnishes, etc. are also therefore important factors to be taken into account so that encouragement is given to the patient to eat the meal provided.

Trays • • •

The use of a tray in a food service facility has several purposes: first, the transportation of the customer's food and beverages from the service counter to the table whether in cafeteria or waiter service; second, it can be used as an aid to portioning control, for example in airline catering and more recently school catering where 'indented' trays are used; third, it can be used in the removal of dishes from the place where the customer has dined, to the dishwashing area and finally, it can be an aid to advertising by printing an establishment's logo actually on the tray and cross-advertising this with outer outlets of the operation, for example a department store's different catering facilities.

The catering situations in which trays may be used as an aid to food service vary therefore from self-service cafeteria arrangements using plastic trays, to high-class restaurants using silver trays, to travel catering situations where complete meals are served on a tray, for example onboard a train or plane.

Finally, a combination of self-service and waiter service is now becoming more popular in some catering operations. Customers select their first course from a buffet arrangement, order their main course from the counter or from the waiter, which is then served to them pre-plated at their table, desserts and coffee subsequently being ordered and served in the same way. Harvester Restaurants, for example, operate this type of service. Customers make their own salad selection from a salad cart, their main courses and dessert being selected from the menu. Alternatively, customers may order their meals from a counter, giving the operative their table number and the food is then served to them at their table, this type of service is particularly popular in pub restaurants. This 'assisted' or 'aided service' enables more customers to be served by fewer service staff as the waiters' time is not divided between taking orders and service as the customers themselves place their own orders. Refrigerated dessert displays are often situated adjacent to the ordering counter and this can result in an increase in impulse purchases, by the customer waiting to give his dessert or coffee order.

Beverage service methods

Beverage service is an area that is sometimes neglected by catering operations, although it can be a most lucrative part of the total catering service, if approached and managed in the correct way.

The method of beverage service employed by a catering establishment should be complementary to the food service method. In a high-class haute cuisine restaurant, for example, it is common to find an adjacent cocktail bar for pre-dinner drinks, where the customer is served at the bar or table by a waiter; after the meal beverages are served at the customer's table, or served in a separate coffee lounge. In a catering facility operating a self-service method of food service, customers would either help themselves to beverages as they moved along the cafeteria line, serve themselves from a vending machine or be served by an operative behind the counter. There is not often a separate coffee lounge in self-service restaurants, although where space requirements permit, one may be provided to help increase customer throughput. Alcoholic beverages are not sold through vending machines in public areas due to licencing restrictions.

Classification of beverage service methods

As with the previously described food service, there are basically two main types of beverage service: self-service, and waiter/barperson service. Unlike food service, however, there are no special service arrangements designed specifically for the service of beverages other than a bar or dispense bar, although beverage service is of course included as part of those special arrangements described earlier, such as in hospital catering.

Self-service • • •

Self-service beverage methods are those in which customers collect their own beverages from a counter or machine, rather than a waiter serving beverages to the customers at tables. Such a method may be completely self-service, such as the vending of beverages, or it may be aided such as in the traditional cafeteria arrangement where an operative would portion drinks into cups and glasses and hand these to the customers.

The cafeteria • • •

In traditional cafeteria arrangements beverages are included in the main counter line, usually at the end, just before the cashier. The serving of beverages is, however, recognized to be one of the slowest points in the cafeteria line and the tendency now is to separate the beverages out from the main line completely and to serve them from a separate counter. This 'breaking down' of the traditional cafeteria line is carried further in the free-flow cafeteria arrangements, which consist of a series of individual counters of which beverages are one.

In some cafeteria arrangements the beverage counters may actually be sited in the dining area. This is an attempt to speed up the throughput of customers in the main cafeteria area to the dining area. Counter staff may either man such beverage stations or vending machines may be used.

Bar or counter service • • •

This method of beverage service is most commonly found in public houses or hotels and restaurants that have licensed bars; customers purchasing their drinks at the bar and then usually carrying them back themselves to a table for consumption. Payment for the beverage is made directly to the barperson. A growing trend in this type of service is the use of computerized automatic measuring devices for beers, spirits and soft drinks, together with an emphasis on displaying and merchandising beverages.

The carousel • • •

Pre-portioned cold drinks may be offered for sale on a carousel. These are usually situated on the refrigerated shelves and such beverages as glasses of wine, fruit juices, milk, iced coffees, etc. may be featured. Hot beverages such as tea and coffee would be dispensed from a separate counter either adjacent or close to the carousel, or again may be sited in the main dining area.

Vending • • •

Beverage vending machines may vend hot or cold drinks separately or together in the same machine and may also dispense alcoholic and non-alcoholic drinks. (Alcoholic vended beverages are studied in the next section under room service.)

1. Hot non-alcoholic beverage machines vend coffee, tea, chocolate and sometimes soups. They offer a range of variations, for example with and without sugar, creamers or whiteners, beverages of different strengths, fresh brew leaf teas, ground and continental coffees, etc.
2. Cold and non-alcoholic beverage machines vend a variety of drinks, mainly syrup and concentrate based, although some powders are used. Examples of cold drinks being vended include still and carbonated bottle waters and juices, cartoned milks and milk shakes, fruit and health drinks, and canned products such as Coca-Cola and Pepsi which it is estimated account for 90% of the canned drink vending market.
3. Hot and cold non-alcoholic beverage machines were developed to meet the growing need for cold drinks in some establishments already using vending machines, yet who did not require a machine vending cold drinks only. Packages of cold vending drinks were therefore designed that could be fitted into most existing hot drinks machines with little difficulty.

Beverage vending has a considerably wide application within the catering industry. First, it may be used in those operations offering a total vended service such as hospitals, where both food and beverages are sold through vending machines. Second, beverage vending may be used as a supplement to an existing method of food and beverage service, such as in cafeteria arrangements where all the food is served in a traditional line, but the beverages are separated out and dispensed from vending machines. Finally, beverage vending may not be used within the actual restaurant operation itself, but it may still be used as part of the establishment's total catering facilities – for example by sighting individual or banks of beverage vending machines throughout the office block, factory layout, or as a supplement to, or in place of, a floor service in hotels.

Room service • • •

Beverage service in hotel and motel rooms is most commonly waiter service, although many establishments have now installed mini-bars or small automatic dispensing machines (also called Bell Captains), from which guests may obtain a drink. A limited choice of alcoholic and non-alcoholic drinks and snacks are placed in the mini-bar, guests simply removing any drinks they may require. The mini-bars may be freestanding or, alternatively, they can be built into existing furniture. During the late 1990s' the introduction of glass fronted mini-bars to promote impulse consumption were introduced. These units were connected with a light that comes on with the room light but were unpopular and have largely disappeared.

There are a number of mini-bar systems available today and payment for items consumed may be made in several ways.

1. The purchase may be automatically registered at the cashier's office and debited directly to the customer's account. The beverages consumed are itemized on the guest's bill, which can also show the time of purchase and the cost. The advantages of this totally computerized system are that every selection from the mini-bar is immediately registered so that the hotel has few lost sales, the guest does not have to be disturbed for a daily stock check of the mini-bar and detailed information such as sales analysis, value of stock held, refill and maintenance requirements, etc. is all available to management. Its major disadvantage is the high cost of installing such a system although this has to be weighed against the savings made in reducing labour costs and the number of lost sales, the increase in efficiency and security to both guests and the hotel, and the additional control information generated for management.

2. On the morning of the guest's departure, the mini-bar is checked and the customer's account debited for drinks consumed. This form of control may either be totally manual or it can be aided by the use of a portable system to process the data normally manually recorded. The manual system is a lengthy process involving the checking of all mini-bars within the hotel on a daily basis and recording by hand those that have been used, those in use, mini-bars requiring re-stocking, etc. With this 'honesty bar' system, however, the guests are either required to remember their purchases from the machine or the mini-bars must be checked early enough so that the customer's account can be correctly debited before leaving the hotel. With such a system, lost sales can sometimes therefore run at a high level.

This manual approach has been greatly improved by the use of hand-held terminals. The mini-bar management system (MMS) is a portable system used by the mini-bar attendant to record consumption from the mini-bars. By using a bar code reader and a bar chart listing the products in the mini-bar, the data can be recorded and relayed to the invoice printer by telephone or read directly. This information can then be prepared as an individual receipt for the room account or entered directly on to the guest's account. As with the totally computerized system, there are labour savings to be made and it can also provide detailed up-to-date management information. Its major advantage over the totally computerized system is its reduced installation cost as it can use existing telephone and electrical cables. Such a system does, however, still require an attendant to physically check the mini-bars daily although a system can be installed whereby an attendant can see those rooms where the mini-bar has been opened, which need to be serviced, etc. via a central display console; this is not only labour saving but also reduces guest disturbance. More recently the wider introduction of 'wireless' technology allows the room attendant to simply enter the details of stock used and 'send' this to the accounting system where it is instantly debited to the customers account. An electronic tag fitted to the mini-bar door signals whether the mini-bar has been used and again reduces un-necessary guest disturbance.

3. The guest may purchase a drink by placing the correct amount of money into the machine and removing the beverage item as with a normal vending machine.

Mini-bars therefore exist as a supplementary service to room service and are used by guests at different times of the day when they may not want to call or wait for room service. Operated and managed efficiently mini-bars can be an independent profit centre generating additional revenue for the hotel.

Welcome trays or hospitality bars are now increasingly found in hotel rooms. These basically consist of a base which can be free-standing or fixed to a unit, or wall-mounted for extra safety and security, a kettle, an ingredient dispenser which would contain sachets of coffee, tea, sugar, pots of milk and cream, and sometimes packets of biscuits, and a detachable tray with cups, saucers, spoons and a teapot. Welcome trays are essentially a free service provided by hotels so that guests may make themselves a hot drink at any time without calling for room service.

The buffet • • •

Beverage service in buffet type arrangement is usually waiter service, although in some cases pre-portioned drinks may be on display on the buffet table to encourage sales. Such beverages that may be offered include glasses of wine, fruit juices, iced coffee, etc.

The takeaway • • •

In take-away operations, beverages are usually served to the customer with the food ordered. When the customer's order has been prepared, the food and beverage items are packaged and handed to the customer. Like the food products offered for sale by the take-away operations, the beverage products are also highly standardized, often offering a limited number of beverages, with a number of variations, for example the takeaway may offer six or eight different flavoured milk shakes. The disposable containers used for the beverages all carry the operation's theme or logo (e.g. McDonald's) so promoting the company's brand image.

Self-service is therefore a method of beverage service in which customers collect their own beverages from a service point rather than waiters bringing beverages to them. In the majority of industrial catering situations today, self-service is the most commonly adopted method of beverage service, because it can aid in speeding up customer throughput, and for this reason beverages are usually separated out from the main food service counter.

Waiter/waitress service ● ● ●

Waiter/waitress beverage service methods are those in which beverages are transported and served to the customer, whether at a table, counter or bar, by a member of the service staff. It is a method of beverage service more commonly associated with higher priced catering facilities rather than some of the self-service operations previously described, and hence is more widely found in haute cuisine and other full service restaurants.

Counter or bar service ● ● ●

In bar service customers may either sit on stools or chairs at the counter or bar and be served directly by the bar staff, or they may sit at individual tables within the bar area and be served by waiting staff who collect the drinks from the bar for the customer. The former method of beverage service in which the customer may remain seated at the bar or table, is most commonly used in public houses and coffee shop styled catering facilities. The latter method is widely used in hotel bars and other restaurants that often feature a separate bar for pre- and after-dinner drinks. In both catering situations the bar is acting as a sales tool for the establishment and must therefore look attractive and feature an appropriate selection of beverages for that particular type of operation and the market at which it is aiming.

Dispensing machines ● ● ●

For the convenience of classification those automatic machines dispensing alcoholic and 'mixer' beverages, may be termed 'dispensing machines', while those offering non-alcoholic beverages may be termed 'vending machines'. Automatic dispensing machines may be used to accurately dispense exact amounts of alcoholic beverages, the types of dispensing machines varying from the very simple to the very sophisticated. In many, the machine's controls are set at the amount required to be dispensed, the bottle is placed inverted into the machine, and the machine will measure and dispense the portions set on the machine. In the more sophisticated machines cocktails may even be mixed and then dispensed.

The use of automatic dispensing machines has several advantages; each portion is accurately measured so there is no over pouring or under pouring; standard drinks are always served to the customer; some dispensing machines can pour and mix drinks quicker than a barperson; if the machines meter the number of drinks dispensed, a precise check may be made on the number of drinks served and the amount of money taken by the bar; their use cuts down breakages, wastage and theft; bar layouts can become more compact and save on space requirements; and finally, those machines that not only meter and dispense drinks, but also maintain a perpetual stock inventory are a very useful tool for re-ordering and management control.

Table service • • •

In the context of this classification table service is being used to describe the service of beverages at the customer's dining table. The customer's order for beverages is taken at the table and the beverages usually collected from the side of the bar or from a dispense bar, which is out of sight from the customer. A dispense bar is a bar for dispensing beverages to service staff, and not directly to customers; because it is not a visual sales tool of the establishment, it is not usually designed to be aesthetically appealing but very functional, as it often has to serve a number of restaurant and other beverage sales outlets in the establishment, for example in a hotel. In some restaurants a trolley or cart may be used for the service of beverages to tables, particularly after the meal when liqueurs are served. The use of such a beverage cart is not only an aid to the service of the beverages but is also an important visual sales tool.

Banquet service • • •

Beverage service at banqueting functions is often very similar to food service in that specific beverages have already been chosen and are served at set times during the course of a meal, to accompany certain foods. Pre-meal drinks in banqueting may either be served by the service staff, for example taking trays of drinks round to the guests, or a bar offering a selection of drinks may be arranged in the room used for guest assembly, and the guests can buy directly from this. During the meal the wines pre-chosen by the host are served, and after dinner beverages such as coffee and liqueurs are also served at the guests' tables. This above system is referred to as an 'inclusive bar'. Any other beverages ordered by the guests are not usually included in the cost of the banquet meal and are therefore paid for separately by the guests. The alternative to an inclusive bar is a 'cash bar' when no drinks have been pre-ordered and the guests themselves pay for all drinks. It is a common practice, however, that in the reception area for a banquet the wine waiters will have set up a table so that customers can choose, and at times pay for, their wines in advance.

Room and lounge service • • •

In waiter service operations the customer orders the required beverages from room or floor service and the drinks are taken to the room; payment may be made directly to the waiter, or as is more usual, is debited to the customer's account. Although self-service machines are being used in some establishments' waiter service is still the most common method used for room service.

As with the service of foods in hotel lounges, beverage service is gradually being confined to the more expensive hotels; some other grades of hotels, resort establishments and pubs, however, do use the service of morning coffees and afternoon teas as a means of extending their service times.

Coffee carts ● ● ●

The use of coffee carts or tea trolleys for the service of beverages have been included here because within this type of service beverages are often served directly to customers at their desk or table. This method of beverage service is still being used today in office blocks and factory buildings although to a large extent it is being replaced by vending.

Liqueur trolleys ● ● ●

Liqueur trolleys may be used in a variety of restaurants and hotels and are usually brought to the customer's table at the end of a meal. An attractively stocked and interesting display of liqueurs can often stimulate customers' interest and increase alcoholic beverage sales.

The waiter method of beverage service is therefore most commonly used in higher priced catering establishments, although it does have an application in a number of other catering situations. By definition this type of beverage service is more labour intensive than the type required in self-service operations. In haute cuisine restaurants for example, employing the French method of food service, in which the food is presented to the guest before service, a similar method of beverage service also exists; the service of wine, for example, would be very similar in style and formality – the wine being presented to the customer and tasted before it is served to the other guests. This type of service contrasts with self-service operations where guests not only help themselves to the food they would like, but also to the beverages. In the majority of catering situations, therefore, the style of beverage service reflects the style of food service, so that the two are complementary to one another.

Summary

- The major food production methods currently in operation in the UK are: conventional or traditional (cook-serve); conventional production with the use of convenience foods: cook-freeze and cook-chill and their derivatives.
- Additional methods employed specifically by the food manufacturer are: canning, dehydration, the use of synthetic foods, etc. but these are not covered in this book.

- The trend is increasing use of convenience and preserved food products as manufactures improve quality, packaging and a wider range of products.
- Where staff costs continue to rise, particularly skilled staff, the cost of technology remains fairly constant. It is possible for restaurant and hotel chains to maintain standards of quality and reduce costs by its utilization.
- The food production system chosen needs to meet the demands of the menu style of service operation and the space available.
- Food and beverage service systems include restaurant service, cafeteria, self-service counters or buffet, room service, bars and vending.
- Increasing costs in land values, capital and equipment, labour and raw materials demands attention to detail at the initial planning stage in order to satisfy the exact requirements of the food production system.

Further study options

Food and beverage production and service is a study area made up from a number of inter-related specialist areas, food production and food service, liquor studies wines beers and spirits, etc. hot beverages and the managing of skilled production staff and discerning customers, all under a wide umbrella of complex legislation. We will therefore examine further study options under a number of headings.

Legislation; anyone working in food and beverage production will need to study for a Basic Food Hygiene Certificate issued by the Chartered Institute for Environmental Health, usually a half-day course run by your local council. As a food and beverage employee, especially if you are in a supervisory position you will be required to have a working knowledge of the provisions in the 1990 Food Safety Act available from Her Majesties Stationary Office (HMSO). For those involved with the sale of liquor, again particularly if you are in a supervisory position then you should be aware of the provisions of the 2003 Licensing Act and the National Certificate for Licensees or the National Certificate in Licensed Retailing are appropriate courses of study. You may also choose to attain a Personal Licence Qualification.

Food Production and service; there are a wide range of textbooks covering various aspects of food production and service, from those that offer recipes or recipes with food production theory to those that offer more complex food production theory and food systems theory. There are of course a huge number of recipe books available including a number containing professional recipe's, for example Gary Rhodes,

Jamie Oliver, Gordon Ramsey, Anthony Worral Thompson, Rick Stein, Raymond Blanc and Anton Mossiman and these are all valid texts for the industry professional. In addition to these and numerous other popular books there are a number of more educationally based academic texts that will provide a deeper understanding of specific areas of food and beverage production and service methods. These include Le Répertoire De La Cuisine by Louis Saulnier a reference of classical preparations, sauces, garnishes, etc. *Practical Cookery*, 10th edition by Foskett, Ceserani and Kinton; or *Advanced Practical Cookery*, 4th edition by Foskett Campbell and Ceserani; both cookery texts for the professional chef. *Food and Beverage Service*, 7th edition by Lillicrap and Cousins which looks primarily at the service side of food and beverage production; *The Larder Chef* by Bode and Leto a modern classic in larder preparations and the *Theory of Catering*, 10th edition by Foskett, Ceserani and Kinton.

Beverages; whilst beverages includes all liquid refreshment most interest appears to centre on wine, cocktails, real ale and coffee. For those with a special interest in wines there are a number of texts available notably The *World Atlas of Wine*, 5th edition by Johnson; *The New Short Course in Wine* by Hoffman, Grapes and Wine by Clarke and Rand; *The Wine Report* by Stevenson together with a number of annual publications on vintages, etc. the *Pocket Wine Book* 2008 by Johnson. For those with an interest in studying Beer the reputed UK experts both on beer production and consumption are the Campaign for real Ale (CAMRA). They have regional offices throughout the UK with a membership of around 87,000. They lobby to retain traditional standards in brewing, hold various festivals, produce a newsletter and publish numerous guides on beer. The study of spirits falls into two broad groups. The first are those that are traditionally consumed on their own, for example some brandy, armagnac, cognac, malt whisky, most liqueurs and we may add here some fortified wines such as fine sherry or port. The second group are cocktails that may contain one or more spirits mixed together with other ingredients to create a unique beverage. There are a number of institutions that can provide further study, the two most popular are The United Kingdom Bartenders Guild (UKBG) established in 1933, a trade association offering bar and cocktail training, and the Wine and Spirit Education Trust (WSET) established in 1969 they provide high quality education and training in wines and spirits up to diploma level. There are also a number of publications including *Decanter Magazine*, 12 issues per year and *Food and Drink Magazine*, 6 issues per year and a number of textbooks, *International Guide to Drinks* authored by the UKBG, *Classic Cocktails* by Calabrese, *The Craft of the Cocktail* by Degroff and *Kindred Spirits* by Pacult.

Study exercise

Executive Chef Sarah Bronston, soon realized that taking this new position might have seemed an exciting opportunity at the time but it seemed that the stock control of the premises she was hired to manage was so unorganized that it was certainly one of the main reasons customer numbers were failing.

During her very first audit Sarah discovered that her team would order foods on an ad hoc basis without keeping any clear stock records. When deliveries arrived at the premises staff appeared too busy to count the items or even check for quality and would simply sign the delivery note without double-checking the products. She was horrified to identify a number of products in the stores that were out of date and prepared goods stored were not labelled so there was no way of knowing what was safe to use and what was not. There was no monthly stock takes and the wine was stored in cellars that would often reach 20°C. An EPOS system that was recently installed was not linked to any stocktaking system so that no stock reports seemed to exist. Sarah realized that she had a lot of work to do if this restaurant was going to keep its licence let alone attract a healthy number of customers.

Consider the implications of the situation described above in terms of:

Health and Safety
Production Control
Quality of Product.

If you were Sarah what steps would you undertake to ensure the quality of the product is not jeopardized?

Further reading

Automatic Vending Association of Britain (1996). *Census Vend Inform*, Automatic Vending Association of Britain.

Coltman, M. (2000). *Hospitality Management Accounting*, 7th edn. New York: John Wiley.

Cracknell, H. L., Kaufmann, R. J. and Nobis, F. (1988). *Practical Professional Catering*. London: Macmillan.

Davis, B. and Lockwood, A. (1994). *Food and Beverage Management – A Selection of Readings*. Oxford: Butterworth-Heinemann.

Fiss, M. L. (2003). Charting a Course to Freedom: Cruise Lines Create Dining Revolution. FoodService Director, 08977208, 6/15/2003, Vol. 16, Issue 6.

Green, E. F. et al. (1987). *Profitable Food and Beverage Management: Planning*. Jenks, OK: Williams Books.

Hyman, H. H. (1982). *Supplies Management for Health Services*. London: Croom Helm.

Leto, m.j. and Bode, W. K. H. (2006). *The Larder Chef*, 4th edn. Oxford: Butterworth-Heinmann.

Lillicrap, D. and Cousins, J. (2006). *Food and Beverage Service*, 7th edn. London: Hodder and Stoughton.

Mintel (2006a). *Number of UK Confectionery, Snacks and Meals Vending Machines, by Type of Food Dispensed, Mintel Estimate, Based on AVA Census Data Trends for 2002–05* Mintel International Group Limited, London.

Mintel (2006b). *Comparison of Performance of Different Sectors in the Eating Out Market, 2001–06* Mintel International Group Limited, London.

Mintel (2007a). *Number of UK Drinks Vending Machines, by Dispensing Method, 2002–06* Mintel International Group Limited, London.

Mintel (2007b). *Vending Performance Key Indicators* Mintel International Group Limited, London.

Mintel (2007c). *Ethical Role of Vended Drinks* Mintel International Group Limited, London.

Perlik, A. (2006). Seal of Approval: Restaurants and Institutions, 02735520 Vol. 116, Issue 8.

Silver, D. (2000). Breaking with Tradition Restaurants & Institutions, 02735520, 11/01/2000, Vol. 110, Issue 29.

Stevens, J. (1987). *Measuring Purchasing Performance*. London: Business Books.

Strauss, K. (2004). *Hotels: Full Scale Production* 38(9), p. 67–70. Reed Elsevier Inc., New York.

Ward, J. (1984). *Profitable Product Management*. Oxford: Butterworth-Heinemann.

Westing, K. et al. (1983). *Purchasing Management*. New York: John Wiley. www.food.gov.uk/consultations/ukwideconsults/2005/genfoodlaw178 www.food.gov.uk/foodindustry

Food and beverage control

Food and beverage control may be defined as the guidance and regulation of the costs and revenue of operating the catering activity in a food and beverage establishment. A successful holistic food and beverage control is imperative for any type of food and beverage operation regardless of its size. The cost of food and beverage can range from 25% to up to 50% depending on the type of operation. In restaurants, food and beverage can be the only source of revenue (e.g. merchandising and room hire can generate additional revenue). In the public sector catering, employee restaurants and similar operations, food and beverages are the main day-to-day expenditure, which is controlled by budgets and possibly a level of subsidy, either on a total company or on a per unit basis. The amount of control is related to the size of the operation. A large group operation would require a much more precise, detailed, up-to-date information, than a small operation. Additionally a larger operation will be able to support the control with a computerized system when a smaller operation may not be able to afford it (however the cost of such technology has been greatly reduced in recent years so much so that even smaller operations can now afford such a system). In both instances the type and volume of data required needs to be selectively determined if control is to be meaningful and effective. Having already gone through Chapters 5 and 6 the reader will be familiar with the concepts of purchasing (Chapter 6) and pricing (Chapter 5) which are two important parts that complete the circle of effective food and beverage control.

It is important at this stage to clarify the limitations of a control system.

- A control system can only identify problem areas and trends in the business. The system cannot automatically correct such problem areas.
- A control system will require constant management supervision to ensure that it functions efficiently.
- A control system will need management action to evaluate the information produced and to act upon it.

Chapter objectives

After working through this chapter you should be able to:

1. Understand the objectives of food and beverage cost control.
2. Perform a break-even analysis and understand the budget.
3. Understand the concepts of standard recipes, yields and portion sizes.
4. Understand the methods of food and beverage cost control.
5. Understand the basics of revenue control and the differences between manual and computerized systems.
6. Understanding some of the basic operating ratios.

THE OBJECTIVES OF FOOD AND BEVERAGE CONTROL

The objectives of a food and beverage control system may be summarized as follows:

- *Analysis of income and expenditure*: The analysis is solely concerned with the income and expenditure related to food and beverage operations. The revenue analysis is usually by each selling outlet, of such aspects as the volume of food and beverage sales, the sales mix, the average spending power (ASP) of customers at various times of the day, and the number of customers served. The analysis of costs includes departmental food and beverage costs, portion costs and labour costs. The performance of each outlet can then be expressed in terms of the gross profit and the net margin (i.e. gross profit minus wages) and the net profit (i.e. gross profit minus wages and all overhead expenses such as rent, rates, insurance, etc.).
- *Establishment and maintenance of standards*: The basis for the operation of any food and beverage outlet is the establishment of a set of standards which would be particular to an operation, for example, a chain of steak house restaurants. Unless

standards are set no employee would know in detail the standards to be achieved nor could the employee's performance be effectively measured by management. An efficient unit would have the set standards laid down in manuals often known as SOPs (standard operational procedures) which should be readily available to all staff for reference. Having set the standards, a difficult problem always for the management of an operation is to maintain these standards. This can be aided by regularly checking on the standards achieved by observation and analysis and by comments made by customers, and when necessary, conducting training courses to re-establish the standards.

- *Pricing*: An important objective of food and beverage control is to provide a sound basis for menu pricing including quotations for special functions. It is, therefore, important to determine food menu and beverage list prices in the light of accurate food and beverage costs and other main establishment costs; as well as general market considerations, such as the average customer spending power, the prices charged by competitors and the prices that the market will accept (Pricing is further explained in the Chapter 5).

- *Prevention of waste*: In order to achieve performance standards for an establishment, targets are set for revenue, cost levels and profit margins. To achieve these levels of performance it is necessary to prevent wastage of materials caused by such things as poor preparation, over-production, failure to use standard recipes, etc. This can only be done with an efficient method of control, which covers the complete cycle of food and beverage control, from the basic policies of the organization to the management control after the operation has been completed (see Figure 8.1).

- *Prevention of fraud*: It is necessary for a control system to prevent or at least restrict the possible areas of fraud by customers and staff. Typical areas of fraud by customers are such things as deliberately walking out without paying; unjustifiably claiming that the food or drink that they had partly or totally consumed was unpalatable and indicating that they will not pay for it; disputing the number of drinks served; making payments by stolen cheques or credit cards. Typical areas of fraud by staff are overcharging or undercharging for items served and stealing of food, drink or cash.

- *Management information*: A system of control has an important task to fulfil in providing accurate up-to-date information for the preparation of periodical reports for management. This information should be sufficient so as to provide a complete analysis of performance for each outlet of an establishment for comparison with set standards previously laid down (e.g. budget standards).

Information overload can be a major issue when managing an operation. Often management will be presented with enormous amount of reports and statistical information that they may not know how to use or do not have the time to act upon.

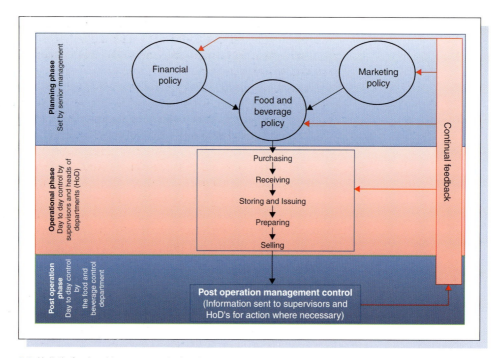

Figure 8.1 Holistic food and beverage control system

It is therefore imperative that depending on the size of the operation appropriate control is applied, for example, a small operation may not require daily, weekly and periodic reports whilst a larger operation will probably require them so that management may take both corrective and preventive action quickly.

SPECIAL PROBLEMS OF FOOD AND BEVERAGE CONTROL

Food and beverage control tends to be more difficult than the control of materials in many other industries. The main reasons for this are:

- *Perishability of the product*: Food, whether raw or cooked, is a perishable commodity and has a limited life. The caterer, therefore, has to ensure that she buys produce in the correct quality and quantity in relation to estimated demand, and that it is correctly stored and processed (beverages are less perishable and this contributes to easier control).
- *Business volume unpredictability*: Sales instability is typical of most catering establishments. There is often a change in the volume of business from day to day, and in many establishments from hour to hour. This causes basic problems with regard to the quantities of commodities to be purchased and prepared as well as to the staffing required.
- *Menu mix unpredictability*: In order to be competitive and satisfy a particular market, caterers must often offer a wide choice

of menu items to the customer. Predicting menu item preference on top of customer volume can be a challenge. Effective forecasting as part of the total food and beverage control system is therefore necessary.

- *Food and beverage operation short cycle*: The speed at which catering operations take place, relative to many other industries, allows little time for many control tasks. It is not uncommon that items ordered one day are received, processed and sold the same or next day. It is for this reason that in larger catering establishments cost reporting is done daily or at least weekly. Further problems, particularly with perishable foods, are that with a short life for produce, items cannot be bought very much in advance of their need; and the problem of availability at times of produce relative to the price that can be afforded in relation to the selling price.
- *Departmentalization*: Many food and beverage operations have several production and service departments, offering different products and operating under different policies. It is, therefore, necessary to be able to produce separate trading results for each of the production and selling activities.

THE FUNDAMENTALS OF CONTROL

Effective control systems and procedures consist of three broad phases: planning, operational and management control after the operation has taken place.

The planning phase

It is difficult to run an effective catering operation without having firstly defined the basic policies. Policies are pre-determined guidelines, laid down by the senior management of an organization, which outline such matters as the market or segment of the market that is being aimed at, how it is to be catered for, and the level of profitability/subsidy to be achieved. Policies in general are particular to individual companies and establishments, although in the public sector operations, there may well be broad national policies, for example, for hospital catering.

A catering operation should have its policies clearly defined before it commences business, and re-defined whenever a major change takes place, for example, when a new theme is chosen for a restaurant to aim for a different market segment. Ideally, in a large organization the policies should be written down and periodically reviewed in relation to the current business and future trends; however, in smaller organizations there is not the communication problem of a large organization and to formally draw up and commit policies to paper is not so vital. There are three basic policies which need to be considered:

1. The financial policy will determine the level of profitability, subsidy or cost limits to be expected from the business as a

whole and the contribution to the total profit, subsidy or cost limit that is to be expected from each unit, and then from the departments within them. This involves the setting of targets for the business as a whole as well as each unit and the departments within them. Thus, the financial policy for a large hotel will set profit targets for the hotel, and departmental profit targets for the accommodation and catering as well as other departments. The financial policy for the catering department will set the overall target for the department itself, which will be further divided into targets for the various restaurants, bars and function facilities. The financial policy for an industrial contract catering operation will set the overall target for the operation, the level of subsidy and the level of management fee, as well as the cost limits per unit (meal or employee).

2. The marketing policy will identify the broad market the operation is intended to serve and the particular segment(s) of the market upon which it intends to concentrate. It should also identify the immediate and future consumer requirements on a continuous basis in order to maintain and improve its business performance. It is obvious from the above that the broad market intended to be served by a large city hotel could be broken down into the specific segments of the various types of users of, for example, the coffee shop, the carvery, the cocktail bar, the banqueting rooms, etc. each having specific and different consumer requirements. The interpretation of the marketing policy for a national commercial catering organization into a marketing plan for the next year may include some or all of the following objectives:

   - *National identity* – to achieve a better national identity for all units by corporate design, and by meeting consumer expectations of what a 'popular restaurant' concept should be.
   - *Customer* – the customer profile being the business person, shopper, tourist of either sex, aged twenty-five years or more, commonly using the high street of any major town, requiring food and beverage of good general standard, waitress served, for a typical price of £n per meal.
   - *Market share* – to achieve, maintain or increase the percentage of 'our' market.
   - *Turnover* – sales volume to be increased by $x\%$ on previous year.
   - *Profitability* – profit to be increased by each unit by $y\%$ on previous year.
   - *ASP* per customer to be increased by $z\%$ – to achieve a new ASP of not less than £n.
   - *Product* – the product to be maintained at a consistently high standard.
   - *Customer satisfaction* – the net result must be the satisfaction of every customer.

3. The catering policy, which is normally evolved from the financial and marketing policies, will define the main objectives of operating the food and beverage facilities and describe the

methods by which such objectives are to be achieved. It will usually include the following:

- The *type of customer*, for example high spending business executive, low spending female shopper, short-stay hospital patient, etc.
- The *type of menu(s)*, for example table d'hôte, à la carte, fast food.
- The *beverage provision* necessary for the operation.
- The *food quality standards*, for example fresh, frozen, canned, etc. and the grade of produce to be used.
- The *method of buying*, for example by contract, quotation, cash and carry, etc.
- *Type and quality of service*, for example cafeteria, counter, waiter, etc.
- *Degree of comfort and décor*, for example square footage per customer, type and style of décor, of chairs, tables, etc.
- *Hours of operation*, for example twenty-four hours, seven days a week; 1200–1500 and 1800–2200 hours, Monday–Saturday, etc.

The operational phase

Having defined the policies (i.e. pre-determined guidelines), it is then necessary to outline how they are to be interpreted into the day-to-day control activities of the catering operation. The operational control is in five main stages of the control cycle. These are:

1. *Purchasing*: There are five main points to be considered.
   (a) *Product testing* – to identify as a result of a series of taste panel evaluations the particular products to be used.
   (b) *Yield testing* – to identify as a result of tests the yield obtainable from all the major commodities used.
   (c) *Purchase specifications* – a specification is a concise description in writing of the quality, size, weight, etc. for a particular food or beverage item.
   (d) *Method of buying* – by contract, quotation, cash and carry, etc.
   (e) *Clerical procedures* – it is necessary to determine who originates, sanctions and places orders and what documentation is required for control.

2. *Receiving*: There are three main points to be considered:
   (a) *Quantity inspection* – a person must be nominated to be responsible for physically counting and weighing goods and checking that the quantity and size of items in the delivery matches the purchase order. If there is a shortage in the delivery the purchasing manager or a member of the management must be informed.
   (b) *Quality inspection* – this is particularly important with perishable foods where inspection may be made by a senior chef. Whenever possible the items should be checked against the appropriate purchase specification.
   (c) *Clerical procedures* – this is a very important aspect as all necessary documentation must follow a set procedure. It

includes the acknowledgement of the receipt of acceptable goods and the delivery person's signature on a 'request for credit' note for returned goods and short deliveries.

3. *Storing and issuing*: There are four main points to be considered:
   (a) *Stock records* – it is necessary to decide what records are to be kept.
   (b) *Pricing of items* – the method of pricing of the various types of items must be decided upon so that there is consistency within the operation. (see Chapter 5)
   (c) *Stocktaking* – the points to be considered here are the level of stock to be held, rate of stock turnover, dealing with discrepancies, identification of slow-moving items, etc.
   (d) *Clerical procedures* – there is a need to determine what documentation is necessary, for example requisitions, record cards, bin cards, stocktaking reports, etc.

4. *Preparing*: This is a critical stage in the control cycle, in particular for food. There are three main points to be considered:
   (a) *Volume forecasting* – a method of predicting the number of customers using the catering facilities on a specific day, and also of predicting as accurately as possible what items they will eat and drink.
   (b) *Pre-costing* – a method of controlling food and beverage costs in advance of the preparation and service stages. It is done by preparing and using standard recipes for all food and beverage items and also by using portion control equipment, for example ladles, scales, optics, standard glassware, etc.
   (c) *Clerical procedures* – what documentation is required and the distribution and destination of this information.

5. *Selling*: This important stage of operational control needs to take into consideration the following points:
   (a) *A checking system* – this is necessary to keep control of the number of covers sold and of the items sold. This may be done through a standard type of waiter's check system or through a till roll or in the case of hospital patients, by the summary and analysis of completed individual patient menu cards.
   (b) *The control of cash* – this is vitally important. It is necessary to ensure that all items sold have been paid for and that the money is received or credit has been authorized.
   (c) *Clerical procedures* – these would be necessary to control items sold and the money received or credit entitled, and would often include a restaurant checking system, meal and sales analysis, cashier's paying-in book, etc.

The post operation phase

This final phase of food and beverage control is in three main stages:

1. *Food and beverage cost reporting*: As mentioned earlier in this chapter, the cycle of production is very short and the product

is perishable. These factors together with the variations in demand for the product necessitate up-to-date reporting at least weekly if not daily.

2. *Assessment*: There is a need for someone from the food and beverage management team in the case of a large unit, or the proprietor or manager of a small unit, to analyse the food and beverage reports and to compare them with the budget for the period and against previous actual performance.

3. *Correction*: A control system does not cure or prevent problems occurring. When the analysis of the performance of a unit or department identifies that there is a problem, it is up to management to take the necessary steps to correct the problem as quickly as possible.

THE REALITY OF CONTROL

No matter how effective a control system may be there are certain realities that do not allow for any system to be 100% efficient. The reasons for the deficiency of a system can be:

- The material product (apart from purchased beverages) is very unlikely to be 100% consistent as to quality or the final yield obtainable from it.
- The employees are unlikely to work to a level of 100% efficiency at all times, in spite of the fact that operational standards may exist.
- The equipment used is also unlikely to work to the level of 100% efficiency at all times, and this could well affect the yield obtainable.
- The customers' choice of dishes can well be different at times to some of the budgeted sales mix, therefore affecting all forecasts.

It is important that the staff should see that control in some form is taking place and that on occasions there is a follow-up and action is taken on irregularities to set standards.

Further, the importance and relevance of using percentages as a yardstick necessitates that any percentages used should be directly related to the amount of money involved. A 1% difference to the required budgeted gross profit may not appear very significant at first but when related in financial terms it becomes more significant. For example, in the case of a unit with a turnover of £400,000 and with a budgeted gross profit percentage of 65% (i.e. £260,000) a 1% difference in the gross profit achievable would represent £2,600. Being aware that they are £2,600 off budget may be more meaningful to unit managers than just being aware that they are 1% off target.

The management of any catering operation has to be fully aware of everything that is taking place within and outside the operation and, to be successful, needs to continually collect, analyse, and evaluate data and take any necessary steps to correct anything which is irregular to the standards set for the operation.

SETTING THE BUDGET AND BREAK-EVEN ANALYSIS

In order to have an effective food and beverage control system a manager needs to have benchmarks where he/she can compare the operations performance.

The budget

A budget is a plan – expressed usually in financial and/or quantitative terms (e.g. total value of payroll, number of customers, etc.) – which reflects the policies of an establishment and determines the business operations for a particular trading period. The trading period is usually of one year, but is often broken down into review (or control) periods of either thirteen four-week periods; or alternatively, of thirteen-week quarters, each quarter consisting of two four-week and one five-week periods. Whichever method is adopted it is necessary that the periods remain the same so as to make it possible to compare results not only with corresponding periods in the same year, but also with the corresponding periods in earlier years. Bank holidays and special events falling into different periods each year should be noted.

The term *budgetary control* refers to a method of control where particular responsibility for various budgeted results is assigned to the managers concerned and a continuous comparison of the actual results and budgeted figures is made. When there are discrepancies between the two, it is necessary to identify the reasons for the variances and to take appropriate action. It is essential that when budgets are set they are clearly seen to be achievable; otherwise they are of little value. The objectives of budgetary control are threefold:

- To provide a plan of action for a set trading period, to guide and regulate a business in keeping with its stated policies, and to maximize the full use of its resources.
- To set standards of performance for management against which their performance can be measured.
- To set out levels of cost responsibility and encourage cost awareness.

Budgets are prepared by the senior management of an organization in consultation with the various managers and departmental heads so as to ensure a greater level of commitment and an awareness of the aims, objectives, problems and possible weaknesses of the establishment. There are two main types: capital budgets; and operating budgets. Capital budgets, as the name implies, are those which are concerned with the assets and liabilities of an establishment, for example equipment, plant and cash.

Operating budgets are those concerned with the day-to-day income and expenditure of an establishment and include sales, cost of sales, labour, maintenance, head office expenses, etc. This is the type of budget that food and beverage managers will be mostly concerned with when looking at the food and beverage control system.

For simplicity, budgeting may be seen as being in six stages. The amount of detail and sub division into departmental budgets depends very much on the type and size of the business. The basic stages are:

1. Determination of the net profit required for the business in relation to the capital invested and the risk involved. Alternatively, in the case of non-profit making establishments, the level of subsidy available or required is postulated.
2. *Preparation of the sales budget*: This determines the volume of sales necessary to achieve the desired net profit or subsidy and also influences the budgeted costs for food, beverages, labour and some overheads.
3. *Preparation of administration and general budgets*: These are for such items as head office expenses, advertising, rates, insurance, etc. Some of these may be regarded as fixed budgets, that is, they are not affected by any change in the volume of business, for example head office expenses, advertising, rates, etc.; while others may be regarded as flexible budgets, that is, they are affected by changes in the volume of business, for example telephones, laundry, etc.
4. Preparation of the capital expenditure budget which makes provision for such items of expenditure as new kitchen equipment, restaurant and bar furniture (including any installation charges), etc.
5. *Preparation of the cash budget*: This is regarded as the most important of the capital budgets and it predetermines the cash inflows, the cash outflows and resulting cash balance at particular points during the period.
6. *Preparation of master budgets*: As stated previously master budgets are prepared for the trading account, profit and loss account and the balance sheet (see Figure 8.2).

Costs, profits and sales

The cost of operating a catering unit or department is usually analysed under the three headings of the elements of cost (see Figure 8.3).

1. *Material costs* – cost of food and beverage consumed and the cost of additional items such as tobacco. (*Note*: The cost of any food and beverage provided to staff in the form of meals is deducted from material costs and added to labour costs.) The food cost is then calculated by the formula:

$$\left.\begin{array}{l} \text{opening stock} \\ + \text{cost of purchases} \\ - \text{closing stock} \\ - \text{cost of staff meals} \end{array}\right\} = \text{material cost}$$

2. *Labour costs* – wages and salaries paid to all employees, plus any employer contribution to government taxes, bonuses, staff meals, pension fund, etc.

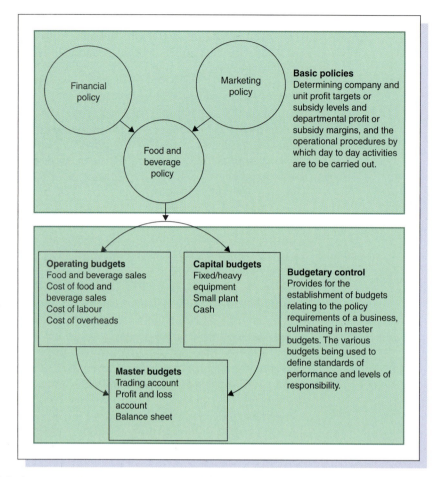

Figure 8.2 Budgetary control as an extension of basic policies

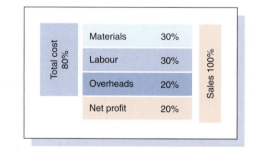

Figure 8.3
A typical example of the elements of cost

3. *Overhead costs* – all costs other than material and labour costs, for example rent, rates, insurance, depreciation, repairs, printing and stationery, china and glassware, and capital equipment.

As most catering operations are subject to changes in the volume of business done, it is normal practice to express the elements of cost and net profit as a percentage of sales. A change in the volume of sales has an effect on the cost structure and on the net profit.

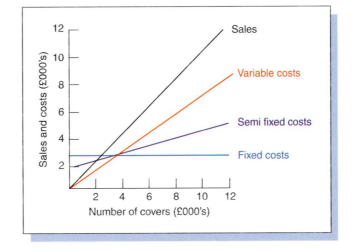

Figure 8.4
Fixed, semi-fixed and variable costs

It is necessary to examine costs not only by their nature (material, labour, overheads) but also by their behaviour in relation to changes in the volume of sales. Using this criteria, costs may be identified as being of four kinds:

1. *Fixed costs*: These are costs which remain fixed irrespective of the volume of sales, for example rent, rates, insurance, the management element of labour costs (see Figure 8.4).
2. *Semi-fixed costs*: These are costs which move in sympathy with, but not in direct proportion to the volume of sales, for example fuel costs, telephone and laundry. Semi-fixed costs contain a fixed and variable cost element, for example, the charge for the telephone service in the UK contains a fixed cost for the quarterly charge for the rental of each phone and a variable cost depending on the number of phone calls made.
3. *Variable costs*: These are costs which vary in proportion to the volume of sales, for example food and beverage (see Figure 8.4).
4. *Total costs*: This is the sum of the fixed costs, semi-fixed costs and variable costs involved.

Three main kinds of profit are normally referred to in food and beverage operations:

1. *Gross profit* = total sales – cost of materials. *Note*: The term gross profit is often referred to as 'kitchen profit' (food) or 'bar profit' (beverages). Room hire is normally treated as 100% gross profit.
2. *After-wage profit* (or net margin) = total sales – (material + labour costs).
3. *Net profit* = total sales – total costs (material + labour + overhead costs).

All of the above are normally used as measures of performance against past results and budgeted targets. For an example of the use of the three main kinds of profit used in controlling food and beverage operations see Table 8.1.

This period					Year to date				
Actual		**Budget**				**Actual**		**Budget**	
£	%	£	%			£	%	£	%
11,000	100	10,000	10	Net sales		20,000	100	21,000	100
5,500	50	4,000	40	Less Cost of sales		11,200	56	8,400	40
5,500	50	6,000	60	Gross profit		8,800	44	12,600	60
2,750	25	2,000	20	Less Wages and staff costs		4,200	21	4,200	20
2,750	25	4,000	40	Net margin less allocated expenses		4,600	23	8,400	40
550	5	500	5	Maintenance		1,200	6	1,050	5
220	2	200	2	Head office services		600	3	420	2
220	2	200	2	Others		200	1	420	2
110	1	100	1	Equipment		200	1	210	1
1,100	10	1,000	10			2,200	11	2,100	10
1,650	15	3,000	30	Operating profit		2,400	12	6,300	30

Note: Budgeted figures are used to compare with the actual operating results. It can be observed that the low operating profit achieved is almost entirely to the failure to achieve the budgeted gross profit on sales in spite of an increase in sales this period

Table 8.1
Example of a restaurant operating a sales statement with the sales budget

The Endsleigh Restaurant		
	April	May
Number of covers	2,000	3,000
Average spend	£10	£10
Total sales	£20,000 (100%)	£30,000 (100%)
Fixed costs	£3,000 (15%)	£3,000 (15%)
Variable costs	£8,000 (40%)	£12,000 (40%)
Semi-fixed costs	£6,000 (30%)	£8,000 (26.7%)
Total costs	£17,000 (85%)	£23,000 (76.7%)
Net profit	£3,000 (15%)	£7,000 (23.3%)

Note: Fixed costs remain the same and variable cost % remains at 40%. Semi-fixed costs increase by £2,000 but in relation to sales there is a 3.3% decrease this is also reflected in the total costs. A change in the volume of sales will reflect a change on the cost structure

Table 8.2
The Endsleigh Restaurant operating statement

The behaviour of the different types of cost and profit relative to a change in the volume of sales can be identified by examining the example of a simple operating statement for a restaurant in Table 8.2. The statement shows the sales, costs and profit over two consecutive months with the May sales figure showing a 50% increase in business.

Break-even analysis

It is very common for food and beverage management to be faced with problems concerning the level of food and beverage cost that can be afforded, the prices that need to be set for food and beverages, the level of profit required at departmental and unit level and the number of customers required to cover specific costs or to make a certain level of profit. Typical questions raised are:

1. What level of sales is needed to cover the fixed costs of a unit?
2. What level of sales is required from a particular unit to achieve £x's net profit?
3. What level of sales is required to increase the net profit of a unit by £10,000?
4. What will the effect of increasing prices by 5% have on net profit?
5. What will be the effect on net profit of increasing the average spend of customers by 50p per meal?
6. What increased level of sales must be obtained to cover the spending of £1,000 on advertising to promote the restaurant?
7. What will be the financial implications of discounting beverages during a proposed promotion?
8. What is the relationship between the capital invested in a restaurant and its sales and profit?

Answers to the above types of question are normally attempted by using the accepted technique of break-even analysis. Break-even analysis enables the relationship between fixed, semi-fixed and variable costs at specific volumes of business to be conveniently represented on a graph. This enables the break-even point to be identified and the level of sales necessary to produce a pre-determined level of net profit. The term break-even point may be defined as that volume of business at which the total costs are equal to the sales and where neither profit nor loss is made. The technique is based on the assumption that: the selling price remains constant irrespective of the volume of business; that certain unit costs remain the same over the sales range of the charted period; that only one product (e.g. a meal) is being made or sold; that the product mix remains constant in cost price and volume and that labour and machine productivity is constant.

Nearly every action or planned decision in a business will affect the costs, prices to be charged, the volume of business and the profit. Profits depend on the balance of the selling prices, the mix of products, the costs and the volume of business. The break-even technique discloses the interplay of all these factors in a way which aids food and beverage management in selecting the best course of action now and in the future.

Pricing is a multi-dimensional problem, which depends not only on the cost structure of a business and its specific profit objectives but also on the level of activity of the competition and the current business economic climate.

Activity 1

Saudi Enterprises is considering the acquisition of the Rumble-Tum Restaurant. The purchase price is £100,000 and the directors of Saudi Enterprises expect any new purchase to show a return on capital of 18%. The proprietor of the restaurant is able to provide the following information:

Rates, insurance, fuel costs, etc. £45,000 per annum
Franchise fee £5,000 per annum
Franchise commission 1% of turnover
Wages £l,000 per week

The restaurant operates for six days a week and for fifty weeks in the year. *Note*: Wages are only paid for fifty weeks.
A typical day's business shows:

200 lunches served with an ASP of £1.50
100 dinners served with an ASP of £3.00

The maximum number of covers which it is possible to serve without physical alterations to the structure is 250 lunches and 125 dinners.
The restaurant is expected to operate at a gross profit of between 55% and 65%.

Using the Saudi Enterprises example:

1. Prepare a profitability statement for the restaurant when operating at gross profit percentage of 55, 60% and 65%.
2. Making the calculations, using the break-even formula, state clearly the break-even points and their margins of safety.

Note: For the solution see the end of this chapter.

Example

A restaurant has seating capacity of 180 covers, enabling to serve a total of 10,080 customers per twenty-eight-day trading period over lunch and dinner. The ASP of the customers is £15 (total maximum sales of £151,200). The fixed costs of the restaurant are £35,000 per period and the variable costs are 40% of sales (maximum £60,480). The break-even chart of the restaurant would be prepared as shown in Figure 8.5. Drawing the diagram shows that 4,000 covers appears to be the break-even point however calculating the break-even point the accurate number would be 3,889. So the number of covers served between 3,889 and 10,080 will bring the restaurant some net profit. The output between the break-even point and the maximum output is known as the margin of safety. The size of the margin of safety is a measure of the stability of the profits.

The output between the break-even point and the maximum output is known as the margin of safety. The size of the margin of safety is a measure of the stability of the profits. The higher the proportion of variable costs (to fixed costs), the greater the margin of safety, while the higher the proportion of fixed costs the narrower the margin of safety. Should the variable costs

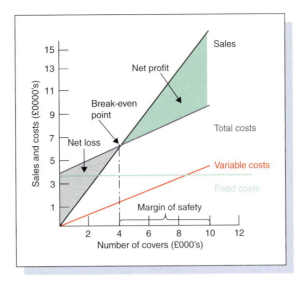

Figure 8.5
Break-even chart

be increased (with the level of fixed costs remaining static) the break-even point will be raised resulting in a lower level of net profit and a smaller margin of safety.

Although a break-even chart shows diagrammatically the varying levels of profit or loss from different volumes of sales, the level of accuracy of the information may at times be in doubt owing to the scale of the graph and the skill of the person drawing it. A precise break-even point may be calculated using the formula:

$$B/E = \frac{C}{S - V} = \text{units of output at the break-even point}$$

where

    C = the total capacity costs, that is, the costs of establishing the particular production capacity for an establishment (e.g. this would include rent, rates, insurance, salaries, building and machinery depreciation)

S = sales price per unit
V = variable cost per unit

Essentials of a control system

With the advancements in points of sale technology, food and beverage control has become even easier to establish even to small operations. There are a number of companies that now offer software that will offer solutions to any restaurant. The main components of such a software system may include:

- *Menu planning* – historical data will enable to forecast menu item popularity and profitability making it easier for the manager to plan future menus.
- *Production control* – menus can be used to determine precise sales and production quantities, ensuring great control over kitchen production and usage of goods, reducing wastage of perishable goods.

- *Stock management* – the system may maintain stock levels in any number of individual store locations, tracking the issues and consumption of raw materials, as well as wastage and weekly or monthly stock checks.
- *Purchase ordering* – the system can base on minimum stock levels and/or forecast demand from production planning and match delivery notes and invoices. Some systems will even place an automatic order once stock levels are detected to be under minimum required.
- *Menu analysis* – individual customer menu choices can be automatically recorded and analysed.
- Financial management reporting.

These components are often fully integrated into the electronic point-of-sale (EPOS) system, so that all data inputting is automatically done.

It is important that when examining an existing control system or preparing to install a system into a new operation that the following points should be taken in consideration.

- Any control system should be comprehensive and cover all the outlets of an establishment and all stages of the food control cycle.
- The cost of maintaining the system should be in relation to the saving to be made, the level of sophistication of the control system usually increasing with the increase in the volume of sales and the complexity of the menu.
- The control system should be easy to operate and to be understood by all levels of staff.
- The control system should be seen by staff to be working. That is, that the management act in a positive way to adverse trading results and follow up on future results to check if the corrective action taken is effective.
- To be effective the information produced must be accurate and up-to-date.

BASIC CONCEPTS

Before we consider methods of food and beverage control we need to have an understanding of the four basic concepts in food and beverage production control. These are planning, standard yields, standard recipes and standard portion sizes (PYRS). When PYRS are practised in a food and beverage operation they should aid management in controlling costs, setting standards and achieving customer satisfaction. The production of beverages needs to be tightly controlled as the contribution to profits from beverages is usually higher than that from food.

Production planning

Production planning, or volume forecasting as it is also known, is the forecasting of the volume of sales for an establishment, for a specified time period, for example a day, a week or a month. The aims and objectives of production planning are as follows:

- To facilitate food and beverage cost control for the establishment.
- To facilitate the purchasing of items, particularly perishable ones, and ensure appropriate stock levels are maintained.
- To reduce the problem of food that is left over and how it is to be re-used, beverage wastage or customer dissatisfaction when insufficient foods and beverages are available.
- To gear production to demand by forecasting the number of meals and drinks to be served for a given meal period.
- To enable a comparison to be made between actual and potential volume of sales, and for corrective action to be taken if necessary.

An initial forecast is made either at a set period in advance, for example a month, or when the major food orders are placed. This initial forecast estimates the total number of meals to be sold by the establishment and the estimated total of each menu item. In the case of a large hotel with a variety of catering outlets, a more detailed forecast would be made for each individual outlet. Factors that need to be taken into account at this stage are the season, and hence the weather forecast for that time of year; past popularity of menu items; major events occurring in the area – fêtes, shows, etc. that are likely to attract a larger than average number to the establishment's normal catchment area, any sales campaigns currently being promoted by the operation, etc.

The initial estimate is later adjusted, usually one or two days prior to the day of production, so that a more accurate forecast may be made. On the basis of this updated information, any changes that may need to be made with regard to staff scheduling, food purchases and requisitions, etc. should be made as soon as possible. There are a number of aids or management tools that may be employed by an establishment to assist the forecasting and planning of production.

Standard yields

The standard yield of a particular food product is the usable part of that product after initial preparation, or the edible part of the product after preparation and cooking; for example, the standard yield for a whole fillet of beef is the number of fillet steaks that will be available for cooking and final sale to the customer after the fillet is trimmed and any unwanted meat removed. Any usable trimmed meat should be taken into account with the standard yield.

In large establishments buying in large quantities of food per week, standard yields may be available for almost all the commodities – meat, fish, vegetables, etc. In smaller establishments standard yields may only be determined for the more expensive cuts of meat or fish such as whole fillets, lobsters, salmon, etc.

The development of standard yields by an establishment has a number of advantages:

- Standard yields determine the most appropriate and advantageous size/weight to buy a particular commodity in.
- They assist in determining the raw material requirements for the production levels anticipated from the production forecasts, and therefore act as an aid in the purchasing of the establishment's foodstuffs.
- They act as a 'double check' for the purchasing department. Should an unsatisfactory delivery of meat, for example, be made to an establishment and is unnoticed at the receiving bay, this delivery is subject to a second 'checking' procedure in the kitchen where the meat should yield a standard number of portions.
- They act as a safeguard against pilferage or wastage occurring in the kitchen as the actual and potential yields can be compared and this acts as a measurement of the efficiency of the production department.
- Finally, they are an aid to accurate food costing for particular dishes offered on an establishment's menu, as the cost factor can be established.

For beverages the standard yields of beverage products may, with few exceptions, be accurately calculated, because for the majority of beverages there is little wastage and all the contents of, for example, a bottle of spirits may be used. For the purpose of beverage control all beverages bought in to an establishment should have standard yields calculated, on which the pricing of each drink may be based, and to control wastage and pilferage. If, for example, a 75 cl bottle of wine is bought in, allowing 15 cl of wine to a glass, five good measures should be obtained.

Standard recipes

A standard recipe is a written schedule for producing a particular menu item, specifying the name and quantity of the item to be produced, the constituent ingredients necessary for its production and the method of preparation. This is the basic information contained in a standard recipe although it may also include such information as the costings of the dish, its nutritional value, etc. Detailed recipe cards are usually kept in the food and beverage control department for cost and price updating, only the basic information needing to be included on those cards that are displayed in the production area – often together with a photograph of the end product. Recipe management software has replaced the manual system. Along with the standard recipes the nutritional information of each item is readily available as well as the recipe costings (see Figure 8.6). Linked to an EPOS total food costs at the end of the day can be automatically calculated and easily reported to managers.

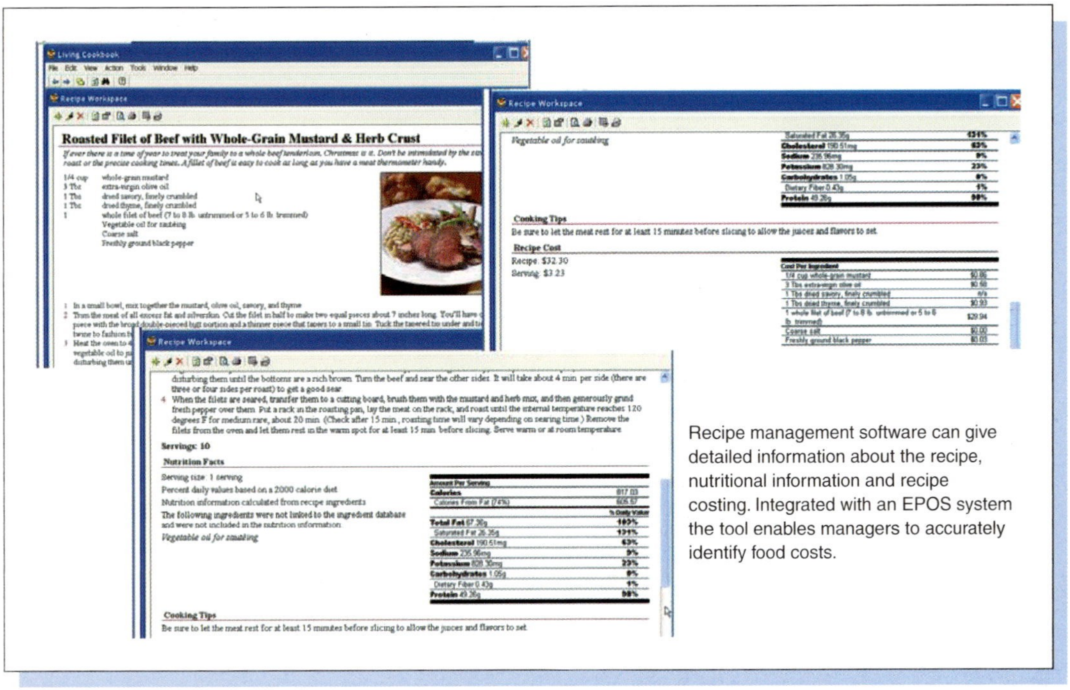

Recipe management software can give detailed information about the recipe, nutritional information and recipe costing. Integrated with an EPOS system the tool enables managers to accurately identify food costs.

Figure 8.6 Recipe management software (*Source*: Reprinted with permission Radium Technologies, Inc)

The use of standard recipes by an establishment has a number of advantages.

- Accurate food and beverage costings can be determined for particular dishes/drinks and from this the cost per portion may be calculated. It is necessary to have the food cost of a dish for the purpose of pricing it for sale to the customer, in order to make the required gross profit. For some items it is not possible to make a gross profit, of, for example 65%, whereas for other items the gross profit made may be higher; by having this type of information, the food and beverage department is able to balance the menu prices so that overall the necessary gross profit is obtained from the menu.

- In certain institutional establishments, such as hospitals, it is important to know the precise nutritional value of the dishes being given to certain patients. By itemizing the ingredients for a particular dish the nutritional value of it is easily calculated.

- They are an aid to purchasing and internal requisitioning. By taking into account the following day's production forecast requirements the head chef is able to use the standard recipes to calculate the quantities of foodstuffs he/she will require the following day. In some catering establishments the head store-man may have a copy of the standard recipes and when the next day's forecast requirements are sent, the head storeman is responsible for calculating the quantity of foodstuffs that need to be sent to the kitchen.

- Standard recipes are particularly useful in the preparation of items in the kitchens, both as a reminder to present staff of the preparation procedure, and also as an aid to the training of new employees. More importantly the use of standard recipes in the production area ensures that the customer will always receive a standardized product.

- Standard recipes are an aid to menu planning. New additions to the menu, for example, may be accurately costed and balanced with the other items on the menu, not only in terms of price, but also in appearance, flavour, colour, etc.
- They may be used as a basis for compiling standard portion sizes which, if used in conjunction with standard recipes and standard yields, will together form the basis of a very effective production control system.

Standard recipes should also be compiled for the majority of beverage products offered for sale by the establishment. Like standard yields, standard recipes may be very accurately produced as all the contents of a drink may be itemized on the standard recipe.

Obviously only a certain number of standard recipes may be produced for an establishment, and this is where the sales histories discussed earlier may be particularly useful – they do at least ensure that the recipes for the most popular drinks have been standardized. With such a variety of components with which to make different drinks, it would not be practical to write standard recipes for every possible combination; so the bar staff should be provided with a book or books chosen by management on how to prepare those varieties of drinks that may be rather unusual or rare. Computer terminals and visual display units may be used in bars where the mixing and service details of various drinks can be displayed to order giving a speedier visual recipe than using a book.

Bar staff should also be provided with the correct equipment for measuring and mixing drinks. Standard bar equipment would include such items as a fruit knife and board, sticks for cherries and olives, ice bowls, fruit squeezers, a cocktail shaker and stirrer, etc.

Standard portion sizes

A standard portion is the quantity of a particular food item that will be served to the customer; the quantity may be measured in terms of ounces (e.g. a 4 oz portion of meat), or a numerical quantity (e.g. one bread roll per person). The portion sizes of the food items are determined by management in conjunction with the heads of both the kitchen and restaurant departments. Standard portion sizes in the operation may be established in several ways.

- By buying in pre-portioned food items, for example 8 oz rump steaks, pre-wrapped packs of butter and condiments, etc.
- By buying in food items in bulk and portioning them in the production kitchen before service, for example, pre-plating salads to be served in a display cabinet in a cafeteria line.

- By portioning food items as they are being served to the customer, for example, food in hot *bain-maries* in a cafeteria line being plated and served when the customer requests the food item.

In establishments operating more than one level of service, there may be varying portion sizes for the same food items, for the different catering outlets. For example, in a hotel the coffee shop offering a table d'hôte menu may serve a 6 oz rump steak, while the silver service restaurant offering an à la carte menu would serve an 8 oz steak.

Standard portion sizes, like standard recipes, are an aid to food costing, as once the standard portion size has been established the gross profit may be calculated for that dish. Any fluctuations in the sizes of the portions, for example serving larger portions, will therefore be reflected in the restaurant's gross profit, particularly so if this is occurring with a number of menu items.

Details of the standard portion sizes should be made readily available to all necessary employees. The food and beverage costing department should regularly review the portion size of a particular food item with reference to its current price, as it may be necessary either to reduce the standard portion size if the cost of a particular food item has increased substantially; increase the selling price; or possibly, remove the dish from the menu for a period until the cost price is acceptable. In the kitchen and restaurant, the standard portion sizes of a dish are often combined with the standard recipes, and together they may be displayed on a wall chart to which all employees may refer.

As with standard recipes, standard portion sizes for beverages should be easier to control than those for food products. With some beverages, for example a bottled baby orange juice, all the contents of the bottle will be emptied into the customer's glass. Other beverages such as spirits need to be measured before being poured into the customer's glass, the use of optics being an accurate method.

Another aid to control the portion size is to use standard glassware for specific drinks. In the UK, for example, alcohol measurements are specified by law and managers can be heavily fined or even lose a licence if they are found not to comply with specifications.

METHODS OF FOOD CONTROL

Depending on the size of the operation food control methods may be automated or manual. In Figure 8.6, we see examples of a recipe management software which can then produce automatic reports of daily/weekly/monthly food costs. Inventory or stock control is an imperative management tool to ensure that food costs are controlled and losses minimized.

The basic tools that enable the correct functioning of the inventory control cycle are:

- *Purchase order*: Completed by the Chef and are normally forms that are in triplicate with one copy for the supplier one for the accounting and one remains with the chef.
- *Delivery note*: Issued by the supplier and delivered together with the goods to the operation.
- *Invoice*: Issued by the supplier and normally send directly to the accounts department.
- *Requisition*: A note issued by the production unit (kitchen) to the storeroom requesting the issuance of goods.

Receiving and storing is explained in Chapter 6 however two methods of storing goods often used in storerooms are worth noting. These are FIFO and LIFO. FIFO stands for First in First out meaning the goods that were received first should be sold to customers. Because of the high levels of perishability of goods, FIFO is the method most commonly used in food and beverage operations. The LIFO method stands for Last in First out and in fine dining restaurants where the freshest ingredients are expected to be used this method is normally utilized. Depending on which method is used closing inventory may be valued differently using the oldest (FIFO) or the latest (LIFO) prices of the stock to value the whole stock. However with computerized systems, it is very easy to use actual cost of each item therefore allowing managers to be far more accurate than ever in the costings of their inventory.

Weekly/monthly food cost report

The following is an example for the calculation of the monthly food costs for an operation where detailed information is not thought to be necessary, or for a small or owner-managed unit where the control is an everyday part of the manager's activity, in order for the operation to be successful. The weekly/monthly food cost report is almost a reconciliation report on an activity that is tightly controlled daily by management (see Table 8.3). The advantages of this method are:

- It is simple and quick to produce.
- It can give and indication of the general performance of the unit.

The disadvantages though are:

- This information is only produced after seven or twenty-eight days of operation.
- It provides no intermediate information so that any undesirable trends (e.g. food costs too high) may be corrected earlier.
- It does not provide the daily or to-date information on purchases, requisitions and sales for a unit with an average of £2,700 a day turnover.

	£
Opening food cost	15,000
Purchases for period (4 weeks day 1–28)	28,525
Subtotal	**43,525**
Less closing food stock level at end of day 28	14,800
= Total cost of food consumed	**28,725**
Total food sales	75,836
Food cost %	37.87%

Table 8.3
A weekly/monthly food cost report

A daily food cost report

This food cost method is suitable for a small to medium-sized operation, or one where a not too sophisticated method is required, or where the costs involved in relation to the savings to be made do not justify a more involved method (see Table 8.4).

Activity 2

Complete the daily food cost report shown on Table 8.4. The formulas for columns **E**, **H**, and **L** are given to you in the table. The opening stock of the next day is the closing stock of the previous so for Tuesday, the 2nd of March it would be 2,541 − 290 = 2,251.

The totals for columns **D** and **F** have been completed so that the closing stock at the end of week 2 is calculated. If you complete this report correctly then the total food available for Sunday, the 14th of March less the food requisitioned will give a total of 2,126.

The advantages of producing this basic food report are:

- It is simple and easy to follow.
- It gives a reasonably detailed account of the general performance of the business on a day-to-day basis.
- It records the daily stock level, daily purchases, daily food requisitioned and daily food sales and enables the daily food cost percentage to be calculated. This information is used for preparing to-date totals (i.e. running totals to date).
- The to-date food cost percentage smooths out the uneven daily food cost percentages and highlights the corrective action to be taken, if necessary, early in the month. The uneven daily food cost percentage is often is often caused when food is requisitioned on one day to be processed and sold on subsequent days.

The disadvantages of this basic food report are:

- Although simple and easy to prepare, the report relies heavily on the accuracy of the basic information to be collected, for example the total of daily purchases, daily requisitions, etc.

A	B	C	D	E	F	G	H	I	J	K	L
				Today				To date			
Date	Day	Opening food storeroom inventory	Purchases	Total food available (C + D)	Food requisitioned	Food sales	Food cost % (F/G)*100	Food purchases	Food requisitions	Foot sales	Food cost % (J/K*100)
		£	£	£	£	£	%	£	£	£	%
March											
1	M	2,220	321	2,541	290	820	35.37%	321	290	820	35.37%
2	T	2,251	385	2,636	370	980	37.76%	706	660	1,800	36.67%
3	W	2,266	404	2,670	440	1,100	40.00%	1,110	1,100	2,900	37.93%
4	T	2,230	480	2,710	480	1,050	45.71%	1,590	1,580	3,950	40.00%
5	F	2,230	890	3,120	405	1,005	40.25%	2,480	1,985	4,955	40.05%
6	S	2,715	203	2,918	535	1,490	35.91%	2,682	2,520	6,445	39.09%
7	S	2,383	0	2,383	240	720	33.33%	2,682	2,760	7,165	38.51%
8	M		380		310	920				8,085	
9	T		402		395	1,015				9,100	
10	W		425		345	925				10,025	
11	T		464		427	1,160				11,185	
12	F		844		463	1,220				12,405	
13	S		185		512	1,405				13,810	
14	S		0		265	690				14,500	
Totals:			5,382		5,477						

Proof of inventory

Opening stock:	2,220
Plus purchases	5,382
Subtotal	7,602
Less requisitions	5,477
Closing stock	2,126

Table 8.4
A daily food cost report

- It is not totally accurate as it ignores such things as the cost of the staff meals; food transferred to bars, for example potato crisps, nuts, salted biscuits, trays of canapes, etc. which are given away free in the bars to customers and items such as lemons, limes, etc. which are included in certain drinks; and beverages transferred to kitchens, for example wine, spirits, beer, etc. for use in the cooking of specific dishes.

A detailed daily food cost report

This food cost report is a development of the previous report and refines the accuracy of the report by taking into account the cost of beverages transferred into the kitchen, the cost of food transferred out of the kitchens to the bars, and the cost of employees' meals (see Table 8.5).

- It is more accurate than the two previous food reports illustrated in Tables 8.3 and 8.4 in that it includes additions to the cost of food for beverages transferred to the kitchen (e.g. cooking wine, etc.) and deductions for the cost of food transferred from the kitchen to the bars (e.g. lemons, oranges, olives, nuts, etc.) and for the cost of all employees' meal. It also separates purchases into those that go straight to the storerooms and those that go direct to the kitchen and are charged immediately to the kitchen.

	Day	March-2001	March-2002	March-2003
		M	T	W
A	Stock levels at beginning of each day	2,220.00	2,250.50	2,265.50
B	Storeroom purchase	120.50	200.00	204.00
C (A + B)	Total food available in storeroom	2,340.50	2,450.50	2,469.50
D	Food requisitioned	90.00	185.00	240.00
E	Direct purchases	200.00	185.00	200.00
F	Beverage transfer to kitchen	0.00	5.00	5.00
G (D + E + F)	Cost of food used	290.00	375.00	445.00
H	Cost of employee meals	35.00	25.00	30.00
I	Transfer of food to bars	0.00	0.00	5.00
J (G − H − I)	Cost of food sold	255.00	350.00	410.00
K	Food sales	820.00	980.00	1,100.00
L	Food cost %	31.09	35.71	37.27
M	Cost of food sold (to-date, running total of J)	255.00	605.00	1,015.00
N	Food sales (to-date, running total of K)	820.00	1,800.00	2,900.00
O	Food cost % (to-date)	31.09	33.61	35.00

Table 8.5
Example of a detailed daily food cost report

The result of these additions and subtractions is that the true cost of the food sold to customers is more accurate than previously.

- The accuracy of the to-date food cost percentage is refined to take into account all daily transactions and these figures should be fully relied upon to be the basis against which corrective action may be taken.

The disadvantages of this type of report are that it is more detailed than the previous reports and it relies very much on the accuracy of the collected information, for example, the collection of all the requisition notes and the accurate extensions of the pricing of items; the collection of the goods received sheet and the checking of it against delivery notes, credit notes, invoices, etc.

Calculation of the potential food cost

The potential food cost is the cost of the food under perfect and ideal conditions. The potential food cost of an operation is the principal and most effective method of evaluating the actual food cost. Any variance higher than 1% between the potential and actual costs should be investigated. The potential food cost may be calculated in a variety of ways, but because of time it is usually costed per menu for each selling outlet twice a year or more frequently if the menu changes. This means that the potential figures will differ between breakfast, lunch and dinner menus and between selling outlets, where the prices of items may vary.

The calculations are in three main steps.

1. For each individual menu item multiply the number of portions actually sold during a 'sample' week as determined by the restaurant sales analysis, by the potential food cost per portion, to obtain the total potential cost of food sold for that week.
2. Multiply the same portions actually sold, as above, by the menu selling prices, and arrive at the potential total sales.
3. Divide the potential total food cost by the potential total food sales and arrive at a figure which, when expressed as a percentage, is the potential food cost percentage.

To be able to do the above calculations it would be necessary to have the following information to hand:

- A detailed sales analysis of all items sold in the various outlets, together with their selling prices.
- Standard recipe cards of all the menu items costed out.
- Summary of potential food cost, obtained from the standard recipe cards.
- Average market price for the main ingredients taken from invoices, food marketing reports or food cost indices reports.

It is not unusual for there to be a difference between the actual and the potential food cost figures. Usually the actual cost of the food sold is higher than the potential for such reasons as

food being a perishable commodity, the difficulty of being exact when forecasting food production requirements and that a small amount of waste is almost unavoidable. Any large differences in the figures will reflect a lack of adherence to established standards, or pilfering or sheer carelessness resulting in an excessive amount of waste. As stated earlier, any variance in excess of 1% should be investigated.

METHODS OF BEVERAGE CONTROL

There are many different methods in use today to control costs, the various methods depending on the size of the operation, the volume of business, owner or managed operation, etc. and the level of sophistication of control required. Each of the different methods in use could be classified under one of the following six basic types of beverage control systems. Whatever method is adopted, it would be of little value unless the previous steps of control had been efficiently implemented and enforced, that is, the control of purchasing, receiving, storing and issuing; production planning; the establishment of standard yields, standard recipes, standard portion sizes and inventory. The inventory control cycle (Figure 8.7) is of course applicable to beverage

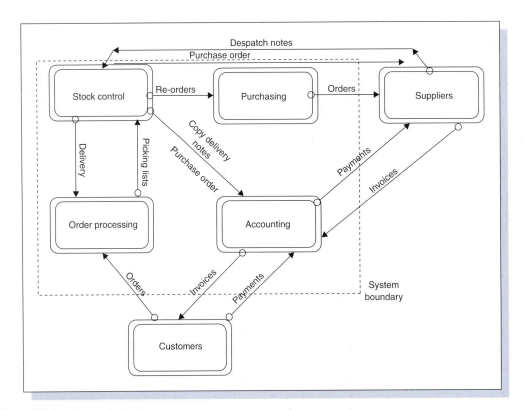

Figure 8.7 Inventory control cycle

inventory as well, with FIFO been the most used method whilst LIFO may find application in situations where some stock may be kept back for later use. For example, some wine may be kept in the cellar and not sold so that it may age a little more.

Bar cost system

This system is similar to that for the basic food cost report and the detailed food cost report. It may be produced for each bar separately or for all of the beverage operations.

Par stock or bottle control system

This is a simple yet effective method of beverage control and is particularly useful for the smaller type operation where there are few full-time control staff. The following points should be noticed.

1. The level of par stock is established for each bar, that is, to establish for each beverage the number of bottles required for a busy day plus a small safety factor. This number is determined to be the stock level to be held in the bar at the beginning of the service each day. To simplify the system only full bottles are counted, partial bottles are not counted.
2. The number and type of empty bottles are noted each day, this being the amount and type to be requisitioned for the day.
3. The potential sales are based on the quantities issued at selling price and are compared to actual revenue received.
4. Adjustments to be made to the initial selling price if many mixed drinks are sold. This may only be necessary if the difference between the potential and actual sales figures gives cause for investigation.

The particular advantages of this system are its simplicity and ease of operation. The system assumes that over a short period the level of partial bottles remains relatively constant so that it becomes unnecessary to count each bottle's contents to determine the total sales. Theoretically, the sales value of today's issues should equal yesterday's revenue. This would be unlikely, however, but over a short period the sales value of issues to date should equal the revenue to date figures.

Potential sales value system

This system is designed to control beverage sales and therefore beverage costs by setting a sales value on each bottle item carried in stock. The revenue value of each bottle is based on the standard size of the drink, the contents of the bottle and the selling price for each drink. The sales value of each drink is called the potential (or standard) sales value. The system requires as a basis for its operation, established standards for a bottle code number system, drink recipes, drink sizes, glassware and par stocks. Whenever the bottle size, drink size or recipe change a new calculation must be made and recorded, as this can affect the price of a drink and should require the price to be reviewed.

The various calculations which have to be made to establish the potential sales values are concerned with:

1. *Full bottles of spirits*: The potential sales value of a full bottle of spirits, etc. which at times may be sold over a bar is equal to the selling price established by management. As little handling is involved in selling a full bottle, its price will usually be lower than when sold by the individual glass.

2. *Spirits, etc. sold by the glass*: The sales value for a bottle of spirits, wine, etc. which is to be sold by the glass is calculated as in the following example.

    Potential sales value for a bottle of whisky:
    Size of bottle 70 cl
    Size of a straight drink 2.5 cl
    Selling price per drink £4.50
    Number of drinks per bottle 28
    (as determined by management)
    28 (number of drinks) × £4.50 (selling price per drink) = £126.00 (potential sales value)

3. *Soft drink and mineral water sales*: The potential sales value of soft drinks, etc. depends on the pricing policy of the establishments; it could, for example, be:

    - A fixed price when sold on its own or when with another drink, for example, gin and tonic water.
    - At a lower price when served as part of a mixed drink, for example, a straight 2.5 cl drink of whisky may cost £4.50; a split bottle of dry ginger may cost £0.99; as a mixed drink whisky and dry ginger may be priced at £4.99 and not £5.49 as would be the case in fixed pricing.
    - The cost of soft drinks is included in the price when selling spirits.
    - It should be noted that if a lower or inclusive pricing system is adopted, adjustments must be made when preparing the control sheets so that an accurate potential sales figure is calculated.

4. *Cocktails, etc*: If all drinks served to customers were sold as straight drinks or full bottles, it would be simple to calculate the potential sales value. When drinks are sold as cocktails containing two or more high selling price items it often requires an adjustment to be made when preparing the control sheet.

When the sales of mixed drinks on analysis are found to be low, there would be little need to go into great detail to calculate the allowances for the various mixed drinks. It is only when the actual money taken in the bars differs from the potential sales value by say more than 2% that detailed analysis of sales and allowances needs to be done.

The millimetre system

This method is recognized as the most accurate (non-automatic) method of determining the amount of beverage sold. It is used at

times when investigating the cause of an unacceptable difference recorded between the actual and potential results in a beverage report. It is, however, a complicated and difficult system to operate for large units with a full range of beverage services unless aided by a mini computer. The system requires:

- An accurate and detailed analysis of all sales by type and brand of drink sold, for each selling outlet.
- The calculation of the actual consumption of each type and brand of drink based on the daily physical stocktake, giving opening and closing stock levels of bars, plus any issues, and minus any transfers out to other bars. All drinks sold are converted back to the number of millilitres of each type and brand of drink sold using the standard beverage recipes. The total consumption of each kind of drink per sales bill has then to be compared with the actual consumption determined from the physical inventory and any adjustments.

The main disadvantages of this control system are:

- The time required to analyse sales and to take stock levels daily.
- The time required to calculate the daily consumption for each selling outlet.
- Additional difficulties if a large number of mixed drinks are sold and if drinks of different sizes are sold in each selling outlet.

Banqueting and function bar system

Should the banquet department have its own storage and bar areas it can operate and be controlled in the same way as any other bar. If, however, a bar has to be set up for each separate banquet or function, it will be necessary for an authorized person to requisition for each event from the main cellar and then immediately at the close of the event to return all unsold beverages. Bottles issued would be the quantity issued from the cellar for that function. Bottles returned are the bottles and part bottles (calculated in tenths of a bottle) unused and returned to the cellar. The number of bottles issued minus bottles returned should be equal to the number of bottles and part bottles used. The actual cost is the purchase price paid per bottle, or half or split. The potential sales per bottle would be the selling price per drink multiplied by the standard number of drinks per bottle.

Automated beverage dispensing system

The use of automated beverage dispensing systems is becoming more and more of a norm. As the cost of technology drops these systems can be afforded by medium-sized operations and when linked to an EPOS system inventory control reports can be compared to sales reports and discrepancies of actual stock can be identified much easier. The bottles of beverage are inverted and connected with small bore pipes within a locked storeroom, to

each selling outlet. Large operations that may often use casual staff (e.g. food and beverage operations in stadia) will normally invest into such technology. The advantages of this method are numerous, but include the following:

- The drink size is pre-set and the drink automatically measured.
- The yield is consistently higher than when using other methods as the bottles drain completely into the dispenser.
- Each drink can be metered by the selling outlet. This helps with inventory control and the calculation of estimated bar revenue.
- It prevents bar staff from handling bottles. Every drink that they need for a customer is obtained by just pressing the correct drink button on the dispenser.
- Many beverage dispense machines are connected to microcomputers so that they can measure the drinks, dispense, display the prices, print the guest's bill, as well as maintain the inventory and analyse drink sales.

There are some disadvantages in using beverage dispensing machines, such as:

- Unsuitability for certain types of beverage operations, for example, a cocktail bar in a luxury type hotel where the clientele expect personal service with the mixing of their drinks.
- The cost of installing dispensing machines is high, although the higher level of control should help to repay the initial costs relatively quickly.
- In general, they are only suitable for use in bars with a very high volume of sales and where the customer is not so concerned with traditional bar service.

The management techniques used in beverage production planning are therefore very similar in concept and method to the techniques used for food production planning; if anything even tighter standards may be laid down for beverage production for the reasons already discussed. A similar recipe file for beverages may also be produced – either manually or by use of a computer and again the use of a computer for beverage planning should be seriously considered for the long-term cost savings and tighter control it can offer the establishment.

EPOS REPORTING

Electronic data storage has both been a blessing and a curse at the same time. The availability of so much information can often overload managers to the point that they end up not using any of the information after all. Here we briefly look at typical reports that a manager can extract from an EPOS system. It is important to understand that a manager can obtain such reports for any specific period be it daily, weekly, monthly or annually or it can even be a report between two dates. In that way reports

Table management

Reporting

Back of house solutions

Front of house EPOS and mPOS solutions

Geac
RESTAURANT *Systems*

Figure 8.8 The Remanco series advance system (*Source*: Courtesy of Geac Computers Inc)

can be customized for the periods that are important to control for that specific operation (see Figures 8.8, 8.9 and 8.10).

Menu item preference

From a control point of view this report is extremely important. It allows the user to identify potential menu items that are not doing very well and possibly eliminate them from the menu, or identify the items that sell extremely well and ensure that enough ingredients are ordered to ensure no customers are left unsatisfied due to a menu item that was not available.

Menu item profitability

This report extracts information from the stock control module of the system and gives accurate profitability per menu item. This together with the menu item preference report can be easily converted into a menu engineering report. The example on Figure 8.9 shows the potential of the EPOS reporting provided the restaurant management wishes to input food costs into the system. In small operations that change their menu weekly and sometimes daily the management decision to not input all the data can often be made.

| Back Office System | | | | | Summary Sales Analysis | | |

Date Printed: 8/9/2007 15:02:39 — Page Number: 2
Selection Criteria: All Product Group — All Sales Areas
Outlet Surrey University
Reference Code: 1000

Date Criteria: Between 8-08-2007 And 8-08-2007

Restaurant

Beverage	Menu Item	Quantity	Voids	Sold	Total Net Sales	Cost of Sales	Cost of Sales%
Wine							
White Wine							
	Sbiraz Rose 175 ml	1.00	0	1.00	3.00	0.00	100.00
	Zonda 175 ml Glass	3.00	0	3.00	8.55	2.79	67.37
	Total For: **White Wine**	**4.00**	**0**	**4.00**	**11.55**	**2.79**	**75.84**
	Total For: Wine	**5.00**	**0**	**5.00**	**13.98**	**3.39**	**75.74**

| **Total For Beverage** | | **33.00** | **0** | **33.00** | **60.61** | **3.39** | **94.41** |

Food	Menu Item	Quantity	Voids	Sold	Total Net Sales	Cost of Sales	Cost of Sales%
Desserts							
Desserts							
	Choccy Tart	2.00	0	2.00	7.23	0.00	100.00
	Lemon Sorbet	1.00	0	1.00	2.95	0.00	100.00
	Mango Sorbet	2.00	0	2.00	7.90	0.00	100.00
	Seasonal Creation	1.00	0	1.00	3.36	0.00	100.00
	Summer Pudding	5.00	0	5.00	16.81	0.00	100.00
	Total For: **Desserts**	**11.00**	**0**	**11.00**	**38.25**	**0.00**	**100.00**
	Total For: Desserts	**11.00**	**0**	**11.00**	**38.25**	**0.00**	**100.00**

Food	Menu Item	Quantity	Voids	Sold	Total Net Sales	Cost of Sales	Cost of Sales%
Mains							
Fish Mains							
	Catch of the day	3.00	0	3.00	21.70	0.00	100.00
	Total For: **Fish Mains**	**3.00**	**0**	**3.00**	**21.70**	**0.00**	**100.00**
Mains							
Meat Mains							
	Chicken breast	3.00	0	3.00	23.85	0.00	100.00
	Home cured Gammon	1.00	0	1.00	8.50	0.00	100.00
	Open Mains	6.00	0	6.00	61.28	0.00	100.00
	Tenderloin of Pork	2.00	0	2.00	17.00	0.00	100.00
	Total For: **Meat Mains**	**12.00**	**0**	**12.00**	**110.63**	**0.00**	**100.00**

Figure 8.9 Extract of an EPOS report (*Source*: Lakeside Restaurant)

Sales by meal period

Identifying how well the restaurant is doing for each meal period is extremely important as it allows the manager to identify the hours of the day that he may need less or more staff, as well as focusing any marketing and promotions to that particular day.

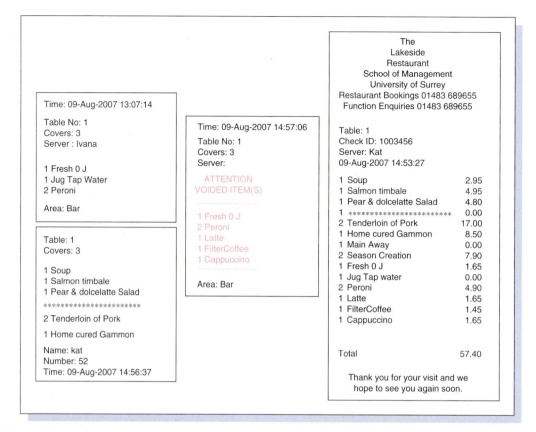

Figure 8.10

An EPOS receipt and bar and kitchen dockets (*Source*: The Lakeside Restaurant. *Note*: The waiter inputs the order and the top left docket prints at the bar whilst the bottom left prints at the kitchen. Pay attention how the starters and mains are clearly separated and information such as the table number, number of covers exact time and date of the order as well as the servers name are displayed. Voided items would appear in red. At a touch of a button the customer receipt can be printed (far right))

Sales by server

Sales by server help identify members of staff that may need further training to enable them to up sale items or reward members of staff that are doing exceptionally well.

Category report

Often food and beverage items are placed in a specific category, for example appetizers, seafood, whiskies or beer. This enables the manager to see at a glance as to how well a particular category of food or beverage might be performing in terms of popularity and profitability.

Table waiting times

Another interesting report is a report that illustrates the time passed between stages of the meal experience. This is not very accurate as the system will only start measuring from the time the order has been put through the system but it can keep records of how long the meal has lasted and time lapsed between courses. Extremely useful tool in helping the manager to ensure quality of the meal experience in terms of service efficiency.

FOOD AND BEVERAGE CONTROL CHECKLISTS

Recent advances in technology have helped with food and beverage control but often one cannot understand the basics of the control system or what they should be looking for when trying to identify errors in the system. Although it would be impossible for us to address every corrective action that should be taken when standards are not being met we can produce a control checklist that can be used as a tool to identify the weak areas of a control system (see Tables 8.6 and 8.7). Although the checklists are not exhaustive for every type of operation, it provides a good starting point and can be adapted to fit the type of operation the reader may have in mind.

The major reasons for food cost (and gross profit) variances from the established standard for a unit include the following:

- Inaccurate arithmetic to paperwork. This also includes the paperwork of suppliers.
- Inefficient stocktaking.
- Poor revenue control. Lack of systematic procedures and practices.
- Poor menu. Unrelated to market conditions and requirements, lack of sales analysis and up-dating of menu.
- Poor purchasing, resulting in higher food costs, overstocking and wastage.
- Poor receiving, inferior goods being accepted, short weight of goods being signed for.
- Poor storing, poor rotation of stock resulting in wastage, poor security.
- Failure to establish and/or maintain standards for volume forecasting, standard recipes, standard yields and standard portion sizes.
- Failure to account accurately for all staff and management meals.
- Food control not being seen by staff to work, resulting in staff failing to maintain desired standards.

As mentioned earlier, beverage control is not so difficult or involved as food control. What at times is a problem is the dishonest employee and this is usually difficult to detect. The typical problems are bar staff who:

- Bring in their own bottles of spirits, etc. sell the contents to customers and then pocket the money. This results in a busy bar with disappointing cash takings.
- Drink at work. Bar staff who help themselves to the odd drink soon get into the habit of it unless it is quickly detected. This results in lower than should be cash takings or customers hav-

Purchasing, receiving, storing and issuing procedures	Food production	Food control procedures
Purchase specifications used for all main items.	Yield and product testing practised to establish and measure standard of products.	Check and marry up all delivery notes, credit notes, invoices and goods received report.
Purchase orders made for every purchase; the exception possibly being to the daily order of fresh fruit and vegetables.	Production to be related to volume forecasts.	Check arithmetic to all paper work.
All purchases made from nominated or approved suppliers.	Maximum use to be made of standard recipes.	Check correct discounts are being allowed.
Deliveries timetabled whenever possible so that quantity and quality checks may be efficiently carried out.	Efficient scheduling of production to be made so as to ensure maintenance of quality of dishes produced.	Check delivery notes to bin cards/ledgers.
All deliveries to be recorded in the foods and beverage received book and credit notes obtained for any variance between what is stated on the delivery note and what is actually delivered.	All equipment to be regularly maintained so as to ensure the standard yields and quality of dishes are maintained.	Maintain certain charges and credits for period inventory.
All deliveries of food to be entered into bin cards/ledgers on the day of delivery.		At set periods complete a full inventory of all chargeable containers.
Issues of all food and beverages from the stores/cellars to be against authorized, signed requisitions only.		At set periods complete a full stocktake of all food stores and food held in the kitchens and compare to ledgers.
Entry to food stores or cellars to be restricted to authorized personnel.		Prepare a stocktaking report and stocktake variance report.
Cellar ledger and any other records kept to be up to date and accurate.		Maintain up-to-date food control reports.

Table 8.6
Purchasing, food production and food control checklists

ing short measure drinks which 'compensate' for the bar staff free drinks.

- Fail to 'ring-up' each drink sold and pocket the money taken from the client. This results again in lower cash taken.
- Provide free drinks for friends, again, resulting in lower bar takings.

Food service	Bar procedures	Beverage control procedures
Food service standards established and practised.	Bar stock to be replenished by written and authorized requisitions, or by using a 'full for empty' bottle system.	Check and cross-reference delivery notes, credit notes, invoices and goods received report.
Standard portion sizes adhered to.	Bars to use standard recipes, standard drink sizes and glassware.	Check arithmetic to all paper work.
Standard portion size equipment always available.	Bars to sell 'house brands' for all drinks unless specifically requested by the customer, as they will normally give a higher gross profit.	Check correct discounts are being allowed.
Careful control made to all food sent to restaurant. All unsold food to be accounted for and returned to the kitchen.	Check that all bar sales are properly recorded.	Check delivery notes, etc. to cellar inwards book.
	Periodically check proof of liquor in open bottles if tampering is suspected.	Maintain beverages perpetual inventory book.
	Check that beverage price lists are displayed and freely available to customers.	Maintain container charges and credits for period inventory.
	Check frequency of 'breakages' recorded.	At set periods complete a full inventory of all chargeable containers, for example crates, kegs, soda syphons, etc.
	Check 'shortages' or 'overs' recorded by accounts department for each bar.	At set periods complete a full inventory of cellar and compare to beverages perpetual inventory book.
	Check that bar staff have no access to till rolls, etc.	Prepare a stocktaking report of value and type of goods, rate of stock turnover, etc.
		At set periods complete a full inventory of the stock of each bar for beverage control reports.
		Maintain daily and to-date beverage control reports, the amount of detail depending on the size of the unit and the volume of business.
		Prepare end of period beverage reports for management and highlight any problem areas for corrective action.

Table 8.7
Food service, bar procedures and beverage control checklist

- Dilute drinks. When a group of customers order their third or more 'round of drinks', they are less likely to identify weak drinks, the difference being pocketed by the bar staff.
- Under-charge the customer. The customer, being an accomplice of the bar staff, orders a drink, pays for it and is then given change in excess of what it should be. This results in bar takings being lower than they should be.
- Short-change customers. This is the all too common problem of bar staff giving customers less change than they should do and pocketing the difference for themselves.

If the spirits are on optics, or beers, spirits and minerals automatically dispensed to controlled measures, any discrepancy will almost certainly mean an error in cash handling made deliberately or by carelessness.

The above types of problems are usually only discovered when good beverage control procedures are in operation, the identification of the dishonest employee being made as a result of such steps as changing bar staff duties and shifts, taking daily bar inventories, changing till drawers during a busy shift and checking the cash with the till reading, and by observation of the bar by an unknown member of the management or security staff. The above only highlights the necessity for the personnel department to carefully interview and take up several references before employing any new bar staff.

Checklist for the smaller operation

A quick checklist for the smaller operation for food cost (and gross profit) variances from the established standard would include the following:

- Check the arithmetic of all major figures (i.e. food report, stock report, etc.).
- Re-check stock figures and total, and in particular look for unusual figures in relation to the norm. The percentage of the total consumption of each category of commodities (meat, poultry, fish, dairy, fresh vegetables, etc.) should be constant for any given menu over a period. Once a standard has been established, variations from it will indicate a problem, for example, if the meat consumption percentage was up it could well indicate pilferage, fraud, wastage or an increase in price and management attention should be focused towards this.
- Re-check sales figures and check against meals served.
- Check for unusual variances in sales. This could be caused by a major change in the weather, a national holiday, etc.
- Check for unusual changes in the sales mix.
- Check for unusual changes in price of major and costly food items.
- Check stores, refrigerators and waste bins for evidence of over purchasing, over preparation and unnecessary wastage.
- Check on meals taken by staff.

REVENUE CONTROL

To control the revenue of a unit, particular attention must be paid to the major factors which can have an influence on the profitability. Therefore it is essential to control the main factors which can affect the revenue of a business, such as the menu–beverage list, the total volume of food and beverage sales, the sales mix, the average spend of customers in each selling outlet at different times of the day, the number of covers served and the gross profit margins.

It is important to note, particularly in commercial operations that somewhere in the total control system there is a need for the accountability of what has been served to the customer and the payment for what has been issued from the kitchen or the bar.

The payment for food and beverage may be made in many forms such as cash, foreign currency, credit cards, cheques, travellers' cheques, luncheon type vouchers and signed bills.

All staff handling cash should be adequately trained in the respective company's methods. It is a common practice for a cashier's or waiter's handbook/manual to be produced so that an established procedure may be followed with the specific aim of ensuring that cash security is efficiently carried out at all times. A typical handbook/manual would contain information on the standard procedure to be followed for such things as:

- *Opening procedure* – instructions here would include procedures about checking the float, having a float of specific denominations, checking the till roll, recording waiters' bill pad numbers, etc.
- *Working procedure* – instructions on how to accept payment and the procedure to follow.
- *Closing procedure* – instructions on any documentation and recordings to be completed, cashing up, recording of credit cards, cheques, etc.
- *Procedure for accepting foreign currency* – what currency is to be accepted, how to obtain the current exchange rates, how this is to be recorded, etc.
- *Procedure for accepting credit cards* – which credit cards are to be accepted, how they are to be checked, method of processing credit cards for payment, recording of credit vouchers, etc.
- *Procedures for accepting vouchers such as luncheon vouchers* – which vouchers are acceptable, how this is to be recorded.
- *Procedure for accepting cheques* – how cheques are to be made out, customers to produce a valid cheque guarantee card, checking that signatures correspond, etc.
- *Procedure for accepting travellers' cheques* – what travellers' cheques are acceptable, what currencies are acceptable, witnessing and checking signatures, how this is to be recorded.
- *Procedure for a complimentary or signed bill* – check against current list of authorized persons and their signature, how this is to be recorded.

PROFIT SENSITIVITY ANALYSIS AND MENU ENGINEERING

Maintaining and improving an adequate level of profit are essential for all businesses today to survive – particularly with the increasing level of competition tempting customers not only to change from their usual type of restaurant, but also from the many other types of leisure businesses all chasing the same customers' restricted amount of disposable income.

Among the problems often facing the food and beverage manager is how can the profitability be maintained or increased. Should the prices for some or all items be increased and by how much, and/or food and beverage items costs be reduced, and/or labour costs reduced, and/or the number of customers increased, etc. Two accepted methods of profit improvement are PSA and menu engineering.

Profit sensitivity analysis

PSA is concerned with identifying the 'critical' or 'key factors' (i.e. the determinants of profitability) of a business and establishing how they rank in influencing its net profit. The emphasis of PSA is on net profit and the examination of those areas that responded positively to change. In order to undertake PSA the 'profit multipliers' (PM) of the business must firstly be calculated. The method is:

1. Identify the 'key factors', financial and operational of the business (Key factors may be number of covers, food and beverage costs, labour costs, revenue, price per cover, etc.
2. Assume a change in one 'key factor' at a time of say 10%, whilst holding all others constant.
3. Calculate the resulting change in net profit.
4. Calculate the PM:

$$PM = \frac{\text{Percentage of change in net profit}}{\text{Percentage of change in 'key factors'}}$$

5. List the PMs in order of size.
6. Analyse the results.

Menu engineering

Menu engineering is a marketing orientated approach to the evaluation of a menu with regard to its present and future content, design and pricing. Its origins are based on the famous Boston Consulting Group (BCG) portfolio technique, a matrix specifically designed to analyse individual business performance in a company with a range of different business interests (see Figure 8.8). The concept of menu engineering requires food and beverage managers to orient themselves to the contribution that menu items make to the total profitability of a menu. It high-lights the good and the poor performers in a menu, and provides vital information for making the next menu more interesting and appealing to the customers, and hopefully more profitable. Menu engineering is a step-by-step procedure that focuses on the three main elements:

1. Customer demand – the number of customers served.
2. Menu mix – an analysis of customer preference for each menu item (popularity).
3. Contribution margin – an analysis of the contribution margin (GP%) for each menu item.

The pre-requisites for using this technique are:

1. The standardization of all recipes (including the presenta-tion), so that the food costs can be accurate.
2. The accurate sales analysis of each menu item, daily and by meal period.
3. The use of a personal computer, so that simple spreadsheets, with standard calculations, may be done accurately and with speed.

Using the simple matrix, menu items can be plotted, repre-senting their performance with regard to volume (popularity) and cash contribution (profit). The four squares of the matrix commonly have names indicating the performance of items in a particular square.

1. *Stars*: Menu items *high* in menu mix (popularity) and also *high* in contribution margin.
2. *Plowhorses*: Menu items *high* in menu mix (popularity) but *low* in contribution margin.
3. *Puzzles*: Menu items *low* in menu mix (popularity) and *high* in contribution margin.
4. *Dogs*: Menu items *low* in menu mix (popularity) and *low* in contribution margin.

The analysis of the data to undertake menu engineering can be done using a standard computer spreadsheet package (see Table 8.8). This takes the form of a large grid compromising of rows and columns where labels, formulae and values can be entered. When in operation, the formulae and values can be changed if required, giving instantaneous re-calculations of the figures, and hard copies printed and retained for easy reference. Whilst spreadsheets can be compiled by hand, the time taken would be lengthy and the opportunity to frequently undertake 'what if' exercises less likely (e.g. What would be the effect on the profitability of the restaurant with a menu of 30 main items, if the price of all the main items were to be increased by 3% or by 4%?). It should be noted here that the success in being able to move menu items 'up' the matrix to the status of a 'star' could

(A) Menu item name	(B) No. sold (MM)	(C) Menu mix%	(D) Item food cost	(E) Item selling price	(F) Item CM (E – D)	(G) Menu costs (D * B)	(H) Menu revenues (E * B)	Menu CM (G – H)	CM category	MM% category	Menu item classification
Chicken blue	420	2.7	5.95	8.5							
Steak	360		4.5	8.5							
Lobster tail	150		8	9.5							
Tenderloin tips	70		4	7.4				M			
Totals	1,000		19.2	31.35		I	J				
						K = I/J (FC%)		O = M/N (Av. CM)		Q = (100%/items) (70%)	

Table 8.8
Menu engineering worksheet

have an undesirable effect on the profitability of the menu, simply because customers do not always behave in a rational manner in spite of the wishes of the food and beverage manager.

Activity 3

Complete the Menu engineering worksheet seen on Table 8.8 and determine the Menu Item classification (Dog, Puzzle, Plowhorse or Star). **Q** is the popularity benchmark and **O** is the contribution benchmark. For the solution see the end of this chapter.

SYSTEMS OF REVENUE CONTROL

There are two basic approaches to recording and controlling food and beverage sales.

1. *A manual system* – which is commonly used in small and in exclusive type catering units.
2. *An automated system* – which is commonly used in units with several outlets, in units with a very high volume of business and in up-to-date companies with many units.

Manual system

As technology is becoming increasingly affordable even for the very small businesses we become more relied on technology without having an understanding of the basics of a system. Furthermore even the best EPOS will at some point malfunction or a printer may be out of order, and then the business will need to have a back up plan and know how to use a manual system. Here we examine two basics of a manual system the sales check and the role of the cashier which in a computerized system it becomes defunct as every server can have his/her own float as the adding and printing of the bill is automatically done.

Sales checks

One of the simplest steps to take when attempting to establish sales control procedures is to require that each item ordered and its selling price are recorded on a waiter's sales check. Using some form of a check system serves the following functions:

- To remind the waiting staff of the order they have taken.
- To give a record of sales so that portion sales and sales mixes and sales histories can be compiled.
- To assist the cashier and facilitate easy checking of prices charged.
- To show the customer a detailed list of charges made.

An additional aid is to use numbered checks and control these tightly, recording all cancelled and missing checks. It is more common to find *duplicate* or *triplicate checks* being used as an aid to control for the following reasons:

- They provide the kitchen, buffet or bar with a written record of what has been ordered and issued.
- They authorize the kitchen, buffet or bar to issue the food and/or beverage.
- They provide the opportunity to compare the top copy of the check with the duplicate to ensure that all that has been issued has been charged and paid for.

The cashier's role

In addition to following precisely the unit's procedure for the handling of all revenue transactions within the restaurant or bars, it is normal practice for the cashier working a manual system to be required to complete the following:

- To issue check pads to the waiting staff prior to a meal period, to record the numbers of the checks issued in each pad, and obtain the waiting staff's signature for them; and on the completion of the meal period to receive from the waiting staff their respective unused check pads, record the numbers, and sign for the receipt of those returned. This information to be recorded on the check number issue control sheet.
- To check the pricing, extensions and subtotals of all checks and to add any government tax charges and to enter the total amount due.
- To receive and check money, credit or, when applicable, an approved signature in payment for the total amount due for each check.
- To complete the missing checklist for each meal period. This is an aid to the cashier in controlling what checks are used. The respective check numbers on the list are crossed out when payment is made. When a missing check is identified, investigation to be carried out to find the reason for this, and if no satisfactory explanation is forthcoming, to inform a member of management on duty. Missing checks to be marked on the missing checklist.
- To complete the restaurant sales control sheet for each meal period. This form requires that all revenue received (or its equivalent) is recorded under specific headings such as cash, cheques, credit card transactions, etc. From this control sheet basic data – such as the number of covers served or the average spend per customer on food and beverages – is quickly obtained.
- To complete the necessary paying in of all cash, etc. in accordance with the unit's established practice. This could be direct to a bank whether a small independent unit, or a unit of a large company, or to the head cashier's office if a large unit with many outlets.

Problems of the manual system

In brief, the basic problems of controlling any food and beverage operation are:

- The time span between purchasing, receiving, storing, processing, selling the product, and obtaining the cash or credit for the product, is sometimes only a few hours.
- The number of items (food and beverage) held in stock at any time is high.
- A large number of finished items are produced from a combination of the large number of items held in stock.
- The number of transactions taking place on an hourly basis in some operations can be very high.
- To be able to control the operation efficiently, management ideally requires control in formation of many types to be available quickly and to be presented in a meaningful way.

The full manual control of a food and beverage operation would be costly, time consuming and data produced would frequently be far too late for meaningful management action to take place. Certain aspects of control such as regularly up-dating the costings of standard recipes, calculating gross profit potentials, and providing detailed sales analysis would seldom be done because of the time and labour involved.

A manual system providing a restricted amount of basic data is still widely used in small- and medium-sized units although they are likely to be replaced in the near future by machine or electronic systems. The day-to-day operational problems of a manual system are many and include such common problems as:

- Poor handwriting by waiting staff resulting in:
  - Incorrect order given to the kitchen or dispense bar.
  - Wrong food being offered to the customer.
  - Incorrect prices being charged to the customer.
  - Poorly presented bill for the customer, etc.
  - Human error can produce such mistakes as:
    - Incorrect prices charged to items on a bill
    - Incorrect additions to a customer's bill
    - Incorrect service charge made
    - Incorrect government tax (e.g. VAT) charge made.
- The communication between departments such as the restaurant, dispense bar, kitchen and cashiers has to be done physically by the waiting staff going to the various departments. This is not only time consuming but inefficient.
- Manual systems do not provide any quick management information data, any data produced at best being normally twenty-four to twenty-eight hours old, as well as being costly to produce.
- Manual systems have to be restricted to the bare essentials because of the high cost of labour that would be involved in providing detailed up-to-date information.

COMPUTERIZED SYSTEMS

EPOS technology and windows based software specifically designed for the food and beverage operation seem to have replaced every other type of machine based system. Although it is tempting to simply talk about EPOS systems only, it is important we also look at some of the older technology that still may be used in some countries and is still used in very small operations around the world.

Pre-checking systems

Pre-check machines are somewhat similar in appearance to a standard cash register and are designed to operate only when a sales check is inserted into the printing table to the side of the machine. The machine is operated in the following way.

- A waiter has his/her own machine key.
- A check is inserted into the printing table and the particular keys, depending on the order taken, are pressed giving an item and price record as well as recording the table number, the number of covers and the waiter's reference number.
- A duplicate is printed and issued by the machine which is then issued as the duplicate check to obtain food and/or beverages.
- For each transaction a reference number is given on the sales check and the duplicate.
- All data is recorded on a continuous audit tape that can be removed only by authorized persons at the end of the day when the machine is cleared and total sales taken and compared to actual cash received.

The advantages of the system are:

- The sales check is made out and a record of it made on the audit tape before the specific items can be obtained from the kitchen or bar.
- Analysis of total sales per waiter is made on the audit tape at the end of each shift.
- No cashier is required as each waiter acts as his/her own cashier, each keeping the cash collected from customers until the end of the shift and then paying it in.
- As each waiter has his/her own security key to operate the machine, there is restricted access to the machines and no other way by which pre-checks can be provided and used in exchange for items from the kitchen or bar.

Pre-set pre-checking system

This is an up-date on the basic pre-check machine. The keyboard is much larger than the previous machines, and has descriptive keys corresponding to all items on the menu which are pre-set to the

current price of each item. A waiter pressing the key for, say one cheeseburger would not only have the item printed out but also the price. A control panel, kept under lock and key, would enable management to change the price of any item, if required, very quickly. It is also possible to have a running count kept of each item recorded and at the end of a meal period by depressing each key in turn to get a print out giving a basic analysis of sales made.

Electronic cash registers

These are very high speed machines which were developed mainly for operations such as supermarkets and were further adapted for use in high volume catering operations. They are robust machines that apart from printing the customer bill they can also provide basic reports such as sales by type of product, payment method, etc. The advancement in EPOS technology and the low costs are making Electronic cash registers (ECRs) a thing of the past, although in small operations that do not require heavy inventory control and detailed reporting an ECR is still the choice due to its much lower cost.

EPOS control systems

At a basic level a point-of-sale control system is no more than a modern ECR with the additional feature of one or several printers at such locations as the kitchen (or sections of the kitchen) or dispense bar. Some systems replace the ECR with a 'server terminal' (also called 'waiter communication' systems), which may be placed at several locations within a restaurant, and is a modification of an ECR in that the cash features are eliminated making the terminal relatively small and inconspicuous. The objectives for having printers are:

1. To provide an instant and separate clear and printed order to the kitchen or bar, of what is required and by and for whom.
2. To speed up the process of giving the order to the kitchen or bar.
3. To aid control, in that items can only be ordered when they have been entered into the ECR or terminal by an identifiable member of the waiting staff and printed.
4. To reduce the time taken by the waiter in walking to the kitchen or bar to place an order and, as frequently happens, to check if an order is ready for collection.
5. To afford more time, if required, for customer contact.

Printers are at times replaced by VDU screens.

Server terminals are part of a computer-based point-of-sale system. These special terminals are linked to other server terminals in the restaurants and bars within one system and, if required to, also interface with other systems so that, for example, the transfer of restaurant and bar charges may be made via the front office computer system. The advantage of a computerized point-of-sale system is that it is capable of processing data as activities occur, which makes it possible to obtain up-to-the-minute reports for

management who can be better informed and able to take immediate and accurate corrective action if necessary.

This type of point-of-sale control system has been taken one step further with the introduction of hand-held terminals or mobile points of sale (MPOS). These hand-held devises can use radio frequencies or infrared or bluetooth technology to communicate from the guest's table direct to the kitchen and bar preparation areas. MPOS offer a number of advantages: food and beverage orders are delivered faster and more efficiently to preparation sites; waiters in turn can attend more tables; with a two-way communication service staff can be notified if an item is out of stock; all food and beverage items ordered are immediately charged to the guest's bill, which is accurate and easy to read; finally, operations can reassess their labour utilization and efficiency, certain members of the service staff, for example, can take the simple orders, while others can spend more time with customers to increase food and beverage sales.

Touch screen technology utilized by the systems enable the server to use EPOS and MPOS technology with minimal training as the systems often resemble a Microsoft windows type interface.

FORECASTING

For food and beverage control to be successful one of the important management tools is successful forecasting. In smaller restaurants managers may often have an intuitive idea about how many customers to expect on any given day. In larger operations however a more scientific approach is required. Lack of storage space and perishability of the produce are only two of the reasons why effective forecasting is imperative for the success of a food and beverage operation. The main considerations of forecasting is not only how many people will turn up at any given period but also what menu items are they likely to consume and at what time of the day. Getting it right all the time is an impossible task however with the correct techniques it is possible to have an educated informative guess that is based on research and not assumptions. Forecasting does not only affect purchasing of food and beverages but it also affect all other areas of the business such as the pricing, production, number of employees to hire, to name a few.

In order to be successful in forecasting accurately some of the type of information would need is:

- Sales history
- Turn down history
- Cancellations and no shows trends
- Competitor data
- Market trends at local, national and international levels
- The weather forecast
- Information about special events and new attractions.

Even a change in the weather can affect menu item sales, on a cold day, for example, chances are that customers would prefer a hot soup rather than a cold salad as a starter. There is a number of

forecasting software that is available to food and beverage managers and these use some of the methods briefly described here:

- *Multiple regression analysis*: Used when two or more independent factors are involved – widely used for intermediate term forecasting. Used to assess which factors to include and which to exclude. Can be used to develop alternate models with different factors.
- *Non-linear regression*: Does not assume a linear relationship between variables – frequently used when time is the independent variable.
- *Trend analysis*: Uses linear and non-linear regression with time as the explanatory variable – used where pattern overtime.
- *Moving average analysis*: Simple moving averages – forecasts future values based on a weighted average of past values – easy to update.
- *Weighted moving averages*: Very powerful and economical. They are widely used where repeated forecasts required – uses methods like sum-of-the-digits and trend adjustment methods.
- *Adaptive filtering*: A type of moving average which includes a method of learning from past errors – can respond to changes in the relative importance of trend, seasonal, and random factors.
- *Exponential smoothing*: A moving average form of time series forecasting – efficient to use with seasonal patterns – easy to adjust for past errors – easy to prepare follow-on forecasts – ideal for situations where many forecasts must be prepared – several different forms are used depending on presence of trend or cyclical variations.

OPERATING RATIOS

Besides the general operating ratios that have been used earlier in this chapter, for example, food cost in relation to food sales, beverage cost in relation to beverage sales, etc. there are many more that are used and found to be of value. The following is a brief explanation of those that are frequently used.

Total food and beverage sales

The total food and beverage sales should be recorded, checked and measured against the budgeted sales figures for the particular period (e.g. week or month).

The analysis of these figures is usually done daily for large establishments and for those that are not operating a manual control system. The analysis would show separately the food sales and the beverage sales per outlet and per meal period.

The importance of this yardstick cannot be emphasized enough other than to remind the reader that it is cash and cash only that can be banked and not percentages or any ratio or factor figures.

Departmental profit

As mentioned in Chapter 7, departmental profit is calculated by deducting the departmental expenses from the departmental

sales, the expenses being the sum of the cost of food and beverages sold, the cost of labour and the cost of overheads charged against the department, and the profit being usually expressed as a percentage of the departmental sales, for example:

$$\frac{\text{departmental profit (£1,200)}}{\text{food and beverage sales (£8,000)}} \times \frac{100}{1} = 15\%$$

The departmental profit should be measured against the budget figures for that period.

Ratio of food/beverage sales to total sales

It is worthwhile for food and beverage sales to be separated from each other and to express each of them as a percentage of the total sales. This would be a measure of performance against the established standard budgeted percentage as well as indicating general trends in the business.

Average spending power

This measures the relationship between food sales and beverage sales to the number of customers served. If food sales are £750 and the number of customers served is seventy, the average spend by each customers is £10.72. The ASP for beverages is usually related to the number of items recorded on the till roll, rather than to the number of customers, and the total beverage sales. Thus if £600 is the recorded beverage sales and an analysis of the till roll showed that 200 drinks had been sold, the average spend per drink would be £3.00. What is different here is that a customer may order several drinks during an evening and therefore the average amount spent on a drink is more important than the ASP per customer. To calculate the ASP for bottled wine sales in a restaurant or at a banquet though could be a useful exercise.

Sales mix

This measures the relationship between the various components of the total sales of a unit, for example:

Sales mix	%
Coffee shop sales	
Food	20
Beverages	5
Restaurant sales	
Food	25
Beverages	15
Banqueting sales	
Food	20
Beverages	10
Cocktail bar sales	
Beverages	5
	100

In addition, a sales mix may be calculated for the food and beverage menus for each outlet under group headings such as appetizers, main course items, sweet course, coffees, etc.; and spirits, cocktails, beers and lagers, etc. This would not only highlight the most and least popular items, but would at times help to explain a disappointing gross profit percentage that occurred in spite of a good volume of business; the reason often being that each item is usually costed at different gross profit percentages and if the customers are choosing those items with a low gross profit this would result in the overall gross profit figure being less than budgeted for.

Payroll costs

Payroll costs are usually expressed as a percentage of sales and are normally higher, the higher the level of service offered. It is vital that they are tightly controlled as they contribute a high percentage of the total costs of running an operation.

Payroll costs can be controlled by establishing a head count of employees per department, or establishing the total number of employee hours allowed per department in relation to a known average volume of business. In addition, all overtime must be strictly controlled and should only be permitted when absolutely necessary.

Index of productivity

This is calculated by the formula:

$$\frac{\text{sales}}{\text{payroll (including any staff benefits costs)}}$$

The index of productivity can be calculated separately for food sales, beverage sales or for total food and beverage sales.

The use of the term 'payroll costs' in the formula includes not only the appropriate payroll costs, but also any other employee benefits such as employers' pension contributions, medical insurance, etc.

The index of productivity would vary depending on the type of operation, for example, a fast-food restaurant with a take-away service would have a high index of productivity, as the payroll costs would be lower than a luxury restaurant employing highly skilled and expensive staff with a high ratio of staff to customers, which may have a relatively low index of productivity.

As payroll costs can be controlled and should be related to the forecasted volume of business, a standard index of productivity can be established to measure how accurately the two elements are related.

Stock turnover

This is calculated by the formula:

$$\text{rate of stock turnover} = \frac{\text{cost of food or beverages consumed}}{\text{average stock value (food or beverage) at cost}}$$

The rate of stock turnover gives the number of times that the average level of stock has turned over in a given period. Too high a turnover would indicate very low levels of stocks being held and a large number of small value purchases being made. This is costly and time consuming for whoever does the purchasing as well as costly for the purchases as no price advantage can be taken of the standard quantity offers made by suppliers. Too low a turnover would indicate unnecessary capital tied up in an operation and therefore additionally a larger control and security problem.

Sales per seat available

This shows the sales value that can be earned by each seat in a restaurant, coffee shop, etc. As in the section about rate of seat turnover, the seat is the selling point and is required to contribute a certain value to turnover and profits.

Rate of seat turnover

This shows the number of times that each seat in a restaurant, coffee shop, etc. is used by customers during a specific period. Thus, if in a 120-seater coffee shop 400 customers were served in a three-hour lunch period, the rate of seat turnover would be 400 divided by 120, that is, 3.33. As the coffee shop staff can only sell food to customers while they are seated at a table, the importance of the rate of seat turnover is highlighted.

Sales per waiter/waitress

Each waiter/waitress will have a known number of covers for which he/she is responsible. This would vary depending on the style of food and beverage service offered. As salespeople for the restaurant or coffee shop, their takings should be of a predetermined target level so as to contribute to a satisfactory level of turnover and profit.

Sales per square metre[2]

This is self-explanatory in that the space of all selling outlets needs to be used to its best advantage so as to achieve a desired turnover and profit. This can be calculated on a square foot/metre basis. As the square footage per customer varies with the type of food and beverage service offered, so must the costs to the customer so that an establishment is earning the desired turnover and profit per square foot of selling space.

Summary

In this chapter the fundamentals of food control both from a cost and a revenue perspective are explored more specifically:

- Basic issues of control at the planning the operational phases.
- Basic issues of control at the post operation phase.

- Basic but essential skills for any food and beverage manager, such as setting up a break-even analysis and the budget are explained.
- Basic concepts such as standard recipes and standard portion sizes, which are essential to a good control system.
- Cost control reports are also examined as well as the flexibilities of today's EPOS systems.
- Concepts of PSA and menu engineering.
- Issues with non-computerized systems are explored.
- Operating rations useful in the assessment of an effective Food and Beverage control system.

Review questions

1. What are the objectives of an effective food and beverage control system?
2. What is a standard recipe?
3. What is a break-even analysis?
4. What are the key parts of an effective food and beverage control system?
5. What are the differences between a daily food cost report and a detailed food cost report?
6. Explain the millimetre system of beverage control?
7. What does 'DOG' mean in menu engineering terminology?
8. How do you calculate stock turnover and sales per waiter?

Further study options

Case study

The 'Coconut duck' restaurant was originally a 40 cover Thai restaurant in London, UK. In the first few years of operation, business was doing well and the restaurant was featuring in major tourist guides and newspapers as a 'must visit' restaurant not only for the great cuisine but also for the fantastic décor. As business picked up the restaurant owner decided to expand so when the opportunity appeared to acquire the lease for the property next door he did so and expanded the restaurant to a 120 seater. Things seemed to be going well and the owner was certain that he would get a good return on his investment. However, the original small team could not cope with the business and the new chefs and servers did not have the rapport that a small team had. Soon the restaurant was faced with problems of stock control especially in the bar area. Stock would go amiss quite often and wastage levels both in food and beverages had hit an all time high. Worst of all the management could not identify if the problem was at the bar or the cellars and had no idea as to how to resolve the issue. Some suspected theft whilst others felt it was merely bad management.

The owner decides to hire a consultant to come up with an effective food and beverage control system that helps alleviate the problem. In his briefing to you he has suggested that money is not a problem.

Question 1: What do you think are the key issues or potential problem areas with the restaurant in terms of food and beverage control?

Question 2: Design a food and beverage control system that ensures that the problems are limited or eliminated.

Solution to activity 1

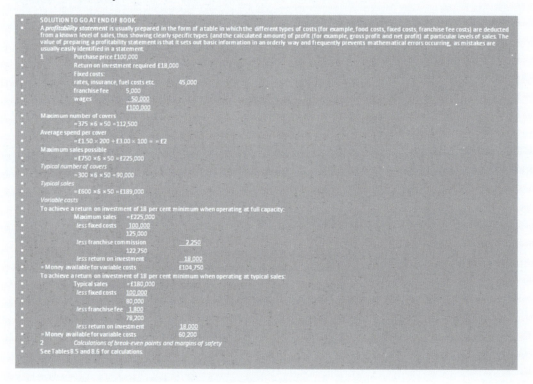

SOLUTION TO GO AT END OF BOOK

A *profitability statement* is usually prepared in the form of a table in which the different types of costs (for example, food costs, fixed costs, franchise fee costs) are deducted from a known level of sales, thus showing clearly specific types (and the calculated amount) of profit (for example, gross profit and net profit) at particular levels of sales. The value of preparing a profitability statement is that it sets out basic information in an orderly way and frequently prevents mathematical errors occurring, as mistakes are usually easily identified in a statement.

1   Purchase price £100,000

     Return on investment required £18,000

     Fixed costs:

rates, insurance, fuel costs etc		45,000
franchise fee	5,000	
wages	50,000	
	£100,000	

Maximum number of covers

     = 375 × 6 × 50 = 112,500

Average spend per cover

     = £1.50 × 200 + £3.00 × 100 = = £2

Maximum sales possible

     = £750 × 6 × 50 = £225,000

Typical number of covers

     = 300 × 6 × 50 = 90,000

Typical sales

     = £600 × 6 × 50 = £189,000

Variable costs

To achieve a return on investment of 18 per cent minimum when operating at full capacity:

Maximum sales	= £225,000	
less fixed costs	100,000	
	125,000	
less franchise commission		2,250
	122,750	
less return on investment		18,000
= Money available for variable costs		£104,750

To achieve a return on investment of 18 per cent minimum when operating at typical sales:

Typical sales	= £180,000	
less fixed costs	100,000	
	80,000	
less franchise fee	1,800	
	78,200	
less return on investment		18,000
= Money available for variable costs		60,200

2   *Calculations of break-even points and margins of safety*

See Tables 8.5 and 8.6 for calculations.

Solution to activity 2

Menu engineering worksheet

Solution

(A) Menu item name	(B) No. sold (MM)	(C) Menu mix%	(D) Item food cost	(E) Item selling price	(F) Item CM (E – D)	(G) Menu costs (D*B)	(H) Menu revenues (E*B)	Menu CM (G – H)	CM category	MM% category	Menu item classification
Chicken blue	420	0.42	2.7	5.95	3.25	1,134	2,499	1,365	Low	High	Cow
Steak	360	0.36	4.5	8.5	4	1,620	3,060	1,440	High	High	Star
Lobster tail	150	0.15	8	9.5	1.5	1,200	1,425	,225	Low	Low	Dog
Tenderloin tips	70	0.07	4	7.4	3.4	280	518	238	High	Low	Puzzle
		0				I	J	M			
Totals	1000	1	19.2	31.35	12.15	4,234	7,502	3,268			
						K = I/J (FC%) 0.564382831		O = M/N (Av. CM) 3.268		Q = (100%/items) (70%) 0.175	

Further reading

Cranage, D. (2003). Practical time series forecasting for the hospitality manager. *International Journal of Contemporary Hospitality Management*, 15(2), 86–93.

Harris, P. and Mongiello, M. (2006). *Accounting and Financial Management: Developments in the International Hospitality Industry*. London: Elsevier.

Kwong, L. Y. (2005). The application of menu engineering and design in Asian restaurants. *International Journal of Hospitality Management*, 24(1), 91–106.

Mayer, K. and Raab, C. (2007). Menu engineering and activity-based costing – Can they work together in a restaurant?. *International Journal of Contemporary Hospitality Management*, 19(1), 43–52.

Sanders, E., Hill, T. & Faria, D. (2007). *Understanding Foodservice Cost Control: An Operational Text for Food, Beverage, and Labor Costs*. NJ: Prentice Hall.

Staffing issues

Introduction

Given that for most managers managing people forms the major part of their job role, the main aim of this chapter is to provide an outline of staffing issues that managers should be aware of. The employment of staff in the UK is highly regulated by both the UK and EU legislature and as with any text covering such issues changes occur frequently. Generally, managers of staff in the normal course of employment will be mostly concerned with issues of staff recruitment, motivation, development, productivity, deployment and retention with hopefully only occasional minor disciplinary matters. It is, however, inevitable those managers will get involved in more serious disciplinary or grievance procedures and although this text does provide some outline of these it would be prudent to seek professional advice before dealing with more serious issues. The hospitality industry is one of a number that attract large numbers of part-time, seasonal and casual employees particularly at lower grades and this tends to exacerbate the high level of staff turnover. This can add pressure to management in terms of recruitment and training, maintaining produce and service quality standards, and keeping employment costs at an acceptable level.

After working through this chapter you should be able to:

- Have a broad appreciation of hospitality employment statistics.
- Understand the process of staff recruitment.
- Be able to calculate staff turnover.
- Link staff motivation, training and retention to company success.
- Understand the process of supervision and communication.

STRUCTURE OF UK LABOUR

Changes taking place in the size and structure of the UK labour pool are considerable with 60% of the adult population, some 29 million, now in employment and by 2009 it is estimated that a third of these will be over fifty-five years of age. In addition, the UK economy has seen a steady move away from traditional manufacturing industries towards those of the service sector with hotel and catering seeing an increase over the past five years of 1.4%. The UK eating out market continues to grow with forecasted turnover expected to be in excess of £28 billion by 2007. One of the major difficulties faced by service industries in general and the hospitality industry in particular is the recruitment, training and retention of staff. Many of the job roles in hospitality are customer facing where the service element forms a major aspect of customer satisfaction or dissatisfaction and it therefore has the potential to be a stressful experience. With the continued drive by hospitality companies to gain strong brand recognition together with a memorable meal experience through excellent service delivery rather than an average one the importance of good staff recruitment and training together with a strategy for improving staff retention becomes very important.

RECRUITMENT

Employment statistics

The latest information available is from 2005 at which time the Labour Force Survey showed that tourism and hospitality employed 1.88 million people, which represents a reduction of 4%, 84,000 on 2004. Of that figure 1.64 million are employed in the hospitality industry and 77% of these are employed in restaurants, pubs and clubs, hotels, bars and food service management. The remaining 23%, 380,000 are employed where hospitality is not the primary purpose, for example hospitals and school catering.

In 2005, the number of female workers represented 59% of the total workforce, ten years earlier this figure stood at 70%.

	Males	Females
Hotels	97,600	140,800
Restaurants	255,300	258,400
Pubs, bars and nightclubs	141,200	192,700
Food and service management	56,600	121,800
Gambling	33,600	44,000
Travel and tourist services	30,900	79,400
Visitor attractions	5,300	3,300
Holiday parks and self-catering	14,300	30,600
Hospitality services	93,500	286,500
Total	**728,300**	**1,157,500**

Source: ONS Labour Force Survey BHA Trends and Statistics, 2006

Table 9.1
Numbers employed in the tourism and hospitality industry by gender, 2005

Occupations	2001	2005
Hotel and accommodation managers	51,099	50,700
Restaurant and catering managers	141,164	160,600
Conference and exhibition managers	11,646	12,600
Publicans and managers of licensed premises	51,255	60,300
Travel agency managers	10,693	7,700
Chefs, cooks	261,467	256,700
Travel agency staff	58,060	48,400
Travel and tour guides	16,945	21,100
Hotel porters	14,502	11,900
Kitchen and catering assistants	416,136	397,100
Waiting staff	221,017	231,800
Bar staff	277,859	284,200

Source: ONS Labour Force Survey BHA Trends and Statistics, 2006

Table 9.2
Total employed in core occupations, 2001 and 2005

Table 9.1 represents that the significant areas where female employees dominate males are in the hotel, food and service management, travel and tourist services, and hospitality sectors. The total employed in core occupations are identified in (Table 9.2).

Table 9.3 represents total employed by sector and age. This would indicate that the industry is predominantly a younger person's industry with 44% below the age of 30, a further 38% under 50 and 16% aged between 50 and 64. The remaining 2% is over 65.

	16–19	20–29	30–49	50–64	Over 65	Total
Hotels	41,800	73,000	82,600	36,000	5,000	238,400
Restaurants	133,800	137,200	180,400	57,300	5,100	513,800
Pub, bars and nightclubs	82,900	128,500	86,000	32,800	3,700	333,900
Food and service management	8,300	30,100	93,300	43,100	3,400	178,200
Gambling	7,000	20,700	33,100	15,600	1,300	77,700
Travel and tourist services	6,200	39,100	45,200	17,700	2,200	110,400
Visitor attractions	1,500	2,700	2,700	1,000	700	8,600
Holiday parks and self-catering	3,700	3,900	16,100	17,600	3,600	44,900
Hospitality services	51,200	62,200	167,100	87,800	11,600	379,900
Total	**336,400**	**497,400**	**706,500**	**308,900**	**36,600**	**1,885,800**

Source: ONS Labour Force Survey BHA Trends and Statistics, 2006

Table 9.3
Total employed by sector and age, 2005

Recruitment criteria

Recruiting staff for successful customer service is the first practical stage in the development of a workforce. We have already discussed in previous chapters the importance of developing the objectives of the marketing policy, the catering policy, and the financial policy, menu design, operational style, etc. and all these will impact on the staff recruitment policy, but essentially the delivery of all the above policies will rely substantially on those front line operatives that deliver the service. From the marketing policy decisions will have been taken concerning how the organizations image will be portrayed to its' target customers. The catering policy will have identified operational aspects, for example how food will be served to customers, the best service style suited to meeting the desired image. The financial policy will in part concern itself with issues of profitability and cost control and it is here where there is often a dichotomy of views, are staff a valued asset or an unavoidable cost? Formally, of course staff are recorded in the business accounts as a cost but it is how they are regarded operationally that can cause difficulties for management. It is popular at the present time to view staff as assets and they are often referred to as the 'internal customer'. Authors such as Heskett, Sasser and Schlesinger have developed a model of this, 'the service profit chain', which suggests that if an organization treats its' staff well they will treat the organizations customers well, the customers will respond to this and remain loyal to the organization and the organization will reap higher or more sustained profit levels. It is important therefore that staff should be properly selected, kept motivated, actively integrated into the organizations culture and empowered (Figure 9.1).

Employee satisfaction	Added value to product/service	Customer satisfaction	Customer loyalty	Profit and growth
From: Good recruitment and high quality support and training	From: Satisfied loyal and productive staff	Because: Happy with product or service	Because: Customers are satisfied with product or service	Due to: Happy customers retention and loyalty

Figure 9.1 Service profit chain adapted from *The Service Profit Chain* (*Source*: Heskett et al., 1997, p. 19)

Methods of recruitment

Selective recruitment remains one of the most difficult areas with recruitment managers getting it wrong almost as often as they get it right. However, there are some practical ways that can help to achieve a greater success rate.

1. Review recruitment practices on a regular basis both those that have been successful and those less so. It provides useful data on how current practices could be improved.
2. Ensure that all candidates go through a process that allows you to properly evaluate both their current skills and also their future potential. For example, in the case of a chef some food preparation and cookery skills could demonstrate current ability with perhaps a short psychometric test to determine future potential.
3. Give candidates the opportunity to tell you what they know about your organization and on the basis of this what they might bring to it.
4. Have a well thought out job description together with a well-defined personal attributes specification. List these under the headings of 'essential' or 'desirable'.
5. Where appropriate the impact on or of any co-workers should be considered and you may choose to include one co-worker in the interview panel.

The rewards for getting this process right are considerable and include increased productivity, higher morale amongst the workforce, a good level of commitment, less time wasted on dealing with disputes which will lead to better use of management time and improved profitability.

STAFF TURNOVER

The hospitality industry operates in an environment of high staff turnover, particularly amongst low skilled employees and this not only generates huge costs but also creates challenges in

finding the right calibre of staff on a continuous basis. Hoteliers are very aware of the demands that this puts on both their managers and on the bottom line and a recent article in the *Caterer and Hotelkeeper* shows how one manager is trying to redress the trend. 'Andrew Silver, Managing Director of Golden Tulip UK, highlights ways to overcome the damaging effects of high staff turnover and low morale' (Silver, 2007).

Recent research undertaken by David Battersby, Managing Director of the consultancy Hospitality and Leisure Manpower (HaLM), for the British Hospitality Association (BHA) reveals the very high cost of staff turnover within the hospitality sector. Based on this research, he has made a conservative estimate that staff turnover stands at about 30% overall, but is noticeably much higher in some areas such as the licensed trade where 100% or even 200% is not unusual. The most conservative estimate of the cost of recruitment for each person is in the region of £500. This figure includes the cost of advertising, interviewing candidates; reviewing CV's checking references, etc. It does not take into account any cost of lost business, training of new recruits or agency fees.

Given the fact that that the hospitality industry in the UK employs around two million people, and that the turnover figure is 30% per annum (some 600,000 people), it quickly becomes clear that the annual cost to the industry amounts to £300,000,000. It is an astonishing figure and is only supportable because the cost is defrayed over so many businesses and because those running hospitality businesses have become reconciled to high staff turnover, and resignedly accept recruitment as part of the 'fixed costs' of running the business. A high staff turnover can have a detrimental effect on any business and where possible an exit interview should be undertaken with all leavers in order to identify the cause. It is inevitable that some staff turnover will be linked to promotions, better salary; move in location or a change of career but some may be avoidable in the short to medium term bringing more stability to the organizations labour force (see Figures 9.2 and 9.3).

Recruitment costs

Recruitment costs can be considerable, advertising expenses or agency fees, time taken to short list potential candidates, collecting references and setting up interview panels are the most obvious and easily quantifiable. Costs that are less obvious are overtime rates paid to other staff covering the vacancy, the natural start up time and 'paperwork' associated with a new employee, induction, uniform, medical check and the time taken to make new acquaintances. Training is also a cost but apart from an initial operational training course, training costs should be part of an operation budget and therefore may not necessarily fall entirely on the recruitment budget. It is with these costs in mind that strategy and spending on staff retention as opposed to staff replacement should be in the forefront of managements

1. Statistics show that, by asking employees to complete a staff opinion survey, they feel more engaged with their business and believe that their views will be listened to and used constructively to their benefit.
2. Some of these benefits could be increased holiday time or birthdays off. Also, an active and effective staff suggestion scheme definitely helps employees feel that their opinions and suggestions are valid.
3. Everyone has different motivations, and our role as managers is to understand them and act accordingly. Retention is greatly helped when your team understands their role clearly and how it affects the performance of the business.
4. One of the greatest motivators is feedback. Giving feedback helps people understand when they are doing a good job and when they fall short of required standards. It helps them to improve their performance and, let's face it, most people come to work wanting to do a good job and derive great satisfaction when they are empowered to do just that.
5. Giving praise and recognition for achievements is vital, while at the same time implementing a performance management programme for when things don't go so well.
6. What matters most is that people enjoy what they do and feel they are making a difference. Businesses that are committed to treating their whole team with openness and honesty, and assuring them that they will be treated with respect, will be rewarded with low staff turnover and a motivated willing team.

Figure 9.2
Strategies to reduce staff turnover (*Source*: Adapted from Silver, 2007, p. 18)

More than three-quarters of senior managers believe that an annual quota for *staff dismissals* would boost their company's performance, according to a survey by management consultancy Hudson. Almost half agreed that shedding up to 5% of *staff* was positively healthy. Hudson described this as a 'taboo area of debate for British business'. But there's no suggestion that the law should sanction an annual cull of underperforming *staff* with no questions asked and immunity from tribunal claims. Such a brutal regime would not be politically acceptable and clearly breach European law. So employers tempted to implement headcount-reduction quotas must follow meticulous performance-management procedures to avoid unfair *dismissal* claims and charges of discrimination on grounds of sex, race, disability, age and so on. A proposal to dismiss a set proportion of the workforce might also trigger a legal duty to consult employee representatives. Legal constraints aside, a majority of respondents cited 'introducing a culture of fear' as a deterrent to a *dismissal* quota. And 72% admitted there would be less need to release *staff* if their recruitment process were tighter – suggesting attention should focus on the start of the employment relationship rather than its termination.

Figure 9.3
A draconian view of enhanced staff turnover (*Source*: Burd and Davies, 2007)

mind particularly in industry sectors that have higher than average staff turnover, for example the licensed trade. In order to accurately determine future recruitment costs and to fully understand the scale of the problem it is first necessary to calculate staff turnover for the particular organization in question. There is a relatively simple formula to decide this as follows and an opportunity to explore this further in the short case study at the end of this chapter.

In the simple version of measuring staff turnover percentage per annum count the number of staff that have left during the preceding year, divide it into the total number of staff employed during that period and multiply by 100. For example if 10 staff have left, perhaps including several from one vacancy during the year, and you employ and average of 40 persons then your staff turnover is 10 divided by 40×100 which equals 25%. However, this simple version does not take into account part-time or seasonal workers that are very common in the hospitality industry. In order to gain a better indication of full-time equivalent staff turnover the following approach should be taken.

- The Dog and Penguin Public house employ the following staff.
- Twelve part-time working six hours per week for fifty-two weeks per year.
- Six full-time working forty-two hours per week for fifty-two weeks per year.
- Four seasonal staff working forty-two hours per week for ten weeks of the year.

Stage 1: Hours worked

	Number of staff	Hours per week	Weeks per year	Total
Part-time	12	6	35	2,100
Full-time	6	42	52	13,104
Seasonal full-time	4	42	10	1,680
Seasonal part-time	1	18	2	36
Total hours worked				**16,920**

Stage 2: Total days worked

Assuming an average working day has eight hours divide total hours by eight $16,920/8 = 2,115$ days.

Stage 3: Full-time equivalent

The standard number of days worked in one year 235, therefore $2,115/235 = 9$ full-time equivalent staff.

Stage 4: Leavers

Leavers exclude seasonal staff that leave at the end of their contract.

During the year, four part-time and two full-time staff left

$$4 \times 6 \times 35 = 840$$
$$2 \times 42 \times 52 = 4,368 + 840 = 5,208$$

5,208 hours divided by 8 hours per day = 651 days, therefore $651/235 = 2.77$ full-time equivalent staff.

A simple calculation of staff turnover would indicate 6 staff left out of a total of 23 therefore 6 divided by 23 equals a staff turnover rate of 26%. More detailed analysis taking account of part-time staff would identify a staff turnover of almost 31% $(2.77 \div 9 \times 100 = 30.78\%)$

STAFF TRAINING

Induction

The staff induction process provides new employees with an overview of the organization. It should contain a session on general issues of health and safety and include specialized health and safety training where demands of the job role require it, for example, when using machinery or equipment or where work involves lifting, etc. Fire escape routes and evacuation procedures together with details of fire assembly points should be clearly identified. Employees should be introduced to their supervisor, work colleagues and staff where appropriate. It is normal at this time to provide staff handbooks uniforms if required and any further information that a new employee may require in the first few weeks of their employment until they settle in.

Staff training

In larger organizations a specialized training department will provide most of the staff training in-house, particularly areas of customer care and customer service. Where these are not provided in-house the training department will facilitate the training provision via specialist agencies particularly where these receive external accreditation for example 'Investors in People'. In smaller organizations, and sometimes in larger ones too training may take the form of 'on the job' where a more senior member of staff provides training instruction and continues to reinforce the training under supervision during the normal working day. Some staff training needs may have been identified at interview, during periodic appraisal, observed/suggested by supervisor, required by an outside body or requested by the employee. The organization will through its' various policies have established standards and procedures for the operation of its' business. Meeting these operational or administrative goals will require staff to be trained to an appropriate level by establishing a set of training objectives. For example, currently, in the UK it is not unusual for companies, particularly in the hotel sector where typically they will have a large proportion of overseas staff, to provide English language classes so that front line staff can communicate effectively with customers. Where an organization is large enough to offer this type of training it facilitates the recruitment process by enabling recruiters a wider choice of prospective employees.

Activity 1

Write a short training plan to enable new service staff to answer the telephone and take an accurate message/booking for your establishment. Include in the plan the information that you need to acquire and a set text for answering an enquiry.

LEGAL FRAMEWORK

Employment in the UK is governed by a wide legislative framework and would require a number of books in order to cover all of these. For the purposes of this chapter the Employment Act 2002 makes provision for statutory rights to paternity and adoption leave and pay and to amend the law relating to statutory maternity leave and pay. It also amends the Employment Tribunals Act 1996 to provide statutory procedures in relation to employment disputes and amend the law in of particulars of employment, compromise agreements and questionnaires on equal pay. It also makes provision in regard to trade union learning representatives, amends Section 110 of the Employment Rights Act 1996; to make provision about fixed-term work, flexible working, maternity allowance, work-focused interviews for partners of benefit claimants and to make provision about the use of information for, or relating to, employment and training and the Employment Relations Act 2004, which is mainly concerned with collective labour law and trade union rights are those that identify the legislative framework that managers generally come across.

Staff discipline and dismissal

As the previous paragraph shows, employment law is very complex and changes to employment regulations occur frequently particularly dismissal procedures. Employers are still free to dismiss employees at any time but unless the dismissal is considered fair the employer may face a case of unfair dismissal bought by the employee through an employment tribunal. In most companies a detailed procedure for disciplinary issues is written and this forms part of the employee's contract of employment (see Figures 9.4 and 9.5).

The contract of employment forms the legal framework on which the employment is based and should as a minimum contain details of the employment as shown in Figure 9.4. Following one year's service an employee can make a claim to an employment tribunal for unfair dismissal provided it is made within three months of the dismissal. If an employee can prove that the employer has pressured them to resign they have the same right to unfair or constructive dismissal.

In the event of the employee winning the case, the tribunal can choose one of the following remedies:

1. Re-instatement which means getting back the old job on the old terms and conditions.
2. Re-engagement which would mean a different job with the same employer.
3. Compensation where the amount can be anything from a relatively small sum to an unlimited amount if the dismissal was due to some form of discrimination.

Figure 9.4
Basic contract of employment

All employees must receive a written statement of their particulars of employment within eight weeks of commencing employment.

The Statutory Minimum Employment Contract is compliant with both the Employment Rights Act 1996 and Employment Act 2002, and contains the following clauses as per the requirements of Section One of the former Act:

1. Name, address, job title
2. Date of employment and continuous employment
3. Duration of employment
4. Place of work and mobility
5. Hours of work
6. Remuneration
7. Overseas employment
8. Holidays
9. Sick pay
10. Pension
11. Collective agreement
12. Grievance procedure
13. Disciplinary procedure
14. Governing law

Figure 9.5
Reasons for a fair dismissal would include the following matters (*Source*: http://www.winters.co.uk/factsheets/dismissal_procedures.html)

1. The person does not have the capability or qualification for the job (this requires the employer to go through consultation and/or disciplinary processes).
2. The employee behaves in an inappropriate manner (the company/firm's policies should refer to what would be unreasonable behaviour and the business must go through disciplinary procedures).
3. Redundancy, providing there is a genuine business case for making position(s) redundant with no suitable alternative work, there has been adequate consultation and there is no discrimination in who is selected.
4. The dismissal is the effect of a legal process such as a driver who loses his right to drive (however, the employer is expected to explore other possibilities such as looking for alternative work before dismissing the employee).
5. Some other substantial reason.

If it can be demonstrated that the dismissal was due to any of the following it will be considered as unfair regardless of the length of service:

1. Discrimination for sex, race, age or disability.
2. Pregnancy, childbirth or maternity leave.
3. Refusing to opt out of the Working Time Regulations.
4. Disclosing certain kinds of wrong doing in the workplace.

It is important that managers are fully aware of the contents and processes of any disciplinary procedures set down by the company and that these processes are followed exactly in order to avoid needless staff disciplinary problems or expensive litigation.

STAFF SCHEDULING

Staff rota

Creating a staff rota is the process of matching staff availability to the work demands of the organization. In its simplest form it will set out which staff will be on duty for any particular shift, start and end times for each shift and day of the week. If staffing includes occasional weekend working or working during public holidays then advance warning should be given so that staff has an opportunity to plan. The unpredictability of the volume of business or sales instability is typical of most catering establishments. There is often a change in the volume of business from day to day, and in many establishments from hour to hour. This not only causes basic problems with regard to the quantities of commodities to be purchased and prepared but also as to the staffing required.

Rota to meet business demand

Accurately meeting the right level of staffing during the peeks and troughs in demand usually associated with a food and beverage service is extremely important. Too many staff will create needless expense and may affect the level of staff morale if they feel under-utilized and get bored. Too few staff will result in poor customer service and increased customer complaints leading to low staff morale as they face complaining customers and struggle to do their work properly. This in turn will inevitably lead to reduced profits. Data produced electronically via an electronic point of sale (EPOS) system can provide managers with a pattern of sales throughout each daily service period. Data can be collected showing patterns for weeks, months and even years if this is beneficial. By careful analysis these trends in trading patterns can be compared against other data that may have had an extraordinary influence on trading, for example exceptional weather conditions, public holidays, local or national events in addition to restaurant trading data, for example number of no shows or turn downs, number of bookings compared to chance or walk-in trade. A brief description of this terminology is as follows:

1. No shows are customers who have booked a table but fail to turn up or cancel.
2. Turn downs are booking that are refused due to capacity having been met. This situation should ideally be due to restaurant bookings/customers having reached capacity as opposed to refusing customers because of production or staffing problems.
3. Chance or walk-in customers are those that have not booked. It is important to be aware of this particularly if there are strong variations.

From a review of this data trading patterns can be established and a staff rota drawn up and whilst on some occasions there may be a certain element of guesswork, it is calculated and informed guesswork.

Activity 2

You are the manager of a fast-food restaurant in a town centre location open from 0900 to 2300 hours, seven days a week and every day of the year except Christmas day. Contribution margins on fast-food items are small and profitability relies on volume and efficiency of service. What data would you need to collect in order to write an efficient staff rota?

Specialized staff scheduling

Specialized staff scheduling applies to food and beverage operations that have relatively little variation in demand because they operate within a controlled system. For example, serving customers at a banquet where the service standard requires one server per table of ten customers, one wine server per three tables, etc. Specialized staff scheduling may also apply in the case where food and beverage service is ancillary to the main service provision, for example stewards on an aircraft whilst they serve your meals are mainly there for your safety and if the aircraft is flying below capacity the number of stewards remains unchanged the same applies to nurses serving meals in a hospital. Current trends in working practices, for example working straight shifts as opposed to split shifts by changing patterns of food production allow better utilization of staff. Cook-chill as opposed to cook-serve is a prime example of an approach to staffing that minimizes staff costs and optimizes food production. In this case modern technology has bought down the cost of establishing a cook-chill system. Once established the system can be accurately staffed during the normal working day, is therefore more appealing to staff and this can be reflected in the rates of pay offered.

Tables 9.4 and 9.5 elucidate typical capacity scheduling at McDonald's Restaurants using sales data from their EPOS system. Distribution of sales throughout the week and distribution of sales throughout the day at a typical branch of McDonald's inform management of staffing levels required.

This is a key information for service resources planning particularly for a high volume low margin operations where labour cost and efficiency have a dramatic effect on profitability.

Table 9.4
Capacity scheduling at
McDonalds Restaurants

Distribution of sales throughout the week	
Sunday	14
Monday	12.3
Tuesday	12.4
Wednesday	13.2
Thursday	14.8
Friday	16.3
Saturday	16.8
Total	**100%**

Distribution of sales throughout the day	
8.00 AM	3.4
9.00 AM	4.1
10.00 AM	4.0
11.00 AM	3.9
12.00 PM	7.5
1.00 PM	14.9
2.00 PM	9.01
3.00 PM	5.0
4.00 PM	3.5
5.00 PM	5.5
6.00 PM	9.1
7.00 PM	8.4
5.00 PM	5.5
8.00 PM	5.6
9.00 PM	5.3
10.00 PM	4.6
11.00 PM	3.4
12.00 PM	2.5
Total	**100%**

Table 9.5
Sales distribution at McDonalds Restaurants

SUPERVISION AND COMMUNICATION

How we communicate

There are a number of myths concerning how we communicate these are some of them. We communicate only when we want to, words mean the same to both the speaker and the listener we communicate chiefly with words. Non-verbal communication equals silent communication, what we say is what you will receive and there is no such thing as too much information. In order to dismiss these myths we need to clarify what constitutes communication.

1. Most communication, about 70% is non-verbal and is concerned with gestures. Laughter, tears, shrugs, raised arms, raised eyebrows, arms folded and understanding this body language are both intuitive and learned.
2. The second commonest form of communication about 20% concerns vocal communication. Pitch and level of voice, from monotone to highly excited, from screaming and shouting to a raised voice and finally to whispers.
3. Lastly, about 10% of our communication is concerned with the words we use.

In an organization it is often necessary to communicate with other people at different levels of the hierarchy so for example, a restaurant supervisor may need to communicate with their manager (upward communication) or with one of the service staff (downward communication) or with another supervisor coming on the following shift (lateral communication). The subject may be the same in all three cases but the communication may be different. In this situation what is most probable is that the words used will be more or less the same, the tone of voice may or may not be different, but the body language is the most likely area to be different. This is because in the hierarchical structure position assumes an importance that is reflected through the body language used and this is the area of communication within an organization that is best learnt at an early stage because understanding body language provides early and in most cases reliable feedback to your communication.

Barriers to communication

Developing effective communication skills often requires more effort being put into receiving information than to giving it. Having said that, developing a speaking style that effectively communicates is important and concerns the speed at which you talk, the tone of your voice and the style of your body language. Verbal communication needs to be succinct so that the listener does not turn off before you have completed the communication. This tie's in with one of the common myths mentioned earlier, that of information overload. We are used to computers providing endless reports with every minute detail examined inside out and upside down, however with a computer you can save the data and absorb it at a more reasonable pace at a later time. With verbal communication this is not possible, unless you record it when it then becomes a message rather than a communication in the true sense. The span of concentration varies in different people but all will eventually switch off when their information threshold is reached. For communication to be effective it needs to be received and understood by the listener and is essentially a two-way process. Listening is a skill that needs to be developed so that listening becomes active listening. In communication situations with active listeners each will send and receive information with signs of acknowledgement, for example the active listener may repeat part of what has been said as a way of confirming that they have heard what has been said correctly. There will also be visual signs in the form of body language that will show that the listener both understands and is interested in the communication or not as the case may be. In the work environment many communications take a written form, for example standard operating procedures, instructions for cashing up tills or the staff rota. In these particular communication situations, a response to the originator is not normally required or available and the communication must therefore be clear and unambiguous. If the written communication is a letter of complaint from a customer then this almost certainly will require a response and if the complaint is badly phrased or indeed the response is badly phrased it may not adequately address the problem (Table 9.6).

Other forms of written communication may involve feedback to staff as part of a periodic review process and again it is important

Communication	Essentials
Speaking (vocal)	Volume, pitch, tone, pace
Listening	Focus, eyes, posture, gestures, body movement
Non-verbal	Facial, eyes, posture, gestures, body movement
Writing	Active short sentences, inverted pyramid

Table 9.6
Essentials of effective communication

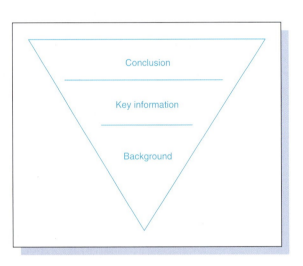

Figure 9.6
Inverted pyramid of background information

that the right form of words are used because different people will read the communication differently, for example 'above average' to the writer may mean 'quite good' whereas the recipient may read it as being 'barely acceptable'.

The inverted pyramid suggests a format for written communication where background information is limited to the essentials that need to be known in order to put the communication in context and comes last in the communication. Second comes the more detailed key information that supports the point/s being made/argued, perhaps in the form of a tabulated list. Most importantly the communication conclusion leads with a succinct summary of all salient points that need to be considered so that the recipient has an overview and understanding of what the communication is about and can decide immediately on its importance and what time to devote to reading it (Figure 9.6).

1. Communication and supervisory channels
2. Supervision and communication structure
3. Levels of supervision and empowerment
4. Measuring effective communication.

Supervision and the communication process

The supervision of others is the first step on the management ladder and utilizes the following processes; planning, organizing, coordinating, staffing, directing, controlling and evaluating. In the hospitality industry and probably in many others the supervisory structure normally starts at the technical skill stage where, for example, the headwaiter will train and supervise a station waiter. As the headwaiters skills develop he may be promoted to assistant restaurant manager where technical skills are still required but more emphasis is placed on man management skills. Eventually if he is successful in this role he may be promoted to restaurant manager and perhaps food and beverage manager at which stage his technical skill will move even further into the background as man management skills take more time and conceptual skills start to develop. If and when there is further promotion to hotel manager then although other skills will not totally disappear most of the effort will be focused on conceptual management decision-making. So why do many supervisors fail fairly early in the career, well for many it is the inability to relate to the employees. Some authors of hospitality books have liked the hospitality industry to a theatrical performance and restaurant service is very often like that where staff are expected to put on a show no matter how tired they may feel or how busy or understaffed the restaurant may be. Under these types of condition it is essential that supervisors can at the very least empathize with their staff. An ill-considered comment or gesture taken out of context creates an incident out of all proportion to the situation it was intended to deal with.

Group activity 1

Role-play: One person should be a member of service staff the other the supervisor. The supervisor is required to reprimand the staff member for being late for shift for a second occasion. The supervisor is looking for a correction in the person's behaviour, not to dismiss them or particularly upset them but just to correct the situation before it becomes more difficult. The staff member feels they need to defend their behaviour. Before starting the role-play you should think what each person wants to get from the meeting, write it down and reveal whether you succeeded at the end.

The second major cause for complaint concerns character and or personality shortcomings. In what is sometimes a very demanding, busy and yet exciting environment, supervisory staff are required to maintain control, not only of any operational situation but maintain control of both their own and their staffs emotions, perhaps deal with distraught staff or angry staff and of course the occasional demanding or dissatisfied customer. Lastly failure to supervise may be the result of an inherent inability to perform management tasks.

Understanding motivation

Through the process of correct recruitment and continued self-development through training, staff are inherently self-motivating. It is therefore management's responsibility to maintain this motivation by monitoring and facilitating in five key areas:

1. Achievement should be recognized and opportunities to achieve should be available by setting realistic targets and goals that can be attained.
2. Recognition for effort and results can be very motivational and encourage further effort.
3. Job interest is an important motivator and management should be aware that any proposed changes in a job specification may effect this.
4. Responsibility enables staff to show their dependability and gives them the opportunity to show their potential to undertake a more senior role.
5. Advancement, most people look to advance within an organization, renews job interest and allows the attainment of the more tangible aspects of career development.

Group activity 2

Hotel service staff have become very de-motivated since the introduction of annualized hours (a system of working long hours during busy periods with extended days off during quiet periods to balance average hours worked over the year so that they aggregate to the hours shown in their contract of employment). Consider both the potential difficulties and benefits for both the staff and the employer of adopting an annualized hours contract and then discuss how the issue of de-motivation may be addressed.

Summary

- Issues to do with staffing are likely to be the most difficult issues that any manager has to deal with. People are naturally demanding, complex, have their own agendas and are sometimes very emotional.
- Problems associated with staff turnover can affect other employees and have the potential to drive profitability down.
- Employment statistics can provide a good benchmark from which it is possible to measure other establishment's performance, for without measurement there can be no management.
- Key elements are recruitment, setting recruitment criteria and understanding some of the methods together with their associated costs.

- Maximizing profitability by accurately forecasting demand and associated levels of staffing with the need for proper staff induction and training.
- Supervision and management can be problematic; some of the pitfalls are being unprepared, ill informed and poor communicators.
- Staff motivation and retention should be a manager's first staff management priority.

Further study options

As this chapter has demonstrated there are a number of specific areas to do with staffing issues that are worthy of further study. Looking at the statistics we can see that staff recruitment, staff retention, staff training and staff development are all key issues. Recruitment consultants seem to be at the sharp end of the staff recruitment business, it is a highly competitive industry and is best suited to those with a ruthless and highly tenacious attitude, and it can be very stressful. 'Human Resource Management' (HRM) is the term most companies use to describe their overall personnel activities and there are many texts available on this subject. For those thinking of a career in HRM the likely route would be to study for membership of the Chartered Institute of Personnel and Development (CIPD). Staff retention, training and development are usually in-house activities although there are specialist companies that will provide special training. Generally, any manager of staff is likely to have some involvement with one if not all of these areas and there are a number of texts designed to help managers manage staff. These include books on organizational behaviour, HRM, staff motivation and managing change.

Study exercise

The Rat and Toad is a large public house situated on the outskirts of a busy market town in the Home Counties. Revenues are down on the previous year despite longer trading hours and overall profitability has reduced even more dramatically. The pub manager believes that the decline is the result of excessive staff turnover, which has slowly worsened since the brewery failed to increase basic pay rates or to address issues of late night working since new licensing allowed the pub to trade later into the night. The manager had previously worked in a hotel bar which had also had staff turnover problems estimated at 25% per year but this had not unduly affect the hotel bar revenue or profits. The Rat and Toad have a total

335

annual workforce of 22 people. They work as follows, twelve part-time staff working an average of twelve hours per week, six full-time staff working forty hours per week and have four seasonal staff working forty hours per week for ten weeks in the year. During the past year ten staff have left, eight part-time and two full-time.

Using the information and formula in this chapter:

1. Calculate the average staff turnover.
2. Estimate the cost of recruitment.
3. Discuss the issues concerning less obvious costs identified.
4. Make a case to bring about change.

Review questions

1. Given the current structure of the UK employment pool what proportion of employees will be aged fifty-five by 2009?
2. How does the 'service profit chain' link satisfied employees with profit growth?
3. What strategies might you consider using to reduce staff turnover?
4. Why is it important for managers to calculate staff turnover?
5. What drives up costs in staff recruitment?
6. What forms the legal framework on which an employment is based?
7. What action can employees take if they believe they have been unfairly dismissed?
8. What are the minimum requirements that a contract of employment should specify?
9. What are the main barriers to effective communication?
10. What does an annualized hour's contract entail?

Further reading

Benny, R., Sargeant, M. and Jefferson, M. (2004). *Employment Law (Blackstone's Law Q&A)*. UK: Oxford University Press.

Burd, M. and Davies, J. (2007). Workplace rights: Don't quota us. *Management Today*, 00251925, March 2007.

Heskett, J. L., Sasser, W. E., Jr. and Schlesinger, L. A. (1997). *The Service Profit Chain. How Leading Companies Link Profit and Growth to Loyalty, Satisfaction and Value.* New York: The Free Press.

Labour Market Statistics (2006). *Office of National Statistics,* London SW1V 2QQ: 1 Drummond Gate.

Silver, A. (30 August 2007). Opinion: Turn down the staff turnover. *Caterer and Hotelkeeper,* 197, 4491.

Trends and Statistics (2006). *British Hospitality Association,* Queens House, 55–56 Lincoln's Inn Fields, London WC2A 3BH.

http://www.winters.co.uk/factsheets/dismissal_procedures.html.

http://www.legislation.hmso.gov.uk/acts/acts2002/20020022html.

Food and beverage marketing

Introduction

Marketing in food and beverage operations can be extremely challenging as managers have to consider how to market both the tangible elements of the meal experience as well as the intangible ones. In order for a transaction to take place the consumer must be present and that makes the consumer part of the product which adds to the challenge of how to market the product effectively. As different customers have different experiences, expectations and perceptions, it can be hard to maintain absolute consistency of the product and service. Furthermore, the Perishability of both the actual products sold and the seats available in a food and beverage operation make marketing an extremely important function for the successful management of any food and beverage business. In this chapter we examine basic marketing definitions as well as the nature of services, market segmentation and market mix. We look at each stage of the product life cycle, and marketing components such as marketing research, advertising, the brand, internet marketing, public relations and merchandising. All of these components need to be given careful consideration in order to run a successful food and beverage operation.

After working through this chapter you should be able to:

1. Understand the essentials of marketing for services.
2. Understand the basics of marketing for food and beverage operations.
3. Understand the basics of advertising for food and beverage operations.
4. Understand the basics of public relations, merchandising and promotions for food and beverage operations.
5. Understand personal selling and upselling.

MARKETING

There are a number of definitions in the public domain as to what marketing is and there is an ongoing debate as to the effectiveness of marketing techniques. According to Kotler (2006), marketing is a social process by which individuals and groups obtain what they need and want through creating and exchanging products and value with others.

The effects of marketing in a business can be an elusive concept. It can be quite hard for a business person to believe in something that is very hard to quantify. If a restaurateur spends a considerable amount of money for a marketing campaign he can never be sure that these customers that turn up through his doors are because of that marketing campaign. Of course there is a plethora of evidence to show that marketing is extremely effective for large organizations that have the necessary budgets to support such activities with impressive results. We can list a number of companies that continually invest in marketing but Coca-Cola or McDonald's, might be the two that easily spring to ones mind.

Matching service and product delivery to customer expectations is no longer enough (Figure 10.1). With increasing competition, exceeding customer expectations has now become a must.

Understanding the marketing concept helps to understand the benefits that marketing will have to any business. For a company to be market oriented it would have to understand and adopt the following elements of the marketing concept:

1. The position of the customer as the focal point of a business is central to the marketing concept.

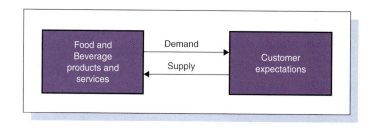

Figure 10.1
The matching process of marketing

2. It is a positive management attitude that permeates through an organization towards the satisfaction of its customers' needs and wants.
3. It recognizes the need for an organization to increase its short- and long-term profits.
4. An organization is aware of its external environment by monitoring, analysing and responding to it.

Furthermore we can distinguish between product orientation and sales orientation.

1. Product orientation is mostly adopted by organizations whose products are currently in demand, producing profit, and the organization is concerned with lowering unit costs by working towards a high volume production and economies of scale. The emphasis, therefore, is towards the product, aspects such as its design, production, quality standards, costs and pricing.
2. Sales orientation is mostly adopted by organizations whose products are not currently in great demand and the organization is concerned with increasing its volume sales. The emphasis, therefore, is towards selling and the generation of increased demand for its products. Many sales orientated businesses are of a high, fixed capital nature, for example, hotels and restaurants.

Of course a combination of these two may be what the specific business needs, or changes in the market may require a shift from one orientation to the other.

Activity

Match the suggested organizations to the type of orientation you believe most fits the particular organization.

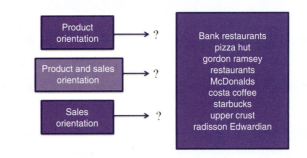

Make a list of food and beverage organizations that you think are most likely to adopt a product orientation. Do the same for organizations that you believe adopt a sales orientated approach in their marketing.

The marketing of services

Services are generally accepted as being 'performed' whereas goods are 'objects' that have been produced. Service industries include, for example banking, insurance, retailing and hairdressing. Manufacturing industries include those producing goods, for example cars, tinned foods, televisions and catering equipment.

However, for the purposes of this book, the following characteristics may be said to be relevant to services in general and food service operations where applicable:

1. The customer is present at the time of both production and service. In service industries, for example, in a restaurant offering conventional food service, customers wait for the food to be prepared, are served their meal at a table and the product is consumed. There is no time delay between production of the meal and service to the customer. In the manufacturing industry, for example, the manufacture of electrical goods, furniture or tinned foods, the customer is not present during the production process. There may also be a considerable time delay between the product being manufactured in a factory, delivered to a shop, its time on the shelf, being purchased by a customer, stored at home and finally being consumed.

2. Exceptions in the food service industry would include cook-freeze, cook-chill and sous-vide operations where production and service are separated, and only at the last stage of production is the customer present, for example, the regeneration process of cook-chill meals in a school kitchen or in a hotel kitchen, prior to banquet service.

3. The customer is involved in the creation of the service. In service industries, the customer involvement is a requirement for the creation of the service, for example in hairdressers, a bank or a self-service restaurant. The degree of customer involvement can vary, simply from their presence in a coffee shop so that the meal may be served and the service element of the product completed, to a self-service vending cafeteria where customers actually contribute to the production of the service by selecting a cook-chill meal, re-heating it in a microwave, taking it to a table, and possibly clearing away themselves afterwards.

4. The service product is consumed at the point of production. Customers go to a bank, or restaurant, for consumption of the service and, in this way, become part of the total product.

5. An exception in the food service industry would be takeaways where, as their name implies, the food is taken away for consumption.

6. Services cannot be examined in advance. In service industries the customer is rarely able to examine the service in advance.

7. Customers entering a supermarket may have a number of different brands of products that they are able to physically compare in terms of appearance, content and price. Customers

using a service such as banking or a fast-food restaurant do not. In the food service industry examples of where the tangible product can at least be seen in advance include self-service food and beverage displays such as cafeterias, buffets, coffee shop trolleys and vending machines.

8. Increased contact time between service staff and customers. Because customers personally go to the operations establishment they have more personal contact time with the service staff and possibly those involved in production.

9. Service industries distribution channels consist of people so that the training of production and particularly service staff in customer relation skills becomes very important. Generally speaking, services which have a high personnel input tend to be more difficult to manage than those with a high equipment input, and the more customized the service, the more contact time between service staff and customers.

10. Services are perishable. An unsold hotel room for the night, or a lunchtime restaurant seat left vacant, is lost forever. Once produced, services must be consumed and, because of their perishability, services are more vulnerable to fluctuation in demand. Sales instability is typical of most catering establishments. There is often a change in the volume of business from day to day and, in many establishments, from hour to hour. This causes basic problems with regard to the quantities of commodities to be purchased and prepared, the staffing required and the availability of the components at times of production in line with the price that can be afforded in relation to the selling price.

11. Services cannot be stored. By their very nature, services cannot be stored. A restaurant open for six and a half hours during the day can only sell its services during those hours. Once closed, it cannot produce any more services to be stored and sold the next day. Peaks of activity are common in service industries. In a hotel, for example, the peaks would typically be breakfast, lunch and dinner service. Resort hotels have peak activity months during the summer and quieter months during the winter. The balance between demand and supply in a service industry is therefore critical; where demand exceeds supply, the result is lost sales and disappointed customers. In terms of marketing implications, an organization may try to spread the level of demand by pricing differentials.

12. Difficulties in quality control. Because there is virtually no time delay between production and consumption of a service, the control of quality becomes very difficult. The speed at which catering operations take place for example, relative to other manufacturing industries, allows little time for many control tasks. It is not uncommon that items ordered one day are received, processed and sold the same or the following day. It is for this reason that in large catering establishments cost reporting is done daily or at least weekly.

13. Services have high fixed costs. Service industries have a high degree of fixed costs relative to any other industries. Customers go to a service operation to purchase a product, services are not taken to customers. A hotel, a bank, a pizza restaurant will still have all the fixed costs every twenty-four hours of trading whether fifty or 250 customers pass through the doors. In the manufacturing industry, supply can be increased or decreased to meet fluctuations in demand much more easily, particularly where production is highly automated.

14. Services have an intangible element. It has been suggested that services represent a performance, whereas goods are produced.

The marketing environment

No business operates in isolation. In a large hotel, for example, there may be a number of different style catering operations – several bars, a coffee shop, a carvery, a speciality restaurant. Although initially they may appear to operate as self-sufficient units, they do, in fact, all have a cause and effect relationship with each other. They are subsystems operating within a much larger system – the hotel. A 'system' may be defined as an interaction of all parts or subsystems, with the whole not equal to but actually greater than the sum of its parts. The food and beverage department in a hotel consists of a series of closely linked subsystems – the kitchen, bars, restaurants, etc. – which, together, form the whole – the food and beverage system.

Often to understand the environment an organization will perform a PESTLE (Political, Economic, Social, Technological, Legal and Environmental issues) analysis. Which stands for Political (The current and potential influences from political pressures), Economic (The local, national and world economy impact), Sociological (The ways in which changes in society affect us), Technological (How new and emerging technology affects our business), Legal (How local, national and world legislation affects us) and Environmental (The local, national and world environmental issues) analysis. Looking closely at each of those components allows businesses to get a better understanding of the environment they operate in and thus gaining a better understanding of their business. One has to keep in mind that each of these factors are constantly changing and that can cause problems when trying to assess the external factors affecting your business (see Figure 10.2).

Market segmentation

Market segmentation is the identification of a group or groups of customers within an organization's total market. The total market may be divided into different segments, each requiring different market mixes. At one extreme there exists the mass market where an organization uses the same strategy to market its products to

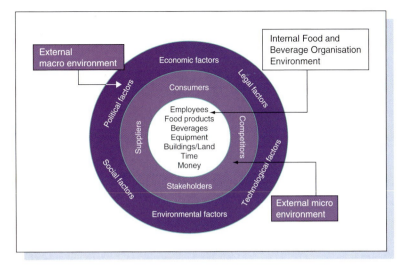

Figure 10.2
The food and beverage
marketing environment

all segments of the market. At the other, an organization is able to identify a very specific market segment and market its products specifically to that segment.

Activity

Identify a major fast-food chain advert or poster that targets kids. Compare that to one that targets a completely different market segment.

Ensure both posters/adverts are from the same company.

What are the key differences and what are the similarities?

Market segmentation is an important aspect of market planning. An organization cannot be all things to all people. To market its products cost effectively, it must clearly identify its customers and the market segments they belong to. Without this clear identification of the organization's markets, its whole marketing activity is wasted in terms of time, resources and finance. A good example of targeting specific market segments is that of children's menus. Family friendly restaurants will always feature such menus ensuring they communicate to their customers that they cater for their children (see Figure 10.3).

In the food service industry some of the following demographic and geographic criteria may be used to identify market segments:

1. *Geographic*: The identification of market segments by geographic area may be at international, national or local level. At the international level different cultures may not be appropriate for the introduction of certain products; regional differences of food exist within the same country; at a local level a fish and chip shop may draw most of its custom from a two or three mile radius, whereas customers may be willing to travel ten times that distance to a specialized quality restaurant.

menu

80	**mini ramen**		£3.35
	slices of grilled chicken breast served on noodles in a tasty vegetarian stack topped with fresh spinach, shredded carrots and sweetcorn		
81	**chicken noodle**		£3.95
	slices of grilled chicken breast served on noodles with a sliced apple, mandarin and sesame tossed salad, served with amai sauce		
83	**mini chicken katsu**		£3.50
	deep fried breadcrumbed chicken breast served with japanese style rice, shredded cucumber and a lightly spiced curry sauce		
84	**mini ramen vegetarian**		£2.95
	deep fried cubes of tofu served on noodles in a tasty vegetarian stock topped with fresh spinach, shredded carrots and sweet corn		
85	**ebi rice**		£4.25
	deep fried breadcrumbed prawns served with japanese style rice, shredded cucumber and an amai sauce dip		

Figure 10.3 Wagamama children's menu (UK) (*Source*: Courtesy of Wagamama.com)

2. *Age group*: Specific market segments may be identified in the food service industry according to their age. The younger 18–30 age group are more willing to experience new ideas, they like to dine and be seen in fashionable restaurants and bars. The older age group may experiment less, but could form a large part of a restaurant's repeat business.

3. *Socio-economic classification*: This is a form of general classification used by JICNARS (Joint Industry Committee for National Readership Surveys), dividing the population into six groups (A, B, C1, C2, D and E) and classifying the head of the household's occupation into the groups shown in Table 10.1. The requirements and expectations of people within each of these groups differ significantly as does the amount of money they have available and are prepared to spend.

4. *Income*: The higher the disposable income, the higher the propensity to spend more on dining out. Areas that have high percentage of ABs are, therefore, able to sustain a higher percentage of expensive restaurants than areas largely made up of CDs.

5. *Family life cycle*: This form of classification is based on identifying stages within the cycle of family life and how each stage affects the family's purchasing behaviour (see Table 10.2).

6. Another example is that of the ACORN classification created by CACI (www.caci.co.uk). This classification clusters the UK population into five categories, seventeen groups and fifty-six

Social grade	Social status	Chief income earner of household	Estimated number	Estimated %
A	Upper middle class	Higher managerial, administrative or professional	1,932	4.0
B	Middle class	Intermediate managerial, administrative or professional	10,573	21.9
C1	Lower middle class	Supervisory or clerical and junior managerial, administrative or professional	13,982	29.0
C2	Skilled working class	Skilled manual workers	9,964	20.7
D	Working class	Semi and unskilled manual workers	7,819	16.2
E	Those at the lowest levels of subsistence	Entirely dependent on state for long-term income	3,916	8.1
Totals			48,186	100

Base: Population of Great Britain age 15+; NRS Jan-Dec 2006; *Source*: National Readership Survey

Table 10.1
Population estimates by social grade 2006

Family status	Twice a week or more	About once a week	About once a fortnight	At least once a month	At least once every three months	Less than once every three months
Marital status:	%	%	%	%	%	%
Married/living as married	8	18	16	24	15	13
Not married	12	17	13	21	11	15
Single	15	18	15	22	10	12
Widowed/ divorced/ separated	9	16	9	20	11	21
Own children in household:						
Aged 0–4	11	15	17	25	15	10
Aged 5–9	12	14	16	24	16	13
Aged 10–14	7	16	13	31	15	13
Any 0–14	9	16	15	26	15	12
No children	10	18	14	21	13	15

Base: 2,029 adults aged 15+; *Source*: Adapted from GFKNop/Mintel, 2007

Table 10.2
Frequency of eating out by family status

types, combining demographics and lifestyle information to enable marketers to target consumers more effectively (see Table 10.3).

The marketing mix

In order for the exchange process to take place in marketing, the organization must decide how to market itself to those segments it has identified, and how to influence customers' behaviour to buy. It does this by means of the marketing mix which according to Kotler it is defined as the mixture of controllable marketing variables that the firm uses to pursue the sought level of sales in the target market.

The four marketing variables that are generally accepted as being the tools of the marketing mix are the *four Ps* (McCarthy,

Category	% of Pop.	Group	% of Pop.	Type		% of Pop.
Wealthy Achievers 1 26.6%		A Wealthy Executives	8.6	1	Wealthy mature professionals, large houses	1.7
				2	Wealthy working families with mortgages	1.5
				3	Villagers with wealthy commuters	2.7
				4	Well-off managers, larger houses	2.6
		B Affluent Greys	7.7	5	Older affluent professionals	1.8
				6	Farming communities	2.0
				7	Old people, detached homes	1.9
				8	Mature couples, smaller detached homes	2.0
		C Flourishing Families	8.8	9	Older families, prosperous suburbs	2.5
				10	Well-off working families with mortgages	2.3
				11	Well-off managers, detached houses	3.7
				12	Large families and houses in rural areas	0.6
Urban Prosperity 2 10.7%		D Prosperous Professionals	2.2	13	Well-off professionals, larger houses and converted flats	0.9
				14	Older professionals in suburban houses and apartments	1.4
		E Educated Urbanites	4.6	15	Affluent urban professionals, flats	1.1
				16	Prosperous young professionals, flats	0.9
				17	Young educated workers, flats	0.6
				18	Multi-ethnic young, converted flats	1.5
				19	Suburban privately renting professionals	0.9
		F Aspiring Singles	3.9	20	Student flats and cosmopolitan sharers	0.6
				21	Singles and sharers, multi-ethnic areas	1.6
				22	Low income singles, small rented flats	1.2
				23	Student terraces	0.4
Comfortably Off 3 26.6%		G Starting Out	2.5	24	Young couples, flats and terraces	1.0
				25	White-collar singles/sharers, terraces	1.4
		H Secure Families	15.5	26	Younger white-collar couples with mortgages	1.9
				27	Middle income, home owning areas	2.9
				28	Working families with mortgages	2.6
				29	Mature families in suburban semis	3.3
				30	Established home owning workers	3.6
				31	Home owning Asian family areas	1.3
		I Settled Suburbia	6	32	Retired home owners	0.9
				33	Middle income, older couples	3.0
				34	Lower incomes, older people, semis	2.1
		J Prudent Pensioners	2.6	35	Elderly singles, purpose built flats	0.7
				36	Older people, flats	1.9
Moderate Means 4 14.5%		K Asian Communities	1.6	37	Crowded Asian terraces	0.5
				38	Low income Asian families	1.1
		L Post-Industrial Families	4.8	39	Skilled older families, terraces	2.8
				40	Young working families	2.1
		M Blue-collar Roots	8	41	Skilled workers, semis and terraces	3.3
				42	Home owning families, terraces	2.8
				43	Older people, rented terraces	1.8
Hard-Pressed 5 22.4%		N Struggling Families	14.1	44	Low income larger families, semis	3.3
				45	Low income, older people, smaller semis	3.0
				46	Low income, routine jobs, terraces and flats	1.4
				47	Low income families, terraced estates	2.6
				48	Families and single parents, semis and terraces	2.1
				49	Large families and single parents, many children	1.7
		O Burdened Singles	4.5	50	Single elderly people, council flats	1.8
				51	Single parents and pensioners, council terraces	1.9
				52	Families and single parents, council flats	0.8
		P High-Rise Hardship	1.6	53	Old people, many high-rise flats	0.8
				54	Singles and single parents, high-rise estates	0.9
		Q Inner City Adversity	2.1	55	Multi-ethnic purpose built estates	1.1
				56	Multi-ethnic, crowded flats	1.1
		U Unclassified	0.3	57	Mainly communal population	0.3

Table 10.3
ACORN targeting classification *Source*: Copyright CACI 2007, reprinted with permission

in Kotler 2006). They may be applied to food and beverage operations in the following way:

1. *Product*: The product basically consists of its tangible and intangible features. Its tangible or physical characteristics include the quality of foods and beverages produced and served, the restaurant decor, table arrangements, menu design, portion sizes, life cycle, etc. The intangible features of the product are those that satisfy the 'feelings' of the customer – the atmosphere of the restaurant, the image it wishes to portray, the attitude of the service staff.

2. *Price*: The prices charged by the catering operation are the balance between the organization on the one side with its need to achieve profitable sales, and the customers on the other with their views as to what they are willing to pay for its products. Varying price levels may be used for different products in different market segments. Pricing variables include à la carte or table d'hôte menus, whether government and service taxes are to be inclusive or exclusive, if discounts are to be given to group bookings, or reductions for meals ordered before a certain hour.

3. *Promotion*: The promotion, or communication mix, is concerned with informing the market about an organization's products and persuading them to buy. It may be on a personal level, for example service staff in a restaurant, or it may be impersonal, for example advertising or merchandising.

4. *Place*: This aspect of the marketing mix is concerned with a number of factors: the location of the catering outlet, for example the haute cuisine restaurant, or coffee shop within a hotel; the siting of a centralized cook-chill operation and its peripheral units; the availability and accessibility of the location and product to the customers; the distribution channels and methods of transportation to be used, the inventory levels to be set.

These basic *four Ps* have been increased to *seven Ps* by Bitner (1991). These three are especially of interest to operations such as food and beverage outlets.

5. *Process*: The actual procedures, mechanisms and flow of activities by which the service is delivered (e.g. seating the guest, taking of food orders, dealing with questions and complaints, etc.).

6. *Physical evidence*: The environment in which the organization and the customer meet and interact, plus the tangible elements that facilitate the performance of communication of the service delivery (e.g. exterior/interior appearance of building, restaurant floor plan, decor, lighting, table layout, staff uniforms, menus, tent cards, etc.).

7. *Participants*: The individual – staff and other customers with whom the customer interacts with (e.g. hostess, restaurant manager, waiter and other customers, etc.).

Different marketing mixes are required for different market segments. In a shopping mall, for example, the marketing mix for a pasta bar would be different to that required for the coffee shop. The more segmented the market, the more detailed the marketing mix can become.

The product life cycle

The concept of the product life cycle (PLC) is that from a product's launch on to the market, until it is withdrawn, it passes through a series of stages. These four stages form an S-shaped curve and are usually described as introduction, growth, maturity and decline. Each stage has a number of particular features in terms of costs, sales, profit and competition (see Figure 10.4).

1. *Introduction*: Costs at this stage are high: research and product development; stock levels to be set; advertising and sales promotion costs for the launching of the new product; managerial time and resources, etc. Sales are from first-time buyers and will be significantly affected by the success or failure of the promotional campaign. Profit is minimal, if any, owing to the high financial commitment at this stage. Losses are common. Competition is also minimal, the new product is at its infancy and many competitors choose to sit back to see the outcome.

2. *Growth*: Costs are lower as marketing research and the high initial publicity costs are more a feature of the introductory phase of a new product. Sales growth is rapid as the market expands – first-time buyers may become repeat purchasers. Profitability can be at its highest owing to increased sales and the overall reduction in costs. Depending on the success of the product launch, competition may now enter the market which has the effect of enlarging the total market for the product due to their additional advertising and promotion.

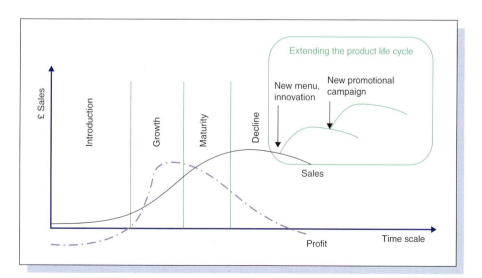

Figure 10.4 Product life cycle and extending the PLC

3. *Maturity*: Costs in the maturity stage may increase again, particularly in terms of promotion as the organization seeks to retain its market share. Sales gradually level out as competition from products of other companies take a share of the total market, and the growth of the organization slows. As the sales levels stabilize, so do the profits – prices are reduced in order to compete, promotional costs erode profitability levels and total demand for the product stabilizes.

4. *Decline*: As the market becomes further saturated with products, some organizations may leave the market altogether. Costs become disproportionately high in an attempt to hold the company's position in the market. Sales and profit levels fall as too many products compete for an ever decreasing percentage of the market, demand falls while supply remains in abundance.

5. At the decline stage a company may reinvent its strategy or create some innovative products or even a new promotional campaign could reinvigorate sales and spur a new growth for the sales of the company (see Figure 10.5). Understanding at which stage of the product life cycle the operation is can be crucial as different strategies would be adopted for a mature organization as opposed to one that is in its introductory stage.

Marketing research

Marketing research involves systematically collecting, storing and analysing information, both internally and externally, for an organization. Once the information has been collected, it may be used for the purpose of examining any aspects of the organization's marketing activities.

1. *Primary information*: Primary information is new information that the organization will usually have to go outside of its own confines to gather. Professional marketing research companies may be used or the organization can tailor-make its own. Primary information is more expensive and time consuming because the data first has to be collected in the field before it can be analysed.

2. *Secondary information*: Secondary information is information that has previously been collected either within the organization itself or it already exists externally. Within the organization 'desk research' often highlights a number of areas that have stored information useful to marketing research, for example:
   - Reservations made in a restaurant, recording client and contact name, address and telephone number, method of reservation, frequency of usage and special rates given.
   - Sales records, identifying products, quantities sold, sales cycles, average spends, methods of payment, cash or credit.
   - Purchasing documents, percentage of convenience and fresh foods being used, food and beverage costs and budgets compared, shortfalls, pilferage and wastage.
   - Staff meetings held between management and staff.

Figure 10.5
Bombardier advertisment.
Celebrating Englishness
campaign (*Source*: Courtesy of
Wells and Young's Ltd 2007)

Outside the organization, there is a wealth of information available:

- Government publications and statistics.
- Professional trade associations, publications, conferences and meetings.
- Educational establishments.
- Other publications, guides, journals, newspapers and television.

The brand

One of the most debated concepts by academics and practitioners alike is that of a brand. According to Walter Landor, of the Landon associates branding consultancy brand can be defined

Owner	Number of outlets	Brands
Whitbread	1,603	Beefeater, Brewer's Fayre, TGI Friday's
McDonald's	1,263	
Spirit Group	798	Chef and Brewer
Burger King	724	
Pizza Express	386	
Wimpy	274	
Mitchells and Butler	263	Harvester
The Restaurant Group	253	Garfunkel's Frankie and Benny's
Little Chef	233	
Ask	186	
Tragus	160	Cafe Rouge, Bella Italia
Nando's	100	
Out of Town Restaurant Group	97	Bitz and Pizza, Bradwells
Greene King	90	Hungry Horse
Compass/EQT	72	Harry Ramsden's
DPP Restaurants	54	Deep Pan Pizza

Source: BHA Trends and Statistics, 2005

Table 10.4
Top restaurant groups

as a promise. By identifying and authenticating a product or service it delivers a pledge of satisfaction and quality. A brand is quite different from advertising and although advertising alone cannot help establish a brand. Some may argue that a brand can only be created by big organizations, however it can be said that even small businesses can create a brand for the market that they are dealing with, the scale is smaller but the concept remains the same. To build a brand a food and beverage organization must first deliver what it promises and if possible not only meet, but exceed customer expectations. Today we have seen individuals becoming a brand, for example, if a celebrity chef opens a new restaurant it can be expected that business will be far better simply because customers will associate the chefs name with a promise of exceptional food. Gordon Ramsay, for example, has created a strong brand around his name due to the effective use of the media. As the brand gets stronger and stronger customers will talk about a business to colleagues, friends and relatives and the business will enjoy loyal customers but also new customers due to positive 'word of mouth'. Some examples of worldwide recognized food and beverage related brands are McDonalds, Starbucks, T.G.I Fridays, Nandos and Burger King (Table 10.4)

Figure 10.6 Website of the Magnolia Restaurant in London, UK (*Source*: Reprinted with permission www.magnolia.uk.com)

Internet marketing

Another effective form of marketing is that of Internet marketing. Particularly for small businesses the Internet provides an opportunity for global exposure. A restaurant card featuring the restaurants web address can enable customers to check the menu before they arrive, they can have virtual tours of the business or even book a table online and take advantage of special promotions (see Figure 10.6).

There are different levels of Internet marketing and the simplest level is that of using a website as a mere electronic billboard with no interactivity for the customer. Even at that stage a website can be a supplementary tool that directs customers from a business card to an area that can provide more information about your business. The other end of the spectrum is a fully interactive website where customers can more than just glance at the operations menu or contact information. They can download recipes, reserve a table and even choose which table to reserve, can read other customers comments, purchase merchandise online and even enjoy interactive cooking lessons.

The web is a fast less expensive medium that potentially speaks to a global audience and can offer wider and deeper material to the consumer. Furthermore every time a customer books a table he or she can be entered in a database which can then make it easy to the restaurateur to communicate direct with customers who are already interested in the product he/she has to offer.

Activity

Internet marketing. Go to www.google.com and type the keyword 'Restaurant'.

Visit some of the sponsored links. What type of websites are the majority of sponsored links?

Also take a note of the top 10 non-sponsored links. Perform the same search one week later. Do you notice any differences in the rankings of the websites? If yes, then why do you think is that?

ADVERTISING

Advertising is concerned with contacting and informing a market of an operation's product, away from the point of sale and is involved with influencing the customers' behaviour and attitude to the product before they enter the service operation.

Advertising has been defined by the American Marketing Association as 'Any paid form of non-personal presentation and promotion of ideas, goods or services by an identified sponsor'. Its purpose, as defined by the Institute of Practitioners in Advertising (IPA) is 'to influence a person's knowledge, attitude and behaviour in such a way as to meet the objectives of the advertiser'.

The aims and objectives of an operation's advertising policy should be contained within the marketing plan. No advertising campaign ought to be undertaken unless it has been properly organized and is going to be efficiently managed. Disorganized advertising will not benefit an establishment; it may, in fact, do a great deal of harm. It is, therefore, wrong to assume that any advertising is better than no advertising.

The size of a food services advertising budget is dependent on a number of factors:

1. The nature of the catering operation, whether it is in the commercial or non-commercial sector.
2. The size of the operation. Generally speaking, the larger the commercial operation, the larger the advertising budget available.
3. The ownership of the catering facility. In a small, privately owned hotel or restaurant, the responsibility for advertising may be in the hands of the owner or manager. In a large multi-unit organization, the responsibility for advertising is either assigned to a specialist department within the organization, or given to a professional outside advertising agency.
4. The number and nature of the market segments being aimed at.
5. The amount of advertising each market segment requires to be adequately covered.
6. The type of advertising to be used. Peak time national television coverage will obviously cost considerably more than a local radio broadcast.

In some sectors of the industry advertising budgets are very large. The fast-food sector, for example, surpasses any others in the catering industry. Generally speaking, advertising expenditure in this sector of the industry varies from 0.5% to 4.5% turnover. Companies within the hotel industry are also increasing their advertising budgets considerably (Table 10.5).

Where small owner-managed or small groups of hotels cannot afford to individually advertise their properties and facilities to any great effect, they may group together to form a marketing consortium to achieve greater advertising impact. By joining together with other small or similar operations, an individual establishment benefits from being part of a large organization.

Whatever the size of the food service facility, however, advertising does have relevance and importance. In order to be effective, there must be a clear understanding of the purposes and objectives of advertising. In a catering operation these would include the following:

- To create awareness of the product.
- To create desire for the product.
- To influence customers attitudes to the product.
- To create brand loyalty.
- To persuade customers to buy.
- To persuade customers to visit an operation in preference to a competitor's.
- To remind customers to buy.
- To inform the market about a product.
- To provide reassurance about the product.
- To be ethical.

The following advertising techniques are all applicable in some way to both commercial and non-commercial operations. However, depending largely on the sector of the industry and

Table 10.5
Main media advertising expenditure for selected chains (UK)

Restaurant chain	Direct mail	Outdoor	Press	Radio	Total
	£	£	£	£	£
Bank Restaurant Group Plc	–	–	1,331	–	1,331
City Centre Restaurants	–	12,648	11,307	391	24,346
Conran Restaurants Ltd	–	–	1,573	–	1,573
La Tasca	–	–	3,711	156	3,867
Loch Fyne	57,310	–	15,915	194	73,419
Ma Potters	–	–	3,875	–	3,875

Source: ACNielsen MMS, 2005

the size of the advertising budget available, the larger commercial organizations are able to utilize many or all of these advertising tools, whereas smaller non-commercial operations will be restricted to only a few. The major forms of advertising that may be employed by food service facilities include the following:

Direct mail, and email

Direct mail involves communicating by post to specified customers; it may be directed at new and potential customers or to past or well-established customers. It involves the direct mailing of personalized letters, brochures, pamphlets and leaflets, and as a form of advertising offers a number of advantages:

1. Specific customers can be targeted.
2. Direct mail and emailing is easy to introduce.
3. The feedback from targeted customers is relatively prompt and easy to appraise.
4. It is a cost-effective method of advertising to specifically targeted groups of customers with very little 'wastage' (Figure 10.7).

However, direct mail also has a number of disadvantages:

1. The market must be specifically targeted or the mail shots are a complete waste of money.
2. The mail must be received, read and acted upon by the specific individual or group or all prior advertising research has also been a waste. An email can be easily deleted or considered 'junk mail'.

Subject: ACORN HOUSE RESTAURANT NEWSLETTER
From: 'R
Date: Thu, August 16, 2007 3:40 pm
To: 'R
Priority: Normal
Options: View Full Header | View Printable Version

```
Summer greetings
Although the weather report might be telling another story, according to the
calendar it's Summer. And if we can't feel it in the temperature outside perhaps
we'll just have to sate ourselves indoors with the Acorn House August menu (see
below to plan your meal). It's a feast of zucchini flowers, black figs and Summer
berries.
How does our garden grow?
The garden is at last starting to resemble a garden - with bright swathes of 'Acorn
House' green springing up.. at least the peas and beans are welcoming the rain!
Morning glory
For those who don't have their coffee loyalty card yet -come and get one -five
stamps and you get your sixth coffee free. It should help brighten up your walk
along Gray's Inn Road. And coming soon. We will be introducing Rude Health mueslis
and cereals in convenient small packs, perfect for taking to the office for a
high-energy start to the day.
Acorn on-line
For a 'virtual' restaurant experience, check out a day in the life of Acorn House on
You Tube. Shot by the friendly guys from Some Like It Shot, the camera follows some
of our future big-name chefs Tom, Nat and Lloyd, and of course Arthur Potts Dawson.
```

Figure 10.7 Extract of the Acorn House Restaurant newsletter (London, UK) (*Source*: email, reprinted with permission Acorn House Restaurant)

3. The production of good-quality mailing literature can be costly. Personalized letters should ideally be used as duplicated material has little impact and is often discarded straight away. The envelope too must encourage the recipient to open it rather than discarding it as a circular. Once the initial mail has been sent out, careful monitoring of subsequent replies is necessary; often further advertising material may need to be distributed to reinforce the initial sales literature.

The identification of the market segments to be aimed at is most important. As with marketing research, the operation may find that through its own desk research – internal and external – it can amass a considerable amount of information about its markets through restaurant reservations, sales records, trade journals, local newspapers, etc. If a restaurant is considering featuring special business lunches, for example, it may consider writing to civic and business associations and asking for their membership lists, as well as contacting any other professional groups in the area. Alternatively, a catering operation may consider using a professional mail service agency. Here again, it is important to specify exactly the section of the market to be aimed at.

Press advertising

1. *Newspapers*: Advertising in national and local newspapers and magazines is probably one of the most popular forms of media used by catering operations. Because restaurant advertisements are generally featured together in a newspaper, it is essential that the design of an advertisement featuring a particular restaurant is such that it will stand apart from the others (see Figure 10.8).
2. *Magazines*: The different types of magazines in which a catering operation may choose to advertise include professional journals and publications, business management magazines and the 'social' type magazines which are read by particular target market groups. The advantages of advertising in specific magazines are that response may be measured, they have a longer 'shelf life' than newspapers and may be re-read many times.
3. *Guides*: There are a number of 'Good Food Guides' produced in which food service facilities may wish to be included. Such well-known guides are the AA and RAC guides, The Michelin Guide, The Egon Ronay Guide, The Good Food Guide and the Tourist Board Guides. To be featured in these guides will often be as a result of passing a professional inspection by the particular organization and at times having to pay a fee for inclusion. As a method of advertising these guides have a special value in that they all have large circulation figures and are purchased by interested and potential customers and are used regularly as sources of reference for eating out occasions.

Figure 10.8 Newspaper Restaurant advertising (*Source*: www.thelondonpaper.com)

4. *Trade advertising*: Trade or 'wholesale' advertising is the selling of an operation's catering facilities through 'middle men' such as travel agents, package tour operators, etc. At present it is mainly the large hotel groups and restaurant chains who have utilized this form of external selling although it is also available to small restaurants that are privately owned. By approaching local tour operators, for example, a country restaurant may be able to secure a regular weekend lunchtime trade of between twenty and thirty covers throughout the summer months.

5. *Electronic guides and magazines*: Ensuring that the restaurants website is linked with popular electronic trade magazines or guides is extremely important as search engines now use links to other sites as a factor for search engine positioning. Meaning that when a customer searches for an Italian restaurant in a search engine, if your restaurant is an Italian one but with no website or with a website that has no links to other websites, your web pages will never be read by that customer simply because your competitors pages would be the first from a list of hundreds or more restaurants of the same type.

Broadcasting

1. *Radio*: Advertising on commercial radio is mainly limited to local radio stations that broadcast within a specific radius. It may be used to advertise local takeaways, restaurants, hotels, wine bars, etc. Its main advantages are that it is a very up-to-date form of advertising, not too costly and has the potential to reach a large percentage of local custom – people at work, driving cars, using personal stereos, people at home, etc.

2. *Television*: Television's major advantage over radio is its visual impact. Its major disadvantage is its high cost, particularly during peak receiving times. Its national use is limited almost exclusively to the larger restaurant and fast food and popular restaurant chains and hotel groups, for example KFC, McDonald's, Pizzaland. McDonalds has a history of TV advertising campaigns with the latest one *'i'm lovin' it'* (see Figure 10.9). Some regional television advertising may be undertaken but at present is very limited. The use of both DVD recorders and cable television are two further extensions of TV and their use in private homes, clubs, hotels, shopping malls, etc. is increasing annually.

3. *Cinema*: Cinema advertising is also highly visual but also very localized. Catering facilities such as fast food and popular restaurants, etc. open until late in the evening are often featured, but are usually quite specific to a certain area.

Signs and posters

Signs and posters advertising a catering facility may be positioned either very close to it or some distance away. They are used

McDonald's is Your Kind of Place (1967)
You Deserve a Break Today (1971)
We Do it All for You (1975)
Twoallbeefpattiesspecialsaucelettucecheesepicklesonionsonasesameseedbun (1975)
You, You're The One (1976)
Nobody Can Do It Like McDonald's Can (1979)
Renewed: You Deserve a Break Today (1980 & 1981)
Nobody Makes Your Day Like McDonald's Can (1981)
McDonald's and You (1983)
It's a Good Time for the Great Taste of McDonald's (1984)
Good Time, Great Taste, That's Why This is My Place (1988)
Food, Folks and Fun (1990)
McDonald's Today (1991)
What You Want is What You Get (1992)
Have you Had your Break Today? (1995)
My McDonald's (1997)
Did Somebody Say McDonald's (1997)
We Love to See You Smile (2000)
There's a little McDonald's in Everyone (2001) – Canada Only
i'm lovin' it (2003)

Figure 10.9 McDonalds TV advertising campaigns over the years (*Source*: www.Mcdonalds.ca)

along streets in towns and cities on hoardings, in airport lounges, railway carriages and the underground subways. External signs on main roads are particularly important for hotels, restaurants and fast-food drive-in operations who rely heavily on transient trade, and it is, therefore, important for these advertisements to be easily read and their messages understood quickly. Traffic travelling at high speeds must also be given adequate time to pull in. Posters displayed in the street, in railway carriages, etc. can afford to be more detailed because passengers and passersby will have more time available to read them.

As with all other forms of advertising, signs and posters must portray the type of image the restaurant is trying to achieve. Fast food and take-away outlets in high street locations, for example, who are attempting to attract as much transient traffic as possible, feature large colourful signs with distinguishing logos and colours, for example KFC, McDonald's, Wimpy, etc. An up-market restaurant situated outside a town, however, would not need to use such obvious external signs, because a higher percentage of the trade would already have made a reservation and such a restaurant would, therefore, display something smaller and more discreet.

Miscellaneous advertising media

This includes other forms of advertising media that may be used in addition to the major channels discussed above, for example, door-to-door leaflet distribution, leisure centre entrance tickets, theatre programmes, shop windows, etc. Another example is credit cards. Credit cards can be used as means of advertising. Featuring the company logo and bestowing discounts or other privileges to customers they can become both a loyalty tool for the customer who has one and an advertising tool for friends and relatives of that customer (see Figure 10.10).

PUBLIC RELATIONS

Public relations is a communication and information process, either personal or non-personal, operating within an organization's internal and external environment. It involves the creation of a favourable environment in which an organization can operate to the best of its advantage. An organization would typically be involved internally in communicating to its customers and employees, and eventually to its customers, suppliers, sales force, local community, council and government departments, etc. Public relations has two main functions:

1. It has a problem-solving or trouble-shooting function to deal with any negative publicity. As with advertising, it is wrong to assume that any publicity is better than no publicity. Detrimental newspaper reports and letters to column writers, bad word-of-mouth and radio news publicity can all have a damaging effect on an operation's image and sales. Through a public relations exercise a company's desired corporate image can be restored.

Figure 10.10 Bank Restaurants credit card (UK) (*Source*: Bank restaurants, UK)

2. It has a forward looking function to creating positive publicity for the organization and may be used at various stages during the life cycle of the facility. For example, if a fast-food unit is to be opened in a busy town centre, a public relations exercise would typically be to create a favourable environment and attitude within the local community before its opening. If this facility is specifically aiming at a younger family market, the public relations function would include informing the identified market segments of the benefits the facility has to offer to them. For example, children's menus and portions will be available at reduced prices, high chairs for babies are to be provided, an informal atmosphere will exist, on certain days entertainment for the children will be organized, a young members' club will be available for those wishing to join, etc.

In institutional catering, the role of public relations may be to explain to a staff committee the need for certain price increases to be passed on to the staff cafeteria, or why different products have been bought to replace existing ones, etc.

The initiation of a public relations exercise should begin with the identification of that sector of the organization's environment that it wishes to communicate with; it may, for example, be a particular segment of its market, the press, local schools, etc. An evaluation of the organization's existing corporate image with that sector will highlight those areas it feels are unfavourable, and would benefit from a public relations exercise. The organization may then choose the most suitable channels for communicating its messages to help create the type of environmental climate it feels would be favourable to its own company's objectives.

The choice of public relations tools to be used depends largely on the target audience, the suitability of one media over another and the budget available. They would include:

1. *Press media*: Newspapers, magazines, trade journals, brochures, leaflets, guides, press conferences and press releases.
2. *Broadcasting media*: Television, radio, cinema, promotional video and cassettes.
3. *Community media*: Sponsorship of local events, individuals, companies, exhibitions, talks, free gifts and samples.

Depending on the size of the organization, the public relations function may be the responsibility of the owner, or manager, it may be an individual's task in a medium-sized operation, a separate department within the organization consisting of a number of employees, or an external public relations company may be used.

Public relations in the hotel and catering industry has a real application whether the catering facility is a small or large operation, is independent or part of a large group, exists in the free market or captive. The importance of public relations is the ability to communicate and inform. The public image, good or bad, of a catering facility is something that develops as a result of the business activity; however, whether it is advantageous or disadvantageous to the organization can be greatly influenced by public relations.

MERCHANDISING

Merchandising is the art in which the brand or image from one product or service is used to sell another. For example, McDonalds will often feature toys from recent cartoon characters with their kids meals. By featuring a favourite character from a recent cartoon as part of the deal kids choose to buy burgers from that chain rather than another. Another example is that of Wagamamas, who have a range of merchandise such as T-shirts, cookbooks and even gift vouchers (see Figure 10.11)

The merchandising of catering operations involves the point of sale promotion of their facilities using non-personal media. Unlike advertising it is not a paid for form of communication, but like sales promotion is more concerned with influencing customer behaviour in the short term.

We have explored menu merchandising in Chapter 5, but here we refer to merchandising in the food and beverage operation in its wider meaning. It is not uncommon to see restaurants

Figure 10.11
Wagamama (UK) Merchandise
(*Source*: Courtesy of
Wagamama)

producing their own labelled bottles of wine, or coffee shops selling their own brand of coffee to customers. Hats, T-shirts, coffee mugs and other promotional materials can both help with extra income into the business and at the same time strengthen the operations brand.

There is a variety of other internal sales tools that may be used by a catering operation. These include place mats, which in coffee shops may contain the breakfast menu with a reminder that the operation is open throughout the day for snacks; napkins; doilies; and pre-portioned condiments which all add to the operation's sales message. In the bars giving away cocktail sticks, matches and drink mats also enables a small part of the operation to be carried out of the establishment and may act as a reminder to customers of their meal experience several days or months later.

Through all aspects of an organization's merchandising approach, there is a very real need for it to complement its advertising campaign. Advertising the facilities will hopefully have stimulated customer interest. The role of merchandising is to convert that interest into purchases and increased sales.

SALES PROMOTION

Sales promotion is a form of temporary incentive highlighting aspects of a product that are not inherent to it. Sales promotion may be aimed at customers, distribution channels and sales employees. It does not necessarily occur at the point of sale, although in many instances it does.

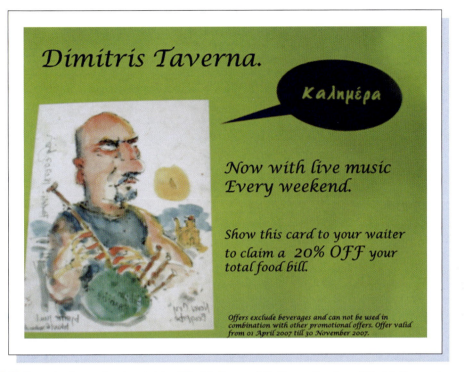

Figure 10.12 Example of promotional materials of Dimitris Taverna (GR) (*Source*: Courtesy of Dimitris Taverna, Leros, Greece)

Sales promotion is used by operations for a number of reasons including the following:

1. To increase the average spend by customers and thereby increase the sales revenue (see Figure 10.6).
2. To promote a new product or range of products being featured by the operation, for example offering a new flavoured milk shake in a take-away facility at a reduced price.
3. To influence impulse purchasers towards a certain product or range of products, for example featuring Australian wine at a special discount price.
4. To aid as a reminder during a long-term advertising campaign, for example on long established main menu items.
5. To help 'level' peak activities of business, for example offering a free glass of wine to customers ordering their meal before 18.30 hours.
6. To celebrate a special event, for example the New Year, Thanksgiving Day Dinner, etc.
7. To 'package' together menu items at an attractive price, for example steak and strawberries. Such 'packages' are seasonal in nature but aid in directing a high proportion of customers' choices towards items of a low preparation labour content (Figure 10.12).
8. To clear slow moving stock, for example pricing specific cocktails at two for the price of one.

The types of sales promotions used are influenced by the targets being aimed at:

1. *Customers*: Sales promotions aimed directly at customers include money-off coupons, discounts or special prices during off-peak periods, free chicken meals for families, a free bottle of wine for every two adult meals ordered, etc. Special events and promotions may be communicated to the customer by advertising, by direct mail, by telephone or by posters and tent cards.

2. *Distribution channels*: Promotional techniques aimed at incentivating third party agents include free restaurant meals, free gifts, competitions and the use of the hotel's leisure facilities.

3. *Sales employees*: Sales promotion incentives are similar to those listed above and include commission related sales, competitions, token and points systems occurring over an extended period to encourage an ongoing sales commitment by the sales force.

Sales promotion is a marketing tool in its own right and should be planned, monitored and evaluated as such. It can be initiated either by the operation itself or by an external organization, and as with all other aspects of the marketing mix must be in line with the marketing objectives of the organization (Figure 10.13).

Figure 10.13 Example of a KFC promotion, featuring a meal package (UK) (*Source*: courtesy of KFC, UK)

PERSONAL SELLING AND UPSELLING

Personal selling is a paid form of promoting a facility on a personal basis. One of the main characteristics of service industries is the increased contact time between service staff and customers, and the attitudes and behaviour of an operation's service employees are important parts of the total product the customer is buying. As with the other aspects of the promotion mix, advertising, public relations, merchandising and sales promotion, the objectives, requirements and techniques of personal selling need to be fully integrated into the overall marketing policy of the organization.

Service employees are one of the most important assets of a catering operation. Too frequently waiters, bar staff, counter assistants, are seen only as 'order takers' and not as sales people. Particularly in large organizations, such as hotels which have their own sales department, it is too easy for service staff to see themselves merely as servers of the facilities' foods and beverages. The fact that an establishment may have a sales department does not relieve the catering department of its sales functions and responsibilities.

When customers enter a restaurant their first personal contact with the restaurant staff is usually the waiter who shows them to their table. How often is that same customer presented with the menu and then left to ponder for a considerable time without being asked if they would like a drink while considering the menu. A potential drink sale is lost immediately. When the waiter comes to take customers' orders there is another chance for the employee to promote the menu, perhaps the restaurant's speciality, a side salad, additional vegetables, wine to accompany the meal, rather than simply being an order taker. At the end of the meal the presentation of the dessert and liqueur trolleys can do much to revitalize a customer's palate, rather than the waiter merely asking if sweet or coffee are required.

Some establishments operate training programmes for service staff to help increase their awareness of the different ways in which they personally can contribute to an operation's sale. These training programmes can include basic sales functions of the waiter, such as asking customers if they would like a drink when they arrive at the restaurant to more in depth sensitivity training. In the US, such techniques can be considered intrusive and when badly performed by the staff it can be seen by customers as 'script' reading. It is important that staff have been trained to be able to 'read' the customer and to offer a personalized service with the goal not the bottom line but increased quality of the meal experience (which would then naturally lead to increased revenue).

Fast-food chains such as Burger King and McDonald's have highly standardized training programmes where service staff are taught selling phrases and responses that may be used when taking a customer's order. Although these highly formalized responses and situational examples are now being modified with the introduction of warmer and friendlier phrases such as McDonald's 'we've got time for you' suggesting that even in an efficiently standardized operation such as their own, they will have time for individual, personalized service.

At the other end of the catering spectrum, where there is a much longer contact time between service staff and customers, such as in haute cuisine or speciality restaurants, the 'personal touch' plays a more important role in the total service product. Also at this level, the technical knowledge of the service staff assumes greater importance.

Some operations encourage their staff to sell by providing incentives. For example, a waiter may receive a sales related bonus for every additional £5.00 spent by a customer over and above a pre-fixed average spend; the additional sale indicating that the waiter sold more food and beverages than the average for that restaurant. Incentives given to service staff in this way, however, needs to be introduced with sensitivity so that the wrong type of competitiveness between staff does not develop to the detriment of the restaurant.

Whatever the level of catering operation and the amount of sales training given, there is a need for service staff to become more alert to customers' needs by listening to and observing and identifying what their needs are for that particular meal; this information may then be quantified by management for possible future action. This aspect of personal selling is discussed as part of the meal experience.

The marketing of a catering operation must be effectively planned, organized and monitored throughout all its stages. The successes and failures of its promotional campaigns and those of its competitors, should be studied and reviewed when possible.

Good advertising, merchandising, public relations and sales promotion are difficult. They are areas of food and beverage management that often require considerable financial outlay, but which have no guarantee of success. Caterers are faced with a variety of promotional tools and techniques and whichever they choose, so will have others; they must compete therefore not only with the other facilities' catering products but also with their marketing campaigns.

Alone, advertising does not sell. It is there to stimulate interest, and to influence a customer towards buying an operation's product above those of its competitors. The customer's action is translated into a purchase at the point of sale, further stimulated by effective merchandising and possibly sales promotion techniques, all working together in a favourable environment created by good public relations.

Summary

Food and beverage marketing is the focus of this chapter. Because of the nature of services marketing for food and beverage operations can differ greatly from that of products, and although the basic concepts of segmentation mix and life cycle remain the same the intricacies of marketing for food and beverage are explored.

More specifically we explored:

- Marketing of services
- Segmentation, marketing mix
- Product life cycle
- Marketing research, the brand and Internet marketing
- Advertising
- Public relations
- Merchandising
- Sales promotions and personal selling.

Review questions

1. Explain the elements of a marketing concept.
2. Why is marketing for services different to that of products?
3. What methods are available to a food and beverage operation in terms of advertising?
4. Which method of advertising is more cost effective for a small operation?
5. Explain merchandising, and its potential benefits to a restaurant.
6. What are the key reasons for an operation to use sales promotion?

Further study options

Case study: Centenary Hotels

Centenary Hotels a small hotel chain in London, UK enjoyed a healthy room occupancy throughout the year. The board of directors were more than happy with the hotel performance in terms of room revenue. However, the same could not be said for the food and beverage department. The hotel restaurants seemed to be doing poorly in terms of customer attendance and it seemed that only a 15% of the hotel residents would eat in the restaurant and a very small number of external customers would ever give their restaurants a try. They decided to revamp all of their five restaurants and spend a considerable amount of money ensuring that a new contemporary design was implemented in all of the restaurants and a new executive chef had redesigned all of their menus. All the restaurants now had separate entrances to the high street so that potential external customers were not intimidated by having to enter the hotel and pass the foyer before entering the restaurant. The board of directors has decided to hire a marketing firm to reintroduce their 'new' restaurants in the market.

Q1: Your company is bidding for this contract and you are expected to prepare a power point presentation illustrating how your company is going to approach the marketing campaign and what tools you are going to use to ensure the restaurants are a success. Consider internal marketing techniques as well as external ones when pitching your ideas to the board.

Further reading

Bitner, M. J. (1991). The evolution of the services marketing mix and its relationship to service quality. In S. W. Brown, E. Gummesson, B. Edvardsson and B. Gustavsson (eds), *Service Quality: Multidisciplinary and Multinational Perspectives*. Lexington, MA: Lexington Books, pp. 23–37.

Davis, B. and Lockwood, A. (1994). *Food and Beverage Management – A Selection of Readings*. Oxford: Butterworth-Heinemann.

Kasper, H. (2006). *Services Marketing Management: A Strategic Perspective*, 2nd edn.. Chichester: John Wiley.

Kotler, P. and Armstrong, G. (2006). *Principles of Marketing*, 11th edn. NJ: Pearson Prentice Hall.

Kotler, P. and Keller, K. L. (2006). *Marketing Management*, 12th edn. NJ: Pearson Prentice Hall.

Kotler, P. and Pfoertsch, W. (2006). *B2B Brand Management*. Berlin: Springer.

Marvin, B. (1997). *Guest-Based Marketing: How to Increase Restaurant Sales Without Breaking Your Budget*. Chichester: John Wiley.

Middleton, V. (2001). *Marketing in Travel and Tourism*, 3rd edn. Oxford: Butterworth-Heinemann.

Zeithaml, V. A., Bitner, M. J. and Gremler, D. D. (2005). *Services marketing: integrating customer focus across the firm*.

CHAPTER 11

Managing quality in food and beverage operations

Chapter objectives

After working through this chapter you should be able to:

- Explain what is meant by quality in food and beverage operations and why it is important.
- Understand the challenges facing the management of quality in F&B.
- Describe a systematic approach to managing quality.
- Compare and contrast a range of approaches to quality management.
- Understand examples of how quality management works in practice.

WHAT IS QUALITY?

The food and beverage industry is a fast moving and exciting business. Looking at the Sunday papers, there are regular news articles about the expansion plans of new theme restaurants or multi-million pound take over deals; there are regular restaurant or hotel reviews and articles about cooking food at home. Television provides growing numbers of programmes on aspects of cookery – from woks to barbecues, from cooking up a feast in twenty minutes to the real feasts of bygone eras. Cookery books, often tied to TV series, regularly top the best seller lists. Chefs are a key part of the current cult of celebrity. The food and beverage manager faces an increasingly knowledgeable and sophisticated customer with broader tastes and experiences than ever before. These customers demand satisfaction but are increasingly difficult to satisfy.

The British Standards definition of quality (British Standard 4778, 1987) is 'the totality of features and characteristics of a product or service that bear on its ability to satisfy a stated or implied need'. It is these 'stated or implied needs' that the operation must satisfy. The customer translates these needs into a series of expectations of the service or product they will experience. If the restaurant meets or exceeds these expectations then the customer will feel satisfied and will feel that they have received 'quality'. If the restaurant does not meet their expectations, then there is a gap between customer expectations and the perceived characteristics of the service or product delivered to them (Parasuraman et al., 1985) and quality will not have been provided. It is implicit in this definition that quality can exist at any level of service, from fast food to fine dining, as long as expectations of that level of service are met.

The totality of features and characteristics that go to make up the meal experience are many and varied. They consist partly of the food itself, partly the service received and partly the environment created by the decor, furniture, lighting and music. One way of looking at these characteristics is to categorize them as

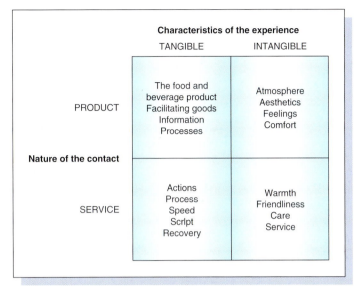

Figure 11.1
The product/service matrix

relating to either the product or the service and as either tangible or intangible, as shown in the Figure 11.1.

The matrix identifies that the food and beverage product consists of a combination of tangible and intangible elements. These relate both to the physical characteristics of the provision (the product) and the interpersonal contact that occurs during the meal experience (the service).

The product tangible elements consist of the food presented to the customer and the facilitating goods used to serve the food on or with. The style and nature of the crockery, cutlery and glassware as well as the linen and napkins are also part of the total experience. The menu also provides tangible evidence of the meal experience by displaying information, through verbal description or pictures, about the dishes available. The final element of this quadrant consists of the machine processes that a customer may come across in a food and beverage outlet. These may range from the effectiveness of the EFTPOS terminal to the way a vending machine dispenses a cup of hot chocolate.

The product intangible quadrant includes the overall atmosphere of the establishment and the aesthetic appeal of the decor, furniture and fittings. Every restaurant and bar has its own feel – some are immediately warm and friendly but others are cold or clinical. Establishing the appropriate decor to engender the right feelings in the customer is obviously important. Compare the clean bright business-like atmosphere of fast-food operations such as Mcdonalds with the warmer, darker, cluttered feel of a TGI Fridays. The product/intangibles help to provide that feeling of comfort, of being at ease or at home that is such an important part of the hospitality concept (Cassee and Reuland, 1983).

Although service is often thought of as intangible, there are still elements that can be seen as tangible. The actions the service staff carry out during service are tangible, as is the way the service process is organized. The speed of service is easily measured and the words service staff use -their 'script' – also provides hard evidence. Another example of tangible service is the action taken to put something right after it has gone wrong – the corrective action.

The service/intangible quadrant is very hard to tie down but undeniably exists. The warmth and friendliness shown through a genuine smile is almost tangible. In some restaurants, customers know implicitly that the staff care about their meal, while in others, customers know that the staff care about very little. All these elements add up to a feeling of service.

Activity 1: A quality experience

1. Consider the following situation and identify the key elements of the experience and classify them according to the matrix described above.
2. At the end of this experience would you have been satisfied or dissatisfied? Why?

At a recent event in France, the 50 or so delegates were entertained to lunch in the upstairs room of an American style restaurant. The restaurant was newly opened, with excellent decor and expensively appointed. It was late November and the upstairs room had been closed down for the winter season. The bar had been cleared of all bottles and glasses and there was an air of emptiness about the place. Fifty people on long tables of ten soon livened the place up – but despite the emptiness, we were crammed into one side of the room so tightly that the service staff could not get between the tables easily to serve food or drinks. It had been a long morning and we were hungry.

The restaurant team has been warned in advance by two-way radio of our arrival but it still took nearly half an hour for our starter to be served – a plated salad. The salad and dressing were crisp and piquant, respectively. The plates were cleared and we looked forward to our main course. Meanwhile the jugs of water that had been ready on the table for our arrival were removed and refilled – but left on the bar and only returned to the table on request. There were no wines or drinks included in the menu price.

Not only was the upstairs restaurant closed for the winter but the upstairs kitchen was closed too. All the food had to be brought upstairs from the kitchen below, some by service staff carrying two plates, some on trays of four. The plates were cold. Fortunately, the food was hot. The main course was two large shallow fried breasts of chicken with a garnish of vegetables. The chicken was of an excellent standard – plump, juicy, tasty and much too large – one would have been generous, two was overkill.

Clearing the main course plates was difficult. The space between the tables was too narrow, the staff not skilled nor experienced at clearing plates from large tables. One waiter managed to drop three half full glasses of wine down one customer's back. The waiter was too embarrassed to apologize but quickly got on with clearing away the broken glass and wiping the floor.

The sweet was a dense white chocolate mousse on a biscuit base. The coffee was black and strong but by now there were only a few minutes left before we were expected back at the next session.

This restaurant is operated by a company that has one of the best international reputations for their attention to quality in the hospitality business.

While it is arguably easier for the food and beverage manager to control the tangible elements of the product, there is some evidence (Parasuraman et al., 1985) that they are more important to the customer than the intangible elements of the product. On the other hand the intangible elements of service are probably more important to the customer than the tangible elements of service but they are much more difficult for any manager to influence.

It is all well and good for an operation to meet customer requirements once, but it is no use to the customers if they receive exactly what they want on one day but, when the chef or their favourite crew member has a day off, the next visit is a disaster. The meaning of quality must also include reliability – what Crosby (1984) calls zero defects. He stresses that this is the only acceptable quality standard. Across the organization, everyone should be striving to deliver to the customer right first time every time.

Some organizations are moving away from seeing quality as simply satisfying the customer and looking to 'delight' the customer by exceeding their expectations. Deming (1982) suggests that if a customer is unhappy they will go to another supplier, but that a customer who is simply satisfied may also go somewhere else because they really have not got a lot to lose. He stresses the importance of repeat customers in generating profit. Customers who tell everyone about how great their meal was and bring their friends with them next time are worth their weight in gold. There are however some dangers in trying to exceed customer expectations. It has been suggested (Tenner and DeToro, 1992) that delight is the result of the added value of characteristics and features that customers did not expect – arousing their latent expectations. Until a few years ago nobody expected their children to be given crayons and something to draw on when they went to a restaurant. Now it is almost commonplace. This highlights the problem of escalating expectations. Little extras soon become the expected norm and new 'delights' have to be found.

Activity 2: Some quotes from businesses on adding value

It can't just be good ingredients. It can't just be fantastic presentation and it can't just be good service. It has to be the whole package ... if anything is not up to the same standard then it just stands out in such a manner that actually some people respond to it and say that it is wrong. That it doesn't belong...

Pub, Monmouthshire

It's very satisfying here. We always try and keep things interesting. We don't have a static menu ... we re-write the menu every single day. We don't change everything on it but something changes everyday. The chefs don't get bored ... the customers who come quite a lot of them come here for their lunch every single day...

Pub restaurant, Belfast

Other aspects of added value come down to being very, very aware of what our customers' want. We have a very good dialogue with our customers ... regularly we'll go around the tables, introduce ourselves and talk to customers. It really works very well ... that has been very well received and again a whole host of comments have come from that...

Restaurant, Bristol

...in Belfast because we've got this small market place ...we can't let people down. We've got to get it right all the time. We're much more focussed on customer care, possibly, in Northern Ireland than you would need to be in, say, central London because there will be another 100 along in a minute. We don't get another 100 along.

Pub restaurant, Belfast

The concept is that you're dealing with individuals. So what is good value to someone may not necessarily be that good value to someone else ... everyone wants individual attention ... they want to be recognised and seen as an individual as opposed to a room number which can be a problem with a good many hotels.

Hotel, Evesham

Source: Lockwood and Bowen, 2003

From the quotes given here, what do you think these entrepreneurs mean by 'adding value'?

Does adding value need to incur additional cost?

Quality in food and beverage operations means reliably providing the food, service and environment that meets with our customers' expectations and where possible finding ways of adding value to exceed expectations and result in delight.

WHY IS QUALITY IMPORTANT?

There are three main sources of pressure on businesses to pay attention to quality. First, customers are more demanding of everything they buy, as well as the way in which those products and services are delivered. Customers are no longer intimidated about complaining in restaurants and are prepared to make a fuss if things do not go right. Second, the development of more sophisticated hard and soft technologies allows managers to offer many possible additional and convenience services, although interpersonal contact is still seen as highly valued for the majority of operations. The effectiveness of methods such as chilling and to a lesser extent sous vide means that a good standard of professionally prepared dishes can be obtained from the local supermarket and prepared at home in a microwave oven. In an increasingly competitive and international marketplace, quality is seen as providing an edge of competitive advantage.

Not long ago some managers felt that providing quality was too expensive or too much trouble to be of any real value. There has, however, been a growing realization that providing quality is an essential part of any operation and brings three main areas of benefits.

The positive impact of quality on profit was shown originally by the Profit Impact of Market Strategy (PIMS) study (Buzzell and Gale, 1987). In this study, the single most important factor affecting a business unit's performance was the quality of its products and services, in comparison to its competitors. Other than Walker and Salameh (1990) who showed similar results for the hospitality industry, there has surprisingly been little further research in this area, although some work is currently being done (Zeglat et al., 2007). A food and beverage operation that customers think has the quality edge over its competitors is partly able to boost profitability through charging premium prices. Quality provides leverage on the price/value relationship. For example, the prices charged by some restaurants are above the market average but high perceived quality can keep their value to the customer high. Over the long term, a quality advantage will result in business growth. This growth in volume will result in economies of scale and superior profit margins on increasing revenue.

Providing high perceived value will lead to loyal customers, who will use the operation consistently over a long period and will recommend the unit to their friends. The now almost obvious value of long-term relationships in services marketing was not always recognized (Buttle, 1994) but good restaurateurs have always realized the key importance of repeat customers.

Quality improvement, without increasing the costs of an operation, results in operational efficiencies which more than recoup the investment. Quality costs are divided into two – the costs of conformance and the costs of non-conformance. The costs of conformance are the costs of assuring that everything comes out right and includes all efforts for prevention and quality education. The costs of non-conformance can be divided into appraisal/inspection costs and failure costs. Appraisal costs are the costs of inspection to make sure that mistakes are kept down and to ensure that any mistakes that are made are identified before reaching the customer. Failure costs are the costs of having made mistakes. They are split into internal and external failure costs. Internal failure costs are those incurred where mistakes are found before they reach the customer or cross the line of visibility. They include scrap, rework, downgrading and excess inventory. External failure costs are those incurred when mistakes are not found before they reach the customer. They include such things as repair and warranty claims, providing replacement goods or services and the potential loss of future business. External failure costs are much more serious than their internal counterparts because by the time the problem reaches the customer it is already too late. While the internal failure costs of excess inventory and waste might be high, the real danger of poor quality for a food and beverage operation lies in those errors that are not discovered until they reach the customer.

Quality provides the opportunity for food and beverage operations to find a winning edge over their competitors, to ensure the long-term loyalty of their customers and to improve both short-term and long-term profitability through cost savings and higher margins. When the benefits are so great, why is it that, with some notable exceptions, few food and beverage companies seem to have made much progress in this area?

MANAGING QUALITY IN FOOD AND BEVERAGE OPERATIONS

The best known approaches to managing quality propounded by the quality gurus such as Deming, Crosby, Juran, Ishikawa, Shingo, Taguchi and others started in the manufacturing sector. The tools and techniques used in manufacturing are well proven to be effective in these environments. Increasingly, attention has been drawn to the service sector and the particular challenges faced by companies wishing to pursue service quality, but recognizing that the challenges can be quite different.

The quality matrix described earlier illustrates the problem facing food and beverage operations. Not only must these operations deal with the manufacturing problems of meal or drink production but they also have to act as a service operation. It is not surprising that the resulting complexity makes managing quality in food and beverage operations a difficult but not impossible challenge.

Looking at the characteristics of service operations that are seen to distinguish them from manufacturing (Fitzgerald et al., 1991), provides some interesting insights for food and beverage operations:

- *Intangibility*: Unlike a 'pure' service operation, food and beverage operations do not simply consist of the service performance and the intangible factors that affect this interaction. A large part of their hospitality consists of the very tangible product elements of food and drink. On the product side there are the tangible elements of the food or drink itself – How hot is the food? What does it look like? How cold is the beer? How large is the glass? etc. – but there are also the intangible elements of the atmosphere created – Does the customer feel comfortable, 'at home', secure? On the service side there are the intangible elements of the friendliness or care offered by the hospitality provider. At the same time it is possible to identify tangible elements such as the time taken to deliver the service or the effectiveness of the service performed – Did the waiter spill the soup? How long between the order and delivery of a cooked breakfast?

- *Heterogeneity*: As service outputs are heterogeneous the standard of performance may vary, especially where there is a high labour content. It is therefore hard to ensure consistent quality from the same employee from day to day, and harder still to get comparability between employees, yet this will crucially affect what the customer receives. While a customer may expect some variability in the service received, the same cannot be true of the product dimension. A hamburger served by one unit of a restaurant chain at one end of the country, must be consistent with every other hamburger served in every other unit of the same chain. The range of tolerance on the product side seems much lower than on the service side.

- *Simultaneity*: The production and consumption of many services are simultaneous, for example having a hair cut or taking a plane flight. Most services then cannot be counted, measured, inspected, tested or verified before sale for subsequent delivery to the customer. The product element of hospitality ranges from simultaneous production – for gueridon service, where cooking is done in the restaurant at the table – to decoupled production – for cook-chill or cook-freeze, where food is batch produced at a central location, cooled and then distributed for later consumption – with many other possible systems in between.

- *Perishability*: Services cannot be stored, and so the buffer of an inventory that can be used to cope with fluctuations in customer demand is removed. Even a restaurant seat is a perishable product. Empty places cannot be stockpiled for a busy day sometime in the future. Once a restaurant seat has been left empty, the potential revenue from the occupation of that space is lost. From the product perspective, raw ingredients or a complete meal can be stored for a limited period depending on the method of storage. Normally, however, that period will be a matter of hours and days rather than years.

Food and beverage operations display many of the characteristics of service industries in general but with the added complication of a production element. However, even the production side of food and beverage is far from straightforward.

- *The cost structure*: The need to provide the appropriate environment within which food and beverages can be delivered means that most businesses need a substantial investment in premises and plant and associated fixed costs. On the other hand, variable costs are low. This high fixed cost/low variable cost structure creates an unusual cost–profit–volume relationship. Generally the break-even volume will be quite high. Exceeding this level will result in high profits, but low volumes will result in substantial losses. The number of hotel and restaurant operations that go bankrupt in their first years of operation bears forceful witness to this fact.

- *The unpredictability of demand*: The cost structure issue would not be too difficult to deal with if it were possible to predict with confidence the levels of demand for the operation. Unfortunately, food and beverage suffers from complex fluctuations in demand. Demand will fluctuate over time – hourly, daily, weekly, monthly, annually and cyclically – by type of customer – group or individual, business or leisure – and by menu item. The result is a complex mixture of patterns that makes forecasting and subsequent resource scheduling, even with sophisticated software, still very difficult indeed.

- *The short cycle of production*: The length of the food and beverage production cycle is short giving little time for monitoring or for the correction of errors. A restaurant operation may well buy in fresh produce in the morning that is prepared during the morning, offered for lunch and consumed by early afternoon.
- *The risk*: The food production process deals with raw ingredients that have a limited shelf life and that, if contaminated, can result in serious illness and death. A customer entering a food and beverage operation is placing themselves in the care of that host and the operation must employ all due diligence to ensure their safety. The customer must place their trust in the operation based on limited available evidence.
- *The technology*: The food and beverage production system is labour intensive but technological substitution is still possible in back of house operations. Recent developments in catering technology have allowed the decoupling of production and service through the use of cook-chill, cook-freeze or sous-vide methods. McDonalds' industrialized service delivery system ensures high speed, high volume with high consistency but over a limited product range and with limited human intervention.
- *The presence of the customer*: Throughout the complexity of the operations described above, the food and beverage operation is pressured by the physical presence of the customer, monitoring progress with the expert eye of someone who has eaten many meals before. Even in home delivery operations the pressure of meeting the delivery time standard, usually thirty minutes, represents that customer's presence.

A SYSTEMATIC APPROACH TO QUALITY MANAGEMENT

To deliver quality to the customer in the face of the complexities identified above, the food and beverage operation must adopt some form of systematic approach. The quality management cycle shown in the Figure 11.2 has been developed from the basis of the Deming PDCA (Plan-Do-Check-Act) cycle (1982). This approach was developed to help identify and correct any errors that occur during production or service and to lead to lasting quality improvement. The foundation of the cycle is one of continual improvement to reduce the gap between customer requirements and the actual performance of the operation. The cycle starts by planning what improvement to make based on a

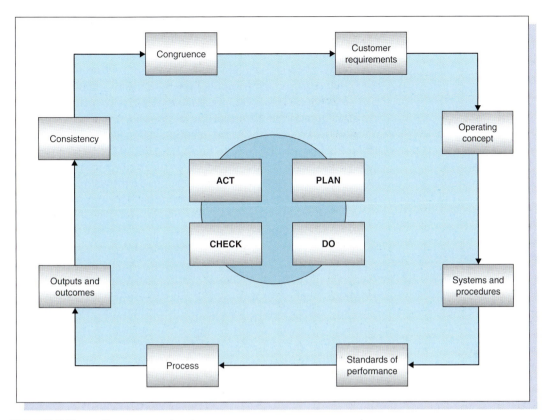

Figure 11.2 The quality management cycle

clarification of the problem and the development of hypotheses about the underlying causes. The 'do' phase implements a small-scale experiment to correct the situation that is then 'checked' through measurement. The final step 'acts' to implement these quality improvements. The cycle is essentially a learning process and after one cycle is completed another one starts. It is, however, useful to extend this four-step approach to the systematic management of quality throughout an organization, while maintaining the elements of learning and continual improvement.

Planning

The starting point for any quality initiative should be to establish the specific requirements of customers in each of the market segments that the food and beverage operation intends to serve. For example, what does a business traveller expect from a hotel breakfast and in what ways is that different from the weekend leisure visitor? In reality, it is more likely that there is already a fairly good idea of what the operation will be like, based on previous experience or an existing brand. Market research can still help to identify the most important characteristics of the operation so that they can be built into systems and procedures from the beginning.

From this customer base, management needs to prepare a detailed operating concept. This should start from an idea of the corporate mission to develop into a series of core product values and then be translated into a practical service delivery system. They can also be developed into a series of operating standards reflecting the core values that the company feels are important. Heskett et al. (1990) have developed a detailed model that describes the integration of the target market segments with the service concept, operating strategy and the design of the service delivery system through positioning, value-cost leveraging and system-strategy integration. This strategic service vision forms the foundations upon which quality can be built throughout the organization. Translating these ideas into a concrete design is a complex challenge that is fundamental to the future success of the operation.

Doing

Once the design of the food and beverage operation has been decided, it is then necessary to fill in the details of the systems, standards and procedures to be adopted. The systems described in the next section can provide the key elements needed here. Most businesses will translate these into detailed standards of performance to be found in the standards manual, which will form part of the induction and ongoing training of employees. With all the design and planning done and all systems, standards and procedures in place, the next stage is to activate the operation and ensure it performs on a day-to-day basis.

Activity 3: Some quotes from businesses on setting and maintaining standards

Consider the following quotes from a range of businesses in the UK:

Everything we do is because of our customer. We don't do anything because we think it looks nice. It's done because that is what the customer is going to want.

Hotel, Edinburgh

What we are trying to do is put ourselves in the position of our customers and say what would they expect … we then write these down and line them all up and then make sure the staff know that standards expected.

Visitor attraction, Devon

We are very particular and precise about the way the whole place runs … none of the staff are left in any doubt that there are two ways of doing things – there aren't! As long as everybody gets into that then the place runs like a machine – albeit a very warm and friendly machine.

Restaurant, Winteringham

We work to the standards that we have and we try to keep it at that level. If we can improve we would but we wouldn't go chasing high level standards just to achieve them … a lot of our customers wouldn't be expecting that sort of thing.

Pub, Berwick upon Tweed

Always asking staff to suggest new ways of doing things, different ways for efficiency or improved service and standards – particularly the new staff who would be viewing the operation with a fresh pair of eyes.

Hotel, Stockcross

It's on a personal basis ... nothing is strict, stringent ... it's not a very formal structured system ... it's just not changing anything ... it's making sure that it's done the same way every single time.

Restaurant, Aunstruther

Source: Lockwood Bowen and Ekinci (2002)

To what extent do these views present a consistent approach to achieving standards? Why might their approaches differ?

Checking

Checking that the operation has performed according to the plan can take place at two levels. Firstly, checks can be made that the process has been carried out correctly and then the outputs or outcomes of the operation can be checked.

Checking the process can be done either as part of the daily operations or as a periodic inspection. Statistical Process Control (SPC) is the term used in manufacturing for the collection of process data that can then be monitored against performance norms to identify when processes have or are likely to deviate from established tolerance levels (Oakland, 2007). There are, however, very few examples of the application of SPC to food and beverage operations. A similar approach that the industry uses more widely, especially but not exclusively, in relation to food hygiene, is Hazard Analysis Critical Control Point (HACCP). This technique, originally developed in food manufacturing to control hygiene risk, identifies the critical points in the production process and puts into place control measures to monitor performance at these points. As long as these measures stay in control, the quality of the whole process should be assured.

Periodic inspection, although not controlling the process as it happens, will check whether all procedures are being followed. The method used here is some form of operational or internal audit, whereby a detailed checklist is developed to cover all aspects of the operation. Some restaurants will have separate checklists for bar/cellar, hygiene, kitchen, restaurant and administration. Each area can then be further divided into headings. For example, a restaurant quality assurance evaluation may be broken down into cleanliness and hygiene, preparation, presentation/moments of truth, service, timing and guest reaction. Each heading can then have a series of items to be looked for. For example, under the preparation heading you might check whether all tables are laid up, cruets and sugar containers are filled, promotional material is displayed and ashtrays are available on smoking tables. Each correct item can then be awarded a number of points and totals can be calculated to compare with acceptable levels, previous performance or other restaurants in a chain.

Monitoring the process should ensure that the service delivery system is performing as it should but it will not check the level of customer satisfaction with the service received. Therefore a checking system also needs to be in place to measure the outputs from the system and the outcomes from the customers' point of view. A commonly used method is to use a mystery shopper or quality audit. Mystery shoppers visit the unit as normal customers but prepare a report on their experiences against established criteria. This technique is widely used in fast-food operations, commercial restaurants and international hotels.

Other approaches may use some form of customer satisfaction survey. The SERVQUAL instrument originally developed by Zeithaml et al. (1990) has been widely researched and customized specifically for lodging operations and a series of food and beverage applications (Knutson et al., 1991), but is not without its critics.

Activity 4: Comparing quality

Find a group of four or five friends and decide on two or three different restaurants that you would all like to visit and put them in rank order based on your expectations of their quality.

Now identify what you all consider to be the five or six key elements of the meal experience that affect customers' perceptions of quality. List these in the left hand column of the table below.

Are they all equally important or are some more important than others? Enter a weighting factor in the second column below if required. If one factor is twice as important as others then enter 2 and so on.

Now visit the restaurants and score each one against your five or six key elements on a scale of 5 = very good to 1 = poor or 0 if it doesn't have it at all.

Multiply the raw score by the weighting factor to get the weighted score for each operation. Total the scores for each operation.

Element	Weight	Operation 1		Operation 2		Operation 3	
		Raw score	Weighted score	Raw score	Weighted score	Raw score	Weighted score
Total							

Do the scores that you have now calculated match with your initial perceptions of the restaurants?

If not, why not?

Which is correct?

Acting

The final stage of the cycle is to act on the information collected. Consistency involves acting on any non-conformance to established standards (i.e. making sure you are doing what you set out to do). Quality improvement to move towards zero defects is a continuing process. The introduction of quality improvement teams, quality control circles or corrective action teams may help this move. The focus here is on improving the process. In looking at congruence the focus is on ensuring that the food and beverage concept still matches the customers' requirements. Over time customer expectations will change and there must be some way of highlighting these gaps between expectations and delivery. Once identified these new or changed requirements are passed on to the design team who then start the next round of the cycle.

DEVELOPING APPROACHES TO QUALITY MANAGEMENT

The development of the main approaches to managing quality is shown in the Figure 11.3. The diagram shows a movement from early approaches to quality relying on inspection of the finished product through quality control and quality assurance to total quality management (TQM).

Quality inspection

The earliest and probably the easiest approach to quality is the inspection approach. This simple approach is based on finding defects in a product or service before it reaches the customer by introducing an inspection stage or stages. There needs to be some specification of what the product should be like against which the product can be checked once it has been produced. The checking would probably be carried out by staff employed

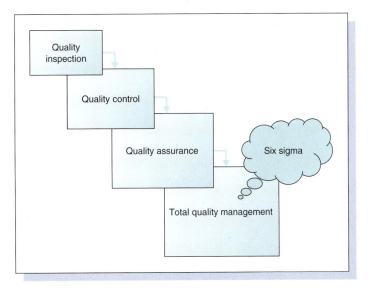

Figure 11.3
The development of approaches to quality management

mainly for that purpose. If any problems are found, that product will be rejected as non-conforming and will be sent back for re-work – to put the defects right – or for scrap. Manufacturing industry has tended to rely on a separate inspection department to carry out this task, but this is not a model that has been adopted in food and beverage operations. A simple example of inspection is the head chef standing at the hot plate during a banquet passing dishes across to the staff when satisfied with the standard reached.

The focus here is firmly on identifying defects. The emphasis is on a lack of quality followed by the rejection of substandard work. The inspection becomes something the staff dread and very negative feelings can be aroused. Quality is a question of checking physical attributes off against a checklist and hoping that nothing has been missed. The emphasis is on putting things right rather than on identifying the cause of the problem and dealing with it at source.

Quality control

The quality control approach still centres on inspection but recognizes the need for a detailed specification and that quality checks should be made throughout the production process. Using sophisticated inspection methods at appropriate points in the production process, the approach is more likely to find errors and will correct them earlier. The emphasis is still on a find and fix mentality. Quality control will not improve product or service quality, it will only highlight when it has gone wrong. A non-conforming product or service must be produced before action can be taken to put it right and this leads to inefficiency and waste. The focus has switched for the staff onto finding others to blame for the defects to avoid the 'disciplinary' action taken against those who make mistakes. The whole focus of quality control is on mistakes. The key features of the approach are shown in Table 11.1.

Quality assurance

Quality assurance recognizes the inefficiencies of waiting for mistakes to happen and strives to design quality into the process so that things cannot go wrong or if they do they are identified and corrected as they happen. Lasting and continuous improvement in quality can best be achieved through planning and preventing problems from arising at source. Moving the emphasis from inspection to prevention is helped by the introduction of a number of quality assurance tools and techniques such as SPC, blueprinting and quality costing. The approach is also likely to include a comprehensive quality system, perhaps based on the ISO 9000 series.

In quality assurance, however, the focus is not just on systems. Effective quality assurance must involve the development of a new operating philosophy and approach; one that is proactive rather than reactive, that includes involving employees in the

Underlying principles and philosophy	Based on a philosophy of inspecting quality in that concentrates on defect detection through post-production inspection.
Responsibility	Responsibility for quality is in the hands of a separate quality control department and individual inspectors.
Costs	It is assumed that there is a trade-off between quality and cost – better quality will cost more. The main costs are concerned with re-work and waste.
Improvement	With a starting point of detailed product specifications and itemized costings, the focus is on the quality of the product and improvement in quality is achieved by increasing inspection to catch more deviations from the specification.
The quality chain	The customers' role in quality is uncertain but at the end of the day they are the final inspection point. Suppliers have no role in quality.
Techniques and approaches	Mainly based around the provision of detailed specifications, such as standard recipes and makes good use of checklists of inspection points as in housekeeping.
Rationale	There are few real benefits of a quality control approach but it is quick to introduce and is better than not doing anything. It also represents a first step on the quality route. There is likely to be no external recognition of this approach.

Table 11.1
Key features of quality control

process from across normal departmental barriers. The key features of the approach are shown in Table 11.2.

Total quality management

The focus on the customer and the scale and nature of internal and external involvement are the main differences between the quality assurance and TQM approaches. In any TQM approach, the driving force is the focus on the satisfaction of customer needs. The whole system must be directed at customer satisfaction and anything that could get in the way of delivering this satisfaction must be removed. This involves the whole organization, including suppliers, looking for ways to improve continually the products or services delivered. TQM places the emphasis on the people in the organization and their roles, through a broadening of their outlook and skills, through encouragement of creativity, through training and empowerment, in measuring their performance and finding ways to improve it. The emphasis is on a management-led move towards teamwork and participation. Taking this holistic perspective can involve organizations in significant changes in their culture. It may be relatively easy to introduce new systems and procedures, but changing the culture is a much more difficult, but necessary, task. The key features of the approach are shown in Table 11.3.

Underlying principles and philosophy	Based on a philosophy of building quality into the hard systems of the operation and organizing quality into the soft systems, the focus is on producing to the design specification through the prevention of errors using in production monitoring. By stopping errors before they happen, there should be substantial cost savings.
Responsibility	The responsibility for quality may be given to a quality assurance department but it is also vested in line management who may even involve some employees.
Costs	The emphasis here is on producing the specified quality at the specified cost. By concentrating on prevention, these costs will increase but the costs involved in making errors – the failure costs – will be reduced.
Improvement	Starting with identifying the costs of quality and blueprinting or flow charting the operation, it is then possible to produce a procedure manual that will allow the introduction of variance analysis – finding out where things went wrong and why. This should lead to an improvement in quality through a clearer product specification, allied with control over the production process and the aim of getting it right first time every time.
The quality chain	The role and importance of customers are appreciated and both external and internal customer needs considered. Suppliers are also recognized as playing an important part in the quality chain and there will be detailed supplier quality agreements and some inspection of suppliers and their quality systems.
Techniques and approaches	The techniques used will include statistical process control, the use of fail-safe devices or poka-yokes, the introduction of quality teams or quality circles and a range of quality measurement tools.
Rationale	By focusing on the process of production, there should be greater control over product quality and reduced cost due to less waste and lower inventory. There will also be clear evidence of the production processes and procedures and with staff involvement the possibility of job enrichment. The approach will take up to two years to introduce but particularly suits those businesses wanting to compete on both cost and quality and who are probably some way down the quality road. External recognition would come for adopting systems that comply with standards such as ISO 9000.

Table 11.2
Key features of quality assurance

Six Sigma

Six Sigma is a set of management tools and approaches first developed by Motorola, who hold the trademark, in the mid-1980s and made famous by its implementation in General Electric. It is a rigorous approach based on the collection of operating data that can improve processes by reducing their variability and eliminating defects from the product or service. It is

Total quality management	
Underlying principles and philosophy	Based on a philosophy of structuring and managing quality into the whole organization of the business, the goals should be consistent satisfaction of the customer, constant improvements in products and processes leading to a highly competitive position in the market. Quality is involved in everything the business does, throughout the organization at all times.
Responsibility	The responsibility for quality is organization wide. Everyone is involved in delivering quality through a devolved strategic vision.
Costs	There is an inverse relationship between costs and quality – as quality increases the cost of quality comes down. However, cost is not really at issue. If there is a choice between cost and quality then quality will always win.
Improvement	By understanding the customers and the commitment of top management, the quality management structure is established that leads to a change in culture where continuous customer driven quality improvement is automatic.
The quality chain	Not only are customers seen as an important part of the business they are actively encouraged to become part of delivering quality. Suppliers are also involved in the quality effort and this may lead to strategic alliances or partnerships.
Techniques and approaches	The techniques used will include the active development of a quality culture and the development of change management, problem solving, quality analysis and quality improvement skills.
Rationale	Through guaranteed quality leading to total customer satisfaction and by competing on value and not on price, the business will achieve competitive advantage and external recognition. This approach will involve a considerable time commitment over a number of years but particularly suits long-term strategies of growing market share, sustained growth and aspirations for market leadership. External recognition would come in the form of awards such as Malcolm Baldridge or the EFQM.

Table 11.3
Key features of TQM

firmly based on the principles of quality control, quality assurance and TQM to drive quality improvement through an operation. For example, it could help a pizza delivery business to reduce the variation in its delivery times to the industry standard of thirty minutes and so maintain high levels of customer satisfaction.

There are three basic ways of looking at Six Sigma:

1. *Six Sigma as a statistical measure*: Sigma stands for standard deviation, a statistical measure of the variation in a set of normally distributed data. Used here it represents how well in control your processes are. It measures how many times your processes are outside the control limit you set, based on the number of standard deviations from the mean. A sigma level

of two standard deviations would mean that you achieved your standards only 68% of the time. In order to achieve Six Sigma you have to get things right 99.9997% of the time. You can only have three or four errors in a million operations.

2. *Six Sigma as a target*: The principal aim here, then, is to give everyone in the organization a target for the number of defects or errors that can creep into the operation. If you serve 100 meals a day over a year and have a success level of four sigma (99.38%) you would still have served almost 250 'bad' meals and had a significant number of dissatisfied customers. By reducing the number of defects, you reduce the associated failure costs and encourage a satisfied and loyal customer base. Six Sigma allows an organization to set a target to achieve and monitor its performance towards reaching this goal.

3. *Six Sigma as a management approach*: Six Sigma is shrouded in some mystery through the wide use of acronyms, detailed training in obscure techniques and the adoption of the green belt and black belt terminology from martial arts. It is, however, primarily a way of focusing management and employee attention on important issues. At Starwood Hotels which adopted the approach in 2001, managers are held accountable for key performance measures including customer satisfaction, key process performance, balanced scorecard measures, profit and loss, and employee attitude (Pande and Holpp, 2002). These measures are reviewed on a regular basis and when the measures do not meet the standard then a Six Sigma team will be charged to investigate and report. These solutions can then be shared with other hotels across the group, so sharing good practice. It provides a way of focusing management attention on improvement and getting the buy-in of employees to identify ways of making the improvement necessary.

Hospitality firms have been slow to adopt the full Six Sigma approach. Apart from Starwood Hotels & Resorts worldwide, who announced in 2001 that it would be adopt all the key tenets of the Six Sigma approach and that it expected this to deliver significant long-term financial benefits of more than $200 million in a five-year period, there has been little obvious interest shown. Six Sigma was part of the philosophy of Ritz Carlton in the 1990s that took them to the incredible achievement of winning two Malcolm Baldridge National Quality Awards in 1992 and 1999 and focused primarily on eliminating waste from their processes.

EXAMPLES OF QUALITY MANAGEMENT IN PRACTICE

This section describes examples of quality management in practice. The first looks at the Institute of Hospitality's Hospitality Assured Scheme which is now widely used across the industry in the UK and also internationally to provide a framework for a company's own approach to quality management. The second part of the section describes the approach of one company – Café

Spice Namasté – drawing on the personal experiences of the owners and managers.

The Hospitality Assured Scheme

The Hospitality Assured Standard for Business and Service Excellence has been developed by the IOH to provide businesses with a standard based on hospitality industry best practice against which they can judge their processes to deliver service. Consisting of some 10 key areas and around 30 individual criteria, the standard allows businesses of any size to judge, initially on a self-assessment basis, whether they have appropriate processes in place to deliver consistently excellent service and achieve their business goals. Following the self-assessment process businesses can elect to be assessed by registered external auditors and if successful be accredited by the IOH. With around 150 separate companies working against the standard, it has recently won the recognition of the British Quality Foundation who have endorsed Hospitality Assured as complying with all aspects of the internationally recognized European Foundation for Quality Management (EFQM) Business Excellence model. Hospitality Assured therefore now represents an international benchmark for either self-assessment or third-party assessment.

The quality map shown here (Figure 11.4) identifies 10 steps on the route to providing the quality your customers expect, which bears a close resemblance to the quality management cycle described earlier. If you are going to satisfy the needs of your customers, you must obviously first know who your customers are and what sorts of things they like. In other words you have to carry out *customer research*. With an existing business this is easy because your customers come into your operation every day and you can find out directly from them.

Having gathered information about your customer needs, you have to turn this into the mix of products and services that you are going to provide. You need to include those things that will make your business different from your competitors. You need to develop *the customer promise* that will form the basis of your business.

You are now in a position to start to think about how you will provide this service concept and how your business will perform. You need to establish your *business goals*. These goals should give a clear picture of where you want to be in a certain period of time and how this will translate into achieving your financial objectives.

Now the detailed work can start of turning the customer promise into a reality for every customer that comes into the operation. This requires some detailed *operational planning*. Time spent on getting the plan right at this stage makes everything that follows much more straightforward. Everybody needs to know what their responsibilities are. All the critical stages in the operation need to be identified and you need to be sure you have the resources to carry your plan out.

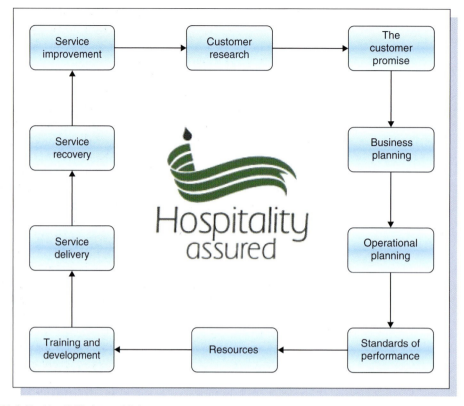

Figure 11.4 The Hospitality Assured Scheme

Before you are ready to open your doors to your customers, three further things need to be in place. First, you need to make sure you have converted your plans into a series of *standards of performance* and it is probably a good idea to have these all written down. Then you need to make sure that all your staff have received the *training and support* they will require to do their jobs to the best of their abilities. Finally, you need to make sure that you have all the *resources* available that you will need to serve your customers.

Now is the crucial stage that will be the ultimate measure of your success. The moment of truth when the customer comes into your operation and orders a meal or asks for their room. The point of *service delivery*. The point at which your promise to the customer should be fulfilled.

It isn't enough to assume that if you planned it all properly it will always work. You have to have some way of checking that everything is going according to plan. You must have some form of check and if that finds that things are not quite as they should be then you need to put things right straight away. You need to take immediate corrective action to ensure full *service recovery* and find ways of making sure that the same problem does not come up again.

You should now have a successful operation that is delivering a range of products and services that your customers want in an efficient and effective way. But the story is not quite over. There will always be ways that you can do things a little bit better and you need to spend some time and effort looking for these to make continuous *service improvement*.

Unfortunately even with these improvements you still cannot rest because customer tastes are constantly changing and you need to keep up to date with what your competitors are doing. In other words you need to start the cycle again with *customer research*.

After the formal external assessment all the scores for all the companies who have been assessed are recorded on the Hospitality Assured National Benchmarking database held at the University of Surrey. Taking a snapshot of the database as a whole and comparing businesses in different sectors, the database provides companies with the mean, minimum and maximum scores as well as the top and bottom 10 percentiles, so that each can judge how they compare to their direct sectoral competitors and how their sector compares to the industry as a whole. At the regular user group meetings, members of the scheme are also invited to share examples of their practices with other members. It is hoped that this process can be extended and developed into a regular series of detailed best practice case studies. There is evidence to suggest from the database that those firms that have been in the scheme for more than a year have consistently improved their performance against the standard year on year.

Café Spice Namasté

This case explores a highly acclaimed mini-chain of Indian restaurants offering authentic Indian cooking. The very highly regarded executive chef enhances the service with some thirty years of international experience and leads the entire operation. There are stringent controls and procedures for the entire operation, with a particular emphasis on staff training and development. The owners offer 'high-class cuisine with good service at affordable prices in a vibrant, friendly atmosphere'. The operation is renowned for its creativity, ingenuity, flair and very attentive service.

Café Spice Namasté was opened in 1995 in Prescott Street in London. The restaurant offers a wide range of authentic, traditional and perhaps 'eclectic' Indian dishes. There is another branch located in Battersea, and fairly recently a third restaurant was opened named Parsee, located in Highgate Hill. The latter is somewhat distinguished from the other two as it offers food mainly from the executive chef's home community. However, there is no shortage of competition.

The restaurants currently employ 46 people. As the business expanded, the number of covers moved from 110 into the range of 250–275. The number of services provided has also increased and currently includes a successful and highly efficient sandwich production unit that offers sandwiches, baguettes and wraps.

The restaurants have won various awards including Most Employee-Friendly Organization. They have also been recipients of numerous Best in Britain Awards starting in 1992 and also included a Catey award for education and training for executive chef and co-owner, Cyrus Todiwala, in 2005. They have won awards for health and hygiene and are very committed to the environment and have won three separate awards for best practice, bringing about various savings in terms of heat, light and power usage.

Due to the area in which the business operates the owners have found it necessary to monitor the market closely and they are currently developing business links in the city. In order to remain competitive they have been conducting some informal methods of market research that basically include observing what is happening in the market. However, the executive chef stated that:

Keeping up with market trends is not necessarily the best form of action. It is not. We can only try but we can't destroy a culture that we have built up just because a trend demands something else. So a focus has to shift on that customer, who is our customer.

The main goals for the business are to make the restaurants rank amongst the best of their kind in London and the world; to give customers good value and good service as well as a good time and finally, to make a profit.

To achieve quality standards, the first thing we do, of course, is to keep on investing in ongoing training. We have our own standards set. We have things, for instance, that we follow all the time, service procedures, for instance. Standards of food etc. are controlled. We have standardised, consistent quality maintaining systems in place so those standards we do maintain. As far as service to the customer goes, yes, that's being operated all the time so we hope to achieve more and more and more.

Controls and procedures • • •

One of the main motives for implementing procedures was the expansion of the business. As the business expanded it also became fragmented and keeping it under control was increasingly difficult.

All of the service standards and procedures for the restaurant are documented, but this is not strictly the case in the kitchen. Strict personal control is used, stressing that everything is kept up to date and of a very high standard. This is achieved by 'checking and having briefings and meetings. Listening, not only to staff but reading all the comments made by guests and checking all aspects (of the operation)'.

Not everything that occurs during service is documented. However, a diary is used to record any incidents and they are reviewed the next day with the requisite staff, if the matter does not require immediate attention. They always try to follow up complaints immediately, this also has a specific procedure, and only the more serious claims are documented.

> *The response is to ensure that that gentleman or that lady is back in my restaurant as a fully committed customer again and that is the main focus. We don't want to lose them.*

Customers • • •

One of the more efficient ways to determine what the customers want is to simply go into the restaurant at a busy period and see what people are demanding. The owners also spend a significant proportion of time chatting with their customers. The executive chef tries to meet as many guests as he can between the three operations, as this is the best way to determine exactly what is happening and assess the service. The executive chef stated that 'we don't hover around the customer but we do make sure that every single table has been asked (about the service)'.

They not only are interested in current customers; they also try to retain repeat customers as well as previous 'one-time' customers, stating that 'We keep abreast as much as possible with our old customers. Try to identify whether they have moved on; whether their jobs have gone; whether their offices have shifted'.

In terms of food controls, a sample system was implemented. On a random basis, samples of food are sent to the Government Food laboratories twice every year for testing. They conduct shelf life tests, try to determine whether the food was chilled properly, whether it was stored in appropriate conditions, whether it is being kept in the right temperature controlled area and so on.

The executive chef creates all of the recipes and then formulas are identified. These are then given to the staff, however, his wife first tests them and samples are given to customers as well. Once they are approved then, 'that's the standard and that standard is set. Nobody can change that standard then because that standard defines the selling price'.

Staff • • •

The organization acknowledges that the 'single biggest asset is our dedicated, hardworking workers'. Thereby they try to '…identify each of the skills within the workforce. Tap on those skills, develop on those skills and do things that skill can best do. That's what we do'.

From the recruitment stage the executive chef stated that 'in this industry what is extremely important is the "gut feeling". There is nothing more vital to us because if we can't trust an individual we can't have them'. Co-operation is crucial. 'With no co-operation you can't go ahead with anything'.

There is a full briefing for the staff everyday at 12 noon. This is an opportunity also to discuss previous lapses in service and customer comments. One of the chefs is also invited to discuss any issues concerning the kitchen.

General suggestions from staff are taken very seriously because 'they are the people on the floor and they are the people who deal with the customers and they are the people who, eventually, are the key to your business'.

Training • • •

Within the operations, training is viewed as particularly important. There are training days at each of the properties (once a week). These are used to reiterate verbally the standards and procedures. There is an ongoing internal training programme and audio-visual facilities are used to further enhance this. The internal training is continuous and comprehensive, using a training room located in the building.

The training needs of the staff are identified via informal chats and a training plan is formulated and they adhere to this for a calendar year. Staff are continuously encouraged to undergo further training. External training is also promoted and several staff members are actively involved in various aspects of training.

Communication with staff can sometimes prove problematic however; the fact that the owners can also speak two or three languages reduces this somewhat. Training classes are held once a month, on Saturdays and the staff are requested to arrive at work one hour early in order to attend.

Outcomes • • •

- 'One of the things that has always kept us abreast of what is happening or ahead of everything else is our reputation. It's a huge reputation that can't be allowed to be tarnished and we have to be on top of things at all times'.
- 'We have to have standards in place otherwise the organization would not have grown'.
- 'The fact that we were a 60 seat restaurant in 1991 and now collectively, we have 225 seats is proof in itself that there are systems in place that allow us to grow'.
- Due to strict procedures any queries or complaints can be quickly followed up and traced from beginning to the end of the process. Basically they can follow up any complaint because of the extensive paper trail. 'We know we can take out sheets for the last five years and follow up'.
- The random testing of the food is one way of checking that the standards are being followed. 'We do it for our own benefit so we are doing the right thing for our customers'.
- Some of the customers have been going to the restaurants for up to eleven years and on a regular basis, some of the more loyal customers have been going to the restaurants every week for eleven years.
- 'That is in itself, an indicator that the standards are being maintained and that the highest level of quality control is being looked into'.

- They have achieved a customer base of 85% repeat and regular clientele.
- In terms of HACCP, this aids in ensuring that food quality controls are in-place and adhered to, as it requires regular daily updates and checks.
- 'Our staff may not have the highest level of competence, but they definitely have the highest level of commitment. That allows us to grow'.
- The executive chef is of the opinion that they have the lowest rate of turnover in the industry. Asserting that, 'the core group of people hasn't shifted in eleven years'.
- 'Good output and productivity are the benefits of good training'.

This organization has acknowledged the significant role that more formal quality management systems can play and are seeking to utilize them within the various restaurants, particularly due to the fact that they are continually expanding and it will increasingly be less feasible for the senior management team to be personally and constantly present during service operations. This shows a clear proactive approach to business operations.

Summary

This chapter has considered:

- The nature of quality, its definition and importance for food and beverage operations.
- The rationale for a systematic approach to quality management.
- The different approaches to quality management and how one approach build towards the next. The advantage and disadvantages of each approach were also considered.
- The experience of two applications of quality management in food and beverage.

Just because a company has introduced a TQM approach does not mean that it can ignore quality inspection or quality control completely, although there should now be very few defects left to find. Each company needs to build its own approach to quality that reflects its own operating environment, its own organizational culture and its own customers' special needs. Although managing quality is a complex problem to tackle, increasing numbers of companies are finding ways of building quality into their operations and improving the standards of service and products they deliver to their customers. Those companies that do not have such a quality approach will find it increasingly difficult to compete.

Review questions

1. Consider the service offered by a fast-food chain and a fine dining restaurant. In what ways are quality issues the same and different in the two establishments?
2. In what ways do food and beverage operations face particular challenges in delivering quality to their customers?
3. To what extent is achieving Six Sigma possible in food and beverage operations?
4. Read the article by Parasuraman, Zeithaml and Berry explaining the development of the SERVQUAL instrument. Now read the article by Francis Buttle reviewing and criticizing their approach. Now search for articles over the last ten years that have used the SERVQUAL approach. Given the challenges made by Buttle, why do you think it has been so widely used?

Further reading

British Standard 4778 (1987). *Glossary of Quality Terms*. London: British Standards Institute.

Buttle, F. (1994). Marketing and merchandising. In B. Davis and A. Lockwood (eds.), *Food and Beverage Management: A Selection of Readings*. Oxford: Butterworth-Heinemann.

Buttle, F. (1996). SERVQUAL: Review, critique, research agenda. *European Journal of Marketing*, 30(1), 8–32.

Buzzell, R. D. and Gale, B. T. (1987). *The PIMS Principles – Linking Strategy to Performance*. New York: The Free Press.

Cassee, E. and Reuland, R. J. (1983). Hospitality in hospitals. In R. J. Reuland and E. Cassee (eds.), *The Management of Hospitality*. Oxford: Pergamon Press, pp. 143–163.

Crosby, P. B. (1984). *Quality without Tears*. New York: McGraw-Hill.

Deming, W. E. (1982). *Quality, Productivity and Competitive Position*. Massachusetts: Massachusetts Institute of Technology, Centre for Advanced Engineering Study.

Fitzgerald, L., Johnston, R., Brignall, S., Silvestro, R. and Voss, C. (1991). *Performance Measurement in Service Businesses*. London: The Chartered Institute of Management Accountants.

Heskett, J., Sasser, W. E. and Hart, C. W. L. (1990). *'Service Breakthroughs: Changing the Rules of the Game'*. New York: The Free Press.

Jones, P. and Lockwood, A. (2004). *The management of hotel operations*. London: Thomson Learning.

Knutson, B., Stevens, P., Wullaert, C., Patton, M. and Yokoyama, F. (1991). Lodgserv – A service quality index for the lodging industry. *Hospitality Research Journal*, 14(3), 277–284.

Lockwood, A. and Bowen, A. (2003). Enhancing customer value for successful small-business operations. *The Hospitality Review*, 5(4), 46–51.

Lockwood, A., Bowen, A. and Ekinci, Y. (2002). Achieving standards for successful small business operations. *The Hospitality Review*, 4(3), 37–43.

Oakland, J. S. (2007). *Statistical Process Control*, 6th edn. Oxford: Butterworth Heinemann.

Pande, P. and Holpp, L. (2002). *What is Six Sigma?* New York: McGraw-Hill.

Parasuraman, A., Zeithaml, V. A. and Berry, L. L. (1985). A conceptual model of service quality and its implications for future research. *Journal of Marketing*, 49(Fall), 41–50.

Tenner, A. R. and DeToro, I. J. (1992). *Total Quality Management: Three Steps to Continuous Improvement*. Massachusetts: Addison-Wesley Publishing Co.

Walker, J. R. and Salameh, T. T. (1990). The QA payoff. *Cornell Hotel and Restaurant Quarterly*, 30(4), 57–59.

Zeglat, D., Ekinci, Y., Lockwood, A. and Li, G. (2007). *An Investigation of the Relationship between Service Quality and Profitability in the UK Budget Hotel Industry*, QUIS 10 The 10th International Research Symposium on *Service Excellence in Management*, June 14–17, The College of Business Administration and The Rosen College of Hospitality Management, University of Central Florida, Orlando, FL.

Zeithaml, V. A., Parasuraman, A. and Berry, L. L. (1990). *Delivering Service Quality*. New York: The Free Press.

Trends
and
developments

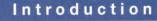

Introduction

This chapter sets out to highlight a range of current trends affecting the food and beverage manager. It is naturally selective and provides only an initial insight into some of the emerging issues facing the industry. The importance of these issues to different industry sectors and in different countries will vary, but the chapter will help you to understand the basics and provide you with a foundation and further details of where to pursue particular issues in more depth.

Chapter objectives

After working through this chapter you should be able to:

- Understand a range of trends affecting the food and beverage manager.
- Identify the possible influence of the media on consumer behaviour.
- Discuss changes in consumer choices in the UK and USA.
- Understand current environmental issues.
- Be aware of recent trends in financing a food and beverage operation.
- Be aware of ethical issues in the industry.
- Understand the definitions of high tech food.

CONSUMER TRENDS

One of the biggest changes in the past decade in the food and beverage area has been the recognition of the importance of consumers and the choices they make. The industry has become more market led and operators who do not take account of their customers' needs and wants have suffered. This change has been partly reflected in the growth of food-related issues reported in the media and the wide array of television programmes with food, cooking, chefs and restaurants as their focus. These programmes range from Jamie Oliver's *School Dinners* to Gordon Ramsay's *the F Word* or Raymond Blanc's *The Restaurant*, alongside long running series of *Hell's Kitchen*, *Ready Steady Cook* or the competition of *Saturday Kitchen* on BBC v. *Saturday Cooks* on ITV. Searching for programmes related to food on UK TV channels at the time of writing, resulted in 40 separate programmes in one week alone and that excludes the UK TV Food Channel! To this can be added increasing numbers of restaurant reviews in all the major newspapers and the emergence of specialist magazines such as *Good Food*, *Delicious* or *Olive*. Media interest and involvement in food and cooking, in the UK at least, has never been higher.

According to a recent Mintel Report (2007a) on the effect of the media on eating out, half of the consumers they surveyed did not believe that the media had affected their eating out decisions but they suggest that the effect of the media is perhaps in some ways so subtle that people do not realize, or do not wish to admit, that they have been influenced. The report suggests that as the amount of media coverage has increased, consumers have become more interested in particular foods, cuisines and ingredients, showing more sophistication in their choices when eating out. Generally, customers have become more knowledgeable about nutrition and healthy eating, especially following the UK government's healthy eating campaign, and how different types of foods should be prepared and cooked, and this is having an effect on where people choose to eat out and which dishes they will select. This in turn has led to more restaurants publishing nutritional information on their menus or websites and introducing more salads, vegetable side dishes and lower fat options. Many fast-food operators have found that customers are increasingly critical of their product offer and have again tried to respond with healthier options. For example, Burger King offer a Garden Salad without dressing that has less than 35 calories and a range of low fat dressings in Honey and Mustard, French, or Tomato and Basil flavours with less than 3% fat. Another interesting finding from this report is that almost one-third of their respondents would be prepared to pay a premium price for 'high quality' food when eating out which perhaps suggests an opportunity for restaurant operators to make profit out of raising their game.

Activity

Visit a number of different websites for restaurants appealing to different sectors of the market. Which of these companies have detailed nutritional information on their websites? Why might there be a difference between operators?

The Mintel Organization also prepare very detailed reports on the eating out market in general, which provide very useful information for food and beverage operators on who is eating what, where and how often. The latest report (Mintel, 2007b) has highlighted the key trends of the last few years. These include:

- Continued growth in the eating out market in the UK with an overall growth in spending of around 25% between 2002 and 2006.
- This growth in the market has been fuelled particularly by the substitution of eating out for 'normal' eating at home – what is called the substitute domestic market.
- The growth has not all been due to replacing cooking at home but has been further encouraged by media coverage and the celebrity chefs, experience of new cuisines while on holiday abroad and by the increasing variety of possible eating out venues.
- From an estimated spend on eating out in 2006 of some £29 billion, the sector is expected to grow to nearly £37 billion in 2012.
- There does appear to be a clear split in the market between operations offering excellent value and being able to compete with home cooking on price and those up-market operations, including the gastropubs, where people are prepared to pay, quite high prices for the more luxurious and indulgent choices. This has left the middle of the market, the casual dining operations, as a particularly dynamic and innovative but especially competitive sector.
- Another dichotomy in the market is between chain operations and individual outlets. The modern consumer has a new

found confidence to choose individual operations without the need for the reassurance and reliability of the brand but at the same time chain operations continue to grow and flourish and are seen as a good target for investment.

- A final dichotomy highlighted by the report is between the innovative nature of the eating out market and operations developing new cuisines, new niche products and processes as against increasing regulation of staffing and food service generally that may make it more difficult for smaller operations to comply and compete and so reducing variety and choice.

A similar report in the United States (Sloan, 2007) has highlighted 10 key food trends. These include:

1. Contrary to trends in the UK, economic pressures are encouraging more Americans to eat and cook more dinners at home, with three quarters of the respondents eating dinner at home at least five days a week – although many of these will be restaurant branded meals from a food store or takeaways. At the same time, however, eating out for breakfast and lunch is continuing to grow.
2. There is a growing 'foodie' culture and many customers are 'trading up' to more exotic and gourmet meals, both in restaurants and as indulgent treats to cook at home.
3. There has been a growth in pre-prepared convenient products, such as peeled and chopped, and even cooked, vegetables and upscale frozen dinners. Portion sizes are however reducing, with TGI Fridays Right Portion Right Price promotion (30% smaller portions for between $6.99 and $8.99) being reflected in smaller cook at home portions.
4. More foods with greater sensual appeal in both flavour, aroma and texture.
5. Increasing numbers of children but increasing awareness of child obesity and so interest in healthier options.
6. For grown ups, there is a trend towards foods 'without' – fat free, dairy free, sugar free, caffeine free and so on.
7. There has been a growing interest in locally sourced, seasonal produce from specialist or artisan producers, with a strong association with a reduction in food miles – the distance between the producer and the plate.
8. This is linked to an interest in more healthy eating, either to reduce the risk of developing a health problem or to help with an existing issue.
9. A new interest in unusual beverages, ranging from high energy drinks to ready-to-drink tea and coffee, and bottled mineral waters and even Health Colas.
10. Snacking and sharing extends from new snack offers in the mid afternoon and late at night growing in popularity in fast-food operations, to ranges of upscale bite size appetizers for sharing and even the appearance of bite size dessert platters.

Activity

Compare and contrast the trends described above for the UK and the USA. Where are the main differences? What possible reasons are there for this?

ENVIRONMENTAL ISSUES

There are a number of environmental issues of which food and beverage operations must be aware. Three of those issues strongly related to food and beverage operations are explored. The issues of waste management, energy and water consumption, and the effects to the environment by procuring products from far away parts of the world.

Waste management

One of the most important environmental issues for food and beverage operations is that of waste management. The importance of recycling and reusing products has become a focus of many local government agencies. The reality of inefficient waste management is becoming more apparent as the shortage of land where waste can be buried is increasing day by day. Furthermore the effects on human health due to pollution, the effects of excess packaging which can be easily witnessed in any supermarket and the fact that waste has to be transported in order to be buried often to large distances adding to carbon emissions and further pollution.

So what can operators do to ensure they minimize waste? Depending on the size of the operation the operator could do some or all of the following:

- Invest in waste minimizing technology such as grinders and incinerators not unlike the ones that are currently utilized in some cruise ships.
- Reuse items such as printer paper, envelopes, packaging.
- Reduce usage of things like paper, for example do not print what does not need printing.
- Compost as much of the waste as possible.
- Recycling glass, paper, aluminium and plastic can reduce an operations waste by up to 35%.
- Invest in a vacuum drainage system (e.g. see www.evds.org.uk).
- Ensure you operate a waste minimization programme and that you evaluate the amounts of waste your business generate regularly.
- Educate your staff, suppliers and customers so that they also minimize waste whilst on your premises. The Acorn House restaurant, for example, offers various portion sizes in an attempt to reduce customer wastage and at the same time offer better value for money.

These are only a few of the things that a responsible and effective food and beverage manager should consider about their business. It is imperative to be informed and keep up with advancements in the area as the more efficient in waste management an operation is the more profitable it will be.

Activity

In groups of 2 to 3, research and identify the waste minimization and recycling programmes that local governments operate in your area. Visit at least two of your local restaurants and ask a few of the staff if they are aware of those programmes and what policies they have in place. Share your findings with the rest of your class.

Energy and water consumption

Another major area of concern is that of energy and water consumption. It is of course highly connected to waste management as an effective waste management programme would also reduce excessive use of energy or water. More governments will soon be imposing a carbon tax or levy which could easily be applied to all companies including hotels and restaurants. In the UK, such a tax was introduced in 2001 and saw the increase of energy bills for hospitality operations to up to 15%. Whilst the EU had introduced the Emissions Trading Scheme (ETS) that enables companies exceeding individual CO_2 emissions targets to buy allowances from 'greener' ones in order to reach the EU targets under the Kyoto Protocol. Energy and water will get more expensive as the years go by and although for energy there may be alternative sources, water could become a rare commodity in the not so distant future. Ensuring that an operations use of energy and water is efficient will reduce costs effectively increasing profits.

Ways of reducing energy and water consumption can be achieved by:

- Using energy efficient equipment and light bulbs.
- Recycling of grey water.
- Utilizing alternative energy sources, such as solar power.
- Adjusting taps and toilet water tanks.
- Minimizing water leakages.
- Training staff to switch off lights when not needed and use water responsibly.

There are a number of companies that are taking steps to minimize their energy and water consumption and its effects to the environment. For example the Orphalese a new cruise liner, features alternative power sources, a wastewater treatment plant, washing machines that utilize sound waves and use 10 gallons of water as opposed to 60 in conventional machines (www.theorphalese.com). Another example in the UK McDonalds is planning to have its 155 strong delivery fleet running on a mixture of in-store cooking oil and rapeseed by the end of 2007 (Druce, 2007).

Activity

If you are a restaurant manager how would you ensure you conserved energy and reduced water consumption in your operation? Do you think the industry is doing enough in this area?

Thinking globally, buying locally

In July 2005, the Department for Environment, Food and Rural Affairs (DEFRA) in the UK released a report that showed that the amount of food transported annually was increased by 23% since 1978, and that the average distance for each trip also up by 50%. The report also showed transport by air was on the increase and the full social, environmental and economic cost effects was estimated at a total of over £9 billion each year (Mae Wan Ho and Gala, 2005). The report identifies the major changes that have affected the increase as:

- The globalization of the food industry with increased sourcing of food within the UK and abroad.
- The consolidation of the food supply base into fewer, larger suppliers, partly to meet demand for bulk year-round supplies of uniform produce.
- Major changes in delivery patterns with most goods now routed through supermarket regional distribution centres using larger heavy goods vehicles.
- Centralized and concentrated sales in supermarkets where a weekly shop by car has replaced frequent pedestrian shop visits (Mae Wan Ho and Gala, 2005).

Although the findings of this report do not concentrate on the hospitality industry alone it is evident that procuring goods that have travelled a number of miles on a plane from another country cannot be sustained. The industry must take the lead and illustrate that procuring goods locally where possible is a way of thinking about the global environment and reducing negative impacts. There are a number of restaurants that have taken such steps to ensure they minimize their food miles. Some examples include The Glasshouse Restaurant in Lyndhurst, UK. The Acorn House Restaurant in London UK, The North Pond Restaurant in Chicago, USA.

The debate of course may be that if we support local farmers what about developing countries such as Kenya that wholly rely on developed countries to purchase their produce. In an article by Corporate Watch in 2004 the author argues the fact that small farmers in developing countries are seen to be marginalized often receiving no more of 12–14% of the export as the supermarkets have total control in setting prices making it unprofitable for these farmers to remain in business (Food Miles, 2004).

Activity

This is a debating activity. It can be done in pairs of two opposing individuals or in two opposing groups, one side defends statement A, and the other statement B.

Statement A: Buying locally reduces the carbon footprint, supports local producers and helps the environment.

Statement B: Buying locally condemns developing countries farmers to poverty and starvation.

FINANCING THE OPERATION

Restaurant operators are always looking at innovative ways to finance their operations with Real Estate Investment Trusts (REIT) being the latest exciting financing option in the industry. Asset financing has also been a widely used option in the last decade amongst small- and medium-size operators. Finally the hotel industry is going down the road of selling rooms to their customers, so arguing the emergence of a similar scheme within food and beverage operations in the future would make sense.

The emergence of REIT

REIT have been around for many years but in the UK only recently have hotels and restaurants been allowed to join into such schemes. REIT allows individuals to invest in property listed on the stock exchange. The added bonus is that investing in REIT you effectively invest on property without having to pay corporation tax. Properties within the portfolio of the REIT must generate their own income and a person can own no more than 10% of each trust.

Vector Hospitality was meant to be the first hospitality firm in the UK to float on the market, however the company pulled out due to lack of investor confidence (Times Online, 2007). The scheme has found success in the USA where hospitality firms were allowed to join in, in 2001 (Hotel and Motel Management, 2007). Today a number of firms exist such as Ashford Hospitality Trust Inc., Diamond Rock Hospitality Company, Highland Hospitality Corporation, Hospitality Properties Trust, Strategic Hotels & Resorts Inc., Supertel Hospitality Inc., to name a few. The success of REIT's in the USA suggests that soon there will be a similar trend soon in the UK and possibly the rest of Europe.

Asset financing

For restaurant companies that are in the growth stage and in need to release capital back into their business, asset financing is one of the solutions that they would often look into. In areas such as London, where property can be very expensive, selling one building under this scheme may be enough to finance another property in another city. More specifically an owner would sell a building (but would retain operational control of the company) and lease it back using the capital released to further expand the companies. Known as an Operating Lease this type of finance sees the asset transferred to the lessor whilst he rents the asset to the lessee over a period which may be from one to five years or in some cases more. As the lease expires the asset returns to the lessor who may sell or rent the property to a new person or the lease can be extended. A successful restaurant owner who may wish to open his second or even third property will often find this method of financing an attractive option, although it carries the commitment of a long-term contract.

Buy a restaurant table

A recent trend in hospitality is that of buying hotel rooms that the hotel operator rents out to guests and returns part of the revenue to the investor. The Chicago Mandarin Hotel is one of the latest hotel properties to announce the use of this type of investment (Manson, 2007). Typically investors are allowed certain use of the hotel facilities and the use of their room for a number of days per year. In London, for example, hotel rooms typically cost from £150,000 to £500,000 to build so the scheme is attractive to investors who are regular travellers to the city and wish to invest a smaller amount of money than buying a small flat which may cost from £300,000 upwards. In the same context it may be possible that in the future, the restaurant industry will witness the 'Buy your Own Table' option where investors buy a table, get certain privileges when booking in the restaurant and enjoy a share of some of the revenue for the particular table.

ETHICAL ISSUES

Ethics in food and beverage management is an important area and one that could easily be the focus of another book. Here, the reader is directed towards two issues that are current and will probably continue to be so in the next few years. Ethical food production and a debate on ethics in tipping practises.

Ethics and food produce

Restaurants may offer in their menu items that are controversial due to the way they are produced and the effect that these techniques have on the living animals. For example, foie gras is a French delicacy where geese are forced fed corn mash through a tube that is placed in the animal's oesophagus. The result is an enlarged liver with a number of possible negative effects. A number of countries such as Denmark, Italy and Germany have banned force feeding whilst the EU is currently considering a ban on foie gras. Another example is that of white crated veal were calves are confined in veal crates no bigger than 2 ft wide, and the animals cannot turn or move at all or see day light in order to produce veal of a pale coloured flesh, which is effectively the product of induced borderline anaemia. Other examples can include the use of types of fish that are extremely depleted or fish that is caught in a way that harms other animals such as dolphins. The list of examples of menu items that are used in the industry can be a long one and although information is abundant about those types of produce we find that still operators continue to feature such items in their menus. The debate as to whose responsibility it is as to whether such food items should be consumed continues. Is it the restaurant manager who should claim responsibility and should not use such products or is it the consumer who should refrain from buying such items? Food and beverage management is about managing the operation effectively and ensuring not only the short-term viability of the operation but also its long-term one. Logic would dictate that utilizing sustainable methods of food production would protect the long-term efficiency of the business. So it makes sense from a business point of view to be an ethical food and beverage manager. But even if the benefits are not that great it is the responsibility of both the consumer and the food and beverage operator to ensure they have the knowledge of where their food or beverage comes from and how it was produced. Food and beverage managers do not just sell food and beverages but an experience, so educating their customers can also become part of that experience enabling such operators to have an innovative advantage such as in the case study of the Acorn House Restaurant in Chapter 4.

Ethics in tipping

For many years numerous writers have proposed theories about the differences between a service and a product. The nature of the tangible and intangibles in service, the perishability of services and the need for the recipient of the service to be present at the time of delivery are just a few. We also know that many products have an element of service and many services have a product attached so how in these situations do we determine whether we are primarily receiving a service or simply acquiring a product? One answer to this, and the basis of a clear ethical debate, is whether or not we are required to give a gratuity.

This view about whether we are primarily buying services or products is more complex than it looks at first glance. For example, if we go to the supermarket and buy our groceries the cashier will put all the items through the scanner and offer to pack them for you or get an assistant to pack them, you pay the bill and leave, there is no notion of giving either the cashier or the packer a gratuity. If however you buy these same groceries 'online' do you give the delivery driver a gratuity?

Consider then the situation in a restaurant. It is perfectly legal to charge for service, provided it is clearly stated on the menu and customers are aware that a percentage will be added to the cost of their meal as a service charge. However what the customer cannot do in this circumstance is not avail themselves of the service. In other words you cannot serve yourself and avoid this additional charge.

The question therefore hinges on whether you believe that it is ethical to be required to pay a gratuity for receiving a service that is an integral part of the product on offer (i.e. the meal). In addition many will argue that without such a gratuity system service would not be as good or as efficient, that in fact the promise of a gratuity somehow motivates staff to do their job properly. Consider going into a self-service cafeteria, you may look at the menu to check the choice available and glance at the prices to see if they are acceptable. The prices will be fully inclusive of all costs including staffing and an element of profit. The price charged would be generally lower than that charged in a serviced restaurant, partly because of the product range but also staff costs will be lower and you are not normally expected to tip the counter staff, although occasionally you do see a dish with small change by the cash desk that is an invitation to tip. So, if a serviced restaurant includes higher staffing costs amongst other things in its pricing then why is it necessary to add an additional charge for service because without the service you would not be able to avail yourself of the product. Consider also the wording that appears on some menus concerning gratuities listed in Table 12.1 with some suggested euphemisms for how they are worded.

One area of hospitality where the gratuity culture is essential to the income of service staff is the cruise ship industry. Most shipping companies whether merchant or passenger sail under what are termed 'Flags of Convenience' (FOC) which means they fly a flag of a country other than the country of ownership. Whilst most of the problems associated with this practice are concerned with merchant vessels, the International Transport Workers Federation (ITWF) also cite a number of related difficulties for

Menu wording	Possible euphemism
Service is not included	We expect you to add at least 10% to your bill as a gratuity
Service is at the customers discretion	Don't be too discreet leave at least 10%
A service charge of 12.5% will be added to parties of eight or more	We want to be sure that when everyone in your party pays separately we still get a decent tip
For your convenience a 15% service charge will be added to your bill	This allows us to attract you with lower menu prices without it affecting profitability

Table 12.1
A cynical view of menu terminology

the staff that work on passenger ships including cruise ships. The ITWF suggest that in addition to tax advantages FOC allow cruise ships to employ cheap labour on minimal wages with very basic living and working conditions. Whilst this is not true of all cruise ship companies, Seabourn Cruises, for example, have banned tipping and instead offer employees a revenue/profit sharing scheme together with a reasonable salary, but there are a number that still rely heavily on passenger gratuities. In most cases these are administered by the pursers desk onboard the ship. Each passenger's account has a fixed gratuity added each day of the cruise as a gratuity for the stateroom (room) attendant. Norwegian Cruise Lines (NCL) for example, charges $10 per day for each passenger aged thirteen or over and $5 per day for those below this age. Royal Caribbean provides vouchers for each passenger printed with prepaid amounts for all service staff other than bartenders. Passengers simply give each of the staff, stateroom attendant, waiter, wine waiter, headwaiter, etc. a signed voucher. Bar drinks are charged to the room account and include a service charge of 20%. Different cruise lines adopt different methods but all allow lower basic wages to be paid, in some cases as low as $50 per month.

Activity

Research and discuss the following. If a cruise ship adopts a fixed gratuity system in order to pay staff a living wage how does this motivate staff? If a passenger believes that the gratuity system is tipping staff in addition to their wages are they likely to consider giving additional amounts? The gratuity system adds about 10% to the cost of a cruise and in some way this becomes a hidden charge, companies like Seabourn, who do not allow tipping but instead charge more for the cruise, so they can pay staff a better salary may either be losing out in market share through higher price or maybe gaining market share as the higher price is viewed as higher quality.

The issue of gratuities will continue to raise debate, some staff see gratuities as a right, some customers feel service staff are just too attentive and somewhat insincere. For managers managing a service where an integral part of the staff income is derived from gratuities there are both practical and ethical issues from deciding whether to be involved at all in the distribution of gratuities to what shifts or work patterns you should allocate to which staff as these may have a bearing on the earning potential. Is a gratuity system the correct way to pay hospitality service staff in the 21st century or will legislation on minimum wages will see gratuities phased out?

In a recent article *Tipping and Its Alternatives* Michael Lynn (2006), Associate Professor of consumer behaviour in Cornell's Hotel School, considers both sides of the argument of conventional tipping, service charges and service inclusive menu pricing. Lynn's research

Activity

In the 21st century are gratuities a good method of ensuring that those who work in front-line hospitality service jobs receive a liveable income or has the gratuity culture that typifies this sector been hi-jacked by employers who see it as both a way of continuing to pay low wages whilst at the same allowing them to make attractively priced menu offerings in the knowledge that customers will pay for service. Divide into two groups and defend the argument from each side's perspective.

reveals that 44% of respondents say they would prefer higher wages for waiting staff to tipping but also 69% say they do not dislike tipping. In addition, his research finds 'only a tiny correlation between tip size and customer evaluation of service or dining experience, and points to several potential negative consequences of tipping. These include servers' giving less attention to persons stereotyped as poor tippers (including African Americans, the elderly, foreigners, teens and others); servers inclination to provide free food and or services in expectation of higher tips; and servers' inclinations to focus only on guests at their tables' (Lynn 2006, p. 14).

HIGH TECH FOOD

As new technologies in food production emerge, this book would not be complete without mentioning the emergence of high tech foods. In more and more restaurants around the world, chefs decide to use convenience products in their menus either because of the lack of staff in their kitchen or because of the lack of kitchen space or equipment.

But what does high tech food really means? Is there a clear definition?

High tech food can be defined in two ways:

1. As food that has been manipulated at a base level.
2. From a more generic point of view; from convenience goods to high tech equipment.

Effects of biotechnology

Biotechnology is an area of scientific research that has developed methods of manipulating genes and ways that would not otherwise naturally occur. The terms Genetically Engineered or Genetically Modified Foods are terms that the consumer today is well aware of. Although the defending side in favour of such foods argues that it is the only possible approach to feed the ever-increasing population, the opposing side argues about the

413

potential threats to both human health and the world ecological stability. The important point if one is looking at high tech foods in this way is that it can be extremely hard for any chef to guarantee that the menu is absolutely free of genetically modified goods.

The effects of genetically modified goods have spurred a trend towards customers wanting more organic produce. Consumers are far more informed than ever before and their expectations are always on the rise. Customers will often expect Food and Beverage Managers to be able to trace to produce back on the farm it was produced at, and European Law has made it very specific as to what can be labelled as organic and what cannot.

Convenience goods and high tech equipment

In kitchens today one can find ovens that interface with property management systems, allowing for reports on temperatures, humidity gas or electricity bills allowing for a better allocation of fixed costs per product and ensuring that the operator remains true to the current health and safety regulations. A chef can simply program the oven to cook what he wants, when he wants, as he wants it, reducing labour costs and achieving consistency of product thus meeting consumer expectations. In 1998, McDonalds tested a prototype where a computer-monitored machine dumps frozen fries into a basket that in turn is dunked into hot oil for cooking. The machine then shakes the fries and prepares them for service into bins. Robots prepare drinks and computers instantly convey new orders to robots. The process to deliver an order takes no longer than two minutes! Such technologies have long-term operational, financial and organizational behaviour implications. Production equipment can be already interfaced with point of sale systems. Robots already do serve customers in establishments such as the Yo! Sushi Restaurant in London, UK. Equipment such as ovens can be linked to a PC for reporting, the equipment are installed with temperature and humidity probes and the PC can regulate these, ensuring the food is cooked to perfection and within the health and safety standards. Digital timers can help chefs keep track of time in a busy kitchen. This can reduce overcooked food and wastage. One can take high tech foods even further and use the example of Mr Cantu, the twenty-eight-year-old executive chef at Moto in Chicago, who prepares his sushi on a Cannon i560 inkjet printer rather than a cutting board. He prints images of maki on pieces of edible paper made of soybeans and cornstarch, using organic, food-based inks of his own concoction. He then flavours the back of the paper, which is ordinarily used to put images onto birthday cakes, with powdered soy and seaweed seasonings (Bernstein, 2005).

Information, service and production technologies have undergone substantial advancements in the past twenty years, as those technologies continue to develop the costs of older technology drops substantially enabling smaller operations to afford such technology. It may not be long until a fully automated restaurant becomes a reality. With today's available technology it is quite possible and for fast-food operations at least, this may very well be the next natural step to their development. In fact in April 2007, 's Baggers® the first restaurant with fully automated service opened in Nuremberg, Germany (see the Case study). The restaurant owner and inventor of the service technology claims to have saved millions of Euros on waiter costs whilst there are mixed feelings amongst consumers (Patterson, 2007).

Summary

The food and beverage industry has always been dynamic and innovative, but the issues discussed above demonstrate that the pace of change, either in consumer choices, ethical operations or technological options, will continue to accelerate and challenge the ingenuity, flexibility and perspicacity of food and beverage managers all over the world.

We wish them every success.

Further study options

Case study: 's Baggers® – Restaurant of the third dimension

's Baggers® Restaurant opened its doors in the town of Nuremberg, Germany in April 2007. A 107-seat restaurant, with plans to expand its capacity by opening a beer garden by mid-September 2007, it has been labelled by the press as the first fully automated restaurant in the world (although it still uses some waiting staff). The restaurant does not require as many service staff as customers order via touch screen electronic point of sale (EPOS) at their tables, enabling a more efficient service and reducing labour costs.

The concept

High quality of food at low prices
Freshly prepared scrumptious dishes cooked with high quality ingredients using minimum fat and a focus on organic produce, offering excellent value for money.

Patented technology
Delicious meals and drinks ordered per touch screen are transported on special metallic tracks directly to the guests at the

Figure 12.1
The 's Baggers® rail system

Figure 12.2
's Baggers® easy to use EPOS

table, simply with the help of gravitation (see Figure 12.1). The German Patent office granted the patent for the transportation system in June 2007. 's Baggers® has also applied for the patent in Europe and USA. Due to the high labour cost saving potential of the technology, the restaurant concept could be very interesting for fast-food restaurant chains and the operation is currently developing franchising and licencing concepts.

Restaurant software

The state-of-the-art information technology offers an incredible increase in comfort for the guests who can get detailed information about food, suppliers, concept, at a touch of a button. Waiting times are minimized and there is no queuing for food. The EPOS technology enables the restaurant to operate a loyalty bonus scheme as well as offering bonuses to customers who evaluate the menu and recommend the restaurant to their friends (Figure 12.2). There is also the added bonus that effective advertising as customers can recommend the restaurant to friends utilizing a word of mouth marketing supported by information technology. One thousand five hundred of the loyalty cards (or Friend Cards) were distributed in the first four and a half months of the restaurant's operation. By allowing clients to evaluate the whole concept the restaurant has constant feedback enabling it to constantly monitor and evaluate the quality of its food and service.

Restaurant characteristics

's Baggers® is in all respects a Franconian restaurant: Franconian food presented in Franconian dialect (with translation). The whole concept is based not only in the system efficiency but also enabling customers to have fun and a totally different experience.

An interview with the inventor and owner, Michael Mack

Interviewer: Michael, how did you hit upon the idea?

Michael: I have always been an enthusiastic cook. Whenever I had a dinner party I was rushing from the kitchen to the dining room. So one day, I thought it would be so much easier if the food slipped along to the guests on its own and so the idea was born. Combined with my experience as a former iron foundry manager I decided to re-invent the traditional restaurant and start a new

Machael Mack, proprietor of 's Baggers® and inventor of the food rail technology

generation of restaurants by developing this invention which helps us increase efficiency and comfort substantially and cut costs nevertheless. To realize such a concept you need state-of-the-art service and information technology.

Interviewer: So how does the system work?

Michael: Well, the customer orders their drinks and food from a computerized touch screen at their table. There are one or two such screens per table. The customers can choose from a variety of delicacies – such as organic beef in buttermilk or sausages with Kraut – all regional Franconian specialities. There are pictures and descriptions of the dishes. Those screens are linked to the kitchen where the chefs put the orders on the rails straight from the oven. The dishes are then delivered to the customer's table on metallic rails. They are gliding down from the kitchen which is located on the upper floor, just by means of gravity. When the food and drinks arrive, they have a colour attached to them which corresponds to the seat so you know who's food is who's (see Figure 12.2).

Interviewer: Do the customers like it?

Michael: Oh yes! They just love it. It is quite difficult these days to get a table in the evenings. So you should ring early to get your reservation! Another evidence for enthused customers is the number of recommendations the customers can place from the touch screens at their tables: On average we get 90 recommendations a day. Also we offer a customer loyalty card (which we call 'Freundekarte' meaning card for friends). It offers all kinds of benefits for our customers such as a bonus

Figure 12.3
The system in action transporting food and beverages

system, an optional newsletter or the possibility of direct debit of the restaurant bills at the end of the month. In the first four and a half months 1,500 guests have subscribed already.

Interviewer: What if someone has a problem with their order – Is there a person to deal with it?
Michael: Definitely! Apart from technology and high quality food another part of the concept is a very high level of comfort for our customers. So there are waiters in our restaurant. But they only do tasks that are for the well-being of our guests. They do not have to take orders or run from the kitchen to the diners. They are there to ensure a friendly atmosphere, to welcome the guests, to answer the questions, to help with problems (to clear the dishes) and so on.

Interviewer: What are the future plans for the restaurant – Will there be more of them in other cities?
Michael: We are currently working on both a franchising system and a licencing concept. We have had enquiries from Germany, Europe, Canada, Australia and even Korea for franchising and we hope that we can soon open another 's Baggers® Restaurant somewhere else. In addition to that, the patent for the restaurant system has been granted for Germany and we have applied for the patent in Europe and North America. So we can now also sell licences to use the transportation system for food and beverage, which by the way is so delightful because of its simplicity: dishes are sliding down to customers just by means of gravity. Due to an enormous cost saving potential in the labour costs – you *could* run the restaurant with a minimum of service staff – this restaurant concept must be very interesting for the major restaurant

chains. An average fast-food restaurant could save about €250,000 in overheads per year by adopting the concept.

Acknowledgements

The Authors would like to thank the team at 's Baggers® Restaurant for their time and the information they provided for the creation of this case study. For more information visit www.sbaggers.de

Case study questions

1. Discuss the unique selling point of the 's Baggers® Restaurant.
2. Perform a SWOT (strengths, weaknesses, opportunities and threats) analysis for the 's Baggers® Restaurant technology.
3. Discuss your views of the concept as a potential customer. What are the things you like about the concept and what are the things you may dislike?
4. Discuss the views of the concept as a manager of such a concept. What are the things you like about the concept and what are the things you may dislike?

Review questions

1. Describe three consumer trends that are likely to affect mid-market restaurant operations in the next five years.
2. What are some of the possible methods an operation can utilize to reduce waste?
3. How can operations reduce their energy bills?
4. How does an operation benefit from buying food locally?
5. What does REIT stand for?
6. Explain asset financing.

Further reading

Bernstein, D. (2005). *When the Sous Chef is an Inkjet*, New York Times, February 3, 2005.

Burger, R. (2005). *Ten Environmental Tips for the Hospitality Industry*, http://www.economicallysound.com/ten_environmental_tips_for_the_hospitality_industry.html#more (accessed 30th August 2007).

Chan, W. W. and Ho, K. (2006). Hotels environmental management systems, creative financing strategy. *International Journal of Contemporary Hospitality management*, 18(4), 302–316.

Chathoth, P. K. and Olsen, M. D. (2007). The effect of environment risk, corporate strategy, and capital structure on firm performance: An empirical investigation of restaurant firms. *International Journal of Hospitality Management*, 26(3), 502–516.

Druce, C. (2007). *McDonald's to Operate Delivery Fleet on Bio-Diesel*, Caterer Online 02 July, http://www.caterersearch.com/Articles/2007/07/02/314695/mcdonalds-to-operate-delivery-fleet-on-bio-diesel.html (accessed 30th August 2007).

Food Miles (2004). *Corporate Watch*, http://www.corporate-watch.org.uk/?lid=2627 (accessed 29th August 2007).

Hotel and Motel Management (19 March 2007). *The REIT Story*, http://www.hotelmotel.com/hotelmotel/article/articleDetail.jsp?id=411421 (accessed 23rd August 2007).

Lynn, M. (2006). *Tipping Points; Restaurants and Institutions*, 1st June 2006, www.chr.cornell.edu

Mae Wan Ho and Gala, R. (2005). *Food Miles and Sustainability*, Institute of Science in Society, http://www.i-sis.org.uk/FMAS.php (accessed 30th August 2007).

Manson, E. (2007). *Chicago Mandarin Hotel to Sell Rooms to Investors*, Caterer online 30 May, http://www.caterersearch.com/Articles/2007/05/30/314070/chicago-mandarin-hotel-to-sell-rooms-to-investors.html (accessed 25th August 2007).

Mintel (2007a). *The Impact of Media on Eating Out*, Mintel International Group Limited. London: Mintel.

Mintel (2007b). *Eating Out Review – UK – July 2007*, Mintel International Group Limited. London: Mintel.

Patterson, T. (2007). *Rails replace Waiters*, The Independent 24 August, http://news.independent.co.uk/europe/article2891206.ece (accessed 30th August 2007).

Sloan, A. E. (2007). Top 10 food trends. *Food Technology*, 61(4), 23–39.

Times Online (20 August 2007). *Business in Brief*, http://business.timesonline.co.uk/tol/business/industry_sectors/article2288863.ece (accessed: 29th August 2007).

Van Alphen, K., Van Sark, W. and Hekkert, M. P. (2007). Renewable energy technologies in the Maldives – Determining the potential. *Renewable and Sustainable Energy Reviews*, 11(8), 1650–1674.

Index